Warner
Brothers
Directors

Warner Brothers Directors

The Hard-Boiled, the Comic, and the Weepers

791.
43
MEY

WILLIAM R. MEYER

ARLINGTON HOUSE·PUBLISHERS
NEW ROCHELLE, NEW YORK

78-11165

Library of Congress Cataloging in Publication Data

Meyer, William R.   1949-
    The Warner Brothers directors.

    Includes index.
    1. Moving-picture producers and directors—United States—
Biography. 2. Warner Brothers Pictures, inc.
I. Title.
PN1998.A2M398   791.43'0233'9022 [B]   77-22194
ISBN 0-87000-397-6

For my wife Antoinette,
whose graceful assistance and good humor
helped make this book possible

Acknowledgments

Dominick Abel
Anna Beleznay
Curtis Bernhardt
Film Favorites (Charles Smith)
Robert Florey
K. Bridget Kenney
Mervyn LeRoy
Lincoln Center Library: Theatre Collection
Terry Morse
Movie Star News
James Robert Parish
Vincent Sherman

Contents

Introduction

"Mammy, this is your little boy talkin'." "Is this the end of Rico?" "On the avenue I'm takin' you to." "I steal."

This movie dialogue comes from four of the most important films ever produced in Hollywood—*The Jazz Singer, Little Caesar, 42nd Street,* and *I Am a Fugitive from a Chain Gang.*

These productions set trends for sound, action, singing, and dancing which Hollywood followed for a decade. Significantly, the films were all made at Warner Brothers, a studio which had to struggle to stay above water in the sea of silent cinema, and then burst into prominence when Al Jolson's show-stopping singing exploded from the screen.

In the 1930s Warner Brothers built a multi-faceted machine of artists who turned out fast-paced, economical yet splendid-looking action, comedy, musical, and melodramatic vehicles.

That Warner Brothers was successful was due in no small measure to the ability of its directors to pool the talent, make enemies work together, wrench classic performances from rebellious stars, and cut corners to create movies which reflected hard times and war times, and that laughed, cried, and dreamt with their audiences.

In order to understand a director's career, it is necessary to know how he came to Hollywood. When most of the Warner Brothers directors began working, there were of course no schools to teach them and no history books to read. If the shaping of the American cinema occurred in the able hands of Griffith, Sennett, Chaplin, and others, the solidifying of film values became the job of ex-cowboys, ex-boxers, and ex-actors who laughed and loved their way to Hollywood, in Hollywood, and, if they were spry, post-Hollywood.

11

Most were born around the turn of the century. They came from all over America, and, indeed, from all over the world. When Raoul Walsh was meeting the likes of Edwin Booth and John L. Sullivan at the family dinner table at 128 East 48th Street in New York City, his future associate and friend William Wellman was cutting up in Brookline, Massachusetts, William Keighley was being admitted into Ben Greet's Shakespeare Repertory Company, Jean Negulesco was moving from his native Romania to the art world in Paris, Howard Hawks was getting closer to the movies by journeying from Indiana to Pasadena, California to finish secondary school, and Delmer Daves was making his film debut playing a choir boy in an early Universal production.

Jobs were plentiful for young men who had ambition or a sense of adventure. Future Warner Brothers directors often felt ambition's nudge to experience a world of adventure. In a way they were twentieth-century counterparts of the nineteenth-century dime-novel hero—John Huston busted broncs in Mexico, William Wellman dropped out of school to join the Lafayette Escadrille in World War I, Curtis Bernhardt spent the summer of 1933 in the anti-Nazi underground in Germany, and Raoul Walsh ran away to sea.

These experiences toughened their hides and kept them alive. Those not formed by revolution or robust, rollicking behavior found vocations which primed them, in one way or another, for Hollywood careers. Edmund Goulding's early years as an actor, writer, and director in the British theatre prepped him for the task of handling very independent actresses such as Bette Davis and Miriam Hopkins. Jean Negulesco's years as a Parisian artist later informed his finely lit and photographed suspense films and somber melodramas of the 1940s. William Keighley and William Dieterle utilized their knowledge from acting in repertory to facilitate the sympathy with which they guided Edward G. Robinson, Paul Muni, and James Cagney to some of their greatest performances.

When the Warner Brothers directors drifted to Hollywood prior to and during the 1920s and 1930s, they were well equipped to deal with tough actors, tougher studio bosses, and impossible production demands. As Howard Hawks so typically declared to a production head, "I don't want you to make the movie in the cutting room. I want to make it myself on the set, and if that doesn't suit you, too bad."

One day in 1935, Dieterle received a call to remedy the excesses of former teacher Max Reinhardt, who was breaking the studio bank endeavoring to film Shakespeare's *A Midsummer Night's Dream*. The student's success led him to direct many of Warner Brothers' most prestigious properties during the next half-dozen years.

The Warner Brothers directors usually knew what they wanted, and they had the know-how to get it. Irving Rapper took ten suspensions in seven years, rather than work on scripts that he didn't like or understand, while William Wellman had to throw a brick through Darryl F. Zanuck's window to show the producer that he meant business.

Not that the directors didn't have to pay for their hard heads and eccentricities. Hollywood was a fickled jungle which gave lucrative assignments and grabbed them away without batting an eye. Jean Negulesco was set to direct the adaptation of Dashiell Hammett's *The Maltese Falcon*, until a fellow named John Huston, who had written the script, reminded Jack Warner that he, not Negulesco, had been promised the detective story first. Michael Curtiz's single-mindedness caused many actors, especially Errol Flynn, to dislike him intensely. Curtiz's "artistic vision," while not solely responsible for the reported deaths during the filming of the flood scenes of *Noah's Ark*, certainly contributed to the emphasis of production values over life. And if William Wellman hadn't fought Darryl Zanuck so hard for the right to film *The Ox-Bow Incident*, he wouldn't have been contractually obligated to direct any two turkeys selected for him in addition.

Yet happy accidents occurred. While Mervyn LeRoy was filming the last shot of *I Am a Fugitive from a Chain Gang*, a light blew out just before the title character (Paul Muni) uttered the immortal answer to a question about his future. Muni's face was dimly lit, and as he was about to say "I steal," the lamp silently conked out, enabling LeRoy to unwittingly film one of the most memorable endings in the American cinema. Soon after Negulesco was fired from *The Maltese Falcon*, friend Anatole Litvak told him of another property, Eric Ambler's novel *A Coffin for Dimitrios*. Filmed as *The Mask of Dimitrios*, the project became an archetypal suspense production of the 1940s. Irving Rapper was heading for a rest trip to get over his mother's death when producer Hal Wallis handed him the reins of *Now, Voyager* after Michael Curtiz had rejected the script. Rapper had just completed another film, and only two weeks remained to prepare Paul Henreid to speak English correctly and to adjust star Bette Davis to the Austrian. The results of the hurried project are classic.

Nineteen biographies containing facts and legends of the filmmakers' professional and private lives are animated herein. The director as artist, the director as man—the twain often met. From the shaky silent period, to the salad days of the 1930s and 1940s, through the dabbling of veterans in the new Hollywood and the television era of the 1950s and the 1960s—we now proudly present the Warner Brothers directors.

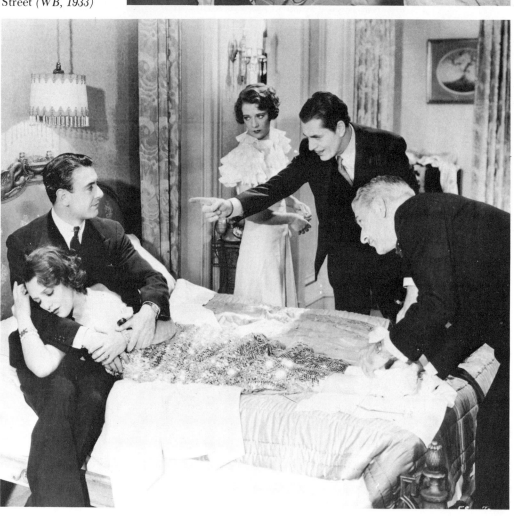

Lloyd Bacon on the set of The Frogmen *(20th, 1951)*

George Brent, Bebe Daniels, Ruby Keeler, Warner Baxter, and George Irving in 42nd Street (WB, 1933)

1

Lloyd Bacon

"I see that the public gets action. Some others may use motion pictures as a vehicle for a psychological study. I haven't that patience." Lloyd Bacon gave four decades of movie-goers action, comedy, action, melodrama, and more action. Over the years 1926-54 director Bacon made ninety-eight films, seventy-three of them at Warner Brothers-First National. "He did things so quickly that I once accused him of taking bribes," James Cagney cracked. Jack Warner expected Lloyd to work rapidly, but no one believed it when the director shot forty-seven takes of the biographical film *Knute Rockne—All American* in one day!

Yet mere speed wasn't the essential factor in Lloyd Bacon's success, for he was equally effective in directing both action dramas and comedies, as evidenced by the top-grade *A Slight Case of Murder, Boy Meets Girl, Marked Woman,* and *Action in the North Atlantic.* Then there was *42nd Street* which was choreographed by Busby Berkeley but directed by Bacon. It was Lloyd who kept up human interest in the film between Berkeley's dazzling production numbers. The greatness of *42nd Street* is its unity of drama, music, and comedy. The film simply wouldn't be the same without even one of these elements, and the classic musical's characters could not possibly have convincingly brought the narrative to its poignant conclusion without the firm, calm hand of Lloyd Bacon.

Lloyd was born on January 16, 1890 in San Jose, California. The son of Frank Bacon, author and star of the hit play *Lightnin'*, Lloyd's show business career almost ended the first time he went backstage at the age of five. His sister Elizabeth was acting in a show called *May Blossom,* and her younger brother stood in the wings of the theatre during each performance, fascinated by the movement of the actors on stage. As the curtain began dropping down, little Lloyd froze, mesmerized by the audience's applause. As Elizabeth caught sight of the boy out of the corner of her eye, she also spotted the curtain rapidly moving to cover the stage and knock Lloyd into oblivion.

"Look out, it's going to hit you!" the sister screamed.

Lloyd jumped past the curtain just in time, and in the future he learned to be intrigued by theatre at a safe distance. He had a lot of practice, touring with his father in such plays as *Hills of California*. After a time Lloyd told his father, "I want to be a lawyer," and Frank Bacon said, "Fine." Among the younger Bacon's early heroes was Clarence Darrow, who defended many controversial people, including Socialist Eugene Debs, John T. Scopes who was arrested for teaching evolution in Tennessee, murderers Loeb and Leopold, and the Scottsboro Boys. He also admired a man named Delmas who defended millionaire Harry K. Thaw in an explosive murder trial of that era.

Before entering Santa Clara College, Lloyd continued acting on stage and was introduced to motion pictures. In 1909 Frank Bacon shipped his son to Omaha to be cared for by two maiden aunts. There Lloyd became enamored of a Nebraska girl whose father managed a film exchange. In the meantime, Frank took over the Burwood Stock Company in Omaha, and when persuasive Lloyd talked the girl's father into buying a movie theatre, the Bacons were ready to exercise control over all visual drama in their little corner of Nebraska—but not for long.

"She was to play the piano, her sister was to sell tickets, and I was to manage the house," Lloyd remembered. "We got there during a flood and went to the best hotel. That afternoon we presented our credentials, only to find that the bill of sale we held was a phony. The man who had sold her father the theatre didn't own it."

Lloyd and company thus had a problem. Determined to enter the film profession, the crafty young businessman obtained a copy of the film of the Gans-Nelson fight, rented a hall, showed the film to receptive patrons, and even provided a first-person narration of the minutes of the battle. Here Lloyd's imagination was particularly useful, inasmuch as he had been nowhere near the site of the fight in San Francisco when it actually took place.

For a time at Santa Clara College, Lloyd's creative aspirations were stifled, but when he performed in a school production of *The Passion Play*, the instinct overwhelmed him.

"I want to be an actor," Lloyd informed his noted father.

"That's fine," Frank said, by now accustomed to the frequent changes of mind in regard to career decisions by his indecisive but enthusiastic son. "But you're going to be a good actor. You're going to work your head off."

Lloyd learned the craft in some arduous environments typical of repertory theatre of the day. The director's performance in a 1907 traveling version of *Salome* was particularly memorable.

"That tour of *Salome* was something to remember," Lloyd recalled. "In Aberdeen, Washington, the theatre was on a wharf and you could hear the water lapping against the piling underneath the stage. Salome was carrying John the Baptist's head and she happened to look into the orchestra pit. The trap drummer was fishing through a hole in the floor, and as she watched him he jerked a fish up into the pit, broke its neck, and then grabbed his drumsticks. She was unable to speak for some few moments."

Years passed and Lloyd overcame the rough conditions, only to be faced with far more discomfort as a location director of action films. In 1911 he became a member of David Belasco's Los Angeles Stock Company, often acting in support of Lewis Stone, MGM's future father of Andy Hardy. Bacon traveled across America, slowly building a small reputation with appearances in the New York presentation of *Cinderella Man* and other hits of the day. He also spent a season in vaudeville.

By 1915 Lloyd Bacon's career changed direction and location. Film was the new challenge, and Lloyd met it in California. He acted in a number of shorts starring Bronco Billy Anderson, graduating to bad guy roles in Lloyd Hamilton comedies. In addition, he served as a double for stars. The rough-and-tumble young man continued developing his film talent in the Photo Department of the Navy during World War I. This started a lifelong love affair with the service, which the director later reflected in a number of films.

In 1918 war veteran Lloyd moved to Mutual with Charlie Chaplin, and the next year he switched again to Triangle comedies. As is peculiar to many silent and early sound filmmakers, Lloyd Bacon's first chance to direct came purely by accident. He was to perform in a Lloyd Hamilton comedy, but production stopped because the original director called in sick. Having expressed an interest in working behind the cameras for some time, Lloyd was allowed to direct the short comedy.

Soon after he worked as a gag writer for Mack Sennett. "Roughly speaking, it was in February [1921] that the director in me won out. That was when they told me I wasn't a gag writer any more."

The 31-year-old man behind the camera had much to learn about the technical and social aspects of directing, as he later recalled: "It was for Sennett that I first began to direct. I did all right, I guess, because he gave me another to do. But you'd never have known it from what he said about my efforts. Nothing was right about it. He ripped it backward and forward, and me along with it, and then left it exactly as it was.

After a little of this, I thought I was pretty fed up with it and went to Fox. I figured I was a director and that Sennett was browbeating me just to keep my salary down and keep me in my place. I wanted to show him I could work anywhere."

It took Lloyd a number of years to realize that the madcap producer was in reality something of a benevolent dictator. In 1931 Bacon smilingly told a *Film Spectator* reporter: "I didn't know Sennett as well as I do now. I didn't realize how much he has to give any director who is willing to learn." Ironically, by then Sennett was an all but forgotten figure in Hollywood, making two-reelers which were merely sad rehashes of things that used to be funny.

Sennett was still a respected figure when Lloyd began directing a trio of three-reelers at Universal. He then began a twenty-year association with Warner Brothers in 1925. The brothers Warner were in the process of building a group of fine contract directors which soon included Alan Crosland, Michael Curtiz, Mervyn LeRoy, John Adolfi, and others. Prolific Lloyd fit into their dynamic production machine as well as any director in Warner Brothers history, including Curtiz.

Lloyd Bacon's first Warner Brothers film was *Broken Hearts of Hollywood* in 1926. He followed that up quickly with *Private Izzy Murphy*, starring stage celebrity George Jessel who made his film debut under Bacon's guidance. "A distinguished 4th cousin to *Abie's Irish Rose*," wrote Mordaunt Hall in the *New York Times*. "It is a feature that has a decided inclination to be melancholy, and to emphasize this mood there is a wealth of tearful close-ups."

Bacon's stylistic accomplishments were certainly modest. Compared to other Warner Brothers directors, Lloyd was technically rather timid. He rarely used the sweeping camera movements and expressive lighting of Curtiz, the gritty pictorialism of Wellman or LeRoy, or the overall intensity of Huston. If any Warner director's filmic signature resembled Lloyd's at all, it was the "eye level" view of Howard Hawks, although Hawks tended to choose rougher stories and frame his characters against a much harsher backdrop. What identifies Lloyd Bacon's best films is a tendency to lay back and rarely give in to the louder, more melodramatic, or broader aspects of his narratives. The classic close-up, used to isolate actors rather than encourage communication, is the primary cinematic mark of the director.

Over the years 1927-28-29, Bacon directed fourteen films, and he was named one of the top ten directors for 1928-29 by *Film Daily*. His first important Warner Brothers film was *The Singing Fool* in 1928, starring the ever popular Al Jolson. The production raked in the then astronomical sum of $4,000,000 in North American rental receipts.

A sound version of Herman Melville's *Moby Dick* in 1930 helped start

Bacon's reputation as an action director. The version in question, along with its silent predecessor (retitled *The Sea Beast*), introduced a love story missing in Melville's classic sea tale and starred John Barrymore, Joan Bennett, and Lloyd Hughes. "*Moby Dick* is stirring, even if you don't believe in whales," quipped *Variety*.

For several years the director was responsible for many competent but hardly memorable productions such as *Fifty Million Frenchmen, Fireman, Save My Child,* and *Miss Pinkerton.* In 1933 he directed his most famous film, *42nd Street,* choreographed by the burgeoning giant of the film musical, Busby Berkeley.

In March the *New York Times'* Mordaunt Hall called *42nd Street* "the liveliest and one of the most tuneful musical comedies that has come out of Hollywood." Irene Thirer of the New York *Daily News* awarded the film a rating of three and a half stars. She commended Bacon's "swift, snappy direction" and Berkeley's "swell dance routines," concluding that the musical should be a box office "smash hit Eastside, Westside, all around the town." Astute critic Richard Watts, Jr. of the *New York Herald-Tribune* called the production "a brisk and alert screen musical show with elaborate dance routines, lively tunes, a plot, and not too many jokes."

Truly *42nd Street* is the film musical of film musicals, not because it is the greatest, but because it came first. Curtiz's *Yankee Doodle Dandy* (WB, 1942) and Stanley Donen's *Singin' in the Rain* (MGM, 1953) are in their own ways equally good. Yet the virtual debut of the screen musical as a viable force in Hollywood occurred with the premiere of *42nd Street.* Warner Baxter (as Julian Marsh, "the greatest musical comedy director in America"), Ruby Keeler (the talented kid), Dick Powell (the singing juvenile), Bebe Daniels (the unlucky leading lady), Guy Kibbee (her sugar daddy), George Brent (her paramour), and Ginger Rogers (a pretentious chorus girl—"She only said 'No' once and then she didn't hear the question") starred in the backstage story of the making of a great Broadway musical. The financing of the play, the choosing of the chorus line, the return of Julian Marsh, the fall of the female star, the rise of the starlet, and the interweaving of the characters to produce a box-office champ, brilliantly punctuated by Berkeley's surrealistic production numbers, all make *42nd Street* an affair to remember. After all is done, the play is a smash, and the leading characters are off with their respective sweeties, director Marsh leans near the stage door, coat on, hat cocked, cigarette in mouth, as the camera pulls back to show him alone, exhausted, but glorified as a great American musical director forever.

The tremendous reception accorded *42nd Street* persuaded Warner Brothers to assign Bacon to other musicals and generally more expensive productions. *Footlight Parade, Wonder Bar, Broadway Gondolier* (in which Lloyd appeared), and *Gold Diggers of 1937* never lived up to the excellence of the film where Ruby Keeler went out there an unknown but came back a star, but they led to better work.

Marked Woman (1937) is one of Bacon's hardest hitting films, a story fresh from the daily newspapers. Bette Davis plays a call girl who informs on the boss (Eduardo Ciannelli) when the dictatorial gangster murders her sister. Co-starring Humphrey Bogart as a district attorney, *Marked Woman* is a slightly veiled narrative of the underworld activities of Lucky Luciano.

Marked Woman "could easily have been a maudlin piece," insisted the *New York Times*' Frank S. Nugent. "It totters every now and then on the brink of pathos and melodramatic hokum. But invariably it is snatched back by Lloyd Bacon's direction or by the honesty of the players." Bacon's "swift precision" impressed *Herald-Tribune* critic Howard Barnes, as well as the "briskly melodramatic treatment of a perennially interesting subject." *Variety* labeled *Marked Woman* "a strong and well-made underworld drama."

"You think I care about money?" snarls jailed gangster Ciannelli. "I only care about makin' people do what I tell 'em." This baldly stated *raison d'être* motivates the criminals to take over an honest nightclub and make hookers out of the entertainers and waitresses. The declaration also symbolizes Bacon's handling of his characters. *Marked Woman* is greatly enhanced by a constant undercurrent of solitude—in the district attorney, the call girls, and even the gangster. The director cuts back and forth for close-ups of Davis and Ciannelli at their first meeting in the club—intensity for intensity. In the final scene, where the girls leave the courtroom after their nemesis has been sentenced to a long prison term, Davis rejects Bogart's advances and disappears in the fog with four other well-worn hucksters of the house. As they descend into oblivion, Bacon focuses on each for one last close-up. Even though the disturbed gangster is imprisoned, there is no pretense of a happy ending, and no armchair solution is offered to the persistent troubles of the group of tough but basically decent women trying to escape the Depression any way they can.

Bacon followed *Marked Woman* in 1938 with a similarly uncompromising crime film, *Racket Busters*, but that same year the director brilliantly parodied the genre in *A Slight Case of Murder*. Starring Edward G. Robinson and Jane Bryan, along with a fine cast of studio stock players, the film is the legendary Little Caesar's first and perhaps finest attempt to make fun of the genre which made him famous. In the future Bacon and Robinson would work together in two similar films,

20

Brother Orchid (1940) and *Larceny, Inc.* (1942), and the actor grew to respect the opinion of his director.

On the set of *A Slight Case of Murder*, Edward G. Robinson asked for Lloyd's help more than once, but the director would say: "Don't kid me, Eddie," somewhat taken aback at being asked to show Robinson how to act. However, Robinson was serious. "I'll listen to anything about acting he has to say, any day," the star insisted.

Others at the studio weren't sure that Bacon had as much control on the set as it appeared. He guided James Cagney, the studio's biggest name, in fourteen films throughout the 1930s, but it was often said that Cagney did a good job of handling himself. Nevertheless, as the premier director of Warner Brothers' top names, Lloyd earned $4,225 a week in the decade before World War II, more than any other contract filmmaker.

One thing was sure—Lloyd looked as flashy as fellow director William Keighley looked sophisticated. Bacon could often be spotted cloaked in huge houndstooth coats, topped with ostentatious hats. He had a reputation at the studio for ruining at least one felt topper per film by throwing it around while guiding actors and camera.

Critical reception was far from unanimous regarding *Boy Meets Girl*, released in August 1938. Bacon's incredibly fast-paced adaptation (it may have been a two-hat affair) of the play by Bella and Sam Spewack does suffer from excessive silliness, which might have been avoided if the film could have shifted locations at the rate of Howard Hawks' *Bringing Up Baby* or even *Twentieth Century*. The wackiness unfolding against different backdrops would necessarily take on a fresh quality absent in repeated and prolonged scenes in the producer's (Ralph Bellamy) and writers' (James Cagney and Pat O'Brien) offices.

Nevertheless, *Boy Meets Girl* is a funny, albeit crazy spoof of the typical Hollywood studio and the contents therein. "Just as gay and impudent as a film," asserted Barnes of the *Tribune*. Yet he felt that Bacon's staging was "more resourceful than imaginative," and he believed that the script was too reminiscent of the play. *Variety* carped that *Boy Meets Girl* "does not approximate the rip-snorting click of the play ... little more than adequate."

Brother Orchid (1940) is a touching and mildly humorous variation on the parody *A Slight Case of Murder*. This time Edward G. Robinson plays a gangster who wants to go straight into a monastery, instead of merely straight. Although his madness has a method (he wants to hide out), the gangster slowly becomes attuned to the ways of men who live in another world.

"A funnier case of hard-boiled impudence hasn't been enjoyed here-

Bette Davis and Humphrey Bogart in Marked Woman *(First National, 1937)*

Willard Parker, Edward G. Robinson, and Jane Bryan in A Slight Case of Murder *(WB, 1938)*

Penny Singleton, Pat O'Brien, Dick Foran, Ralph Bellamy, Paul Clark, and James Cagney in Boy Meets Girl (WB, 1938)

Herbert Anderson, Dan Dailey, Nancy Guild, and Charles Winninger in Give My Regards to Broadway (20th, 1948)

abouts since ... *A Slight Case of Murder,*" asserted Bosley Crowther in the *New York Times.* "Lloyd Bacon has directed this film with a sure grasp of its divine elements of farce and religious sentiment," insisted the *New York Post's* Archer Winstein.

That same year Bacon produced his magical forty-seven takes in one day for *Knute Rockne—All American.* Starring Pat O'Brien as the legendary sports figure, the stirring, misty-eyed script features Ronald Reagan as the "Gipper." Eileen Creelman of the *New York Sun* called *Knute Rockne—All American* "a sentimental tribute to a man who was America's best football coach." *Variety* summed up the best of the film: "[It] carries both inspiration and dramatic appeal on a wide scale."

A number of mediocre but usually enjoyable films followed. *Honeymoon for Three* (1941) was shot in twenty-six days. *Footsteps in the Dark* (also 1941) proved that Bacon could direct a breezy, thin affair in such a way that an audience could be entertained and not realize until later that it had seen a patchwork film skipping by on thin thread. *Silver Queen* (1942), along with *The Oklahoma Kid* (1939), proved that Westerns weren't Lloyd's forte.

Over the years the director made several films about a beloved subject, the Navy, but none were more than modest in quality. *Wings of the Navy* (1939) is a million-dollar production which employs six hundred planes to tell the story of Olivia de Havilland, George Brent, and John Payne fighting and loving. During the shooting, Lloyd restated his philosophy of directing, but tacked on another proviso: "You can't get too much action in a motion picture. And you can't get too much Navy in a picture either, particularly one demanding excitement."

Bacon's best sea film, *Action in the North Atlantic* (1943), concerns the Merchant Marine rather than the Navy. Humphrey Bogart, Raymond Massey, Alan Hale, Julie Bishop, Ruth Gordon, Sam Levene, and Dane Clark star in a solid tribute to the men who fought World War II without weapons. *Action in the North Atlantic* "is often spectacular and generally instructive, but it is too rambling to be more than moderately entertaining," Howard Barnes opined in his *Herald-Tribune* review. The *New York Times'* Bosley Crowther disagreed, labeling the Bogartstarrer "a tingling, informative picture."

Shooting *Action in the North Atlantic* was a tough assignment. The model of the *Liberty* ship filled a whole stage, and photographer Ted McCord found it difficult to illuminate the set for many day and night scenes. Moreover, the ship was too big to stand on rockers, so the camera had to do the rocking. The machine was mounted on a huge crane which allowed the camera to move as the *Liberty* itself would tumble in the ocean. During the studio storms, McCord had to deal with lighting actors who were being drenched by torrential rain and waves. Conversely, the arc lights and special effects fires became so strong that Lloyd and his assistants often donned masks. Once while directing a scene in the wheelhouse of the construction, he was choked by smoke. Ripping off his mask, he stumbled through the set, alarming the twenty-five firemen who maintained a constant vigil during the production.

For all his trouble shooting the tribute to the Merchant Marine, *Action in the North Atlantic* was Lloyd Bacon's last film at Warner Brothers. In 1944 he made his debut as a Fox director with *Sunday Dinner for a Soldier,* starring Anne Baxter, John Hodiak, and Charles Winninger. For the next decade Bacon made a number of Fox films concerning the family—*The Sullivans* (1944), a factual war drama of five brothers, *Home Sweet Homicide* (1946), a comedy about murder, the dignified musical *Give My Regards to Broadway* (1948), and *Mother Is a Freshman* (1949)—as well as Columbia's *Kill the Umpire* (1950), in which a rabid baseball fan becomes the most hated man in the ball park.

Starring Dan Dailey, Charles Winninger, Nancy Guild, and Charlie Ruggles, *Give My Regards to Broadway* is a sentimental story of the break-up of a family of vaudevillians. The father (Winninger) simply fails to realize that his career is over and that his children wish to pursue other goals. Bacon's knowledge of the power of close-ups is never so evident as in the scene where the son (Dailey) tells his father that a family life on stage is an impossible dream. An extremely close frame of Winninger's sad face sensitively evokes all the crushed dreams of a man who had hoped to regain his former glory.

Critics couldn't see the subtle quality of the film back in 1948. "A dull, sentimental family drama poorly disguised with technicolor and occasional music," wrote Otis L. Guernsey, Jr. in the *New York Herald-Tribune.* Crowther of the *Times* criticized the film as suffering from "redundancy, want of originality, dullness, and sheer lack of drive."

Bacon's other Fox musicals such as *Golden Girl* (1951) and *The I Don't Care Girl* (1953) have the same modest virtues as *Give My Regards to Broadway.* The former is a competent, occasionally touching Civil War drama with music, and the latter is a perky, nostalgic biographical film about musical star Eva Tanguay. All three films have a quiet, tuneful, human touch, with light drama and comedy blended well, and the trio is about as far removed from Bacon's Berkeley-choreographed musicals as was Bacon's drama from Berkeley's production numbers. At the end of Bacon's career, the director realized the undemanding, sentimental unity of drama, comedy, and music in the solid if unspectacular Fox productions.

Lloyd hopped over to Universal and RKO for four more productions during 1953-54. His last released film was *The French Line*, shot in 1953 but held up by producer Howard Hughes until the next year. The millionaire fought with censors over the ample display of Jane Russell's breasts on publicity posters.

Like fellow director Michael Curtiz, Lloyd Bacon made films until he died. Lloyd entered a hospital near Burbank, California on October 20, 1955 and died there on November 15 of a cerebral hemorrhage. He was survived by his wife, Margaret Balch Bacon, two children, and a grandchild.

The filmography of Lloyd Bacon isn't littered with classics. There are no stories of failed productions or unmanageable ego. Bacon's career stands as an example of a filmmaker who was always competent, occasionally brilliant, and rarely incapable of telling a story, whether it was good or not.

The Films of Lloyd Bacon

Broken Hearts of Hollywood *(WB, 1926)*
Private Izzy Murphy *(WB, 1926)*
Finger Prints *(WB, 1927)*
White Flannels *(WB, 1927)*
The Heart of Maryland *(WB, 1927)*
A Sailor's Sweetheart *(WB, 1927)*
Brass Knuckles *(WB, 1927)*
The Lion and the Mouse *(WB, 1928)*
Pay as You Enter *(WB, 1928)*
The Singing Fool *(WB, 1928)*
Women They Talk About *(WB, 1928)*
Stark Mad *(WB, 1929)*
No Defense *(WB, 1929)*
Honky Tonk *(WB, 1929)*
Say It with Songs *(WB, 1929)*
So Long, Letty *(WB, 1929)*
She Couldn't Say No *(WB, 1930)*
A Notorious Affair *(FN, 1930)*
The Other Tomorrow *(FN, 1930)*
Moby Dick *(WB, 1930)*
The Office Wife *(WB, 1930)*
Kept Husbands *(RKO, 1931)*

Sit Tight *(WB, 1931)*
Fifty Million Frenchmen *(WB, 1931)*
Gold Dust Gertie *(WB, 1931)*
Honor of the Family *(WB, 1931)*
Manhattan Parade *(WB, 1931)*
Fireman, Save My Child *(FN, 1932)*
The Famous Ferguson Case *(FN, 1932)*
Miss Pinkerton *(FN, 1932)*
You Said a Mouthful *(FN, 1932)*
Crooner *(FN, 1932)*
Picture Snatcher *(WB, 1933)*
42nd Street *(WB, 1933)*
Mary Stevens, M.S. *(WB, 1933)*
Footlight Parade *(WB, 1933)*
Son of a Sailor *(FN, 1933)*
Wonder Bar *(FN, 1934)*
A Very Honorable Guy *(FN, 1934)*
He Was Her Man *(WB, 1934)*
Here Comes the Navy *(WB, 1934)*
6-Day Bike Rider *(FN, 1934)*
Devil Dogs of the Air *(WB, 1935)*
In Caliente *(FN, 1935)*

The Irish in Us (WB, 1935)
Broadway Gondolier (WB, 1935)
Frisco Kid (WB, 1935)
Sons O' Guns (WB, 1936)
Cain and Mabel (WB, 1936)
Gold Diggers of 1937 (WB, 1936)
Marked Woman (WB, 1937)
Ever Since Eve (WB, 1937)
San Quentin (FN, 1937)
Submarine D-1 (WB, 1937)
A Slight Case of Murder (WB, 1938)
The Cowboy from Brooklyn (WB, 1938)
Boy Meets Girl (WB, 1938)
Racket Busters (WB, 1938)
Wings of the Navy (WB, 1939)
The Oklahoma Kid (WB, 1939)
Indianapolis Speedway (WB, 1939)
Espionage Agent (WB, 1939)
Invisible Stripes (WB, 1940)
A Child Is Born (WB, 1940)
Three Cheers for the Irish (WB, 1940)
Brother Orchid (WB, 1940)
Knute Rockne—All American (WB, 1940)
Honeymoon for Three (WB, 1941)
Footsteps in the Dark (WB, 1941)
Affectionately Yours (WB, 1941)
Navy Blues (WB, 1941)
Larceny, Inc. (WB, 1942)
Wings for the Eagle (WB, 1942)
Silver Queen (UA, 1942)

Action in the North Atlantic (WB, 1943)
Sunday Dinner for a Soldier (20th, 1944)
The Sullivans (20th, 1944)
Captain Eddie (20th, 1945)
Wake Up and Dream (20th, 1946)
Home Sweet Homicide (20th, 1946)
I Wonder Who's Kissing Her Now (20th, 1947)
You Were Meant for Me (20th, 1948)
Give My Regards to Broadway (20th, 1948)
Don't Trust Your Husband (UA, 1948)
Mother Is a Freshman (20th, 1949)
It Happens Every Spring (20th, 1949)
Miss Grant Takes Richmond (Col., 1949)
The Good Humor Man (Col., 1950)
Kill the Umpire (Col., 1950)
The Fuller Brush Girl (Col., 1950)
Call Me Mister (20th, 1951) (choreography by Busby Berkeley)
The Frogmen (20th, 1951)
Golden Girl (20th, 1951)
The I Don't Care Girl (20th, 1953)
The Great Sioux Uprising (Univ., 1953)
Walking My Baby Back Home (Univ., 1953)
The French Line (RKO, 1954)
She Couldn't Say No (RKO, 1954)

Busby Berkeley (in the late forties) and a bevy of beauties plus Tony Martin

2

Busby Berkeley

"He was a forceful, positive man bursting with ideas. He was into everything and seemed to know everything. He would argue with cameramen and composers and producers who would tell him that what he wanted couldn't be done. But it would be done, and done exactly as he wanted it. He was energetic, tireless, tough, and sometimes rough, but look at his pictures and tell me how any other kind of man could have achieved what he did." Ruby Keeler wrote these words in *The Busby Berkeley Book** in 1973.

The man who knew everything had another version of his *modus operandi.* "I don't know one note of music from another and I never took a dancing lesson in my life," Berkeley told a *Newsweek* reporter in 1970. "I always tried to think of a great entrance and exit. And never have them fall down."

They rarely fell down, to say the least, in the films choreographed or directed by Busby Berkeley. From the opulent, razzle-dazzle, surrealistic, realistic pillow fluff of the production numbers in *42nd Street, Gold Diggers of 1933,* and *Dames,* to the overall directorial splendor of the later *Babes in Arms, Strike Up the Band, Babes on Broadway, The Gang's All Here,* and *Take Me Out to the Ball Game,* Berkeley evoked an amazing visual cinema equal to the French and German *avant-garde* of the 1920s, yet he managed to charm even the most depressed, war-torn audiences of the 1930s and 1940s. The name Busby Berkeley has been so closely associated with the Hollywood musical that the *American Thesaurus of Slang* defines the director's moniker as a "very elaborate musical number."

*A+W Visual Library.

Busby Berkeley William Enos was born on November 29, 1895 in Los Angeles, California. His parents, Gertrude and Francis Enos, named him, their second son (George was the first), after two actor friends in the Tim Frawley Repertory Company, Amy Busby and William Gillette. His mother, whose stage name was Gertrude Berkeley, performed with the group, as did father Francis, who also took directorial charge on occasion.

The Enoses did not want their children following in their tired footsteps to the theatre. By the time Busby was born, brother George was already in military school. The future dance director toured the country with his parents, but he was forbidden to enter the theatre except for Saturday matinees. Brother George couldn't be stopped from walking the boards for pay, and he joined Frawley's Company. Five-year-old Busby wasn't going to be put off either. "I had sneaked away from Annie [his nurse] and managed to slip by the stage doorman," he recalled. "I stood in the wings goggle-eyed as the company played the Arabian desert drama *Under Two Flags*. George was one of the Arabs. He spotted me, and on his next entrance shoved me under his robe and walked onstage. There I stood, hidden from the audience, holding my brother's leg, scared stiff."

Despite Busby's official debut in 1900, almost twenty years passed before he really entered show business. The young man was packed off to the Mohegan Lake Military Academy, fifty miles from New York City. He graduated in 1914 and accepted an offer from a family friend to become the equivalent of a management trainee at a shoe factory in Athol, Massachusetts. By 1917 Busby had seen enough of shoe leather, and the day before America entered World War I, he traded it for military khaki. Busby enlisted in the U.S. Army at Fort Banks, Massachusetts, choosing the artillery because that group would be the first to sail to France. After requesting officers' training, Busby was sent to Oglethorpe, Georgia. At the end of the year, Busby Berkeley William Enos rose to the rank of second lieutenant in the 312th Field Artillery, 79th Division.

Assigned to conduct parade drills, among other things, Berkeley was initiated into the rites of maneuvering men on stage. "I got tired of the old routine," he recalled, "and to make things more interesting, I asked the colonel to let me try something different. I had worked out a trick drill for the twelve hundred men. I explained the movements by numbers and gave the section leaders instructions for their companies and had them do the whole thing without any audible orders. Since the routines were numbered the men could count out their measures once they had learned them. It was quite something to see a parade square full of squads and companies of men marching in patterns, in total silence.

The French Army asked if I would do the same for them, but our people refused permission."

After almost being court-martialed for going AWOL on a lark, Berkeley was appointed an Assistant Entertainment Officer in occupied Germany, but in late 1917, when he was mustered out of the service, he had no career plans. One day Busby and his mother met John Cromwell while walking down Broadway. A family friend, stage director Cromwell persuaded Gertrude to allow her son to perform in a stock company version of *The Man Who Came Back*.

Busby played the role successfully for a year, but he decided that it would be his last drama, since comedy was his forte. Berkeley himself had to do a lot of laughing soon after, inasmuch as he was unemployed for a long time. The road company of *Hitchy-Koo of 1923* provided work for Busby, and he fattened his income by doubling as assistant stage manager. During this time he also acted in and directed stock productions in Rochester, Baltimore, and Springfield, Massachusetts.

The next three years were occupied by a Broadway revival of *Irene*. Busby approached producer James Montgomery and asked to be in the show. Impressed with the young man's gall, Montgomery assigned him the role of Madame Lucy, the limp-wristed fashion designer. In 1926 Berkeley left the play to direct a stock company in Somerville, Massachusetts. He received only a small percentage of the salary that he had earned for *Irene*, but Busby wanted to direct, and he couldn't do that on Broadway—at least not yet.

Soon afterward Broadway beckoned and Berkeley answered the call to stage dances for *Holka Polka*. The show didn't last, and the 31-year-old man again found himself without a source of income. After some complications, he finally found temporary employment directing dances for *Castles in the Air*. The next show, *Lady Do*, served as Berkeley's "comeback" vehicle as an actor. He had by then realized the value of performing—he could continue to draw a salary while in front of audiences, whereas a dance director's services ended after the numbers were staged.

Busby created the dances for *Sweet Lady*, but the show which featured young Archie Leach (soon to be Cary Grant) folded due to insufficient funds. The show nevertheless came to the attention of agent Louis Shurr, and Shurr obtained the job for Berkeley which became his first break. He was hired as dance director for Rodgers and Hammerstein's *A Connecticut Yankee*. The musical debuted on November 3, 1927 and closed 421 performances later. Berkeley got noticed. "A new dance director has been born on Broadway," one critic wrote.

That dance director didn't know the first thing about the mechanics of

31

movement. Busby's nerve outshone his ignorance, and then, as later, his unstinting confidence financed much on-the-job training. Thinking about *A Connecticut Yankee*, he remembered, "The second act opened with Queen Guinevere's dancing class in the castle. I thought it would be a good ploy to start the scene with the Queen teaching the first five positions of the dance. The trouble was I didn't even know the first position, let alone the others. So I walked around the stage rubbing my head and pretending I was thinking up something. I said to one of the girls, 'I think I'll have the Queen start off by showing the first position.' She said, 'Oh, you mean this,' and pointed her feet in a certain way. I looked out of the corner of my eye to see what she was doing and then pointed to another girl. 'Second position,' and so on. In this way, and without their knowing it, I learned the first five positions of the dance."

Employment offers multiplied, and Busby choreographed five Broadway shows in 1928. The next year he worked on a revue starring Texas Guinan called *Broadway Nights*, but he only agreed to do the Shuberts' show after the brothers promised to allow him to direct a musical of his own. The musical was *The Street Singer*. Signed as producer, Berkeley hired himself to direct and choreograph the production. It was the first time in the history of the American theatre that a producer was so involved in a presentation. In a way, Busby Berkeley followed Frank Capra's "one man, one film" philosophy before ever going to Hollywood. Yet Berkeley's degree of participation followed the pre-talkie tradition of filmmaking in Hollywood and the rest of the world. The director was the thing, and the 32-year-old triple-threat talent was going to be *the* thing in American cinema a short time later.

While creating the choreography for *Lew Leslie's International Review*, Busby was asked by the William Morris Agency if he would be interested in going to Hollywood. The respected and well-paid theatrical mastermind didn't like movie musicals, rightly considering them static affairs, but he consented when Sam Goldwyn offered him the job of staging dances for *Whoopee*, produced by Florenz Ziegfeld and starring Eddie Cantor. Busby and his wife came to Hollywood in 1930, and with the exception of a quick return to Manhattan that year, the director didn't come back to the Broadway stage for fifteen seasons.

Berkeley entered Hollywood as ignorant of the ways of filmmaking as he had been of the techniques of dancing. "I soon realized that in the theatre your eyes can go any place you want, but in pictures the only way I could entertain an audience was through the single eye of the camera," he said in 1969. "But with that single eye, I could go anywhere I wanted to."

Whoopee's art director, Richard Day, also gave Busby some valuable basic advice about the cinema image. "All you have to remember is that the camera has only one eye, not two. You can see a lot with two eyes but hold a hand over one and it cuts your area of vision."

In *Whoopee* Busby used overhead shots of the chorus girls for the first time. Conversely, he also filmed extreme close-ups of Goldwyn's showgirls, causing the mogul much consternation, until Berkeley explained, "Well, we've got all these beautiful girls in the picture. Why not let the public see them?"

But Hollywood's new arrival almost didn't get to shoot his dance sequences in *Whoopee*. Once the choreographer created the production numbers, he left the filming of those scenes to the director, and the footage came together in the editing room. Berkeley cut out the middle men. He insisted that the crew use only one camera instead of the usual four, thus allowing him to edit each sequence in his head. Goldwyn liked what came out.

Soon after *Whoopee* Busby met Warner Brothers' director Mervyn LeRoy. LeRoy convinced the dance director who couldn't even do a time step that unemployment in Hollywood was often cyclical. Musicals which couldn't sell one day would become gold mines a year or two later. Therefore Busby stayed on the Coast, working at Fanchon and Marco, a Los Angeles production house which created stage prologues for movie theatres.

Goldwyn brought him back on screen via *The Kid from Spain* in 1932. Shortly Busby realized that LeRoy was right. Darryl F. Zanuck, the assistant production head at Warner Brothers, asked Berkeley to do the musical sequences for *42nd Street*. Mervyn LeRoy had signed to direct the $400,000 production, but he was forced to withdraw due to illness. Lloyd Bacon took over, and with Busby he created one of the greatest musicals ever made.

When *42nd Street* opened, it lit up Hollywood with bright reviews. "Busby Berkeley's dance numbers are rapidly paced and rather imaginatively conceived," wrote Richard Watts, Jr. in the *New York Herald-Tribune*. "Swell dance routines," chimed Irene Thirer in the New York *Daily News*. Jimmy Starr of the *New York Herald Express* insisted, "*42nd Street* is a cinematic effort by which Busby Berkeley, and he alone, is responsible for the current return of celluloid musicals. The beauty and originality of his dances top anything yet shown on screen."

Busby originally signed for one film, but ultimately he penned a seven-year contract at Warner Brothers. He credits Darryl Zanuck with allowing him the necessary freedom to revolutionize Hollywood's concept of the movie musical: "He [Zanuck] came to the set that evening with an entourage of executives and I prepared to show him what we had planned for the number 'Young and Healthy.' I staged this with three revolving platforms, and I explained to Zanuck that I couldn't

*Joan Blondell
(center) in* Gold
Diggers of 1933
(WB, 1933)

*Adolphe Menjou
in* Gold Diggers
of 1935 *(WB,
1935)*

show him exactly what he would see on the screen because I planned to shoot in cuts. I outlined the continuity for him and showed him my camera placements, then had Dick Powell and the boys and girls go through the number in sections. Zanuck and the others seemed very pleased."

Gold Diggers of 1933 followed. LeRoy directed and Berkeley stepped in for the musical sequences. The results are not up to the standards of *42nd Street*, but the film contains one of Berkeley's greatest production numbers, "Remember My Forgotten Man." It's an intense plea, etched in song and dance, for the fair treatment of war veterans, reduced to selling apples in the street and marching on Washington for the piece of the American pie they had fought to preserve in 1918. The number employs one hundred and fifty extras in soldiers' clothing, filing through a three-story half-moon set placed against a studio sky, while Joan Blondell vocalizes (dubbed) their plight, and men and women fall to their knees around her on a long block of thin steps. The sequence is as powerful as anything in *42nd Street*.

"It's a dazzling, eye-paralyzing, ear-tickling creation that makes all the other musical films look like Delaney Street peep shows," insisted critic Relma Morin of the *Los Angeles Record*. "The star of the picture is the gentleman who does not appear in it. Busby Berkeley, the geometrically minded lad who created the dance sequences, has done a perfectly amazing job."

In his first two years at Warner Brothers, Busby worked on eight films, all but one of them expensive musicals. The rising genius of the West Coast commented later that his routines cost about $100,000, or $10,000 a minute. Naturally the Warner Brothers executives were vitally concerned with the work schedule of their contractee. Unfortunately, Sam Goldwyn signed Busby to choreograph *Roman Scandals* as a condition of releasing him to Warner Brothers. When the cameras rolled on the Goldwyn production, Berkeley was involved in *Footlight Parade*. A lawsuit ensued, with both projects happily receiving pages of free publicity, and Goldwyn had to wait for "The Million Dollar Dance Director" to finish *Footlight Parade*.

Gold Diggers of 1935 was Busby Berkeley's first film as a director. Three musical numbers, "The Lullaby of Broadway," "The Words Are in My Heart," and "I'm Going Shopping with You," punctuate a sparse and cliché-ridden script. The first sequence is clearly the best.

"A great part of my work has not been the work of a choreographer strictly speaking, because, for me ... it is the camera that must dance," Busby said. And dance it did in "The Lullaby of Broadway." Berkeley had a special monorail built to monitor the boom microphones secured throughout the rafters. On a typical day, the director could be seen sixty feet in the air, casually traversing the catwalks, plotting out movements of his camera and dancers. "The Lullaby of Broadway" opens with a pinprick of light on the screen which becomes Wini Shaw, crooning about Broadway. Slowly her face swallows more and more of the black space around it; then suddenly the camera dashes around and re-frames her face, with the forehead in front, and the sides of the image slipping down to meet in a curve, broken only by the cigarette butt in her mouth. Berkeley dissolves to a like-shaped view of Manhattan, and then to a montage of fast and furious New York, including shots of Wini coming home to her rotting tenement in the early daylight, while neighbors get ready for work. Soon Dick Powell arrives in top hat and tails for another neon-lit session of night clubbing. Wini and Dick are alone in a ballroom, until two Latin dancers glide in and separate, returning to the frame with one hundred tap dancers snapping at the floor to a crescendo of "The Lullaby of Broadway." Wini attempts to escape the mad, gay life and plunges to her death from the balcony of a skyscraper. The chorus quietly sings "Good Night, Baby," while the camera reflects on Manhattan, and returns to brush Wini's tenement room (à la Ophuls' *Libeleli* and Litvak's *Act of Love*). A final shot of Wini's face ends the brilliant sequence. "Nobody but me ever knew what the number would look like on the screen until it was in the can," said Busby. The statement can be applied to most of his other song and dance extravaganzas.

Despite some excellent parts, *Gold Diggers of 1935* received mixed notices. "Merely a framework—and not a very exciting framework, I fear—for the lavish production numbers of the resourceful Busby Berkeley," lamented *Herald-Tribune* critic Richard Watts, Jr. Andre Sennwald of the *New York Times* was more enthusiastic: "Busby Berkeley, the master of scenic prestidigitation, continues to dazzle the eye and stun the imagination in the latest of the Warner Brothers musical comedies."

Busby's good reviews didn't last. On the night of September 8, 1935 Berkeley drove down the unpredictable Pacific Coast Highway from a party given by Warner Brothers production manager Bill Loenig. The left front tire of his roadster blew out above the Santa Monica Canyon, and the car went out of control. With the director frantically attempting to jerk the vehicle into the right lane, he crashed head-on into another car, instantly killing two of its passengers. Busby was pulled unconscious from the burning roadster. A third person died in the hospital. Berkeley found himself faced with three charges of second degree murder and accused of being drunk while driving on the wrong side of the road. At one of his three trials, nurse Katherine Schneider testified, "Mr. Berkeley sustained a physical shock which left him in a confused mental state for hours afterward." To all who saw him in the dirtied white tie and jacket, disheveled dark shirt, and bandaged right eye, that seemed an understatement. Relatives of the three killed in the collision settled their suits against the director privately. Some at Bill Loenig's party refused to swear about Busby's sobriety, but others did so freely. After his third trial, on September 26, 1936 the superior court found the director to be innocent of drunk driving.

Berkeley's mother and his work helped preserve his sanity through the ordeal. The director's films were popular for another two years. In 1937 the last two big Warner Brothers musicals, *Varsity Show* and *Hollywood Hotel,* came out to dwindling critical and public acceptance. Music became a smaller factor in the typical studio production, and this turn of events pleased Busby, since he had wanted to move into the non-musical areas of comedy and drama.

His chance arrived with vehicles such as *Garden of the Moon* (1938) and *They Made Me a Criminal* (1939). *Garden of the Moon* was his last musical under the seven-year Warner Brothers deal. Starring Pat O'Brien and John Payne as a night club owner and band leader who battle over a girl (Margaret Lindsay), the film isn't exactly a satire on Hollywood, but it hits Los Angeles square in the jaw a number of times. "A bright musical," asserted *Variety.* "A delightful satire on LA manners," wrote the *New York Times'* B. R. Crisler.

They Made Me a Criminal wasn't nearly so delightful. Filmed in the gritty, realistic Warner Brothers tradition, the production concerns a young boxer (John Garfield) who mistakenly believes he has killed a man and flees west. Relentlessly pursued by a has-been detective (Claude Rains), John is reformed by a hot air version of the Dead End Kids and the love of a good woman (Gloria Dickson), and freed by the detective.

They Made Me a Criminal was one of Berkeley's favorites among his films. It is certainly the most atypical production of his career. Although the film indulges in excessive Dead End Kids-style comedy and pathos with Billy Halop, Leo Gorcey, Huntz Hall *et al.*, it does indicate that Busby could have brought a unique touch to other crime dramas if they had been offered to him.

That year the director moved to MGM because Warner Brothers refused to raise his salary as promised. After working on a mediocre Jeanette MacDonald film, *Broadway Serenade,* Berkeley directed, among others, *Babes in Arms, Strike Up the Band,* and *Babes on Broadway* over the next three years. The trio starred the popular team of Mickey Rooney and Judy Garland.

Babes in Arms (1939) was called "one of the finest musicals we have seen on stage or screen" by Robert W. Dana of the *New York Herald-Tribune.* The production is genuinely charming, if not among the greatest screen musicals, with Rodgers and Hart's book, lyrics, and

Mickey Rooney,
Douglas
MacPhail, and
Judy Garland in
Babes in Arms
(MGM, 1939)

Judy Garland and
Mickey Rooney in
Strike Up the
Band *(MGM,*
1940)

Mickey Rooney and Judy Garland in Babes on Broadway *(MGM, 1941)*

Alice Faye, Frank Faylen, and James Ellison in The Gang's All Here *(20th, 1943)*

music providing Berkeley with dreamier material than he had ever had at hard-boiled Warner Brothers. The production numbers are perhaps overdone, with one in particular extremely reminiscent of sequences in *Footlight Parade*, *Roman Scandals*, and *Gold Diggers of 1933*. Here Berkeley has his actors moving back and forth on a stage with little of the motivation that inspired his earlier productions.

Strike Up the Band (1940) was a quickly conceived sequel to the successful *Babes in Arms*. Garland and Rooney head a group of high school students who transform the school band into a swing orchestra to compete in a national band contest sponsored by Paul Whiteman. Mickey Rooney at the drums and a musical fruit sequence highlight the film's production numbers. "Spanking good entertainment," wrote Theodore Strauss in his *New York Times* review. "The lenses are constantly restless, moving from dancers' feet to upraised trombones or zooming down from the ceiling. And the sequences have been assembled as if the cutting room assistants were rhythm crazy." The *Philadelphia Record* supported *Strike Up the Band* as "one long live jamboree from beginning to end."

Strike Up the Band does suffer from excessive sentimentalizing, surfacing in long, lofty discussions between Rooney and his screen mother, and also between Rooney and Whiteman. When Whiteman counsels ambitious Rooney not to leave his friends, he makes the point by stating that life is like a continuous rhythm, full of ups and downs, until one reaches the "last eight bars" in the sky. This brand of schmaltz would have been stomped to death on Warner Brothers' editing room floor.

Babes on Broadway (1941) was the last of the trio of Garland-Rooney musicals, and it proved to be as solid as the others. The thin plot revolves around the efforts of some youthful show biz types to put on a show for a settlement home. The two top numbers are the "Chin Cup, Cheerio, Carry On" number sang by Judy Garland, surrounded by fifty British refugee children, and the ghost segment of the song-story in which Mickey Rooney moves through a creaking stage impersonating legendary actors. Perhaps the liveliest section of *Babes on Broadway* is the "Hoedown" scene, which reflects a slightly toned-down style emphasizing song and dance, with angular set designs and expressionistic camera angles at a minimum.

The Gang's All Here (1943) was Busby's first film for 20th Century-Fox. The studio, headed by former Berkeley booster Darryl F. Zanuck, had tried to borrow the director's services while he was at Warner Brothers, but the "Berkeley look" wasn't allowed to surface under any other banner. Fortunately MGM was a little more flexible.

"The trouble is that the book and music do not live up to the production or the performers," lamented Otis L. Guernsey in the *New York Herald-Tribune*. "The most imaginative things in the show are the sets and costumes," said Theodore Strauss of the *Times*. *Nation* critic James Agee labeled it "as torturing a piece of torching as the war has evolved." However the revival of *The Gang's All Here* precipitated a large flow of critical praise. In 1971 Rex Reed proclaimed in the New York *Daily News*: "Nothing could have been so innocent or so much fun as the Hollywood musical of the Forties.... None of it makes the slightest sense, but it's been a long time since I've had so much fun watching pure escapist nonsense.... Since the whole thing was designed and directed by Busby Berkeley, almost everything was conducted for some kind of colossal effect."

As usual, the story is skin deep, but *The Gang's All Here* is closer to the Berkeley extravaganzas of the 1930s than anything the director shot at MGM. The show-stopper in the light, opulent film is the finale, "The Polka Dot Polka." "I built a great kaleidoscope," the director recalled, "two mirrors fifty feet high and fifteen feet wide which together formed a V design. In the center of this I had a revolving platform eighteen feet in diameter, and as I took the camera up high between these two mirrors, the girls on the revolving platform below formed an endless design of symmetrical forms. In another shot, I dropped from above sixty neon-lighted hoops which the girls caught and used in their dance maneuvers."

Ironically, Berkeley's next film came from the studio which had refused to loan him out. He shot *Cinderella Jones* early in 1944 (released in 1946) and Jack Warner offered him a five-year contract with an increase in salary if he would leave MGM. Berkeley did so, and was given the life of Ziegfeld musical comedy star Marilyn Miller to put on film, but the property was dropped as a result of legal complications.

Other problems arose. Busby wanted it contractually agreed that he should produce as well as direct, but Jack Warner rebelled at the suggestion. Berkeley's well-known chutzpah, which enabled him to take his career to such heights, this time proved to be his undoing. Annoyed at not being able to reach Warner on the telephone, he told the studio boss' secretary that if a meeting could not be arranged, their contract should be terminated. Jack Warner happily ended their association.

Glad to See You, a Broadway musical with songs by Jule Styne and Sammy Cahn, revived the director's sagging spirits, but the show was only a moderate success.

During the 1940s Gertrude Berkeley's health rapidly deteriorated. The former stage actress had been a good friend and business adviser to her son, and her death in 1946 was a great blow to the director. His mother's medical bills were enormous, and Busby had to separate from his new wife, the former Marge Pemberton, in order to stay at Gertrude's side. He sold his valuable antique collection as well as property in New Hampshire, Oklahoma, and California. The final shock was discovering that he owed $120,000 to the government.

On July 17, 1946 Busby Berkeley entered the bathroom and slashed his neck and wrists. Saved by his houseboy, the man whose fall from the heights was accomplished in a matter of months was taken to a nearby hospital and then sent to a sanitarium to recuperate. "There's no comeback trail for a has-been," he said dejectedly. His mother had died, his fifth marriage had disintegrated, his career was at an all-time low, and he was broke. Nevertheless, Busby Berkeley came back.

Two years after his suicide attempt Busby called George Amy, an old friend at Warner Brothers, and Amy succeeded in getting the completely cured filmmaker the job of supervising the musical sequences in Michael Curtiz's *Romance on the High Seas*. From there, MGM producer Arthur Freed suggested that Berkeley shoot *Take Me Out to the Ball Game*. Busby convinced Louis B. Mayer of his sincerity in wanting to work hard, and, indeed, that he wanted to live.

Take Me Out to the Ball Game won Berkeley *Photoplay*'s Blue Ribbon Award for 1949 and the industry's Laurel Award. The tale of two pre-World War I vaudevillians (Frank Sinatra and Gene Kelly) who were also famous baseball players is a charming, bright piece of Americana which allowed Busby to stage musical sequences in one of the largest theatres in existence—the baseball park. Kelly and Stanley Donen, who penned the original story, also choreographed the dances, leaving Berkeley to focus on the narrative and comedy shtick.

Despite the applause of moviegoers, *Take Me Out to the Ball Game* was not a critical favorite. "For all its high spots ... the show lacks consistent style and pace, and the stars are forced to clown and grimace much more than becomes their speed," lectured Bosley Crowther in his *New York Times* review. "Busby Berkeley directed the book as though he were trying to drive home jokes with the nearest thing at hand—a baseball bat," lamented Barnes of the *Herald-Tribune*.

Although *Take Me Out to the Ball Game* was Berkeley's final film as a director, he returned eight times to the sound stage to supervise or conjure musical sequences, the last being for *Billy Rose's Jumbo* in 1962. Busby was known as the man whose films cost plenty, and in a penny-pinching Hollywood of the 1950s which was reacting to the very real threat of television, there was little room for an expensive director who didn't turn out spectacles such as *Quo Vadis* or *The Greatest Show on Earth*.

The best thing that occurred during the quiet decade for Berkeley was his sixth and final marriage—to Etta Dunn, on January 23, 1958. The union lasted until Busby's death in 1976. In the 1960s the Berkeleys lived in a small pink stucco house in a residential community near Palm Springs, California, with seventeen cats to keep them company.

After *Jumbo* Berkeley retired, but he remained open to job offers. Without compensation, he directed plays at a local theatre and waited for the wave of critical appreciation that he knew would eventually come. In 1965 he was represented at the San Francisco Film Festival by *For Me and My Gal* (MGM, 1942). A more complete retrospective took place in New York City a short time later. Soon a compilation film titled *An Evening with Busby Berkeley and the Glorious Era of Hollywood* circulated at festivals and on college campuses. Jack Haley even wanted to produce a film on the director's life.

Like so many veteran directors, Berkeley disdained the increasing cynicism in the American cinema. "In my musicals people forgot the Depression; they forgot their troubles. My God, why can't we do the same today?" he asked. A happy response was provided by the reappearance of a 1925 Broadway hit called *No, No, Nanette*. The show opened to rave reviews on January 19, 1971 with Berkeley's name on the credits as supervisor. He proved to be just as tough in rehearsal at the age of 76 as he had been for years. Time may have taught him how to cope with life, but not to be timid about it. The show, which reunited him with Ruby Keeler, had dazzling production numbers. A large tap-dancing chorus, gigantic staircases and pianos, and an Atlantic City sequence where the girls balanced balls brought back, if only for a moment, the magic of Busby Berkeley and what many have termed a less complicated era. The only negative reaction toward the filmmaker's stage comeback surfaced in a book by Donald H. Dunn entitled *The Making of No, No, Nanette*, which was critical of Berkeley's work in the show.

"You know, if someone came along today and made a *Gold Diggers of 1970* he'd make himself a bloody fortune," Busby insisted. "And I'd like to do it. Wow! What I could do with wide screen and color. I didn't have those things back in the thirties."

That chance never came. What Busby Berkeley did have was the ability to take the cinematic form to its purest heights in a Hollywood obsessed with the star. No other American director of the period even came close to Berkeley's sense of imagery in his elaborate musical sequences.

Busby Berkeley's life ended on March 15, 1976. Before his death he roughed out a summary of that old Hollywood religion which provides a fine epitaph for the man: "Never ask the whys and wherefores of a Berkeley number. I don't know myself. I kept you entertained, didn't I?"

The Films of Busby Berkeley

As Choreographer:
Whoopee *(UA, 1930)*
Kiki *(UA, 1930)*
Palmy Days *(UA, 1931)*
Flying High *(MGM, 1931)*
Night World *(Univ., 1932)*
Bird of Paradise *(RKO, 1932)*
The Kid from Spain *(UA, 1932)*
42nd Street *(WB, 1933)*
Gold Diggers of 1933 *(WB, 1933)*
Footlight Parade *(WB, 1933)*
Roman Scandals *(UA, 1933)*
Fashions of 1934 *(FN, 1934)*
Wonder Bar *(FN, 1934)*
Twenty Million Sweethearts *(FN, 1934)*
Dames *(WB, 1934)*
Go into Your Dance *(FN, 1935)*
In Caliente *(FN, 1935)*

Stars Over Broadway *(WB, 1935)*
Gold Diggers of 1937 *(FN, 1936)*
The Singing Marine *(WB, 1937)*
Varsity Show *(WB, 1937)*
Gold Diggers in Paris *(WB, 1938)*
Broadway Serenade *(MGM, 1939)*
Ziegfeld Girl *(MGM, 1941)*
Lady Be Good *(MGM, 1941)*
Born to Sing *(MGM, 1941)*
Girl Crazy *(MGM, 1943)*
Two Weeks with Love *(MGM, 1950)*
Call Me Mister *(20th, 1951)*
Two Tickets to Broadway *(RKO, 1951)*
Million Dollar Mermaid *(MGM, 1952)*
Small Town Girl *(MGM, 1953)*
Easy to Love *(MGM, 1953)*
Rose Marie *(MGM, 1954)*
Billy Rose's Jumbo *(MGM, 1962)*

As Director:
She Had to Say Yes *(FN, 1933)* (co-directed by George Amy)
Gold Diggers of 1935 *(FN, 1935)*
Bright Lights *(FN, 1935)*
I Live for Love *(WB, 1935)*
Stage Struck *(FN, 1936)*
The Go-Getter *(WB, 1937)*
Hollywood Hotel *(WB, 1937)*
Men Are Such Fools *(WB, 1938)*
Garden of the Moon *(WB, 1938)*
Comet Over Broadway *(WB, 1938)*

They Made Me a Criminal *(WB, 1939)*
Babes in Arms *(MGM, 1939)*
Fast and Furious *(MGM, 1939)*
Forty Little Mothers *(RKO, 1940)*
Strike Up the Band *(MGM, 1940)*
Blonde Inspiration *(MGM, 1941)*
Babes on Broadway *(MGM, 1941)*
For Me and My Gal *(MGM, 1942)*
The Gang's All Here *(20th, 1943)*
Cinderella Jones *(WB, 1946)*
Take Me Out to the Ball Game *(MGM, 1949)*

Jeffrey Lynn and Olivia de Havilland in a publicity pose for My Love Came Back *(WB, 1940)*

Curtis Bernhardt, Alexis Smith, and Humphrey Bogart on the set of Conflict *(WB, 1945)*

Curtis Bernhardt

"The first thing that hit me here, and hit me hard, was that I no longer had the authority that I had had before," said Curtis Bernhardt, reminiscing about his thirty years in Hollywood. "In Germany, France, and Italy before World War II, the director was in charge of the whole artistic side of the film including the script and the choice of story. The producer had very little influence on actual filmmaking; he was only the business head of the organization."

The career of Curtis Bernhardt has been shaped by timing more than anything else. Much of his apparently inventive early European work seems to be lost, or is rarely available today. It is clear that the German-born director evinces a talent for pictorialism amid period settings, and his filmography contains a number of impressive "women's" pictures, along with finely detailed performances by the women themselves. However, Bernhardt's first American production didn't occur until 1940, and that was the main problem. A decade later Hollywood began to end the middle-budget property that the director made so well, with roles for women largely reduced to a Marilyn Monroe-type as a blonde, brunette, or redhead. Nevertheless, his credits include *Devotion*, *My Reputation*, *Possessed*, and *The Blue Veil*, four excellent films, ably supported by a series of light comedies, melodramas, and costume dramas which indicate that Bernhardt could have been as prolific as similarly inclined directors such as Edmund Goulding and Clarence Brown had he started in Hollywood when the talkies were new.

Kurt Bernhardt was born on April 15, 1899 in Worms, Germany. He began as an actor on the German stage before his career evolved into directing. In the mid-1920s a film producer came backstage and asked Kurt if he could make a film for 60,000 marks. Like many other filmmakers who entered the profession in the early years, Bernhardt was ignorant of production procedure: "I had no idea whether a motion picture cost sixteen thousand, sixty thousand, or six hundred thousand marks, but I said: 'Yes.'"

The film, titled *War*, reflected the overwhelming pacifist sentiment throughout Europe in the 1920s. Bernhardt's lack of awareness regarding cinema history may have actually helped him to create an original, striking work. He later recalled: "In it I used what I think must have been one of the first traveling shots ever attempted: during a big Berlin public demonstration I put the camera in a taxi and had it photograph the demonstrators through the rear window as they followed the vehicle on their march."

In 1926 Bernhardt received recognition for his direction of *Qualen der Nacht (Torments of the Night)*, which he also co-scripted with Carl Zuckmayer. The film stars Wilhelm (William) Dieterle and was a big hit in Europe. That same year he filmed a version of Charlotte Bronte's *Jane Eyre*, retitled *The Orphan of Lowood (Die Waise von Lowood)*. "I tried to give the film a grey, Gothic kind of mood as demanded by the story," the director remembered, "although it's not as somber as, say, *Wuthering Heights*." It might be valuable to compare the German's silent effort with *Devotion*, the biographical film of the Bronte sisters he shot twenty years later.

After several years of soundless filmmaking, the director, who barely understood English, traveled to London to see *The Jazz Singer*. Shortly afterward Bernhardt filmed his (and Germany's) first talkie, Ufa's *The Last Company* (1930), a popular production still revived in Europe. He shot it on the stage next to Josef Von Sternberg's *The Blue Angel*. "I looked at Sternberg's rushes and Sternberg looked at my rushes, and I sometimes took his advice because he came from America, and he had made talkies and I had not."

The next year Kurt filmed *Der Mann, der den Mord Beging (The Man Who Killed)*, starring Conrad Veidt. Adapted from Claude Farrere's novel, the story concerns international diplomacy in turn-of-the-century Constantinople. In a Renoiresque fashion, Veidt escapes punishment for the murder of an English lord because the dead man was a brute with his own wife. "*The Man Who Killed* is one of my favorite films— not necessarily one of my most successful—because it had a certain romantic, brooding mood."

The Tunnel was an ambivalent project for Kurt. Shot in 1933, it gave the director a chance to leave Germany for good—or so he thought. Upon arriving in Paris, he was informed that unless he returned to Munich to make a German version of the script, he would be blacklisted in France. Hitler had come to power, and Bernhardt had no illusions about the National Socialists' goals. He returned home under a guarantee of freedom by the German government, but the promise was worthless. Bernhardt recently informed me how he was "arrested by the Gestapo in the summer of 1933" and how he "escaped from Germany in October 1933 after having lived underground for about two months."

Perhaps needing a complete change from his traumatic existence, the director co-scripted his first comedy, *L'Or dans la Rue*, with Henry Koster in 1934. In 1936 he made *Carrefour*, released in 1938 and reshot in 1942 by MGM and Jack Conway as *Crossroads*, and in England in 1938 by Thomas Bentley as *Dead Man's Shoes*.

When World War II erupted, Kurt found himself in the unenviable position of being considered a Jew by the Nazis and a German by the French and English. America was the answer. He crossed the ocean late in 1939 and found that his reputation had preceded him. "Warner Brothers and MGM on the merits of *Carrefour* offered me jobs," Curtis told me. He signed with Warner Brothers because of the studio's reputation for hard-boiled realism. The director also discovered that he had lost his freedom and his given name. "In America, I found that the producer was the number one man and that the director was supposed to take a script, make a few changes if he felt like it, and then shoot it," Bernhardt related to Charles Higham and Joel Greenberg in *The Celluloid Muse: Hollywood Directors Speak*.

The studio handed the director a script with only days to prepare. "And I was used to having three, four, five months of preparation: selecting the story, writing one shooting-script with the writers and then a second shooting-script, and when I was ready I went on the stage and started shooting."

Illness forced him off that project, and his first American film was the charming comedy *My Love Came Back*, starring Olivia de Havilland as a violinist looking for love and finding it in Jeffrey Lynn. "A pleasant disarming picture," Howard Barnes wrote in his *New York Herald-Tribune* review. "Has a unity of mood and an engaging variety of incident." *Variety* termed the film "light, fluffy, musical, and human."

That last quality permeates the films of Curtis Bernhardt. One cares very much about the Bronte sisters in *Devotion*, about Joan Crawford's plight in *Possessed*, about Jane Wyman's sacrifices in *The Blue Veil*, and about Stewart Granger's courageous, witty, but flawed *Beau Brummell*. Characters feel for each other in the director's films, and those feelings are honest, more so than in comparable works of the period. It is ironic, yet fitting, that one of Bernhardt's final works to date should be the quintessential *Damon and Pythias*, a story of two men who were willing to die for each other.

After a hair-raising session directing Miriam Hopkins as Mrs. Leslie Carter in a biography of David Belasco (Claude Rains) entitled *The Lady with Red Hair* (1940), Warner Brothers assigned Curtis to handle two films that he isn't particularly fond of today. According to the director, *Juke Girl* (1942) was a "sort of semi-Western laid among fruit-pickers and incorporating orgies of fights; I don't know why they gave it to me." Neither did the critics. The earlier *Million Dollar Baby* (also 1942) with Priscilla Lane warmed the hearts of some, including Paramount executive Buddy de Sylva, who borrowed the director to film a musical, *Happy Go Lucky*, in 1943. The loan-out was Warner Brothers' way of slapping Bernhardt's wrists for turning down a script. In those days, a Warner contractee could be suspended for such blasphemy, so Curtis' "punishment" was light indeed. (The director had already been suspended several times previously.)

This was a difficult professional period for the director, since several of his projects of the early 1940s were canceled, including *Manhattan Fury* in 1941, and also *Hot Nocturne*, starring John Garfield and originally scheduled for Anatole Litvak. In addition, there were long delays in the release of his finished films. *Conflict* (1945) was ready for two years before the public saw it, *My Reputation* (1946) sat on the shelves for two and a half years, and *Devotion* (also 1946) gathered dust for three years.

Conflict is an atmospheric though slightly ludicrous tale of a man (Humphrey Bogart) who murders his wife (Rose Hobart) and attempts to marry her sister (Alexis Smith). Bernhardt creates pounding, reverberating suspense during Bogart's murder of his wife on a lonely, washed-out road, and again when the killer mistakenly believes he sees the dead woman enter an apartment building. The final scene at the crime site is almost haunting in its evocation of spiraling doom.

James Agee of the *Nation* called *Conflict* "quite well done, but its story is so fancy that it becomes tiresome." "Melodrama addicts will find it to their liking," suggested *Variety*.

In *My Reputation*, Barbara Stanwyck plays New England widow Jess Drummond, a woman who becomes involved with a serviceman (George Brent) too soon after her husband's death to suit her community. It is one of Bernhardt's personal favorites among his films, and certainly one of his finest. *My Reputation* may be described as a typically "glossy" film of the 1940s, a term the director rightly disdains. "Films in those days, the 1940s, derived their 'dense,' 'crowded' visual texture, their extraordinary rich surface look, largely from the fact that most of them were in black-and-white, and not in color. ... I think the conventional, square 35mm ratio was ideal. Nowadays the image is not as *concentrated* as it was then; directors and cameramen have to cope with a vast expanse of space on either side of people photographed at close quarters, and they don't know what to do with it."

My Reputation contains a wealth of complex formal arrangements which enhance a surprisingly low-key melodrama. The introduction of Jess Drummond is a fine example. The camera pans left in a dark room distinguished by New England artifacts, then drifts down to a close-up of the recent widow in dim light. She sits up into a patch of brightness. The camera pulls back. The moment is luxurious: it captures the atmosphere as well as the depressed figure of the wife. In another case, a single shot tells all. Jess refuses to wear black, committing herself to a promise she has made to her husband Paul never to look back. Bernhardt frames Stanwyck in a medium-close shot, bordered by stern bedposts reminiscent of prison bars, surrounded by the floral pattern of the wallpaper. It is evident from the set-up that Jess will not have an easy time with her neighbors.

Sharp-eyed Bette Davis was impressed with *My Reputation*. With her knowledge of the power of camera placement and lighting on a performance, and Bernhardt's knack for bringing the best out of an actress, it was obvious to the star that Curtis should be her next director, and she insisted that he guide her through the difficult *A Stolen Life* (1946).

Bosley Crowther of the *New York Times* considered the film "a moderately intriguing slick-fiction yarn," but Curtis considers it a troubled production today. Davis stars as twins of radically different character. Warner Brothers wanted to create a new look in double exposures: previously one image resided on a section of the screen, the other completely opposite, and the twain never met. In *A Stolen Life* the twins are pictured passing each other and generally intermingling. A double was only used on over-the-shoulder shots.

The star and Bernhardt started arguing soon after the production began, but they settled their altercations amiably. At one point Bette might have thought that her director was out for revenge. "The climactic storm sequence was staged in the studio tank," Curtis recalled. "It was very difficult and Bette almost drowned in it. In these tank scenes, you see, we have a boat with wires underneath it to control it and jiggle it around whenever you want it. Well, in this tremendous tank we had chutes coming down and waves coming up, and one of them was supposed to swish her overboard. She should have come up immediately but she went down and she didn't come up. I was horrified because I realized that she had been caught in one of the wires." Divers rescued the star, and she admirably continued work soon afterward.

Curtis would have preferred to film *Devotion* in England, but the war prevented it, and he had to settle for a Warner backlot. The director was by 1943 allowed to sit in on story conferences, and as a result Curtis was largely responsible for the final look of the film about the Bronte

Warner Anderson and Barbara Stanwyck in My Reputation *(WB, 1946)*

Olivia de Havilland, Paul Henreid, Ida Lupino, and Nancy Coleman in Devotion *(WB, 1946)*

Van Heflin and
Joan Crawford
in Possessed
(WB, 1947)

Elizabeth Taylor
and Steward
Granger in
Beau Brummell
(MGM, 1954)

sisters and their brother. Starring Olivia de Havilland and Ida Lupino, with Arthur Kennedy as the favored brother, *Devotion* is a soft, pictorial biography quite removed from the traditional Warner Brothers style. It isn't full of action, world-shaking ideas or political radicalism, but instead captures the flavor of Victorian England and something of the creative spirit.

A particularly difficult sequence to film was the death dream on the moors that had been partially created by the director. A man in black atop a black horse rides toward one of the sisters and shrouds her in a black cloak. Shot in the studio, because the cinema technique of the time prohibited anything else, the scene is something of a throwback to the Expressionist mood sometimes dominant in the early Warner Brothers work of Curtiz and Dieterle.

Bosley Crowther of the *Times* called *Devotion* "a ridiculous tax upon reason and an insult to plain intelligence." Conversely, the *Herald-Tribune*'s Howard Barnes felt that it was an "eminently rewarding piece. ... Curtis Bernhardt has staged the Keith Winter screenplay with imagination and considerable realism, but he has wisely relied on artful players to sustain the quiet burden of emotional excitement."

In 1947 the director's seven-year contract with Warner Brothers ended, and so did his association with the studio. Two more projects with Bette Davis (*Ethan Frome* and *The Life of Sara Bernhardt*) failed to materialize, and Curtis' final Warner Brothers film was the excellent *Possessed*. Originally called *The Secret*, the director and star Joan Crawford toured the Los Angeles General Hospital in preparation for the narrative of a mentally unbalanced woman and her two lovers (Raymond Massey and Van Heflin). In addition, Bernhardt read thirty books on the subject.

The result was a touching, suspenseful, and honest film. Geraldine Brooks shines as Massey's daughter, and the Crawford-Brooks, Crawford-Massey, and Crawford-Heflin scenes are full of intensity and total eye-to-eye confrontation. "I wasn't happy, I wasn't sad," says melancholy Louise (Crawford), thus diagnosing her own mental illness. *Possessed* opens with long, then progressively closer shots of a disoriented Louise wandering the streets of the city in the late night and early morning hours. The grit of the story is established in the stark lines of tired Louise's face, in her hysterical ramblings, and in the urban grey. As she is pushed down hospital halls, the camera assumes a subjective position, quickly framing the white, angled ceiling whizzing by, symbolizing spiraling confusion by its very indistinctness. From there, the Ranald MacDougall script moves back and forth in time, capturing a piece-by-piece build-up of Louise's descent from neurosis to madness. The transformation is complete when Crawford poses herself in one of the most hateful masks of her career and pumps a half-dozen slugs into Van Heflin. Bernhardt then dissolves into a medium-close shot of Louise screaming in the hospital ward.

Possessed received mixed notices when released in June 1947. "A gripping screenplay that's been translated into celluloid with unusual frankness," announced *Variety*. In *Time* magazine, James Agee wavered: "*Possessed* is not quite top grade, but most of it is filmed with unusual imagination and force." Barnes of the *Tribune* labeled it "occasionally striking, generally lachrymose, and dramatically laggard."

Next Bernhardt moved to MGM for two 1949 films, *High Wall* and *The Doctor and the Girl*. He had originally signed with Warner Brothers in preference to MGM, but he became tired of the mechanical ways of Jack Warner's production line. Twenty years later, Curtis voiced admiration for the fine standards at the studio that the talkie built. Conversely, he lamented, "MGM was like a big, big opera-house, where you had to please this star and that prima donna." He went ahead irregardless and lensed *High Wall*, a sharp suspense film starring Robert Taylor and Audrey Totter as a former pilot trying to clear himself of a murder charge and a psychiatrist, respectively. *The Doctor and the Girl* is a quiet tale featuring Glenn Ford as an idealistic doctor who practices in the slums. The production has the realistic flavor then favored at MGM by Dore Schary, much to the consternation of Louis B. Mayer. Ironically the switch came a decade too late for Bernhardt's tastes, inasmuch as he had chosen to sign with Warner Brothers in 1940 because of "their pictures' greater realism compared with other studios' concentration on fantasy and schmaltz."

Payment on Demand (RKO, 1951), similar to *Possessed* in that it is a story of tormented male-female relationships, also features frequent temporal discontinuity. Bernhardt recalled, "That had some very fascinating flashback effects using negatives and transparent sets, incorporating a technical innovation of my own invention. Frankly, I cannot understand why it hasn't been used since."

The Blue Veil (RKO, 1951), a remake of *La Maternelle*, is one of Curtis' best films. Starring Jane Wyman as a nursemaid who gives her life to her charges and their families, the story is sentimental, yet never mawkish, and represents Bernhardt's direction of actors at its finest. Yet Crowther of the *Times* panned *The Blue Veil* as "a whoppingly banal tear-jerker based on the hawkline premise that the mere prospect of childless old age, plus quality advertising, will lure multitudes of moviegoers who like nothing better than a good cry." Otis L. Guernsey of the *New York Herald-Tribune* found the film "not so hard to take as might be expected."

The Merry Widow (1952) and *Beau Brummell* (1954), both from MGM, mark a brief return to Metro's lush, exquisite, big-star costume productions of the 1930s. The first is a workmanlike remake of the property that Ernst Lubitsch had turned into a witty 1934 film, the second a very good version of the 1925 John Barrymore starrer. The relationship between Stewart Granger (in the title role) and Peter Ustinov (a British prince) in *Beau Brummell* is another one of Bernhardt's exceedingly human exchanges, this time particularly distinguished by a glorious period setting.

Always interested in location work for heightened realism, the director tried to shoot *Sirocco* (1951) in Damascus, but wound up on a Columbia lot. "It looked like it," he later commented. *Miss Sadie Thompson* (Col., 1953) was shot in Hawaii, but the natural vistas couldn't cloak the creaking nature of Somerset Maugham's original story.

When Curtis made *Damon and Pythias* (MGM, 1961) in Europe, he worked near the ill-fated *Cleopatra* set. "We were the little retail operation, they the wholesale," the director quipped. Like other Hollywood filmmakers who traveled to Europe to work in the 1950s and 1960s, Bernhardt learned much about the ways of Italian production. "The only way you can save money there is by using an Italian manager," he advised, contradicting the myth that filmmaking is always cheaper in Europe. "Someone who can handle the crew. You don't get smeared that way.... The Italian is a great believer in improvisation." There's nothing a director likes less than a crew that executes its own ideas without benefit of the counsel of the filmmaker.

Archer Winstein's *New York Post* critique of *Damon and Pythias* typified the apathy which greeted many films directed by Hollywood veterans in their twilight (not that this production is particularly memorable): "The direction of Curtis Bernhardt is adequate, the color fair, the looks of the people tolerable, the costumes very clean."

Kisses for My President (WB, 1964), also produced by Bernhardt, has been his last Hollywood film to date. Starring Polly Bergen as a woman who becomes President of the United States, with Fred Mac-Murray as her "first husband," the production was attacked by a number of racial groups. Controversy raged over the content of the White House staff, but Curtis was determined to accurately characterize the people. "The White House police, I noticed, are all white, as are the chief housekeeper and the head administrator, and that is the way they will be depicted," he said in 1964. "In fact, Negro servants at the White House are very poised and dignified and are treated with respect, which is exactly how they will be shown on the screen."

One can easily picture *Kisses for My President* as a hit in 1940, featuring Rosalind Russell in Bergen's role, with MacMurray twenty-five years younger. The comedy received mixed reviews. Kate Carroll of the New York *Daily News* awarded the film three stars, but Robert Sal-maggi of the *Herald-Tribune* termed it a "one joke dud."

In the late 1960s the director worked with Westinghouse to produce nine features over a period of two years. He planned to shoot most of them himself, but he actually finished only *The Widow Maker*, filmed in Hungary. Based on a book by Mrs. Ladislaus Bus-Fekete, the intriguing film is set in a World War I Hungarian village, where women whose men are fighting take in Russian POW's, feed them, love them, then murder them. Bernhardt told Charles Higham, "This story has unfortunate parallels with the present-day general breakdown in moral fibre everywhere. Killing has become the accepted thing."

"Sickness has prevented me from further work," Curtis Bernhardt related to me. Hopefully his health will improve to the point where he can return to filmmaking and turn out more graceful productions, wrought with deep, sensitive images, and human beings who really touch each other on screen. Until then we can cherish *Devotion, My Reputation, Possessed, High Wall, The Blue Veil,* and, possibly, some rediscovered European productions.

The Films of Curtis Bernhardt

War *(German, 1925)*

Qualen der Nacht (Torments of the Night) *(German, 1926) (and co-script)*

Die Waise von Lowood (The Orphan of Lowood) *(German, 1926)*

Kinderseelen Klagen Euch an *(German, 1926)*

Das Mädchen mit den Funf Nullen (Das Grosse Los) *(German, 1927)*

Schinderhannes (The Prince of Rogues) *(German, 1928) (and co-script)*

Das Letzte Fort *(German, 1928)*

Die Frau, Nach der Man Sicht Sehat (Three Loves) *(German, 1929)*

Die Letzte Kompagnie (The Last Company, Thirteen Men and a Girl) *(German, 1930)*

Der Mann, der den Mord Beging (Nachte Am Bosporous) *(German, 1931)*

L'Homme Qui Assina *(French version of above) (German, 1931)*

Der Rebell *(German, 1932) (co-directed by Luis Trenker)*

Der Grosse Rausch *(German, 1932)*

Der Tunnel *(German and French versions, 1933)*

L'Or dans la Rue *(French, 1934)*

Le Vagabond Bien-Aimé *(French, 1936)*

The Beloved Vagabond *(British version of above) (Col., 1936)*

Carrefour *(French, 1938)*

Nuit de December (December Night) *(French, 1939)*

My Love Came Back *(WB, 1940)*

The Lady with Red Hair *(WB, 1940)*

Million Dollar Baby *(WB, 1942)*

Juke Girl *(WB, 1942)*

Happy Go Lucky *(Par., 1943)*

Conflict *(WB, 1945)*

Devotion *(WB, 1946)*

My Reputation *(WB, 1946)*

A Stolen Life *(WB, 1946)*

Possessed *(WB, 1947)*

High Wall *(MGM, 1947)*

The Doctor and the Girl *(MGM, 1949)*

Payment on Demand *(RKO, 1951) (and co-script)*

Sirocco *(Col., 1951)*

The Blue Veil *(RKO, 1951)*

The Merry Widow *(MGM, 1952)*

Miss Sadie Thompson *(Col., 1953)*

Beau Brummell *(MGM, 1954)*

Interrupted Melody *(MGM, 1955)*

Gaby *(MGM, 1956)*

Damon and Pythias *(MGM, 1961)*

Stefanie in Rio *(Casino, 1963)*

Kisses for My President *(WB, 1964) (and producer)*

The Widow Maker *(Hungarian, 1967)*

Alan Crosland (on platform in center) on the set of The Jazz Singer *(WB, 1927)*

4

Alan Crosland

"How's the picture going?" queried the weak director from his hospital bed. A half-hour after an assistant reported the condition of the production to his boss, Alan Crosland was dead.

The film in question was *The Case of the Caretaker's Cat*. It was re-titled *The Case of the Black Cat*, finished by William McGann, and released to good reviews.

In the early morning of July 10, 1936, Alan Crosland drove along a quiet Sunset Boulevard, probably thinking about the film that he wouldn't live to finish. Somewhere along the street his car hit an obstruction and careened off the road. No one saw the accident, but a passer-by eventually called for an ambulance. Crosland was rushed to the Beverly Hills Emergency Hospital, with a broken right arm and leg and possible skull fracture. On July 14, Dr. Frederick Bergstrom revealed that the director had contracted pneumonia and wasn't expected to live out the week. Yet to his last hour Crosland acted like the consummate professional he was. Overcome by a broken body and with pneumonia rampaging through his system, the director died on July 16, 1936, less than a month before his forty-second birthday.

The next day, production of Alan Crosland's last assignment was halted. Several of his co-workers spoke on-the-set tributes to the sophisticated, self-assured man who had helped bring Warner Brothers and the world into the realm of the talkie via his direction of *Don Juan* and *The Jazz Singer*.

Although few of his films are available to the general public at the moment, the name Alan Crosland lives on in at least three fine silent costume spectacles starring the inimitable John Barrymore. *Don Juan*, *When a Man Loves*, and *The Beloved Rogue* are occasionally shown in revival theatres and on television. Crosland's revolutionary part-talking

The Jazz Singer is more important as a signal of the public's acceptance of the sound film, and the studio's faith in him, than as cinema art. His subsequent musicals don't fare well today, and they showed to critics of the time that Crosland was a stager of action, not song. Yet historically they represent the beginnings of a genre that Hollywood producers made better than anyone else. And Crosland didn't fumble for long when the operetta adaptation became a stale commodity in the early 1930s and Busby Berkeley's cinematic gyrations over surrealistic sets won mass appeal. He did what he knew best, on a less significant level. During the last few years of his life, the director shot a dozen or so modestly budgeted comedies, love stories, and action dramas which were received more favorably than their current absence from both movie and television screens would indicate.

Alan Crosland was born on August 10, 1894, in New York City, but the family didn't stay in Manhattan long enough for Alan to attend a city high school. They moved to the fair pastures of East Orange, New Jersey, sometime during the first decade of the twentieth century. Alan went to East Orange High, not too far from Thomas Edison's new movie studio, and he also traveled to England for a taste of British education.

A frisky boy who found it hard to stay in one place, Alan enrolled at Dartmouth, but he got restless and left before graduation. The desire to write and act inspired the smart, smooth-talking young man to devise ways of bringing his dreams to fruition.

Crosland secured a letter of introduction to Fox's future replacement for Will Rogers, sour-pussed Irwin S. Cobb, then an editorial writer for the *New York World*. One scorching summer day, with the letter in hand, Alan entered Cobb's office. The veteran journalist was uncomfortable in the heat and suffering from a boil on the back of his neck, all of which left him in a foul mood. Young Crosland, in contrast, was the epitome of summer cool, and he cut a dashing figure in his snappy pre-World War I suit of clothes. His curious accent, a blend of British culture, Manhattan tough, and New Jersey twang, set him apart from the hordes of faceless youths who crossed the irascible newspaperman's path in search of a job—once the man let him speak, that is.

Sweating Cobb must have retched at the sight of calm, collected Crosland, who stood in the editor's office for a half-hour before anyone acknowledged his existence. Cobb then looked up from the papers on his desk and growled: "What 'n hell d'you want to be a journalist for? Why d'you want to write? It's a dog's life." Undaunted, Crosland replied: "Because I always read your stuff, Mr. Cobb, and I know if I could write like that it would make me happier than anything in the world." The middle-aged man paused, then snapped: "You'll make a success."

That chutzpah coated with sincerity got Crosland the job. He eventually moved over to the *New York Globe*, and he also wrote short stories and articles for movie magazines.

In 1909 he reportedly joined the Edison Company as a 15-year-old movie actor, thus juggling his studies with performing in the new art form. Three years later he was appointed the studio's first publicity director, which led to the position of casting director. Sandwiched into Crosland's busy life at Edison were his jobs at the New York papers and a free-lance writing career! But the studio was his primary concern, and he learned enough about moviemaking to win several directing assignments for the Curtis Publishing Company.

Five years after entering the Edison Company as an actor, 20-year-old Crosland signed with Famous to direct the films of the celebrated 21-year-old stage star Alice Brady. In February 1915, William H. Brady, a theatrical producer affiliated with Famous, started World Features and brought the new director/star team with him. Under the banner World-Selznick, they made such melodramas as *La Boheme* and *The Fear Market* (both 1916).

Before being drafted into the Army Photo Service shortly after America joined the Allied effort in World War I, Crosland helmed the last Edison production, *The Unbeliever* (1918), shot with the help of the United States Marine Corps. Adapted from Mary Andrews' novel of a slacker who learns the value of patriotism, the film stars Marguerite Courtot, Raymond McKee, and Erich Von Stroheim as a villainous Hun, a role he played in a number of silent war films. Crosland got along well with the notoriously difficult Stroheim, once nonchalantly commenting, "He made forty dollars a week and worked like everybody else."

The ability to deal with difficult performers proved a godsend for the director who led such iconoclastic stars as John Barrymore and Al Jolson to some of their most notable performances. On the set of *Enemies of Women* (1923), Crosland handled a problematical situation with extreme cunning. The film stars Lionel Barrymore, Alma Rubens, William Collier, Jr., and Gareth Hughes in a complicated melodrama set in Czarist Russia. Along with the regal settings, bits and pieces of royal existence are the most memorable aspects of the production. One particularly effective element came close to exclusion.

Barrymore played a Russian prince in the film and was having difficulty adjusting to the huge wolfhound that Crosland had secured to follow the character around. When the cameras rolled, man's best friend showed a decided apathy toward its master. "You've got to pat that dog and make friends with him," the director reasoned, "or he'll never follow you." But Barrymore wasn't going to make the first move. "Tell it to the dog," he growled. Rather than continue battling on the set, crafty Crosland saw to it that a piece of freshly cut meat was concealed in the pocket of Barrymore's costume before each day's shooting began, thus guaranteeing that the wolfhound would follow hungrily in the star's footsteps.

At Goldwyn-Cosmopolitan, the director filmed *Under the Red Robe* in 1924, which firmly placed him with John Ford and King Vidor as one of the bright young Hollywood directors of the 1920s. Based on the famous novel by Stanley Wigmon, the plot is laid in the court of King Louis XIII of France and revolves around the efforts of the unscrupulous Duke of Orleans (William Powell in an early role) to unseat Cardinal Richelieu (Robert Mantell). The *New York Times* liked the production and was particularly impressed with its direction: "The scenes in many sequences of this film are so attractive that without much else they would be worth viewing."

With a reputation for visual excellence amid royal or historical surroundings already forming, Crosland was selected to direct the cinematization of Elinor Glyn's popular novel *Three Weeks*. The best of five films that he made in 1924, *Three Weeks* concerns a queen who runs away from her throne for twenty-one days to romance a commoner. Glyn's melodramatic novels, all written before World War I, virtually overflow with bluebloods, and the popularity of the titled rich in America of the 1920s made the author a valuable commodity to a Hollywood which reflected the public's taste.

As such, Glyn was powerful in a way almost unknown to any other writer in movieland. She chose 26-year-old Conrad Nagel and unknown Aileen Pringle for the leads, and Crosland directed them in what was to be a hit film. Apparently author and director worked well together, and the *New York Times* reviewer claimed that the filmed *Three Weeks* "has all the fantastic flavor of her red-covered book."

The next year Crosland unfortunately chose to veer away from regal tales, opting instead to film a trio of forgettable productions, *Contraband, Compromise,* and *Bobbed Hair.* Mordaunt Hall of the *Times* summed up the worth of all three in his criticism of *Contraband:* "This production is filled with exaggerations, impossible conflicts, and wonderful coincidences."

Despite the mediocrity of those three films, there was a revolution in the works at Warner Brothers, and Crosland was to be part of it. With Bell Telephone and Western Electric, the studio developed a sound-on-film system called Vitaphone, and Crosland was signed to direct the first production using the technique, *Don Juan.* His ability to stage such lush historical spectacles had already been proven, and Warner Brothers needed a sure hand to introduce its new device. John Barrymore agreed to star as the heart-throb of all women of all times and ages, fighting and loving for the first time to the strains of a synchronized score. Supporting the "great profile" were Mary Astor, Estelle Taylor, Montagu Love, Helene Costello, Warner Oland, and Willard Louis.

The filming of *Don Juan* set the pattern for many Crosland/Barrymore efforts to come as the two became great friends. The vibrant actor worked hard for his director, and he often reduced both cast and crew to laughter with his sizzling panache. "John Barrymore seldom loses his temper in the ordinary way," Crosland told a reporter after the shooting of *Don Juan*. "But he can say the most diabolical things in a suave and almost gentle tone." In one scene Barrymore had to scale a balcony while wearing a white ermine cloak. The first two attempts to do so ended with the garment sliding off the star's body. Temperamental Barrymore suffered both failures in silence, but when the same thing occurred on the third try, Crosland smilingly reminisced: "He flung it to the floor and jumped on it with both feet, uttering one word— but what a word!"

And what a film! *Don Juan* has everything the archetypal Warner Brothers swashbuckler could ask for—a dashing, handsome hero, vicious, shifty-eyed villains, beautiful heroines (a pair yet), breathtaking bravado in front of magnificent baroque sets, and a breakneck escape.

Barrymore is everywhere and into everything in *Don Juan*. His simple presence is a paradigm for the archetypal attractiveness, excitement and A-to-Z thrills of Crosland's film. He's a lover, a fighter, and a mimic when necessary. While masquerading as a torturer, Barrymore twists his face into such horrible contortions sans make-up that he completely (but not unalterably) reverses the godlike image of Don Juan.

The look on the actor's hooded face as he glares at innocent Mary Astor on the rack matches the intensity of his escape across the Tiber River. Crosland and his cameraman had to shoot part of the scene in a glass tank underwater. The cutting from gushing liquid to racing Barrymore is a masterpiece of suspense along the lines of current "disaster" films (man against the elements), equaled in subsequent Warner Brothers adventure spectacles only in the finale of Curtiz's *The Charge of the Light Brigade* (1936).

The climactic duel between Barrymore and baddie Montagu Love is as animated as any in film history. The pair swing swords at each other in a ballet of death, running over marble steps and elegantly designed floors, swirling around lushly angular columns, their battle witnessed by soldiers, royalty, and pretenders. One shot perfectly frames the battle, with Barrymore lunging like a dancer and Love parrying thrusts as they move over a squared floor design featuring all sorts of dark circles. The silver line in Barrymore's tights perfectly clashes with the floor, thus promoting his figure over Love's drab attire. The scene is quite an eyepiece.

Don Juan premiered on August 6, 1926 at the Warner Theatre in New York City, and the affair still stands as one of the greatest events in Hollywood history. Although Will Hays gave a slightly out-of-synch on-film lecture on the future of what he termed the "speech film," the program of synchronized music and song was a real treat to a sound-hungry audience. The New York Philharmonic Orchestra, consisting of 107 musicians, performed on screen that night, along with Giovanni Martinelli, Efrem Zimbalist, and Anna Case, among others.

"Perhaps the most brilliant motion picture premiere that was ever held," chimed H. David Straus of the *New York Morning Telegraph.* "*Don Juan* will bring joy to the heart of the flapper," he exclaimed. Most other reviews were just as ecstatic. "By the time the first stretch of *Don Juan* faded out," wrote Mordaunt Hall of the *Times,* "the spectators were in the mood of a person who does not wish to leave an interesting novel." The *Boston Herald* took the opposite view, stating, "It is a pity that Warner Brothers chose to announce the Vitaphone with so crude and old-fashioned a piece of 'movie' craftsmanship." The same reviewer also disliked Crosland's direction "in the style of the romantic of three years ago, when such a thing as camera subtlety or subtlety of any sort was quite foreign to the cinema."

The following year, 1927, was another big one for the director, Warner Brothers, and Hollywood. Crosland continued his association with John Barrymore in two more costumed spectacles, *When a Man Loves* and *The Beloved Rogue. When a Man Loves,* based on Abbé Prevost's story *Manon Lescaut,* is set in the France of Louis XV and features Barrymore as adventurer Fabier Des Grieux. Mordaunt Hall of the *New York Times* called it "a good entertainment," but he took a negative stance on *The Beloved Rogue* which had been adapted from Justin Huntley McCarthy's *If I Were King.* Hall saw the film version of poet François Villon's life as a "fanciful affair which has none of the clever and impressive situations that marked Mr. McCarthy's masterpiece." He also took the director to task. "Alan Crosland, producer of this film, delights in extravagances, exaggerations that are presumed to have a popular appeal." This judgmental reversal on the director's formerly praised quality, typical of the critical backlash that Crosland felt in the late 1920s and early 1930s, is a common phenomenon in reviewers' circles.

The Jazz Singer, which was Crosland's next important production, marked the end of one era and the beginning of another. The synchronized score of *Don Juan* was topped in this movie by a few scenes containing songs and dialogue, using the story of a cantor's son who goes

John Barrymore and Mary Astor in Don Juan *(WB, 1926)*

Conrad Veidt, Marcelline Day, and John Barrymore in The Beloved Rogue *(UA, 1927)*

*May McAvoy and
Al Jolson in* The
Jazz Singer *(WB,
1927)*

*Richard
Barthelmess and
Clare Dodd in*
Massacre *(First
National, 1934)*

into show business. In terms of narrative this was certainly a step downward from the exciting *Don Juan*, but nevertheless it featured what the brothers Warner thought had the best future in the sound film—music.

In *My First Hundred Years in Hollywood*, Jack Warner asserts that his brothers frowned on the theory of a talkie. He recalls the following conversation: "'But don't forget you can have actors talk,' Sam broke in. 'Who the hell wants to hear actors talk?' Harry asked testily. 'The music—that's the big plus about this.'"

Al Jolson immortalized the heartfelt cry "Mammy" on screen, but he wasn't the first choice to play the boy who becomes a vaudeville star. George Jessel was headlining in the show on Broadway, and he signed a contract for $2,000 a week to appear in the film. Publicity had already been prepared when the 29-year-old star insisted on receiving additional money for proposed recordings of *The Jazz Singer's* songs.

Jessel's contract was quickly torn up, and he was replaced by Jolson who thought a movie lead might give his career a fresh slant. However, Jolson was unsure of his acting potential. This anxiety had led to his walking out on a production called *Black and White* in 1923 after viewing himself in the daily rushes. "I thought all along I was an actor," the singer reportedly lamented. "Why, I'm only a song and dance man." The film's director, intuitive D. W. Griffith, disagreed with Jolson about his adaptability to the screen, and the pioneer filmmaker's opinion was borne out by Crosland in *The Jazz Singer*.

Associates begged Crosland not to make the same mistake with Jolson which closed the Griffith production. The director disagreed, insisting that the crooner could learn by watching himself. "I'm going to show him his mistakes," Crosland decided, "so he can tell what to avoid and how to change his technique."

Something clicked on screen for the man with the jutting eyes, broad mouth, and powerfully emotional singing voice. *The Jazz Singer's* New York premiere on October 6, 1927 was even more auspicious than *Don Juan's* opening the year before. "The premiere of Al Jolson in *The Jazz Singer* at the Warner Theatre, New York last night had all the gala gilt-edged trimmings," wrote *Motion Picture Daily*.

Yet even then critics sensed that the film was little more than a showstopper of the moment, that it would not endure the test of time, that it would be a curio and not a classic. "The Warner Brothers astutely realized that a film conception of *The Jazz Singer* was one of the few subjects that would lend itself to the use of the Vitaphone," wrote Mordaunt Hall of the *New York Times*. The implication is there if one wishes to look for it, but Richard Watts, Jr. of the *New York Herald-Tribune* was more to the point, stating, "This is not essentially a motion picture, but rather a chance to capture, for comparative immortality, the sight and sound of a great performer."

Crosland's 1928 production, *Glorious Betsy*, his first all-talking film, also marked a return to the world of the imperial past, where he was on solid footing. Set in turn-of-the-nineteenth-century Europe, the melodrama revolves around two love affairs, featuring none other than Napoleon as one of the partners! Mordaunt Hall of the *Times* called it "an appealing sentimental romance of the old days" and congratulated Crosland "on his direction of the film."

On with the Show, a 1929 musical, was advertised as the first "100% natural color talking film." Its creaky plot concerns a stranded troup of performers, featuring Betty Compson, Arthur Lake (in an imitation of the "Dagwood" character he later created in the *Blondie* series), Joe E. Brown, Louise Fazenda, and silly Sally O'Neill as the heroine. This production held a dim prophecy regarding the acceptance of future Crosland musicals by critics and a public growing weary of sound films for sound's sake. The thrill of the talkie quickly diminished, and the business of producing good films which didn't rely on faddish gimmicks was again practiced. However, Crosland simply couldn't handle filmed operettas with the light touch of a Lubitsch, so productions such as *Song of the Flame* and *Viennese Nights* (both 1930) fell on a public with deaf ears, and they are badly dated today.

After several years of uninspiring musicals and a series of improbable melodramas, the director who broke the sound barrier for Warner Brothers was eclipsed by not younger, but newly popular studio craftsmen, including Michael Curtiz, Howard Hawks, Mervyn LeRoy, and William Wellman. When Busby Berkeley came to Hollywood in 1930 to create a new kind of film musical, Crosland's fate seemed to be sealed in the numerous B films he made at Warner Brothers and Universal.

As Crosland's directorial star dimmed, his marriages faded also. He divorced his first wife, the former Juanita Crawford, at Cannes in 1930, but retained custody of Alan, Jr. Soon after he wed actress Natalie Moorhead, but they too were divorced in 1935.

Of the twenty-three films that Crosland directed after *The Jazz Singer,* only *Massacre* (1934) has been revived or written about recently. Yet many of the productions released in 1934-35 were popular in their day, and unlike the stale musicals and melodramas of the period before them, they have plots which may very well sparkle with the fast pace, wit, and action so typical of the best Warner Brothers products of the 1930s. Aside from *Massacre*, Crosland's *The Case of the Howling Dog* (1934), *It Happened in New York, The White Cockatoo, Mister Dynamite, Lady Tubbs,* and *The Great Impersonation* (all 1935) look intriguing enough from a distance to fare well with a modern audience.

Charles Emmett Mack and Dolores Costello in In Old San Francisco *(WB, 1927)*

While one waits for an Alan Crosland revival, Alan Crosland, Jr. is keeping the family name alive, filming a number of episodes of action television series such as *Adam 12* and *The Bionic Woman*. In this way the director of *Don Juan* will not suffer complete anonymity.

The real irony of Alan Crosland's fatal car crash could have been its timing. By 1936 the director had discarded the ill-fitting robe of the heavily melodramatic and musical filmmaker for the double-breasted suit of the topical action drama. Just when he was back in his element and the swashbuckler was regaining its former popularity, Crosland was killed.

The Films of Alan Crosland

La Boheme *(World-Selznick, 1916)*

The Fear Market *(World-Selznick, 1916)*

The Light in Darkness *(Edison, 1917)*

Apple-Tree Girl *(Edison Perfection, 1917)*

Kidnapped *(Forum, 1917)*

The Whirlpool *(Select, 1918)*

The Unbeliever *(Edison-Kleine, 1918)*

Country Cousin *(Select, 1919)*

Broadway and Home *(Select, 1920)*

The Flapper *(Select, 1920)*

Youthful Folly *(Select, 1920)*

Greater Than Fame *(Select, 1920)*

A Point of View *(Select, 1920)*

Worlds Apart *(Select, 1921)*

Is Life Worth Living? *(Select, 1921)*

Room and Board *(Par., 1921)*

Why Announce Your Marriage? *(Select, 1922) (and co-story, co-script)*

Shadows of the Sea *(Select, 1922)*

The Prophet's Paradise *(Select, 1922)*

Slim Shoulders *(W. W. Hodkinson, 1922)*

The Snitching Hour *(Clark-Cornelious Corp., 1922)*

The Face in the Fog *(Par., 1922)*

Enemies of Women *(Goldwyn, 1923)*

Under the Red Robe *(Goldwyn, 1924)*

Three Weeks *(Goldwyn, 1924)*

Miami *(W. W. Hodkinson, 1924) (and co-producer)*

Sinners in Heaven *(Par., 1924)*

Unguarded Women *(Par., 1924)*

Bobbed Hair *(WB, 1925)*

Contraband *(Par., 1925)*

Compromise *(WB, 1925)*

Don Juan *(WB, 1926)*

When a Man Loves *(WB, 1927)*

The Beloved Rogue *(UA, 1927)*

Old San Francisco *(WB, 1927)*

The Jazz Singer *(WB, 1927)*

Glorious Betsy *(WB, 1928)*

The Scarlet Lady *(Col., 1928)*

On with the Show *(WB, 1929)*

General Crack *(WB, 1929)*

Big Boy *(WB, 1930)*

The Furies *(FN, 1930)*

Song of the Flame *(FN, 1930)*

Viennese Nights *(WB, 1930)*

Captain Thunder *(WB, 1931)*

Children of Dreams *(WB, 1931)*

The Silver Lining *(UA, 1932) (and producer)*

Week-Ends Only *(Fox, 1932)*

Massacre *(FN, 1934)*

Midnight Alibi *(FN, 1934)*

The Personality Kid *(WB, 1934)*

The Case of the Howling Dog *(WB, 1934)*

The White Cockatoo *(WB, 1935)*

It Happened in New York *(Univ., 1935)*

Mister Dynamite *(Univ., 1935)*

Lady Tubbs *(Univ., 1935)*

King Solomon of Broadway *(Univ., 1935)*

The Great Impersonation *(Univ., 1935)*

The Case of the Black Cat *(FN, 1936) (co-directed by William McGann)*

Michael Curtiz and Priscilla Lane on the set of Four Wives *(WB, 1939)*

Lionel Atwill in Mystery of the Wax Museum *(First National, 1933)*

5

Michael Curtiz

"He's tough talking, labels people 'nice bums,' 'bad bums,' and 'ten cent bums' as he barks orders in broken English. He often storms into a room bedecked in a gorgeous suit, dazzling jewelry, and a fur-trimmed overcoat. He's one of the most powerful guys around."

Is this a description of a gangster in a Warner Brothers action drama of the 1930s? No. The man in question is Michael Curtiz, the director of eighty-eight Warner Brothers films, probably a record for one man's direction of features at a single studio. Half of these films were made over the years 1930-39, an average of four and a half films a year. Curtiz undoubtedly made more money for his studio than any other director in Hollywood. Seven of his films are listed in *Variety*'s all-time list of box-office blockbusters. Considering that the bulk of these were typically frugal Warner Brothers productions, made in Hollywood's prolific days before the institutionalization of the budget-eating multi-million dollar epic in the 1950s, Curtiz's economic credentials are staggering.

Curtiz received only a single Academy Award for direction (*Casablanca*), but one counts the classics *Captain Blood, The Charge of the Light Brigade, The Adventures of Robin Hood, The Sea Hawk,* and *Yankee Doodle Dandy* among a filmography virtually littered with minor gems including *20,000 Years in Sing Sing, Black Fury, Angels with Dirty Faces, Dodge City, Mildred Pierce, The Breaking Point, Force of Arms,* and *The Proud Rebel*. His bread-and-butter films were vital to Warner Brothers' growth, and as Andrew Sarris observed in *The American Cinema*, the typical Warner Brothers film of the 1930s and 1940s was often the film Curtiz was directing at the time. Like so many Hollywood craftsmen blessed with talent but not genius, Michael Curtiz never gave second-hand treatment to an assignment once it was accepted: he went ahead and graced plot and character with fluid camera movement, exquisite lighting, and a lightning-fast pace. Even if a script was truly poor and the leading players were real amateurs, Curtiz glossed over inadequacies so well that an audience often failed to recognize a shallow substance until it was hungry for another film a half-hour later.

Carriages clacked down cobblestone streets, carrying happy passengers to the bosom of their baroque homes to await Christmas on the eve of December 25, 1888 in Vienna, the night of Mikhaly Kertesz's birth. Although Vienna was Middle-Europe's industrial center, it was vibrant with the symphonies of Beethoven and Brahms and the gay waltzes of Johann Strauss. The arts flourished, and opera houses and theatres were common sights along the thoroughfares. Although the Hapsburg Empire slowly withered under its own weight, a temporary equilibrium was achieved between the rich and the city's ruling middle-class which was rapidly organizing into trade unions.

A son born to an architect who possessed a fine singing voice and an opera star mother would naturally be exposed to the world of show business at an early age. Little Mikhaly made his stage debut in 1899 in a bit role in an opera starring his mother. The Kerteszes had moved to Budapest, Hungary three years earlier, and by this time Mikhaly had two younger brothers, Gabriel and David.

Mikhaly (he didn't change his name to "Michael Curtiz" until arriving in America in 1926) attended both Markoszy University and the Royal Academy for Theatre and Art, but it is unclear whether he graduated from either institution. When not studying, the young man worked to become a fine athlete, and in 1912 he was already showing the prowess that impressed colleagues years later as a member of the Hungarian fencing team in the Stockholm Olympics. He was such an aggressive competitor that by the time he reached Hollywood, he had already broken both ankles playing polo.

By 1910 he had worked as an actor in the Hungarian Theatre and had joined a circus to learn the art of pantomime, possibly in anticipation of a film career. Curtiz also directed plays, which may have led to his directing the first Hungarian film in 1912, *Má ès Holnap (Today and Tomorrow)*. While the extent of his employment on the set of the production which marked the birth of the Hungarian cinema is unknown, he definitely made his acting debut in the filmed drama.

The first established directorial credit for Curtiz is *Rablelkek*, made in 1913. However, aware that Hungary was not the place to learn film production and technique, Curtiz then journeyed to the more advanced Nordisk Studio in Denmark to master his craft. He returned to Hungary six months later and directed a number of films for different producers.

Bank Ban (1914) was Curtiz's first popular success, but World War I temporarily ended his film career.

Drafted into the Austro-Hungarian artillery, Curtiz slipped back into civilian clothes a year later to become a newsreel cameraman. Soon afterward he was directing feature films again.

Curtiz married 17-year-old Lucy Doraine in 1915, allegedly over the objections of the bride's parents. Lucy was a ballerina who wanted to act, and the budding director put his wife to work quickly, starring her in such profitable efforts as *A Farkas (The Wolf)* and *A Magyar Fold Ereje (The Strength of the Fatherland)* (both 1916). The next year he became managing director of the Phoenix Studio, but he continued film-making. At this time Curtiz started making public sounds that fore-shadowed the hard director he would be known as in Hollywood. "An actor's success is no more than the success of the director," the rising moviemaker declared, "whose concept of the whole brings into harmony the portrayal of each character."

Shortly after April 12, 1919, tough guy Curtiz had to get out of the country. The Communist revolution spread to Hungary on that day, and Béla Kun's government quickly nationalized all film studios. Realizing that his freedom would be severely curtailed, Curtiz and spouse fled to Vienna, even though he was halfway through a version of Molnar's *Liliom*.

Some sources claim that Curtiz directed films in Sweden and Germany before settling into Count Alexander Kolowrat's Sascha studio in Vienna. He may have guided 14-year-old Greta Garbo in a film called *Odette et L'Histoire des Femmes Illustrés*, but scholars have cast grave doubts on this possibility. It is also said that he filmed the first part of Fritz Lang's *Die Spinnen: Der Golden See*, which is now lost.

During the next seven years Curtiz directed twenty-one films for Sascha-Film. By then Lucy Doraine had given him a daughter, Kathe-rine, and the director starred his wife in the first nine. The last and most notable was *Sodom und Gomorrha* (1922-23), a two-part epic shot in Sievering and the most expensive Austrian film up to that time. Curtiz continued using his personal discoveries in Austrian films, a practice he maintained with great success in Hollywood. A young Walter Slezak is featured in the biblical epic, and Willy Forst can be seen in a bit role. Curtiz's assistant cameraman on the second part of the lavish tale, Gustav Ucicky, continued with him through most of his Austrian productions.

While Curtiz's professional life was on the upswing, conflicts with Lucy led to a divorce in 1923. In the next few years he used a number of actresses in her place, such as Lily Marischka *(Die Lasvine)*, Agnes Esterhazy *(Der Junge Medardus)*, and Mary Kidd *(General Babka)*.

Die Slavenkönigin, released in 1924, proved to be a turning point in Curtiz's career. The expensive epic brought him to the attention of Harry Warner, one of the brothers whose new movie studio was tottering on the verge of bankruptcy. Years later the director recounted their first meeting: "It was in Paris that I first met Harry Warner. I remember that well because his American clothes attracted a lot of attention. At first I thought he was just a tourist." But the odd-looking Yankee had a project in mind called *Noah's Ark*, and he wanted Curtiz to direct it.

As the latest of a number of European filmmakers brought to Hollywood (after Lubitsch, Victor Seastrom, Mauritz Stiller, and others), Curtiz expected to receive a triumphant welcome when he entered the United States. He had heard about the many glittering Hollywood publicity ploys, and when he landed in New York, he mistakenly thought that a gala July 4th celebration was for him!

In the next few years, Michael Curtiz, the Hungarian director with the sparkling new American name, learned the customs of his adopted country (he became a citizen in 1938). Warner Brothers put him to work directing five melodramas (including his first with dialogue, *Tenderloin* in 1928), before assigning him the property for which Harry Warner tapped him in 1924, *Noah's Ark*. The lavish biblical spectacle, which paralleled man's greed and lust in ancient times with his amoral existence in the torrential 1920s, boasted a huge cast including Dolores Costello, George O'Brien, Noah Berry, and Louise Fazenda, each of whom was featured in both parts of the narrative. Released in 1929, *Noah's Ark* bowled over the *Variety* critic who exclaimed, "They show everything conceivable under the sun—mobs, mobs, and mobs, Niagaras of water, a train wreck, war aplenty, crashes, deluges, and everything that goes to give the picture fan a thrill." The *New York Times* was lukewarm about the film, stating, "The latter sequences of the film ... are imposing ... but the long stretches with the World War ... are somewhat wearisome."

Perhaps this is the film whose production initiated the rumors about Curtiz's obsession with quality at all costs. It is said that the Hungarian ordered the flood scenes in the film to gush with such power that an extra died as a result. Some years later, Errol Flynn asserted that Curtiz removed the safety catches from the tips of the swords for the climactic dueling sequence in *Captain Blood*, in order to make the performers' reactions real. Other such stories were bandied about, and they must be taken into account in any examination of Curtiz's character, although not necessarily believed.

By 1928 Curtiz's successful filming of Darryl F. Zanuck's original story for *Noah's Ark* had ensured for him a place on Warner Brothers' roster of young talent, along with Alan Crosland, Lloyd Bacon, and Mervyn LeRoy. Four more forgettable ventures came before Curtiz boosted his rising star with Al Jolson's fourth film *Mammy* (1930), based on Irving Berlin's musical, *Mr. Bones*. Critics and public alike applauded *Mammy*, with *Variety* labeling the bouncy effort "a lively picture, playing fast."

Filmed partly in color, this story of a singer (Jolson) who solves a backstage murder offers a clue to the secret of Curtiz's longevity as a film director (his last film, *The Comancheros*, was released in the fall of 1961, only months before his death). It must be remembered that the Hungarian had only been in America for four years before tackling a tale loaded with Yankee schmaltz. His adaptability and quick understanding of an alien culture facilitated his professional direction of all types of productions, from adventures, Westerns, detective and suspense films, to comedies, musicals, and melodramas. Admittedly Curtiz's forte was in the arena of action, but the musicals *Yankee Doodle Dandy* and *This Is the Army* are fine examples of their genre, and the comedies *Four's a Crowd* and *Life with Father* have a host of fans. Early in his career, the director asked himself these questions: "For whom to make the picture? What to do?" The simple answer says it all about Curtiz as an artist: "I compromise. I take a simple story and try to handle it artistically." And he stuck to that conviction. This explains in good part why, although a great admirer of geniuses like Eugene O'Neill, Theodore Dreiser, and Sherwood Anderson, Curtiz rarely adapted acknowledged classics of another medium to film.

Unfortunately he found it impossible to compromise with those he disliked. While filming *Under a Texas Moon* in 1930, the director had the first of his famous fights with actors. This film, which Mordaunt Hall of the *New York Times* called "a pleasing entertainment," was anything but entertaining to produce. Curtiz and his male star, Frank Fay, were diametrically opposed personalities whose animosity toward each other continued for several years. Fay was an easy-going man who could not respond to the Hungarian's need to work night and day, eschewing any social life. Thus their conflict continued through *God's Gift to Women* in 1931.

The year before, Curtiz shot a mild comedy, *A Soldier's Plaything*, co-starring the doomed silent favorite Harry Langdon, who was scratching out a living in cheap one- and two-reel comedies by the early 1930s. After filming a German-language version of William Dieterle's *Moby Dick*, Curtiz had his first big failure, *The Mad Genius*, starring John Barrymore in a caricature of his role as the hypnotist *Svengali* the preceding year. Barrymore's peccadillos were anathema to hardworking, supposedly solemn Curtiz, so the pair did not get along at all. Despite the difficulty in production and the poor critical reaction to the film, *The Mad Genius* got a semi-favorable notice from the *New York Times*, which stated: "From the viewpoint of production and John Barrymore's portrayal, the current picture is admirable."

The year 1932 was a good one for Curtiz, as three of his five films still intrigue viewers today to varying degrees and are seminal indications of work to come. *The Strange Love of Molly Louvain* contains the shabby streets, shady characters, and lower-class angst that Warner Brothers formularized into a box-office bonanza in the 1930s. Mordaunt Hall of the *Times* dismissed the film as "weary and unsavory," but the latter criticism is the quality that Curtiz riveted into later social melodramas like *20,000 Years at Sing Sing*, *Black Fury*, and *Angels with Dirty Faces*.

Doctor X, the first of Curtiz's three horror films, reflects the combination of macabre sets, morbidly suggestive lighting, and eerie long silences so haunting in *The Mystery of the Wax Museum* and in segments of adventures starring Errol Flynn. Mordaunt Hall of the *Times* was more responsive to Curtiz's Germanic horror melodrama, describing it as a "parcel of thrills streaked with fun."

The Cabin in the Cotton was one of Richard Barthelmess' last major starring films, but 24-year-old Bette Davis made strides toward stardom as a planter's daughter who toys with a cotton picker (Barthelmess). Curtiz used similar tensions as the framework for action in the coming years. Refined examples of such deft footwork can be seen in films as diverse as *Black Fury* and *Dodge City*. *Variety* claimed that *The Cabin in the Cotton*'s "subject has dramatic power but it doesn't come through to the audience from the screen." Hereafter poor scripts were blamed for the frailty of certain Curtiz films, while the director emerged with reviews which insisted that he gave a frail property a "good try."

By this time Warner Brothers knew that it had a gold mine in Curtiz. The director's philosophy of moviemaking allowed him to accept stale plots and awkward actors and try to concoct a saleable yet artistic commodity. If he was something of a "yes man" to superiors in the early years, there is no doubt that Curtiz was boss on the set, and he put his personal stamp on even the lowliest property.

His direction of rebellious Bette Davis in *The Cabin in the Cotton* convinced director John Cromwell to cast her in *Of Human Bondage*, the film which really shot her star across the sky and made Hollywood take notice. However, Curtiz didn't have to like those he helped. He reportedly once called Davis that "God-damned-nothing-no-good-sexless-son-of-a-bitch," and developed a truly intense dislike for Errol Flynn, an actor he piloted to stardom. On the other hand, Spencer Tracy, John Garfield, and Doris Day were quietly given a boost by the

Hungarian who also directed Joan Crawford's Oscar-winning comeback performance in *Mildred Pierce*.

The 1933 film *20,000 Years in Sing Sing* was Spencer Tracy's most important up to that time and his finest role until his classic portrayal of the Portugese fisherman in 1937's *Captains Courageous*. Tracy plays a convict who takes the rap for his girl friend's (Bette Davis) killing of the man who fraudulently sent him to jail. The film, one of Hollywood's best prison dramas, received disparate reviews upon release. Mordaunt Hall of the *Times* insisted that it contained "some extraordinarily interesting glimpses of prison routine," while Richard Watts, Jr. of the *New York Herald-Tribune* condemned the production as "a well-meaning but rather complete bore."

Although little or no background music in an early talkie film was not unusual, Curtiz's elimination of such melodious noise in his near-great color horror film, *The Mystery of the Wax Museum*, helped create a foreboding atmosphere. Although Kingsley Canham (in *The Hollywood Professionals, Vol. 1*) claims that the production has roots in the horror comedies of silent Swedish director Benjamin Christenson, Curtiz's blend of terror and laughs is a workable overstatement of the archetypal Hollywood mixture of histrionics and laughs.[*] Glenda Farrell as an acerbically witty reporter is as funny in her horror as Lionel Atwill is chilling in his depiction of a maniacal sculptor. *Variety* called the gruesome tale "a loose and unconvincing story," but Warner Brothers considered the film good enough to remake in 1953 as an inferior 3-D production called *House of Wax*.

Even though the director came of age professionally at a time when cinema Expressionism dominated Middle-European filmmaking, and though he did indeed embrace those values in a number of productions, he sensed a need for something different than the low-key shadowy lighting and Gothic surroundings then popular in the suspense film. Curtiz never appreciated that kind of story anyway, cracking: "Ha! Detective come in with magnified glass." He must have taken particular delight in filming the Philo Vance yarn, *The Kennel Murder Case* (1933), in the cheerful setting of an eighteen-room house done in Georgian colonial furniture, with a pristine backdrop of white walls.

The Kennel Murder Case, starring William Powell as detective Vance, was the forerunner of the classic trend-setting comedy thriller, *The Thin Man* (1934), that also starred Powell. *Variety* called Curtiz's light detective tale "a good film," thus paving the way for acceptance of

---

[*] In 1955 Curtiz's *We're No Angels* contained the same blend of comic yet morbid narrative, by then termed "black comedy."

further deviation from the dark house, creaky door, and crazed villain school of suspense.

The director's most interesting film of 1934, *British Agent,* stars Leslie Howard, Kay Francis, and William Gargan as a trio caught up in the Russian revolution. The film is notable for the presence of Curtiz's seldom seen but strikingly black sense of humor. In *Hollywood in the Thirties* John Baxter describes "an odd vignette concerning one of the diplomats, who goes out to contact a Russian Army officer. Curtiz cuts promptly to the two men walking through a gate as part of a group. The diplomat, smoking nervously, says with a grin, 'Well, Colonel, at least I found you.' The next shot shows them lined up against a wall with the others and executed." Andre Sennwald of the *New York Times* praised *British Agent* for its "momentous and delicate climaxes which crowd the story" and "come to life on the screen in vigorous melodramatic style."

Without question 1935 was the year that Michael Curtiz came into his own as a Warner Brothers director. It started with *The Case of the Curious Bride,* a sort of "detective with magnified glass" film, being a Perry Mason (Warren William) mystery. *Variety* deemed the production a "good whodunit entertainment," but it is important because on its set Curtiz met a man who would be an important force in his life. "Errol Flynn was an extra boy making $50 a week when I first saw him," the director recalled. "I was making *The Case of the Curious Bride* and needed a man to walk into a darkened room to be hit on the head and lie under a piano for a whole scene. Errol was handy, so I gave him the part.

"The next time I saw Errol Flynn," Curtiz continued, "I was testing for *Captain Blood,* looking for a chap to play opposite Olivia de Havilland. Errol was standing behind the camera reading lines for actors who were trying for the part." Robert Donat was the first choice for the role of Peter Blood, but he withdrew because of illness. Flynn's energy and pizzazz eventually won him the part of the idealistic doctor who becomes a pirate after being enslaved on a tropical island plantation for treating a wounded revolutionary. *Captain Blood* was released in December 1935 to glorious reviews. Richard Watts, Jr. of the *New York Herald-Tribune* praised the costume drama as "hearty romantic fiction, picturesquely produced," and Sennwald of the *New York Times* concurred, writing that the subject was "treated with a visual beauty and a fine, swaggering arrogance."

Flynn and de Havilland were wonderfully supported by Basil Rathbone as the effeminate and vile French pirate Levasseur, along with many members of the Warner Brothers stock company, including Alan Hale, Lionel Atwill, Ross Alexander, and Henry Stephenson. But the camaraderie achieved by the men in the adventure wasn't shared by the two most important figures on the set, Curtiz and Flynn. This is where their mutual animosity began—perhaps with the removal of the safety tips for the climactic fight between Blood and Levasseur, perhaps with the instant incompatibility of their life-styles, perhaps with the inevitable jousting of two egomaniacs.

Historically speaking, *Captain Blood* is significant in that it marked the comeback of the swashbuckling hero in the Fairbanks tradition. Although Flynn was no acrobat, the absence of gymnastics is more than made up for by Curtiz's deft manipulation of camera movement and editing, and by his knack for staging mass action. There is no doubt that the Hungarian is to the swashbuckler what John Ford is to the Western. Curtiz is the master of the costumed spectacle. The chemistry between subject, star, and director was perfect in *Captain Blood* and in three more classic action films, *The Charge of the Light Brigade*, *The Adventures of Robin Hood*, and *The Sea Hawk*, a set unequaled by any other director.

"blood—Blood—BLOOD!" the titles exclaim (in progressively larger type). From the unjust condemnation by the English court to the dismal, sweaty imprisonment on the tropical isle, to the frolicking, adventuresome and morally-correct pirating on the high seas, Peter Blood is a man of action and a man of the people. He is a bourgeois in knickers, a radical-liberal with long hair in lace shirt. He is Michael Curtiz's shady idealist who emerges heroically. He is Warner Brothers' prototype of democracy flaunted in the face of fascistic pervert Levasseur. The battle of philosophies erupts on a lonely beach over the hand of the jailhouse governor's daughter (Olivia de Havilland).

Curtiz's camera follows as the pair crosses swords, exchanging verbal sparks along the way à la all good cinema swashbuckling. As Erich Korngold's score heightens, Blood plunges his sword into Levasseur. The evil pirate collapses to the ground, and the ocean stumbles in to cover his reddened body as if in cleansing.

Although *Captain Blood* smacks of social criticism in its tropical locale, *Black Fury* is a middle-of-the-road film, condemning a nebulous organization which causes a strike in a mining town, then hires out its toughs as strike-breakers. In the *New York Post*, Richard Watts, Jr. saw the film "as effective as a compromise picture on a subject could be." But it was hailed by Sennwald of the *New York Times* as "the most notable social drama since *Our Daily Bread* (1934)" and praised for its "melodramatic vigor and an air of cumulative power which is rare in Hollywood cinema."

Unquestionably, *Black Fury* seeks to please everyone. The criminal organization is vague enough to be taken as a symbol of labor unions, while the "worker as victim" theme runs wild through the story. The turning point comes when miner Mike Shermansky (John Qualen) is beaten to death by a member of a brutal police force hired to keep the restless toilers in line. After the bloodied Shermansky slumps to the ground, another cop screams, "Hey McGee, I think this guy's kicked the bucket!" McGee sneers, "So what?" If there are any doubts about the extent of the film's sympathy for the workers, they are disspelled by the image of mean-looking Barton MacLane as club-wielding McGee towering over the body of the dead man.

Despite the obvious melodrama, the incident is based on a true occurrence in a 1929 Pennsylvania mining town. Michael Musmanno, the judge who presided over the trial of the accused policeman, wrote one of the pair of stories (the other was a play called *Bohunk* by Harry R. Irving) on which the taut film is based.

Despite the effort to please everyone, *Black Fury* ran afoul of censorship boards throughout the country, and it was banned in some states, including Pennsylvania. The only people who liked the film were middle-of-the-road critics, whereas left-wing reviewers remained unimpressed by the film's allegedly "social" content. But even the most hard-nosed critics, such as William Troy of the *Nation*, acknowledged Curtiz's direction.

The filmmaker saw his work in terms of story and character, with social intentions merely along for the ride. "*Black Fury* was an interesting picture, but not box-office," he commented. "Too extreme in thought and ideology—very socialistic, very real." Yet there is no denying the power of Paul Muni's portrayal of miner Joe Radek who decides to avenge the death of his friend and simply states, "I got to fix for Mike," or the brooding atmosphere and explosive thrills.

Back in the saddle of adventure, Curtiz directed another classic with Flynn, *The Charge of the Light Brigade*, but the production did little to patch things up between the two. Olivia de Havilland, once more Flynn's enchanting co-star in the venture, remembered her director as "an angry man." Nevertheless, he could respond surprisingly well to brashness in others. One hot morning, Warner Brothers sent over 25-year-old David Niven to audition for the supporting role of Captain Randall in the $1.2 million spectacle. Curtiz himself supervised the test, which was to be with de Havilland. Niven was the seventh to try out, but when he stepped up to speak his lines, he discovered that he didn't have a script. When Curtiz inquired as to the volume's whereabouts, Niven told him it was back in the make-up tent at the other end of the studio. "Run and get it," Curtiz ordered. With the wool costume sticking to his sweaty body, the young actor let his temper flare up, figuring that the goof had cost him the part anyway. "You can damn well run and get

84

it yourself," Niven snapped. The stage was suddenly quiet. Curtiz paused, then roared, "Dismiss the others and give him the part."

The studio allowed no such spontaneity with the lavish production. The story, liberally adapted from British history and the Tennyson poem, was photographed by Sol Polito at a number of California locations. A huge fort was built west of the San Fernando Valley, and most of the thundering charge was shot in Chatsworth. In this dynamic film about the conflict between Britain and the Khan's native forces, as well as the personal bout of Major Geoffrey Vickers (Flynn) and the Khan (C. Henry Gordon), Curtiz reportedly shocked the A.S.P.C.A. by his brutal treatment of the Lancers' horses, as the soldiers rode to their death amid the ringing of the battle cry; "Onward, onward, men!"

But what a charge! Vickers fakes an order to permit the Light Brigade its revenge against the Khan for massacring women, children, and defenseless soldiers. The camera, like the charge, starts out slowly, cutting from relatively close shots of the men trotting in formation to portraits of Vickers and others in their death run. As the dust flies, the image widens to capture the whole brigade, then cuts to the incredulous Russians as they watch a mere six hundred men advancing against so many thousands. As the British cut through the pregnable Czarist forces, the faces of generals and the Khan drop. When the flag falls with a wounded soldier, another raises it high. The camera pans back and forth between the battlers, with much of the action obliterated by smoke. When the Khan's horse is shot out from under him, however, the conflict is focused. The Khan shoots Vickers, but there's enough stuff in the major to sear the body of the mass murderer, and his fellow brigadesmen riddle the Khan's carcas with lances. "For conspicuous gallantry," grunts Sir Benjamin (Henry Stephenson), as he throws Vickers' written confession into the fire.

The Charge of the Light Brigade was hailed as a "smashing and spectacular adventure film" by Frank S. Nugent of the *New York Times*. Howard Barnes acknowledged in the *New York Herald-Tribune:* "Most of the credit for the production must go to Michael Curtiz.... He has sustained suspense admirably and he has effected arresting pictorial compositions."

The next year, Curtiz directed his only boxing film, a solid effort called *Kid Galahad* (dubbed *The Battling Bellhop* for television so that it wouldn't be confused with the inferior remake starring Elvis Presley). Nugent of the *Times* labeled it "a good little picture, lively, suspenseful, and positively echoing with the bone-bruising thud of the right hooks to the jaw." Although Bette Davis has little to do as promoter Edward G. Robinson's girl friend, Wayne Morris gives one of the best performances of his unspectacular career in the title role.

Paul Muni and Karen Morley in a publicity pose for Black Fury *(WB, 1935)*

Olivia de Havilland, Basil Rathbone, Melville Cooper, and Errol Flynn in The Adventures of Robin Hood *(WB, 1938)*

In a publicity stunt for *The Perfect Specimen* (1937) starring Errol Flynn as a sheltered but muscular millionaire who cuts the apron strings from his grandmother, Curtiz and his leading man engaged in a test of physical strength. The director, described as a former circus strong man in press releases, supposedly astonished onlookers by lifting the side of a car, thus illustrating his own perfection, much to the dismay of hard-living Flynn.

William Keighley was originally assigned to film *The Adventures of Robin Hood* in 1938. The director of such fun films as *The Prince and the Pauper* and *The Man Who Came to Dinner* proceeded to shoot most of the outdoor sequences with assistant B. Reeves "Breezy" Eason before being replaced by producer Henry Blanke due to his "light-hearted approach." Curtiz, now an American citizen, was brought in to direct the interiors, and he also shot extra scenes depicting Sherwood Forest.

As usual, sparks flew on the set of this Curtiz production. Reportedly the director ordered real spears to be heaved at Errol Flynn, a move which caused the actor to physically attack the volatile Hungarian. Another time he is supposed to have criticized Flynn's handling of a love scene with Olivia de Havilland. "That kiss—she would not melt butter," Curtiz barked. "Don't hold her like she was a hot potato. Crush her! Maybe you break a rib! That is all right if we get a good scene." Whether or not the first tale has any truth at all, the second may be an example of the director's peculiar sense of humor, already illustrated in his films.

"Have you eaten well, friend?" Robin asks a victim of Prince John, now enjoying a meal on the righteous spoils of the Merry Men. Robin Hood, like Peter Blood before him and privateer Thorpe (in *The Sea Hawk*) in the future, translates William S. Hart's good-badman into a period English setting in the person of Errol Flynn.

It's up to the unmasked bandit to save England from the usurper Prince John. *The Adventures of Robin Hood* warns against a Middle Ages military-industrial complex takeover while the true ruler is off fighting foreign wars. It was all very topical for a 1938 peacetime U.S.A.

This exciting swashbuckler, shot in the new three-color technicolor process, is top-notch from beginning to end. Comedy, adventure, and romance blend perfectly to mask the studio's patriotic rhetoric, and Curtiz captures the natural look of Sherwood Forest, the castle, and the inn with a crackling fireplace. Perhaps the most poignant moment in the film occurs at the finish when the men of Sherwood surrender their arms to King Richard and Robin's lands are returned, along with the hand of fair maid Marian.

"What say ye?" Richard asks, directing his question to a Robin whom he assumes is hidden in a crowd of congratulating Merry Men. Then the king looks up in royal astonishment at the pair waving from the gate. Sex was around the corner in just about every Warner Brothers film of the period.

The Adventures of Robin Hood was the third classic adventure production by the trio of Curtiz-Flynn-de Havilland. Nugent of the *Times* wrote enthusiastically about the film: "A richly produced, bravely bedecked, romantic, and colorful show, it leaps boldly to the forefront of this year's best and can be calculated to rejoice the eights, rejuvenate the eighties, and delight those in between." Barnes of the *Tribune* asserted that Curtiz "set off the whole show with his staging of the suspense-laden encounters between Robin Hood's followers and the Norman rascals." *Film Daily* picked *The Adventures of Robin Hood* as the best film of 1938, and it was nominated for an Oscar as best picture, while its original Erich Wolfgang Korngold score, editing, and art direction won Academy Awards.

Curtiz's next important discovery was John Garfield. Although a sensation performing in socially relevant plays at New York's Group Theatre, Garfield seemed destined to be a flop in Hollywood. "He had failed a test at MGM and was given train fare back to New York," the director recounted. "I saw a screen test and sent him a wire in the Kansas City station telling him to come back."

Garfield came back and Warner Brothers got him. Hollywood finally took notice of the intense young performer in Curtiz's *Four Daughters* (1938) in which he plays a young rebel at odds with his girlfriend's father (Claude Rains). Originally titled *Sister Act* (after Fannie Hurst's short story), the film was nominated for the best picture Oscar and graced the *New York Times*' Ten Best list. Writing in the *Times*, B. R. Crisler declared *Four Daughters* to be "a charming, at times heartbreakingly human little comedy." Curtiz directed two successful sequels to the film, *Daughters Courageous* and *Four Wives*.

The director was now getting much recognition from critics. In a day when stars were mentioned by name more than any other contributor to a film, the Crown Prince of Malaprops (if producer Sam Goldwyn was king, Curtiz deserves a royal title too) was often singled out for fine work in even poor films. This was especially true in the 1950s when the quality of the projects he was handed dropped considerably from that of the 1930s and 1940s.

By this time the former Mikhaly Kertesz was also renowned as a man who used an English language all his own. Journalists constantly joked about his grammatical errors, which they dubbed "Curtizisms." Once he was heard chewing out a prop man who failed to execute an order by thundering, "Next time I send a damn fool, I go myself!"

Another time, after interviewing a child actor, Curtiz dismissed him by saying, "By the time I was your age, I was 15." And once, faced with a confused child playing in a sandbox during a scene, be begged the boy to improvise some dialogue. "Ad-lib, ad-lib," the Hungarian shouted. "Say, 'Jesus Christ, you ruined my sand castle!'" The stories are infinite, but the feeling persists that Curtiz wasn't entirely unaware of his hatchet job on the language. For instance, he constantly referred to enemy Errol Flynn as "Erl Flint," a mistake the director probably enjoyed making to the actor's face. And Curtiz liked the sympathy letters he received from fans who decried his "persecution" in the newspapers.

Michael Curtiz didn't make a habit of joking on the set. It is said that he "lived to work," and that very well may be, considering the one hundred and sixty-five films he directed over a period of a half-century. The Hungarian had little patience with incompetents, and he bawled out people with such a heady stream of vulgar verbiage that some of his actresses complained to the Hays Office. It is also said that he was anti-social, a rather strong characterization for a man who would rather make films than attend parties. Curtiz dismissed the typical Hollywood gathering as "beautiful bubble talk—a few glasses highball and you're greatest man."

The rest of that quote reveals much about Curtiz the man. "I am scared to death of all this honey, this saccharine," he mused. "Our success—it's so flimsy." Although the need to work pushed him to create films at an assembly line rate, those films nevertheless reflect the hand of a concerned artist. While it is true that all men and women in Hollywood who opted for quality over quackery in their work had to be mindful of money and mass appeal, Curtiz's films are striking examples of modest budgets being stretched by superb craftsmanship in the gleaming Warner Brothers' tradition.

Yet Curtiz cannot be labeled a purely cautious or temperamental man. He helped David Niven to stardom by ignoring the green actor's rudeness in an audition for *The Charge of the Light Brigade*, and he wisely chose a totally inexperienced Doris Day for a starring role in *Romance on the High Seas*, even though the 25-year-old singer burst into tears instead of song when she tried out for the film. The Hungarian was obviously not afraid to take chances. He entered the movie business in a country where no films had been made until he made them. Why else would he leave a budding career acting and directing in Hungarian theatre, if not to jump into something new and exciting?

By 1939 the movie business was a firmly entrenched industry, and the industrious Curtiz helmed five productions that year. His two-reel *Sons of Liberty*, about Revolutionary War patriot Haym Solomon, won an Academy Award as best short subject.

But frugal Warner Brothers practically tapped a gold vein to finance Curtiz's first Western, *Dodge City*, starring two of the studio's best sparring partners, Errol Flynn and Olivia de Havilland. With Curtiz, they made a troublesome yet acclaimed trio, and the powerhouse supporting cast, including Bruce Cabot, Alan Hale, Frank McHugh, and starlet Ann Sheridan, helped them shoot life into a rather simplistic script. However, the film's gala opening in Dodge City, Kansas was far from simple. The size of the middle-American town increased tenfold as Warner Brothers hired a special train to carry hundreds of performers and executives to view a film which contained one of the costliest barroom brawls in filmdom's history.

Dodge City was a vastly entertaining Western in the year of such adult fare as *Stagecoach, Ninotchka*, and *Mr. Smith Goes to Washington*. As Wade Hatton, Flynn etches a cardboard yet charming character like his period English counterparts. More so than its swashbuckling cousins, the film thrives on jokes and brawls, with romantic interludes and threads of plot keeping the characters respectable.

Originally dubbed *The Lady and the Knight, The Private Lives of Elizabeth and Essex* brought Curtiz and Flynn together with fighting Bette Davis, and a battle royal raged throughout the production. Some historians say that the psychological scars of the off-screen brawling show up in Flynn's performance, but others insist that his dramatics are practically on par with those of Davis, which surprised many, including the actress herself, who had doubts about her co-star. The tense production was loosened up by Curtiz's comical slips of the tongue. Once a mob of extras assembled for a scene in which the Duke of Essex (Flynn) was to be welcomed home from the wars. Curtiz commanded, "Now, when I yell 'Issacs,' you yell 'Issacs.'" Apparently nobody had the courage to correct him, so they followed the orders precisely. Nugent of the *New York Times* was unscathed by the backstage skirmishes, and he deigned the film "well worth seeing."

Yet 1939 was also a sad year for Michael Curtiz, for it was the year that his daughter attempted suicide. According to one account, Katherine Curtiz was found "moaning in her room, with blood dripping from razor slashes on both wrists and one arm." She arrived in Hollywood on July 23, after leaving City College of New York where she was an art student. "I tried to kill myself," she told a reporter from the *Los Angeles Times*. "But the blood—the blood, it flowed so red. My parents are divorced and I've been going to school most of my life." Katherine feared the consequences when her father found out what she had done, but she went to him anyway. Yet the newspapers knew she was in town before Curtiz did. Perhaps such detachment from loved ones is the tragic price a man pays for working too hard.

Despite the director's personal problems, he prepared three expensive action films, *Virginia City, The Sea Hawk,* and *The Santa Fe Trail,* for release in 1940. Premiering in April, *Virginia City* is in many ways a twin to *Dodge City,* yet it doesn't seem to have been directed by a man with peace of mind. It has some of the same actors (including Errol Flynn, Frank McHugh, Guinn Williams, and John Litel), the same screenwriter (Robert Buckner), the same director of photography (Sol Polito), the same editor (George Amy), the same art director (Ted Smith), and a score created by the same composer (Max Steiner).

Yet *Virginia City* doesn't begin to compare to the quality of its predecessor. The Civil War conflict between Northern and Southern forces to obtain a Confederate cache of gold is dragged out interminably (the film itself is sixteen minutes longer than *Dodge City*), the action sequences are misplaced, and the Flynn-Randolph Scott rivalry is weakened by the script's sympathetic portrayal of both characters. Two vital roles are played by the wrong actors. Miriam Hopkins' brashness is harmful in a part which should have been done by a sweet Olivia de Havilland, and Humphrey Bogart's snarling like a Western bandit is all wrong, as he demonstrated in *The Oklahoma Kid* (1939). Considering atypical errors like these, *Virginia City* may very well have been the product of a man who couldn't devote full attention to his work. At one point in the production, clouds obscured light that Curtiz needed to get a shot, and he said sadly, "God is against me." Maybe this time the Hungarian used the language correctly.

The Sea Hawk was the director's last swashbuckler with Errol Flynn, and it caused great problems. The production costs reputedly spiraled to $1,700,000, due to the necessary construction of such devices as a huge hydraulic jack to shake a studio-built ship for a storm effect. Rising above the myriad problems, Curtiz came back in this classic adventure yarn about a privateer named Thorpe (Flynn) who preys on Spanish ships for the good of Queen (Flora Robson) and country. *Variety* claimed that the 1940 version of *The Sea Hawk* "retains all the bold and swashbuckling adventure of its predecessor" (in 1924).

With Brenda Marshall instead of captivating Olivia de Havilland capturing Errol Flynn's attention, there was room in his screen life for another woman—Queen Elizabeth (Flora Robson). Thorpe and Elizabeth engage in humor-edged battles over his piracy, his aggressiveness, and his pet monkey. This time around, the hero's ego lands him in chains.

The secret expedition to the New World ends with the crew dropping dead from battle and disease. Scenes depicting Thorpe and others as slaves aboard a Spanish ship rival the prison sections of *Captain Blood* for their graphic, brutal details. Thorpe is a visible wreck chained to an oar—hair stringy, beard dangling, sweat oozing from his hard, beaten body, all presenting quite an atypical picture of Flynn's self-assured screen image.

The most dramatic scenes in the film occur when the King of Spain announces his plan to rule the world. Another international despot has emerged on the scene, and as also occurs in the later inquisition of Thorpe, the long shadows of evil men and cold decor creep on the walls in flickering sun or candlelight. A stentorian voice pronounces the world's and Flynn's doom with the same foreboding inevitability. But the only sure thing in a Warner Brothers production of the period was the triumph of the just.

The production of *The Santa Fe Trail* caused the Curtiz-Flynn clash to heighten to such an extent that studio executives had to make a decision regarding the future of their scrapping yet top box-office team. The actor was constantly delaying the shooting (the film debuted five months after *The Sea Hawk,* a long time between premieres for fast-working Curtiz), and his director's blood pressure was rising daily. When *The Santa Fe Trail* had been wrapped up, the fighting pair were teamed for what turned out to be the last time in the mediocre *Dive Bomber* (1941). Then Flynn refused to work with Curtiz on *They Died with Their Boots On* (1941), so Raoul Walsh was handed a script which he turned into a fine film, containing one of Flynn's best performances.

James Cagney and Humphrey Bogart admirably picked up the star slack in Curtiz's next few productions. Cagney acted in a fast-paced film about the Canadian Air Force, *Captains of the Clouds* (1942), before going on to one of the greatest film musicals ever made, *Yankee Doodle Dandy,* which was nominated for best picture of 1942 and won five Academy Awards. Cagney copped an Oscar for his portrayal of producer-writer George M. Cohan and once again exhibited his marvelous hoofing ability that hadn't been in evidence since *Battling Hoofer* five years earlier. Bosley Crowther of the *New York Times* praised the blockbuster highly, calling it "as warm and delightful a musical picture as has hit the screen in years."

Despite the lofty status of the Errol Flynn swashbucklers, *Casablanca* is the film for which Michael Curtiz will undoubtedly be most remembered. Released at the end of 1942, it qualified for the 1943 Academy Awards. With a dream cast of Humphrey Bogart, Ingrid Bergman, Paul Henreid, Claude Rains, Sydney Greenstreet, Peter Lorre, Conrad Veidt, and others, Curtiz constructed a tale of romance and intrigue, with a soupcon of cynicism, which is even more popular today than it was three decades ago.

Casablanca won three major Academy Awards (best picture, best director, best script), and Crowther of the *New York Times* deemed it "one of the year's most exciting and trenchant films." On the other hand, acerbic critic James Agee of the *Nation* had a way of deflating even the most highly praised film, and *Casablanca* did not escape his sharp eye. "Apparently, *Casablanca*, which I must say I liked, is working up a rather serious reputation as a fine melodrama. Why? It is obviously an improvement on one of the world's worst plays; but it is not such an improvement that that is not obvious. Any doubters should review the lines of Claude Rains. Rains, Bogart, Henreid, Veidt, Lorre, Sakall, and a colored pianist whose name I forget were a lot of fun, and Ingrid Bergman was more than that; but even so, Michael Curtiz still has a twenties' director's correct feeling that everything, including the camera, should move; but the camera should move for purposes other than those of a nautch-dancer, and Mr. Curtiz's bit players and atmospheric scenes are not even alien corn."

The odyssey of this classic is extremely peculiar, yet typically Hollywood. Writers and actors came and went, and the film's script wasn't completed until the shooting was over. Julius and Philip Epstein concocted the screenplay for *Casablanca* from an unproduced play called *Everybody Comes to Rick's*. Howard Koch was then hired to polish the characters. As the story goes, his main contribution was the transformation of cafe owner Rick (Bogart) from a heel to a scarred fighter for liberal causes who masks wise thinking in wisecracks.

Bogart, Bergman, and Henreid were not the original choices for the roles they immortalized. Believe it or not, the characters of Rick, Elsa, and Laszlo had been assigned to Ronald Reagan, Ann Sheridan, and Dennis Morgan! If ever there was a case of across-the-board miscasting, this was it. But Curtiz's uncanny sense for matching actors to roles saved the day and established Humphrey Bogart's screen persona for all time. There is a bit in the film in which unsavory Senor Ferrari (Sydney Greenstreet) asks Rick why he came to Casablanca. Replies Rick, "I came for the waters." Flabbergasted, Ferrari counters with, "But we are in the middle of a desert!" "I was misinformed," Rick offers coolly. Imagine Reagan sparring with glandular Greenstreet, affecting anything resembling the biting wit of a Bogart!

After the casting shuffle, the *Casablanca* production still lacked a suitable script. Curtiz must have been a literal rock in the changing rivers of the project, and his cast knew it. Paul Henreid once complimented the Hungarian's directorial acumen: "Curtiz has an instinctual visual sense. It's quite different from the way actors visualize. Every now and again he would stop the camera and say, 'There's something wrong here. I don't know what it is.' By and by he'd realize what it was and we'd begin the scene again." The director himself acknowledged the day-by-day method of building the classic film.

Gilbert Roland and Errol Flynn in The Sea Hawk *(WB, 1940)*

Irene Manning, James Cagney, Joan Leslie, Walter Huston, and Rosemary DeCamp in Yankee Doodle Dandy *(WB, 1942)*

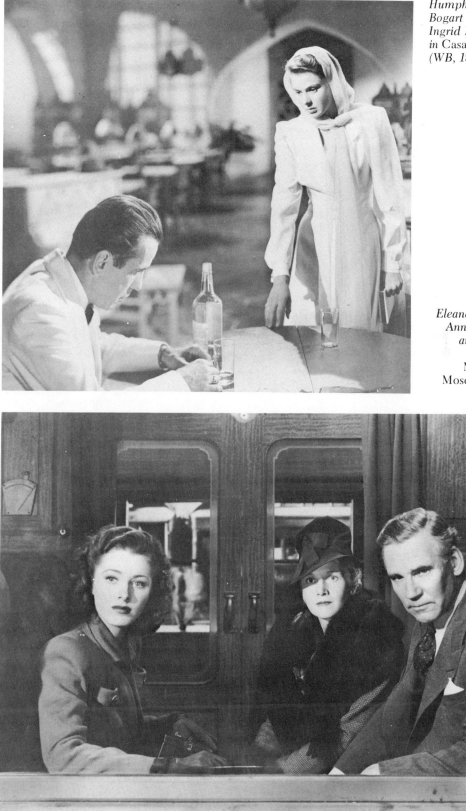

*Humphrey
Bogart and
Ingrid Bergman
in* Casablanca
(WB, 1943)

*Eleanor Parker,
Ann Harding,
and Walter
Huston in*
Mission to
Moscow *(WB,
1943)*

"That picture was made good on set. I have three writers working on set every day as we shoot." And so it went.

"Louie, this could be the beginning of a beautiful friendship," says Rick to the not-so-corrupt chief of police (Rains). They have just watched the patriots (Bergman and Henreid) go off in a plane and are depicted in an overhead shot walking down the rain-soaked pavement between the terminal and the runway. A Gestapo officer lies on the asphalt, killed by Rick and overlooked by Louie.

Rick, the idealist-turned-nilhist-turned-idealist, has just given all for love. "The problems of two people don't amount to a hill of beans in this world," he tells Elsa (Bergman).

The greatness of *Casablanca* lies in the commitment made by those of vastly different character to further the Allied cause. Romantic to be sure, propagandistic to be certain, very possibly silly, but such traits are revealed in exotic Casablanca, where one can meet all kinds of people—the Nazis, the heroic American, the European patriot, the barterer of souls, the innocent, the poor, and the wretched. That many of these confrontations occur in Rick's saloon and gambling house is particularly ironic, yet never dwelled on. Come and take a chance, the film says. Fortunately Curtiz never spends too much time on one aspect or character in a given scene. He moves the camera and cuts to opposed emotional tones. It's something like a merry-go-round of drama—everything is there and everything whizzes by just slow enough to allow a glimpse. Unlike the relatively static *To Have and To Have Not*, which models itself on *Casablanca*, the conflict of the leading characters from different sides of the world of opinion and the map of culture—cynical Rick, idealistic Elsa—produces a formidable sizzle, and it proceeds from there.

Koch's success with the *Casablanca* script led to the assignment of writing *Mission to Moscow* (1943), which Bosley Crowther of the *New York Times* called "clearly the most important picture on a political subject any American studio has ever made." Allegedly President Roosevelt asked Jack Warner to produce a film version of Ambassador Joseph E. Davies' memoirs of Stalinist Russia.

Curtiz agreed to direct, and he then began a search for an actress to play the Davies' (Walter Huston and Ann Harding) daughter, finally hearing about a possibility in a small theatre group: "I found Eleanor Parker at a community playhouse performance. I'd come to see another promising actress, but I forgot all about her when I saw Eleanor in the second row of the theatre."

Mission to Moscow was lauded by Crowther of the *Times*, but the critic questioned the truth of many of the film's contentions about the quality of Soviet life. Many condemned the film's blatant support of Stalin's purge trials of the 1930s. It even praised Russia's signing of a non-aggression pact with Germany. John Dewey and Suzanne La Follette, chairman and secretary respectively, of the International Commission of Inquiry into the purges, wrote a searing attack of the film in the *New York Times*. Howard Koch, who merely transferred Ambassador Davies' rhetorical approval of Russia to the screen, wrote a stinging reply, and the battle raged. A group spearheaded by Illinois state attorney George F. Barrett demanded that *Mission to Moscow* be boycotted. Columnist Westbrook Pegler and the Hearst papers also jumped on the Warner Brothers film.

Some critics praised the effort, which is now regarded as a propaganda classic. Otis L. Guernsey of the *New York Herald-Tribune* called *Mission to Moscow* "good screen entertainment, and it is abundant food for thought." In the *Nation*, James Agee wrote: "As cinema and warfare, *Mission to Moscow* is an important piece." Jack Warner defended his film and bore the brunt of the blame for its distortions of Soviet life. Not only was the production a box-office dud, as propaganda films are wont to be, but it came back to haunt him during the hearings held by the House Committee on Un-American Activities in Washington in 1947. As with Goldwyn's *The North Star* (1943), the winds of change had left *Mission to Moscow* out in the cold.

This Is the Army (1943) was received by Theodore Strauss of the *New York Times* as "the freshest, the most endearing, the most rousing musical tribute to the American fighting man that has come out of World War II." The film got Curtiz out of an unseemly affiliation with pro-Stalinist forces via his direction of *Mission to Moscow*, but it didn't please everybody. Writing in the *New York Herald-Tribune*, Howard Barnes admitted that the large-scale musical extravaganza was staged by Curtiz "with skill and feeling," but he didn't like the overall product.

Even though his last two films were propaganda items, ranging from heavy and inaccurate to light and airy, Curtiz was impressed with the strides made by American cinema since his arrival in the country in 1926. "Past generation got used to phony melodramas, everybody's perfect; gallant hero fight for perfect woman, on horseback. Villain very evil. But this generation very sensitive against anything not like life." He admitted, "I have progressed too. I was too European, too stagey, too sentimental. Now at 56 I do better work. Like Flaubert who didn't get success until after he wrote *Madame Bovary* at 51. Like De Maupassant who was an unknown lawyer and Chekhov who was not recognized until the last three years of life, after he wrote *The Cherry Orchard*. Talent and success do not always go together, you know. Many people cannot get proper foothold." Curtiz admittedly put himself in lofty company here, but the man who had just shored up the many weak spots in a script called *Casablanca* to emerge with a multi-Oscar winner was no mere amateur in his field.

In 1945 Curtiz directed *Roughly Speaking*, starring Rosalind Russell, whom he paired with Ingrid Bergman as one of the "finest actresses in Hollywood; no phony, no fake, no fool the audience." The director worked closely with author Louise Randall Pierson, who adapted the script from her best-selling novel chronicling forty years in the life of an American woman (Russell).

Curtiz and Pierson fought over the script, but she reacted surprisingly well to his criticisms. The author said at the time, "He brings me something he doesn't like, and always the same phrase, 'God-damned symbolism, terrific dull, take away; do better.' He reduces me to ashes constantly." The Hungarian undoubtedly was amused by Pierson's comparison of his classic malaprop, "Bring me the empty horses," with Gertrude Stein's playful devastation of the English language.

Roughly Speaking was the only film Curtiz and Rosalind Russell made together, and the star recalled her director fondly. She described him as "a soft pushover when he's off the set, away from the camera. A perfectionist, a terribly hard-working, able, ambitious man driven by a love for his work." *Film Daily* responded similarly to *Roughly Speaking*, calling it "a warm, human film."

Mildred Pierce (1945) has been widely hailed as Joan Crawford's comeback film, and she was indeed magnificent in the film version of James M. Cain's novel about a mother's efforts to control her spoiled daughter (Ann Blyth). Crawford won an Oscar for the part Bette Davis rejected, playing a role which decidely tarnished the glamorous image that MGM had created for her.

Yet the film itself was harshly criticized by some. In the *New York Times*, Thomas M. Pryor wrote of the absence of "the driving force of melodrama" in the film, but he admitted that Curtiz directed "with cunning dramatic artifice for most of its 111 minutes." Howard Barnes of the *New York Herald-Tribune* derided the production for trying "to be audacious. It is merely anemic." James Agee of the *Nation* disagreed, calling *Mildred Pierce* a "nasty, gratifying version of the James M. Cain novel."

Night and Day (1946) was one of Curtiz's biggest box-office triumphs, although the fictionalized biography of composer Cole Porter does not hold up well today. The film raked in $4,000,000 in North American rentals, so many must have been charmed by Cary Grant's lukewarm portrayal of one of the kings of popular music. Barnes of the *Tribune* described the film as "a highly entertaining screen musical, and Pryor of the *Times* deemed it "generally pleasant."

Curtiz cannot be praised too highly for his fine handling of *Life with*

Father (1947), Warner Brothers' version of the hit play by Russel Crouse and Howard Lindsay, starring William Powell and Irene Dunne. Powell had tried for years to interest Louis B. Mayer in securing the screen rights to the Broadway hit, but the mogul thought that the $500,000 asking price was excessive. Warner Brothers bought it and wisely allowed Curtiz to direct. He handled an alien subject, an American family in New York City of the 1880s, so well that his foreign birth certificate can almost be called into question. The fine screenplay by Donald Ogden Stewart, which eliminated the profanity of father Clarence Day, was filmed so successfully that Thomas M. Pryor of the *Times* announced: "Warner Brothers can be proud of a job well done." James Agee of the *Nation* admired the production, although with reservations. "Rich, careful, rather heavily proficient," he opined. But *Life with Father* was good enough to win four Oscar nominations, make the *New York Times'* Ten Best list, and cop *Film Daily's* award for best film.

In 1950, Curtiz directed *The Breaking Point,* one of the best film versions of a published literary work. It was taken from Ernest Hemingway's *To Have and Have Not.* The author considered his novel a poor choice for film treatment, and he challenged Warner Brothers director Howard Hawks to produce a cinematization, which he did in 1944 with mediocre results. Curtiz's film shifted the focus from political gangsters to the apolitical variety, featuring John Garfield in Humphrey Bogart's role. Garfield is brilliant as the gun runner, a guy who makes the decision to "get involved" at the last minute, "with nothing left but his guts to sell." The able supporting cast includes Phyllis Thaxter as Garfield's wife (eliminated in Hawks' version), young Patricia Neal in Lauren Bacall's role, Juano Hernandez, and a particularly slimy characterization by Wallace Ford.

In the *New York Times,* Bosley Crowther asserted: "All the character, color, and cynicism of Mr. Hemingway's lean and hungry tale are wrapped up in this realistic picture," and he commended Curtiz's "beautifully crisp, commanding style." Barnes of the *Tribune* concurred, stating, "Under Michael Curtiz's pizzicato direction, it has color, violence, and suspense, even though incidents have a frayed look."

Most film historians rightly contend that Curtiz's career took a nosedive after World War II. In *The American Cinema,* Andrew Sarris asserts that after 1951's *Force of Arms,* Curtiz's "career went to the dogs." Jack Edmund Nolan is less severe in his article on the director in *Films in Review,* deciding that of the Hungarian's thirty-two films directed over the years 1945-61, "three or four of them still have value." Kingsley Canham expresses the same sentiments in Volume I of *The Hollywood Professionals.*

Curtiz's decline wasn't as severe as the above statements have indicated, but there is no denying the inferiority of many of his last two dozen films. With the coming of television the studios panicked and altered their stride to accommodate a new generation of movie-goers which could turn on video shows for free. Consequently, those involved in middle-budget films felt the squeeze quickly. In the early 1950s Warner Brothers put its employees on half-salary, MGM let many of its people go, and RKO disintegrated. The blockbuster film was in, and all else was out, or handled more and more by independent producers, directors, and actors.

Force of Arms (1951) is a good example of a moderately budgeted film which wouldn't have gotten the careful production accorded it as a matter of policy just a few years later. *Variety* called the unacknowledged adaptation of Hemingway's *A Farewell to Arms* "excellent," and the *New York Times'* A. H. Weiler labeled the moving drama "a forceful amalgam of ruggedness and romance." *Nation* critic Manny Farber, along with James Agee the earliest critic to recognize the value of Hollywood's middle-budget-genre film, gave *Force of Arms* one of his six-inch "Emmanuelle" awards for being an "also ran" in 1951.

When Warner Brothers instituted pay cuts for all its employees, Curtiz left the studio. His last few films there had been lackluster efforts. The Hungarian moved to 20th Century-Fox for a $5,000,000 ton of bricks, *The Egyptian*. An early Cinemascope venture, the epic featured an all-star cast, including Jean Simmons, Victor Mature, Gene Tierney, and Edmund Purdom in the title role, along with 5,000 extras.

Bosley Crowther of the *New York Times* echoed the most widely held view that the "script and that excavated decor are a little too heavy for him [Curtiz] to move." William K. Zinsser of the *New York Herald-Tribune* appreciated "the pomp of the pharaohs ... in this sweeping pageant of Egypt's great age." Even the production crew was less than awed by the spectacle. Cameraman Leon Shamroy later said, "It might have looked better if Marlene Dietrich had been playing the old hooker—the old whore. And Marlon Brando should have been the man; but he hated Mike Curtiz, he disliked Bella Darvi, and he wasn't too fond of the script."

White Christmas (Paramount, 1954) brought Curtiz back into the winner's circle. Loosely based on the 1942 film musical *Holiday Inn* starring Bing Crosby and Fred Astaire, Curtiz's version grossed $12,000,000 and offered some nicely tuned sentimental nonsense involving Crosby, who repeated his role, and Danny Kaye. However, the critics weren't impressed. "If *White Christmas* is partially flattened under a weight of importance," said Otis L. Guernsey in the *New York Herald-Tribune,* "it at least gives everybody plenty of working room and plenty of time." Crowther of the *New York Times* stated, "Director Michael Curtiz has made his picture look good. It is too bad that it doesn't hit the eardrums and the funny bone with equal force."

Although *White Christmas* ended happily and Curtiz's box-office clout was once more illustrated, 1954 was a hard year for him personally. A 22-year-old woman named Beth Jill Gerrard accused the director of fathering her illegitimate child. The 66-year-old Curtiz reportedly admitted the charge and signed a statement agreeing to pay mother and daughter Deborah $400 a month for life. Sadly, as we shall see, this was not the end of the sordid affair, but it didn't stop Curtiz's prolific picture-making. He made seven films in his last seven years of life. The productions were shot at a variety of studios, including Warner Brothers, and a marked inadequacy is evident in four of these.

His finest film of this last period is *The Proud Rebel* (Buena Vista, 1958) which stars father and son Alan and David Ladd as a father and son who attempt to save rancher Olivia de Havilland's property from ruthless opponents. The quiet Western was praised by most critics. A. H. Weiler of the *New York Times* called it "a genuinely sentimental but often moving drama."

Michael Curtiz was not happy at the eminent end of the structured studio system in Hollywood. With more and more actors, directors, writers, and producers free-lancing, assignments were up for grabs, and a director could no longer count on receiving a certain number of scripts a year. Many of Curtiz's contemporaries, including Lewis Milestone, Mitchell Leisen, and Robert Florey, made the transition to directing in television, but the Hungarian stayed with the cinema until he died.

When he was filming his next-to-last work, *Francis of Assisi* (20th Century-Fox, 1961), Curtiz offered his views on the new Hollywood, and, indeed, the new world of filmmaking: "The combination of unions and stars, with their sky-high demands, is driving productions abroad. It's a shame to watch what's happening. There is no reason for it, except that some of us are just too greedy. If people were more reasonable, and recognized that they are destroying the wonderful machine that was—and still is—Hollywood, the Europeans today would not be reaping the rich harvest of American production investment."

Although *Francis of Assisi* was a failure along the lines of *The Egyptian*, Curtiz's last film, *The Comancheros* (20th Century-Fox, 1961), a rip-roaring Western starring John Wayne, pleased the public and some critics. Bosley Crowther of the *New York Times* felt the film was "so studiously wild and woolly it turns out to be fun," and he imagined "making it under the direction of Michael Curtiz must have been back-breaking fun." But Paul V. Beckley of the *New York Herald-Tribune* decided that *The Comancheros* was "just too stuffed with feathers."

John Wayne and Ina Balin in The Comancheros *(20th, 1961)*

John Garfield, Patricia Neal, and Juano Hernandez in The Breaking Point *(WB, 1950)*

David Ladd, Olivia de Havilland, and Alan Ladd in The Proud Rebel *(Buena Vista, 1958)*

Afflicted with cancer, Michael Curtiz died on April 10, 1962. His estate was valued at $338,000. In his will, the director ordered his executor, The Bank of America, to stop paying Beth Gerrard the $400 a month support he had agreed to in 1954, claiming that the paper was signed under duress. Beth Gerrard, then thirty years old, sued the estate for $6,000, the money she claimed Curtiz owed her, since the director had stopped payments in 1960. In May 1962, the court ordered Curtiz's executors to pay the sum, and to continue the $400 a month allotments.

Wherever the truth lies in this unfortunate conflict, Michael Curtiz was seen as a decent human being by more people than Hollywood gossip-mongers and some film historians would like to admit. In her autobiography, *Doris Day: Her Own Story*, the sweetheart of millions of moviegoers in the 1950s and 1960s tells of the time she auditioned for mean Mike Curtiz.

"Curtiz had his own bungalow on the Warners lot, a tribute to his eminence at the studio. I could tell from the furnishings that Mr. Curtiz was a man of good taste. Tall, handsome, expensively tailored, steel-grey hair, thick Hungarian accent."

Interviewing her, Curtiz discovered that she was a singer with no previous experience as an actress. Therefore, he asked her to sing, but the screen's future sunshine lady was beset with problems at the time and didn't feel up to it. She broke down crying twice while trying to warble, but Curtiz saw something in her. He gave her a script, and asked her to audition two days from then. "You mean, after all this, you're still going to test me?" she asked, astonished. "You're very sensitive girl," Curtiz assured her. "To be good actress is to be sensitive." "What part?" she asked. "The lead," he responded. With script in hand, the 25-year-old singer blurted out, "How can I possibly be the lead? I haven't had any experience—I don't know how to act. That seems pretty crazy to me." Unwavering, and decidedly cool, the director insisted, "You let me decide that," and explained her charm. "I sometimes like girl who is not actress," he said. "Is less pretend and more heart."

Pretense was one quality absent in Michael Curtiz's make-up. The anger, the love, and the dedication were all there. They came out as he felt them.

The Films of Michael Curtiz

Má ès Holnap (Today and Tomorrow) *(Hung., 1912) (and co-script, actor)*

Az Utolsó Bohèm (The Last Bohemian) *(Hung., 1912)*

Rablelkek (Captive Souls) *(Hung., 1913)*

Házasokik Az Uram (My Husband's Getting Married) *(Hung., 1913)*

Az Éjszaka Rabja (Prisoner of the Night) *(Hung., 1914) (and actor)*

Aranyáso (Golddigger) *(Hung., 1914)*

Bank Ban *(Hung., 1914)*

A Tolonc (The Exile) *(Hung., 1914)*

A Kölesonkèrt Csecsemök (The Borrowed Babies) *(Hung., 1914)*

A Hercegnö Pongyolában (The Princess in a Nightrobe) *(Hung., 1914)*

Akit Ketten Szeretnek (One Who Is Loved by Two) *(Hung., 1915) (and actor)*

A Farkas (The Wolf) *(Hung., 1916)*

A Karthauzi (The Karthauzer) *(Hung., 1916)*

Makkhetes (Seven of Spades) *(Hung., 1916)*

A Fekete Szivárvány (The Black Rainbow) *(Hung., 1916)*

Doktor Ùr (Mr. Doctor) *(Hung., 1916)*

A Magyar Fold Ereje (The Strength of the Fatherland) *(Hung., 1916)*

A Medikus (The Medic) *(Hung., 1916)*

Zoárd Mester (Master Zoard) *(Hung., 1917)*

A Vörös Samson (The Red Samson) *(Hung., 1917)*

Az Utolsó Hajnal (The Last Dawn) *(Hung., 1917)*

A Senki Fia (Nobody's Son) *(Hung., 1917)*

A Szentjóbi Erdo Titka (The Secret of St. Job Forest) *(Hung., 1917)*

A Kuruzsló (The Witchdoctor) *(Hung., 1917)*

A Halász Csengö (The Fishing Bell) *(Hung., 1917)*

A Fold Embere (Earth's Man) *(Hung., 1917)*

Az Exredes (The Colonel) *(Hung., 1917)*

Egy Krajacár Törènete (A Penny's History) *(Hung., 1917)*

A Bèke Ùtjà (Peace's Road) *(Hung., 1917)*

Az Arendás Zsidó (Jean the Tenant) *(Hung., 1917)*

Tatárjárás (Tartar Invasion) *(Hung., 1917)*

Az Orvos (The Doctor) *(Hung., 1917)*

Tavasz a Telven (Spring in Winter) *(Hung., 1917)*

A Napra Forgos Holgy (The Sunflower Woman) *(Hung., 1918)*

Lulu *(Hung., 1918)*

Kileneven Kilenc (Ninety Nine) *(Hung., 1918)*

Az Ördög (The Devil) *(Hung., 1918)*

A Csúnya Filu (The Ugly Boy) *(Hung., 1918)*

Alruha (The Disguise) *(Hung., 1918)*

Judas *(Hung., 1918)*

A Vig Özvegy (The Merry Widow) *(Hung., 1918)*

Varázskeringö (Magic Waltz) *(Hung., 1918)*

The Films of Michael Curtiz (continued)

Lu, a Kokott (Lu, the Cocette) (*Hung.*, *1918*)

Jön az Ocsem (My Brother Is Coming) (*Hung., 1919*)

Liliom (*Hung., 1919*) (*unfinished*)

Wellington Rejtely (*Swedish, 1919*)

Odette et l'Histoire des Femmes Illustrés (*Swedish, 1919*)

Die Dame mit dem Schwarzen Handschuh (*Austrian, 1919*)

Der Stern von Damaskus (*Austrian, 1919*)

Die Gottesgeissel (*Austrian, 1920*)

Die Dame mit den Sonnenblumen (*Austrian, 1920*)

Labyrinth des Grauvens (*Austrian, 1920*)

Wege des Schrecken (*Austrian, 1921*)

Frau Dorothys Bekenntnis (*Austrian, 1921*)

Miss Tutti Frutti (*Austrian, 1921*)

Herzogin Satanella (*Austrian, 1921*)

Sodom und Gomorrha (*Austrian, part one-1922; part two-1923*) (*and co-script*)

Die Lasvine (*Austrian, 1923*)

Der Junge Medardus (*Austrian, 1923*) (*co-directed by Sascha Kolowrat*)

Samson und Dalila (*Austrian, 1923*)

Namenlos (*Austrian, 1923*)

Ein Spiel Ums Leben (*Austrian, 1924*)

General Babka (*Austrian, 1924*)

The Uncle from Sumatra (*Austrian, 1924*)

Avalanche (*Austrian, 1924*)

Harun Al Raschid (*Austrian, 1924*)

Die Slavenkönigin (Moon of Israel) (*Austrian, 1924*)

Das Spielzeug von Paris (Red Heels) (*German-Austrian, 1925*)

Der Golden Schmetterling (The Road to Happiness) (*German-Austrian, 1926*)

Flaker Nr. 13 (*German-Austrian, 1926*)

The Third Degree (*WB, 1926*)

The Million Bid (*WB, 1927*)

The Desired Woman (*WB, 1927*)

Good Time Charley (*WB, 1927*)

Tenderloin (*WB, 1928*)

Noah's Ark (*WB, 1928*)

Hearts in Exile (*WB, 1929*)

Glad Rag Doll (*WB, 1929*)

Madonna of Avenue A (*WB, 1929*)

The Gamblers (*WB, 1929*)

Mammy (*WB, 1930*)

Under a Texas Moon (*WB, 1930*)

The Matrimonial Bed (*WB, 1930*)

Bright Lights (*FN, 1930*)

A Soldier's Plaything (*WB, 1930*)

River's End (*WB, 1930*)

Damon des Meeres (*WB, 1931*)

God's Gift to Women (*WB, 1931*)

The Mad Genius (*WB, 1931*)

The Woman from Monte Carlo (*FN, 1932*)

Alias the Doctor (*FN, 1932*)

The Strange Love of Molly Louvain (*FN, 1932*)

Doctor X (*FN, 1932*)

The Cabin in the Cotton (*FN, 1932*)

20,000 Years in Sing Sing (*FN, 1933*)

The Mystery of the Wax Museum (*FN, 1933*)

The Keyhole (*WB, 1933*)

Private Detective 63 (*WB, 1933*)

Goodbye Again (*FN, 1933*)

The Kennel Murder Case (*WB, 1933*)

Female (*FN, 1933*)

Mandalay (*FN, 1934*)

British Agent (*FN, 1934*)

Jimmy the Gent (*WB, 1934*)

The Key (*WB, 1934*)

Black Fury (*WB, 1935*)

The Case of the Curious Bride (*WB, 1935*)

Front Page Woman (*WB, 1935*)

Little Big Shot (*WB, 1935*)

Captain Blood (*WB, 1935*)

The Walking Dead (*WB, 1936*)

The Charge of the Light Brigade (*WB, 1936*)

Mountain Justice *(WB, 1937)*
Stolen Holiday *(WB, 1937)*
Kid Galahad *(WB, 1937)*
The Perfect Specimen *(WB, 1937)*
Gold Is Where You Find It *(WB, 1938)*
The Adventures of Robin Hood *(WB, 1938) (co-directed by William Keighley)*
Four Daughters *(WB, 1938)*
Four's a Crowd *(WB, 1938)*
Angels with Dirty Faces *(WB, 1938)*
Dodge City *(WB, 1939)*
Daughters Courageous *(WB, 1939)*
Four Wives *(WB, 1939)*
The Private Lives of Elizabeth and Essex *(WB, 1939)*
Virginia City *(WB, 1940)*
The Sea Hawk *(WB, 1940)*
The Santa Fe Trail *(WB, 1940)*
The Sea Wolf *(WB, 1941)*
Dive Bomber *(WB, 1941)*
Captains of the Clouds *(WB, 1942)*
Yankee Doodle Dandy *(WB, 1942)*
Casablanca *(WB, 1943)*
Mission to Moscow *(WB, 1943)*
This Is the Army *(WB, 1943)*
Passage to Marseilles *(WB, 1944)*
Janie *(WB, 1944)*
Roughly Speaking *(WB, 1945)*
Mildred Pierce *(WB, 1945)*
Night and Day *(WB, 1946)*
Life with Father *(WB, 1947)*
The Unsuspected *(WB, 1947)*

Romance on the High Seas *(WB, 1948)*
My Dream Is Yours *(WB, 1949) (and producer)*
Flamingo Road *(WB, 1949)*
The Lady Takes a Sailor *(WB, 1949)*
Young Man with a Horn *(WB, 1950)*
Bright Leaf *(WB, 1950)*
The Breaking Point *(WB, 1950)*
Jim Thorpe—All American *(WB, 1951)*
Force of Arms *(WB, 1951)*
I'll See You in My Dreams *(WB, 1952)*
The Story of Will Rogers *(WB, 1952)*
The Jazz Singer *(WB, 1953)*
Trouble Along the Way *(WB, 1953)*
The Boy from Oklahoma *(WB, 1954)*
The Egyptian *(20th, 1954)*
White Christmas *(Par., 1954)*
We're No Angels *(Par., 1955)*
The Scarlet Hour *(Par., 1956) (and producer)*
The Vagabond King *(Par., 1956)*
The Best Things in Life Are Free *(20th, 1956)*
The Helen Morgan Story *(WB, 1957)*
The Proud Rebel *(Buena Vista, 1958)*
King Creole *(Par., 1958)*
The Hangman *(Par., 1959)*
The Man in the Net *(UA, 1959)*
The Adventures of Huckleberry Finn *(MGM, 1960)*
A Breath of Scandal *(Par., 1960)*
Francis of Assisi *(20th, 1961)*
The Comancheros *(20th, 1961)*

Eleanor Parker and John Garfield in Pride of the Marines *(WB, 1945)*

John Garfield and Delmer Daves (far right) on the set of Pride of the Marines *(WB, 1945)*

6

Delmer Daves

In 1972 Delmer Daves recalled his early years in filmmaking: "The principal source of lighting was an endless skylight slanted over eight three-walled sets in which eight films were being shot simultaneously; it was a cacophony as each director of these far from silent films gave instructions to the silent actors, often through a megaphone."

The name Delmer Daves has indicated many things in Hollywood for the past fifty years—actor, writer, director, and producer. Daves participated in the making of war films, comedies, Westerns, swashbucklers, crime films, soap operas, musicals—every genre of film that Hollywood ever produced—but it is as a director of Westerns that his place in the pages of film history has been justified. Neither a romanticizer of Western culture like John Ford, nor a rugged realist with the golden soul of a Hart, he was the most prolific director of the "liberal" Western: one ruled by modern theme rather than by two-fisted cowboys and gunplay. There is little black and white in a Daves Western. The contrasts seep into each other, often resulting in an ugly shade of grey. The grey is often evoked against a studied background of the sun-baked browns of prairies and mountains, with flashes of other colors as rare as the savage depiction of a nineteenth-century ethos is frequent.

Delmer Daves was born on July 24, 1904 in San Francisco, California. When he was 10 years old, he made his film debut portraying a choirboy in a Universal production starring future director Robert Z. Leonard and Ella Hall. He worked sporadically in movies for the next dozen years, but after receiving a law degree from Stanford in 1927, he approached director James Cruze (*The Covered Wagon,* 1923) with a letter from a college chum, and Cruze hired Delmer as a prop man.

Young Daves learned Cruze's habit of cutting inside the camera, not leaving the choice of a take for a scene to the boys in the editing room. Cruze produced his dissolves and fades in the camera, doubtlessly the way this pioneer filmmaker had done it since becoming a feature director in 1918. Delmer worked his way up to technical director and made a "comeback" as an actor. Then Sam Wood hired him to write scripts in 1929, and Daves free-lanced at many studios until 1943, when he was taken out of a Warner Brothers' cubbyhole to direct his own screenplay, *Destination Tokyo*.

Always willing to talk about the technical side of filmmaking, Delmer recalled that in 1929 all sound production took place on a single stage that was used twenty-four hours a day. "Our primeval microphones were so sensitive to high frequencies that they'd burst their valves if you even opened a letter: the prop man had to dampen all envelopes, letters, etc. An actor had to fake clapping his hands or we'd hear the oft-repeated cry, 'Valve broke.'"

During the 1930s Delmer was a popular bachelor in Hollywood. In 1936 rumors intimated that he would wed Warner Brothers star Kay Francis, but the real thing didn't come until 1938 when Daves married Mary Lou Leider. A year later he wrote a script called *Crazy About Him*, which entered the headlines in 1941 during the writer's suit against MGM for plagiarizing the material in *Love Crazy*, starring William Powell and Myrna Loy.

In 1943 Jack Warner asked Delmer to write a follow-up to the studio's successful *Action in the North Atlantic*, and he penned a paean to the men who manned submarines deep in the Atlantic and Pacific. Called *Destination Tokyo*, and co-scripted by Albert Maltz, the film was made with the cooperation of the Navy. Daves guided the building of the submarine Copperfin, utilizing a complicated blueprint. When it was discovered that he knew more about submarine warfare than anybody else at Warner Brothers, Delmer became the director of *Destination Tokyo*.

Destination Tokyo stars Cary Grant, John Garfield, Alan Hale, Dane Clark, William Prince, and a number of other solid supporting players. The overlong (135 minutes) film does move at a brisk pace considering its length, but it often sags during bouts with sentiment and rhetoric. Holing a number of men up in the confines of a submarine for almost an entire film is a dangerous proposition in itself, since it is difficult to create evocative camera movements in such a cramped space, or to set mood lighting which adds so much to a suspenseful script (which *Destination Tokyo* has when it counts).

Nevertheless, Daves' directorial debut was received enthusiastically by audiences and critics. According to Howard Barnes of the *New York Herald-Tribune*, *Destination Tokyo* "is so good that it adds an impressive chapter to the screen's chronicle of the present conflict." "A pippin of a submarine action film," wrote Bosley Crowther in the *New York Times.* In the *Nation,* James Agee asserted that the film "combines a good deal of fairly exciting submarine warfare with at least as much human interest, which I found neither very human nor at all very interesting."

After making a dull musical called *Hollywood Canteen* and the banal *The Very Thought of You* in 1944, Daves co-authored *Pride of the Marines* with Albert Maltz. In general the film is a solid, moving tribute to blinded Marine Al Schmid (John Garfield) who overcomes all odds on the homefront as well as the battlefield. The film is marred by patches of rhetoric, but nothing close to the near disastrous extent found in *Destination Tokyo.* The most flawed sequence occurs in the hospital when Schmid and a group of men debate America's treatment of war veterans. Another topic which would receive further analysis in post-war Hollywood is anti-Semitism. Dane Clark plays Garfield's Jewish buddy, and there are some brief interludes about religious bigotry admirably integrated into the narrative. There is also a bit with a black porter played with extreme dignity. In *Pride of the Marines* war equalizes all races, colors, and creeds.

Daves was much praised for his handling of the battle sequences, particularly the one in which the soldier is struck blind. The director used the technique of double printing with a 60% positive and 40% negative image to evoke the horror of a grenade exploding in Schmid's face. The night fight is stretched out for agonizingly real moments as the GIs are picked off one at a time, leaving Schmid to contend with the unseen Japanese in total darkness.

The *Times'* Bosley Crowther insisted that Daves directed *Pride of the Marines* "with brilliant pictorial realism and emotional sympathy." However, the *Nation's* James Agee wasn't impressed: "Long drawn out and never inspired, but very respectably honest and dogged, thanks considerably, it appears, to Albert Maltz's screenplay."

Next Daves wrote and directed *The Red House* (UA, 1947), the story of a farmer (Edward G. Robinson) who knows the secrets of a foreboding house in the forest. Once more Delmer displayed his technical expertise by shooting the recurrence of the farmer's warning to a young boy in infra-red film.

Continuing to distinguish himself with cinematic bravado, Daves employed a subjective camera to record the first five reels of *Dark Passage* (WB, 1947). Humphrey Bogart stars as an accused murderer who escapes prison and finds refuge with a young woman (Lauren Bacall). In order to search for his wife's killer and elude the police, the man undergoes plastic surgery. Bogart's face is not seen until the bandages

111

are removed. The camera dips and bends in the convict's place, looking into the eyes of other characters as they watch the lens. Since the camera had to replace a person, the director needed especially light equipment to simulate the pulse of human movement. Delmer obtained a captured German camera from the Enemy Property Custody Office in Washington, D.C. for this purpose.

Dark Passage's script, written by Daves, is a winding, often hysterical narrative, offering weak motivations. For instance, it is difficult to believe that a woman would shelter a convicted murderer simply because her father was a victim of the courts. She evidences no neurosis, psychosis, or obsession which could explain such actions. Furthermore, why would a cab driver agree to supply the fleeing prisoner with the name of a plastic surgeon? And Agnes Moorehead's plunge out of an open window is too contrived. Everything seems too pat.

Yet the production is bolstered by the fine support of Tom D'Andrea (the taxi driver), Clifton Young (a blackmailer), and Moorehead. Combined with Bogart and Bacall—under the advertisement "Together Again ... in danger as violent as their love!!!"—*Dark Passage* was favorably reviewed by *Variety*. "Sterling, sultry performances by the duo in a grim story that has plenty of killings and suspense."

After the tepid *To the Victor* (WB, 1948), the sporadically humorous *A Kiss in the Dark* (WB, 1949), and the solid but uninspired *Task Force* (WB, 1949), Daves left Warner Brothers for 20th Century-Fox and one of the ground-breaking Westerns of all-time, *Broken Arrow* (1950).

Broken Arrow was Daves' first Western, and many contend that it is his best film. Along with *The Gunfighter* (20th, 1950) and *High Noon* (UA, 1952), *Broken Arrow* ushered in a new era for the Western. Stereotypes disintegrated, psychology wore down images of outlaws and heroes, a sheriff could abandon his macho and ask a town for help routing bandits—anything was possible in the new West. *Broken Arrow* is one of the very few films to treat Indians with dignity and respect, besides giving a major, adult role to an Indian character (essayed by Jeff Chandler). Chandler plays Cochise, an Apache chief, with James Stewart as an ex-Army man and Debra Paget as the Indian maiden who marries Stewart.

Perhaps the director harkened back to memories of early twentieth-century movie locations, the same country where the story of *Broken Arrow* unwinds decades earlier. Delmer takes full advantage of natural vistas in the film, with the simple blue sky, brown teepee, and white horse giving a striking effect to the wedding of Stewart and Paget.

Broken Arrow received mixed notices. "Believe it or not, 20th Century-Fox has come up with a socially significant Western," announced Howard Barnes in the *Herald-Tribune*. The critic included ho-hum

James Stewart
and Debra Paget
in Broken Arrow
(20th, 1950)

Lauren Bacall
and Humphrey
Bogart in
Dark Passage
(WB, 1946)

praise: "Pictorial, amusing, and, in passing, constructive." The *Times'* Bosley Crowther damned the film with the editorial comment: "We cannot accept this picture as either an exciting or reasonable account of the attitudes and ways of American Indians."

Two decades later, William K. Everson evaluated the impact of *Broken Arrow* in *A Pictorial History of the Western Film* (Citadel Press): "*Broken Arrow*, while it may have been prompted by the controversial but commercially successful race problem (Jewish and Negro) films of the 1940s, managed the rare movie trick of making a social comment without overloading the scales. The side issues of *Broken Arrow* were rapidly commercialized to the hilt: it established Cochise ... as a 'regular' horse opera hero, prompted sequels, established a pattern by which big male stars ... could profitably play Indians, ushered in a whole new era of villainous whites ... and misunderstood noble Redmen, and finally prompted a long-running TV series, with all the attendant merchandising of bows and arrows and Indian outfits for the kiddies. Its controlled documentary qualities were also copied shamelessly by many lesser Westerns. But the original film was good enough to survive even this subsequent exploitation; it was and is a warm, poignant, and often poetic film."

After *Broken Arrow*, Daves didn't make another exciting work until 1956. *Jubal* (Col.) and *The Last Wagon* (20th) both came out that year, and while they are notable additions to the director's oeuvre for different reasons, they have a sort of savage psychological tension in common.

In *Jubal*, Glenn Ford plays the title character of Jubal Troop, a drifter hired by ranch owner Ernest Borgnine. The movie is essentially one large set piece about the relationship of Ford, Borgnine, Felicia Farr, and Rod Steiger, who brilliantly evokes a psychotic cowhand called Pinky. It is almost as if *Jubal* were adapted from a stage play, yet it remains free of a static theatrical outlook.

The Last Wagon doesn't match the character conflicts in *Jubal*, but is much better from pictorial and action standpoints. The primary color of *The Last Wagon* is various tones of brown. From the parched brown prairies and distant mountains, to the plain brown clothing, to the tanned skin and blonde hair of Comanche Tod (Richard Widmark), the ruling hue matches the consistent undercurrent of the base conflict, Indians vs. whites. Raw emotions are displayed throughout. Bigotry, lust, sadism, and revenge motivate the narrative, with human reason coming to rescue the bitter Tod from the hangman.

Daves continued to explore the land for emotional effect in *3:10 to Yuma* (Col., 1957), starring Van Heflin as a farmer who captures outlaw Glenn Ford. The director shot much of the footage through red

114

filters in order to further the feeling of drought, giving the tough narrative an arid, leathery tone, which in turn complements the performances. There is a sense of necessity in the film, something one man has to do, almost a mission. This pattern was established in the "liberal" Western of the 1950s and repeated in *High Noon*, *The Gunfighter*, *The Last Wagon*, and many others. Despite the very modern psychological explorations of power, bigotry, fear, and immorality, these films have an ancient preoccupation with fate and the necessity to make a moral choice.

Bosley Crowther of the *New York Times* called *3:10 to Yuma* "a respectable second section to *High Noon*," while Paul V. Beckley in his *New York Herald-Tribune* critique insisted that "it is a strong, taut drama which builds to a climax almost painfully tense."

After *Cowboy* in 1958 and *The Hanging Tree* the next year, Delmer Daves' career deteriorated with a series of melodramatic projects which he often wrote and produced as well as directed. *A Summer Place* (1960), *Parrish* (1961), *Susan Slade* (1961), *Rome Adventure* (1962), *Spencer's Mountain* (1963), and *Youngblood Hawke* (1964) were all produced under the banner of the new chiefs at Warner Brothers. Every one of these productions is dominated by turgidity (except warmhearted *Spencer's Mountain*), featuring superficial characters and stories. Blond male hair is a constant here, ranging from the paper-thin Troy Donahue in the first four, to the more substantial but undistinguished James MacArthur *(Spencer's Mountain)* and James Franciscus *(Youngblood Hawke)*.

Daves' last film is another Warner Brothers soap opera, entitled *The Battle of the Villa Fiorita* (1965), featuring more mature leads Rossano Brazzi and Maureen O'Hara. That love stories weren't the director's forte is painfully obvious, yet he spent the last half-dozen years of his career filming such projects.

In 1972 there was a retrospective of nineteen of the director's films at the 18th Annual Film Festival of Oberhausen, West Germany. Among those productions screened were *Destination Tokyo*, *The Red House*, *Dark Passage*, *Broken Arrow*, and *Youngblood Hawke*.

Delmer Daves died on August 17, 1977 at the Scripps Hospital in La Jolla, California. Until the end, he attempted to generate film projects through his Diamond D Production Company. He left his wife Mary Lou Lawrence, a son, two daughters, a sister, three grandchildren, and a series of fine Westerns which helped redefine their genre.

The Films of Delmer Daves

Destination Tokyo *(WB, 1943) (and co-script)*

The Very Thought of You *(WB, 1944) (and co-script)*

Hollywood Canteen *(WB, 1944) (and script)*

Pride of the Marines *(WB, 1945) (and co-script)*

The Red House *(UA, 1947) (and script)*

Dark Passage *(WB, 1947) (and script)*

To the Victor *(WB, 1948)*

A Kiss in the Dark *(WB, 1949)*

Task Force *(WB, 1949) (and script)*

Broken Arrow *(20th, 1950)*

Bird of Paradise *(20th, 1951) (and script)*

Return of the Texan *(20th, 1952)*

Treasure of the Golden Condor *(20th, 1953)*

Never Let Me Go *(MGM, 1953)*

Demetrius and the Gladiators *(20th, 1954)*

Drum Beat *(WB, 1954) (and script)*

Jubal *(Col., 1956)*

The Last Wagon *(20th, 1956) (and co-script)*

3:10 to Yuma *(Col., 1957)*

Cowboy *(Col., 1958)*

Kings Go Forth *(UA, 1958)*

The Badlanders *(MGM, 1958)*

The Hanging Tree *(WB, 1959)*

A Summer Place *(WB, 1960) (and producer, script)*

Parrish *(WB, 1961) (and producer, script)*

Susan Slade *(WB, 1961) (and producer, script)*

Rome Adventure *(WB, 1962) (and producer, script)*

Spencer's Mountain *(WB, 1963) (and producer)*

Youngblood Hawke *(WB, 1964) (and script)*

The Battle of the Villa Fiorita *(WB, 1965) (and producer, script)*

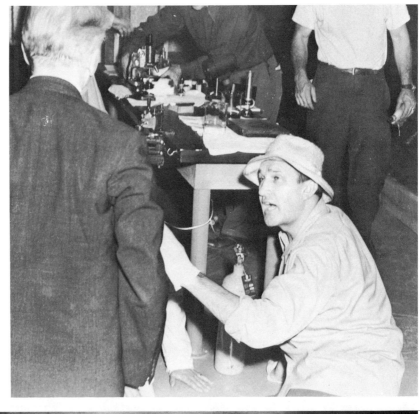

William Dieterle on the set of This Love of Ours *(Universal, 1945)*

Richard Barthelmess, David Manners, Johnny Mack Brown, Walter Byron, Helen Chandler, and Elliot Nugent in The Last Flight *(First National, 1931)*

7

William Dieterle

"To discuss Hollywood problems is like discussing love," mused William Dieterle. "There are a million aspects to the subject which always remain the same. 'Escape' versus 'message' and 'profit' versus 'art.'" Those were the contradictions that the director had to resolve in his thirty-year Hollywood career. He was in the best of all possible worlds in the 1930s when his biographical films won both critical and popular kudos, which translated into big money. For his achievements in *The Story of Louis Pasteur, The Life of Emile Zola, Juarez,* and *Dr. Ehrlich's Magic Bullet,* Dieterle was labeled the "Plutarch of the screen" by Bosley Crowther.

The director once explained his way of turning history into film art. "I prefer the direct, forceful method. I believe that a picture's basic idea is more important than the story that is told. A story can be trivial." Expounding further, he asserted: "In order not to distract attention, the events of the story being told must come in an orderly, consistent progression, the one following the other in logical sequence."

A relegation of narrative to a lesser role in the cinema resulted in some leaden productions in Dieterle's later career. Yet the force of his biographical pictures, in addition to *A Midsummer Night's Dream* and *All That Money Can Buy,* proved that the director was more often right than wrong.

The ninth and last son of poor parents, Wilhelm Dieterle was born on July 15, 1893 in Ludwigshafen, Germany. Mr. and Mrs. Dieterle wanted the boy to become a carpenter and glazier, but Wilhelm rebelled early, opting instead for a life in the theatre. As the years passed, the young actor achieved recognition in Munich, Heidelberg, and Zurich, and he soon became a protégé of theatrical genius Max Reinhardt. The relationship was a long one, and in the future Jack Warner would assign

Dieterle to co-direct Reinhardt's expensive and expansive adaptation of Shakespeare's *A Midsummer Night's Dream.*

By 1921 Wilhelm had decided to make the cinema his career. The future director was fascinated by the Expressionist films made by F. W. Murnau, Fritz Lang, E. A. Dupont, Arthur Robison, and Dr. Robert Weine in Germany during the 1920s. Dieterle would be adept at handling the new cinema style, since Expressionism was rooted in theatre rather than film, and he learned much about the school of drama, which proffered distorted sets, symbolic lighting, and make-up, and a broad acting style, from Reinhardt, who was an acknowledged master in his field.

After two years of acting in German films, Wilhelm Dieterle wrote, directed, and performed in *Der Menschen am Wege.* He continued in important cinema roles in the likes of Murnau's 1926 *Faust,* and then in 1927 he scripted, acted in, and directed *Das Geheimnis des Abbe X.*

With the advent of sound movies, Dieterle was more in demand, since his theatrical training enabled him to make an easy transition from silence to dialogue. During this period Hollywood studios frantically searched for directors with Dieterle's kind of stage experience. In addition, the fact that Wilhelm (soon changed to William) was heavily versed in German Expressionism, a style which influenced American films of the late 1920s and early 1930s, made him a particularly valuable commodity.

Dieterle started out filming German versions of First National Productions' *Those Who Dance, The Way of All Men* (both 1930), and *Kismet* (1931). His first American assignment was in 1931 with an F. Scott Fitzgerald-like story called *The Last Flight.* Richard Barthelmess, Johnny Mack Brown, Helen Chandler, and Elliott Nugent star in a film of the post-war angst of aviation pilots. The director was praised for his handling of an American narrative at a time when he could hardly speak English, and Dieterle himself said it was "the best picture I ever made."

"It is for the most part an impressive piece of work," wrote Mordaunt Hall in the *New York Times.* "And although it is replete with bizarre ideas, it is always interesting." Hall felt that Dieterle "performed his task most skillfully."

For the next several years Dieterle directed a group of varying films at Warner Brothers and Fox. Melodramas such as *Scarlet Dawn* (originally called *Revolt*—WB, 1932), *Six Hours to Live* (Fox, 1932), and *The Devil's in Love* (Fox, 1933) are modest efforts that are greatly enhanced by Dieterle's fluid camera movements and expressive lighting. *Scarlet Dawn* impressively collates documentary footage of the Russian revolution into a story of two White Russians. The director also filmed more

Americanized narratives, most notably an extremely funny comedy about the bridge craze then sweeping the United States. *Grand Slam* (WB, 1933) stars Paul Lukas as a Russian emigré who may very well represent Dieterle in his absolute confusion and disdain for American fads!

Dieterle, along with Howard Hawks, was mentioned as the possible director of *Shanghai Orchid,* starring Richard Barthelmess, but the project fell through. Then William started *Female* (WB, 1933), but he became ill during the shooting, and William Wellman replaced him.

In 1935 William Dieterle became an American citizen. That year *Dr. Socrates* provided him with his first experience with Paul Muni, an actor he greatly admired, and gave him a taste of the Warner Brothers gangster cycle. Muni plays a small-town doctor involved in a scheme to treat wounded criminals. Kate Cameron of the New York *Daily News* gave the firm a solid three stars, and the *New York Mirror*'s Bland Johaneson called *Dr. Socrates* "a lively story, packed with surprise and commotion."

In October 1935 Dieterle's biggest production up to that time, *A Midsummer Night's Dream,* was released. Co-directed by Max Reinhardt, the film received mostly positive reviews. "Whatever its flaws, it is a work of high ambitions and unflagging interest," asserted Andre Sennwald of the *New York Times.* The film "is a beautiful and expansive spectacle imaginatively conceived and handsomely photographed which captures to a striking degree not only the play's dreamlike mood of moonstruck fantasy but also the hearty and hilarious gusto of the Elizabethan clowns," proclaimed the *New York Herald-Tribune*'s Richard Watts, Jr. "Fairly tedious," sighed *New Republic* critic Otis Ferguson.

In the mid-1930s Americans rummaged through bookstores in search of intelligent biographies and European novels, the more voluminous the better. The studios reacted to this surge of culture and interest in period romances mixed with dashes of religion and philosophy by purchasing many such works of that era. Warner Brothers led the field in literary and biographical adaptations. LeRoy directed *Anthony Adverse,* Curtiz lensed opulent adventures, Litvak made *Tovarich,* and Dieterle dallied with Shakespeare.

The making of *A Midsummer Night's Dream* was anything but tedious. Warner Brothers producer Henry Blanke signed Max Reinhardt, at the time producing a play in the Hollywood Bowl, to adapt the comedy, but Jack Warner insisted that Dieterle be made co-director. The long association of Reinhardt and Dieterle did little to stop the endless arguing which arose regarding the direction of the players. After three weeks of shooting, the production was almost shelved when it was discovered that designer Anton Grot's forest could barely be photographed. Grot's Expressionistic creation consisted of trees composed of burlap coated with plaster of Paris, real leaves applied one at a time, and painted silver. The tree branches were so huge that the camera could only pick up small sections in one shot—and the forest ran over two sets.

Ernest Haller, the original cameraman who worked so well with Edmund Goulding, was replaced at Dieterle's insistence by Hal Mohr. Mohr, an expert at lighting, immediately informed Warner and Dieterle that the set would have to be severely altered. The following weekend, Mohr and crew proceeded to unclutter the forest, and they substituted a single light source in place of Haller's variety.

Even today *A Midsummer Night's Dream* arouses controversy among film specialists. The cast, including James Cagney, Olivia de Havilland, Dick Powell, Mickey Rooney, and Victor Jory, has also been criticized as suffering from Dieterle's plodding direction, but with the possible exception of Jory, all are perfect in their roles.

The Story of Louis Pasteur (1936) was a film that Jack Warner did not want to make. Henry Blanke and Edward Chodorov wrote a script of Pasteur's life, but the effort was deemed unacceptable. Then contract writer Pierre Collings, himself a drug addict, assumed the job because of his interest in medical research. Collings synopsized Pasteur's life and work, and then Sheridan Gibney stepped in to pen the final script. Paul Muni was approached with the material and agreed to star as Pasteur, but Hal Wallis disliked the scenario. Muni fought for *The Story of Louis Pasteur*, citing his contract which gave him final word on subjects. In a vindictive mood, Warner and Wallis allotted the film the lowest possible budget, $330,000, ordered old sets to be adapted for the production, and said that only contract players could fill out the cast.

According to Charles Higham, Dieterle shared Warner's and Wallis' opinion of the script but was coerced into directing the project. The director himself later claimed to have been fascinated by the idea from its inception, and he labeled his approach to Pasteur's life "Man meets microbe," thus symbolically contradicting the feeling held by studio executives that the absence of a love story was a serious mistake.

"An excellent biography," insisted Frank S. Nugent of the *New York Times*, "just as it is a notable photoplay, dignified in subject, dramatic in treatment, and brilliantly played." Regina Crewe of the *New York American* called *The Story of Louis Pasteur* "a cinematic masterpiece," adding that "William Dieterle's direction breathes moving life into history's pages." The *New Republic*'s Otis Ferguson confessed that the film "holds one ... but ... continually disappoints with a wasting of substance."

The Story of Louis Pasteur was nominated for an Oscar as best picture, and star Muni copped the award for his portrayal of the scientist. The film also made the *New York Times'* Ten Best list.

Since Jack Warner was glorified for having the "courage" to make *The Story of Louis Pasteur* and since the film was popular with critics and moviegoers alike, both he and Hal Wallis were sure that future biographical films starring Muni would also be successful. *The Life of Emile Zola* came next for both Muni and Dieterle.

After Henry Blanke received, from Ernst Lubitsch, a story about Zola written by two Hungarian playwrights, he convinced Hal Wallis to prepare the finest production in Warner Brothers history for the property. Anton Grot brilliantly designed the homes of Zola and Dreyfus, the Devil's Island prison, the French court, and the Army barracks, while the playwrights, Heinz Herald and Geza Herczeg, helped Norman Reilly Raine to create a top dramatic script.

Dieterle completely enmeshed himself in *The Life of Emile Zola*, familiarizing himself with the period, yet remaining flexible as far as the material was concerned. Several years later he discussed the film in *Cinema Progress* (Dec.-Jan., 1938-39) and his position as a filmmaker in general: "The job of director is, in my opinion, like that of a gardener, who puts a stick here, to help a plant to grow straight, and cuts a branch there, that the whole tree may thrive better and a good harvest result. Of course, this way of directing requires intelligent actors. At this point I would like to mention Mr. Paul Muni, whom I consider one of the most intelligent actors of our day. Imagine, Zola's tremendous scene in the courtroom was the first and only take! Contrary to common opinion, I believe in first takes."

Sometimes he was asked to shoot a scene more than once. Originally Dreyfus was supposed to leave his Devil's Island cell directly, but Dieterle decided instead to have the imprisoned officer leave, re-enter, and leave again three times. The scene was shot the new way, with actor Joseph Schildkraut slowly passing with faint disbelief through the door which had confined him to years of torture. In a long shot, Schildkraut almost saunters back and forth, rays of sun shining on his battered body, illuminating the dust. Dieterle then refilmed the bit in close-ups, without the repeated movement. This scene proved to be one of the film's most memorable moments.

Zola's stirring defense of Dreyfus before the French court caps *The Life of Emile Zola*. The innocent man accused of traitorous activity by a trumped-up, anti-Semitic judiciary wins his freedom on the basis of that speech, which ends as follows: "By all that I have done for France, by my works, by all that I have written, I swear to you that Dreyfus is innocent. May all that melt away, may my name be forgotten, if Dreyfus be not innocent. . . . He is innocent."

123

Paul Muni and Josephine Hutchinson in The Story of Louis Pasteur *(First National, 1936)*

Ross Alexander, Dick Powell, Anita Louise, and Olivia de Havilland in A Midsummer Night's Dream *(WB, 1935)*

*Paul Muni,
Walter Kingsford,
and Robert
Warwick in*
The Life of
Emile Zola
(WB, 1937)

*Donald Crisp,
Brian Aherne,
Mickey Kuhn,
Bette Davis,
and Gilbert
Roland in*
Juarez *(WB,
1939)*

"The finest historical film ever made and the greatest screen biography," proclaimed Frank S. Nugent in the *New York Times*. "One of the more mature jobs Hollywood has turned out," Otis Ferguson wrote in the *New Republic*. Regarding the character of Zola, the *New York Herald-Tribune*'s Howard Barnes asserted: "The film has distilled something of that genius and soul in a great screen biography."

"The message of *Zola*," said William Dieterle, "is that there are millions of people in the world today like the persecuted Dreyfus, and there is not always a Zola." The premise of *The Life of Emile Zola*, the attack on anti-Semitism and injustice, was a veiled warning to Hitler's Third Reich, and like an even more remote cinema prophecy, *The Adventures of Robin Hood*, it represented Warner Brothers' social conscience at its finest.

The Life of Emile Zola won an Oscar as best picture, and Paul Muni was nominated for his brilliant performance in the title role. The film received many foreign prizes, graced the Ten Best lists of the *New York Times* and *Film Daily*, and was considered the year's finest film by the New York Film Critics.

Director Dieterle, as a native German, was becoming increasingly concerned with the European crisis, and his film work reflected that alarm. His manner and personality did much to focus great attention on anything he said. Dieterle was a tall man, 6'4", who never started a film unless his astrologer deemed the stars in the sky to be in the proper position. It is said that he once began shooting exactly at 3:12 A.M. on a Saturday morning on the advice of those stellar lights. Dieterle was allowed to indulge his eccentricity on that particular occasion since just minimal costs were involved, inasmuch as the scene only required gloved hands to enter a drawer. Moreover, since the director himself always wore a pair of white gloves on the set, he served as his own actor for the scene. The gloves weren't considered a bow to superstition. Dieterle claimed that he had formed the habit of wearing them in the 1920s while working in the German theatre, when he would often be asked to move scenery right before going onstage, and he didn't want to get his hands dirty. If the director's odd habits, distinguished frame, and lofty statements gave the impression that he was a pious, "superior" European, the reality didn't follow suit. Dieterle could often be seen on the set in a baggy woolen sweater, with ruffled hair and bangs slipping either way on his forehead, guiding an actor in what was described as "a bundle of concentrated energy" by Alexander Kahn of the *Daily Worker*. And every morning his wife Charlotta drove him to the studio.

In the late 1930s the Dieterles toured the Soviet Union, and the director was impressed, stating: "The eagerness among the people to learn anything and everything is the outstanding impression I brought back with me from Russia." For a while he toyed with the idea of making a biography of Karl Marx. He was also quoted as saying that Russian film actors were the best in the world.

In 1938 Dieterle directed his first non-Warner Brothers film in five years, United Artists' *Blockade*. Produced by Walter Wanger and starring Henry Fonda and Madeleine Carroll, the picture was a vague anti-Fascist story of the Spanish Civil War, but the script made it difficult to tell the good guys from the bad guys. A publicity man declared that *Blockade* had been banned in Spain by Franco, but that did little to bolster the film's lax box-office reception in America.

Sam Goldwyn originally planned to make *Maximilian in Mexico*, starring Gary Cooper, Joel McCrea, Miriam Hopkins, and Merle Oberon, but the project was soon shelved and it passed on to Warner Brothers. John Huston, Aeneas Mackenzie, and Wolfgang Reinhardt based their script on the play *Juarez and Maximilian* by Franz Werfel and the book *The Phantom Crown* by Bertita Harding. A team was chosen from the ranks of the men who made the Warner Brothers prestige films to handle *Juarez*. Henry Blanke and Hal Wallis produced, Dieterle directed, Anton Grot was art director, and Tony Gaudio photographed the expensive production. Research consisted of 372 volumes of printed material and photographs which were studied by the writers, Dieterle, and the cast. Designer Grot made 3,643 sketches, and the engineers produced 7,360 blueprints for the sets, consisting of twelve villages and four cities, castles on the Adriatic Sea and in France, and the Chapultepec Palace in Mexico City.

The cast is magnificent. Paul Muni plays the Indian Juarez as a god, but a god with a leathery stone face and an earthy voice who speaks in slow, mellifluous tones, mouthing a philosophy of justice in slogans. Bette Davis remains on the edge of an alien culture as the bizarre Carlotta, a loving and supportive wife who cannot stand sanity once her royal world collapses. Brian Aherne essays the naive Maximilian von Hapsburg, Emperor of Mexico, as a light, airy, perfumed character with a conscience. John Garfield, Claude Rains, Gale Sondergaard, and Joseph Calleia are all excellent in their supporting hues of intensity.

For *Juarez*, photographer Tony Gaudio discarded the normal floodlighting technique in favor of spotlights with dimmers that were located on lamprails above the sets at all times. In this way, individual beams of light could be distinguished and their strength could be varied. One of the most poignant scenes in the film takes place in an opulent room in Louis Napoleon's castle in France. Carlotta has become deranged after learning that the French emperor has disowned Maximilian and the whole Mexican enterprise. She sits in front of a tall window, from which

127

multi-beamed light illuminates a sharp angle in the room and no more. The camera has already drifted in. As Carlotta psychologically realizes her husband's impending execution, she screams, "Max!" The light drenching Carlotta, surrounded by the omnipresent grey oblivion, creates a contrast image which symbolizes the end of royal imperialism.

"A distinguished, memorable, and socially valuable film.... A stirring re-statement of faith in the democratic principle," wrote Frank S. Nugent in the *New York Times* about another thinly veiled prophecy of the fate of Hitler's Germany. Others weren't as impressed. "William Dieterle was unable to bring out their natural talent," lamented Otis Ferguson in the *New Republic*. Nevertheless, *Juarez* won spots on the Ten Best lists of the *New York Times* and *Film Daily*.

Continuing his interest in the European problem, Dieterle next focused his attention on the plight of refugees. He organized the Continental Players, a group composed of those who had fled the Nazis. The Players' director was Professor Leopold Jessner, former head of the state theatre in Germany. Other members included Lionel Royce and Norbert Schiller of Vienna and Erica Hyde of Munich. All profits from the presentations went to European refugees. Yet that organization didn't satisfy the director's feeling of obligation. In 1940 he sent emergency ambulances to the Allies. "I can no longer think of Germany as being the land I once loved," he commented. "I have watched the land of Goethe, Kant, and Beethoven led into horrible barbarism. I have watched German science and German genius methodically exploited for murder and destruction."

After filming a solid version of *The Hunchback of Notre Dame* (UA, 1939), starring Charles Laughton as Quasimodo, Dieterle returned to biography, this time depicting the life of one of his countrymen in *Dr. Ehrlich's Magic Bullet* (1940). Perhaps this was an effort to illustrate a humanistic German during a time when the entire nation of Germany took on the quality of a monster. The life of the man who discovered a treatment for syphilis makes for a drama of integrity, subtlety, and extreme emotional power.

The story was bought in 1939 by Warner Brothers, and its author, Norman Burnside, with help from John Huston and Heinz Herald, fashioned a screenplay which reflected the triumph of a Jew, Dr. Paul Ehrlich, against bureaucratic indifference and anti-Semitism. With *Dr. Ehrlich's Magic Bullet*, Edward G. Robinson made a distinguished entrance into the studio's biography series.

A Dispatch from Reuters, also released in 1940 and featuring Robinson, wasn't as well received as its predecessor. The story of the man who started the first news service in Europe, the film missed the high intensity, crisis-ridden situations of Dieterle's other cinema biographies. Despite the lack, or perhaps because of it, *A Dispatch from Reuters* has a lighter overall mood; Robinson is a bit more flighty in the lead, and he is even allowed to fall in love.

"A decidedly interesting tale," wrote Archer Winstein in the *New York Post*. Thomas M. Pryor of the *Times* disagreed. "A slow paced drama of mixed values," he insisted. *Variety* admitted that *A Dispatch from Reuters* was "provided with careful production and authentic research of the times and customs."

Perhaps *A Dispatch from Reuters*, along with the following statement, was a reaction from William Dieterle regarding the "seriousness" of his production: "One thing that has bothered me about our films probably cannot be blamed on Hollywood at all, but on the whole nation. That is the reluctance to take a stand for fear of that dreaded accusation, 'propaganda!' But until December 7, anyway, the people in this country branded any talk of ideas as stuffy. You could quote neither history nor the Bible without being suspected of an ax to grind. As if we should be ashamed of grinding axes in the first place! What good is a dull one?"

A Dispatch from Reuters was also significant as the last film Dieterle ever shot at Warner Brothers. In 1940 he severed his ten-year association with the studio in order to form William Dieterle Productions. For a time he considered filming a biography of the recently deceased writer Thomas Wolfe, and also *Johnny Belinda*, starring Marlene Dietrich (ultimately directed by Jean Negulesco in 1948, starring Jane Wyman).

Obviously Dieterle was unhappy being a contract director when he left Warner Brothers, but he understood the need for a studio to watch its filmmakers closely. "There was a time when the director was in supreme command of the production of the film. But today the supervisors take over the picture, and when it is released it is very often totally different from what it was like when the director finished it. Frankly, I must confess that the supervisor is the inevitable result of directorial inefficiency. Unable to get ideas, directors in the past very frequently wasted days and days trying to figure out certain problems while large and expensive casts stood by doing nothing. As a result the producers had to curb this extravagance and created a supervisor." To circumvent this, Dieterle became his own supervisor.

For a long time Dieterle had wanted to film versions of legends such as Sleepy Hollow and Rip Van Winkle, but he settled for an adaptation of Stephen Vincent Benet's *The Devil and Daniel Webster*. Released by RKO in 1941, it is considered by many to be Dieterle's greatest film. Many a title was suggested for the film, among them *A Certain Mr. Scratch* and *Soul vs. Heel*, but finally the more commercial *All That*

Charles
Winninger,
James Craig,
and Anne Shirley
in All That Money
Can Buy
(RKO, 1941)

Ruth Gordon
and Edward G.
Robinson in
Dr. Ehrlich's
Magic Bullet
(WB, 1940)

*Lizabeth Scott
and Charlton
Heston in* Dark
City *(Par., 1950)*

*Cornel Wilde and
Debra Paget in*
Omar Khayyam
(Par., 1957)

Money Can Buy was chosen. Starring Walter Huston as "Mr. Scratch" (the Devil) and Edward Arnold as Daniel Webster, the film is seldom seen today, and the television version was cut considerably, but even a scissored copy of the work is worthwhile.

Critics were generally enthusiastic. "One of the season's best pictures," exclaimed the *New York Post*'s Archer Winstein. "He [Dieterle] has succeeded in welding truth both timeless and timely in a picture which does not follow the lines of the old classic any more than it adheres to the happy ending routine of Hollywood." A final close-up of Scratch's devilish countenance proves the point. "A striking and provocative film," added Howard Barnes of the *Herald-Tribune*.

From this point on, William Dieterle's career slowly became less distinguished. The descent was not completed until he made his last American effort, *Omar Khayyam* in 1957, but his films of the 1940s and 1950s were usually very slow melodramas, which sometimes worked efficiently, yet often didn't. Among the director's better productions of the 1940s are *The Searching Wind* (Par., 1946), about the rise of Fascism in Europe, and *The Accused* (Par., 1949), a suspense story of a teacher (Loretta Young) who accidentally kills one of her students. *Love Letters* (Par., 1945) and *Portrait of Jenny* (Selznick-International, 1949) have their admirers, but none of these films can match Dieterle's best at Warner Brothers, or *All That Money Can Buy*.

The 1950s were even worse. *Dark City* (Par., 1950) and *The Turning Point* (Par., 1952) were both solid crime films which benefit from Dieterle's thick unwinding of cynical narratives (like at least half of *Juarez*), but there were many bad films. *Paid in Full, September Affair, Peking Express, Red Mountain, Salome, Elephant Walk*, and *Omar Khayyam* all suffer from a lethargic pace and melodramatic, trite narratives.

In 1955 Dieterle started filming *Joseph and His Brethren*, but he was replaced by Otto Preminger, and the film was never finished. By the late 1950s he had returned to Germany to direct a series of films, some of them European co-productions.

In 1961 William Dieterle was awarded the Goethe Plaque for fifty years of contributions to the theatre. He directed the Bad Hersfeld Summer Festival, and the individualistic veteran was criticized in some quarters for modernizing the productions. Toward the end of his life he moved from Triesen, Liechtenstein, to Lochau-Bregenz, Austria, but he returned to Germany. William Dieterle died on December 9, 1972 at Ottobruner, near Munich, West Germany.

William Dieterle was a vital force in American cinema during the 1930s and 1940s. In a very real way his best films reflected Hollywood's social conscience, striking out against intolerance, injustice, and bigotry, and supporting democratic principles at a time when the soul of America was in dire need of reaffirmation.

The Films of William Dieterle

Der Menschen am Wege *(German, 1923) (and script, actor)*

Das Geheimnis des Abbe X *(German, 1927) (and script, actor)*

Die Heilige und Ihr Narr *(German, 1928) (and actor)*

Geschlecht in Fesseln *(German, 1928) (and actor)*

Fruhlingsrauschen *(German, 1929) (and actor)*

Ich Lebe fur Dich *(German, 1929) (and actor)*

Ludwig der Zweite Konig von Bayern *(German, 1929) (and actor)*

Eine Stunde Glucke *(German, 1930) (and actor)*

Der Tanz Geht Weiter *(German version of* Those Who Dance*) (FN, 1930) (and actor)*

Die Maske Fallt *(German version of* The Way of All Men*) (FN, 1930)*

Kismet *(German version) (FN, 1931)*

The Last Flight *(FN, 1931)*

Her Majesty Love *(FN, 1931)*

Man Wanted *(WB, 1932)*

Jewel Robbery *(WB, 1932)*

The Crash *(FN, 1932)*

Scarlet Dawn *(WB, 1932)*

Six Hours to Live *(Fox, 1932)*

Lawyer Man *(WB, 1932)*

Grand Slam *(WB, 1933)*

Adorable *(Fox, 1933)*

The Devil's in Love *(Fox, 1933)*

From Headquarters *(WB, 1933)*

The Fashion Follies of 1934 *(WB, 1934)*

Fog Over Frisco *(FN, 1934)*

Madame Dubarry *(WB, 1934)*

The Firebird *(WB, 1934)*

The Secret Bride *(WB, 1934)*

Dr. Socrates *(WB, 1935)*

A Midsummer Night's Dream *(WB, 1935) (co-directed by Max Reinhardt)*

The Story of Louis Pasteur *(WB, 1936)*

The White Angel *(WB, 1936)*

Satan Met a Lady *(WB, 1936)*

The Great O'Malley *(WB, 1937)*

Another Dawn *(WB, 1937)*

The Life of Emile Zola *(WB, 1937)*

Blockade *(UA, 1938)*

Juarez *(WB, 1939)*

The Hunchback of Notre Dame *(RKO, 1939)*

Dr. Ehrlich's Magic Bullet *(WB, 1940)*

A Dispatch from Reuters *(WB, 1940)*

All That Money Can Buy *(RKO, 1941) (and producer)*

Syncopation *(RKO, 1942) (and producer)*

Tennessee Johnson *(MGM, 1942)*

Kismet *(MGM, 1944)*

I'll Be Seeing You *(UA, 1944)*

Love Letters *(Par., 1945)*

This Love of Ours *(Univ., 1945)*

The Searching Wind *(Par., 1946)*

Duel in the Sun *(Selznick, 1946) (not credited, along with Josef Von Sternberg, William Cameron Menzies, Sydney Franklin, Otto Brower: directed by King Vidor)*

Portrait of Jenny *(Selznick, 1949)*

The Accused *(Par., 1949)*

Volcano *(UA, 1949) (and producer)*

Rope of Sand *(Par., 1949)*

Paid in Full *(Par., 1950)*

Dark City *(Par., 1950)*

September Affair *(Par., 1951)*

Peking Express *(Par., 1951)*

Boots Malone *(Col., 1952)*

Red Mountain *(Par., 1952)*

The Turning Point, *(Par., 1952)*

Salome *(Col., 1953)*

Elephant Walk *(Par., 1954)*

Magic Fire *(Republic, 1956) (and producer)*

Omar Khayyam *(Par., 1957)*

Herrin der Welt *(European co-production, 1959: two parts)*

Il Vendicator *(European co-production, 1959) (and actor)*

Die Fastnachtsbeichte *(German, 1960)*

The Confession *(Golden Eagle, 1965)*

Peter Godfrey in the mid-forties

Peter Godfrey

During a period when the *film noir* dominated the crime genre, with its psychopathology, realistic backgrounds, and topical stories, Peter Godfrey successfully harkened back to the old-style Gothic drama in *The Woman in White, Cry Wolf,* and *The Two Mrs. Carrolls.* Each of these is complicated by characters every bit as twisted as the antagonists in *White Heat* or *Crossfire,* yet the narratives unfold among the remote rich, living on country estates, and, in one case, in an earlier time. The director's penchant for creating somber moods, where dark and light cut across the screen, the camera moves to florid music, and glazed eyeballs stare, stylishly frames narratives where the movie-goer discovers a perfectly obvious, sinister secret long before the protagonist. If Godfrey had been a cinema director in the 1920s, his films probably wouldn't have been too far below the best German horror movies of the time. In post-war Hollywood, however, his forte was an antique.

Peter Godfrey was born on October 16, 1899 in London, England. Early in life he founded the Gate Theatre on Villiers Street in London, and he served as its director for fifteen years. Later a branch opened in Dublin. Godfrey directed over two hundred and fifty plays during this period—many of O'Neill's greatest works, Shakespeare, John Gielgud in *Ghosts,* and Claude Rains in *From Morn till Midnight,* to name but a few.

In 1937 he guided *Close Quarters* for the Shuberts, and around then he wrote a play about a Negro opera singer in England. That year Peter came to America to stage *Thank You, Mrs. Bryant,* but he managed to delay the project to direct Paul Vincent Carroll's *Shadow of Substance,* a drama of Ireland. Godfrey succeeded Arthur Shields, but he himself left the play on January 5, 1938. Producer Eddie Dowling assumed the direction, but when the show opened on January 25 at the Dohn Golden Theatre, *New York Times* critic Brooks Atkinson sensibly credited Godfrey for much of the drama's quality: "Add to the beauties of his script the glories of a fine performance [by Sir Cedric Hardwicke] under Peter Godfrey's direction."

In 1939 Godfrey arrived in Hollywood to film *The Lone Wolf Spy Hunt* at Columbia. Considered by many to be the best in the series starring Warren William as the dapper sleuth, the modest production received mild reviews at a time when spy stories were being produced at a faster clip than machine gun fire in Europe. "Whatever merits it has are offset by the presence of an equal amount of stuff and nonsense," wrote William Boehnel in the *New York World Tribune*. "Should be right in there with the sort's current spy scare," opined the *New York Times*' B. R. Crisler. *The Lone Wolf Spy Hunt* is distinguished by the colorful performances of Ida Lupino as William's wacky girl friend, young Rita Hayworth as a spy, Ralph Morgan as the chief of the spy ring, and Virginia Wiedler as the leader's precocious daughter.

Two years later Peter switched to RKO for *Unexpected Uncle,* "a lightweight piece of whimsy," according to Richard W. Dana of the *New York Herald-Tribune*. Charles Coburn gives flair to his role of a crotchety old man who helps a girl (Anne Shirley) romance a rich boy (James Craig). Godfrey was set to direct a version of Clarence Buddington Kelland's novel *The Silver Spoon* in 1942, but the proposed star Dorothy Comingore (the unmelodious mistress in *Citizen Kane*) proved most difficult, and the project dissolved. *Highway by Night* (1942) is a modest production which ended the director's association with RKO.

During the war Godfrey plied his talents as an amateur magician at Army camps throughout America, and he staged shows at the Masquers Club in Hollywood. Then he signed a five-year contract with Warner Brothers in 1944, and he immediately directed *Make Your Own Bed*, featuring Jack Carson and Jane Wyman as a couple who masquerade as a butler and a maid to get the goods on gangster Ricardo Cortez.

Hotel Berlin (1945) is one of Godfrey's best films, a solid reworking of *Grand Hotel* transformed into a war drama. Set during the decline of Nazi Germany, a group of fine supporting actors helps to promote the violence-hewn bent of the narrative. Hitler's Third Reich is patched by gum and spit here, with Kurt Kreuger as one of Hollywood's first sympathetic Nazis in his endeavors to unite the shards of a broken existence.

"The direction of Peter Godfrey and the acting hold a shaky script in some sort of outline of violence," analyzed the *Herald-Tribune* critic, who called it "certainly an engrossing chase film." The *Times*' Bosley

Crowther saw the production as a "sleek and suspenseful show." Individualist James Agee of the *Nation* could destroy a film with a flick of the pen. "*Hotel Berlin,* the most heavily routine of Warner Brothers' political melodramas, is stuffed with sympathetic veterans like Peter Lorre and Henry Daniell and George Coulouris and Raymond Massey, and with sympathetic and understandably more eager young people like Andrea King and Faye Emerson and Kurt Kreuger, but the only thing that had even a chance for any pure quality was a bit by Helene Thimig."

Christmas in Connecticut (1945), starring Barbara Stanwyck as a food critic who can't cook but is stuck entertaining a soldier (Dennis Morgan) for dinner, is one of the more charming war comedies. Peter and his leading lady became friends, and he named his eldest daughter after her.

Sydney Greenstreet excels as a magazine magnate, with the scenes between Stanwyck and her boss running around the house attempting to bedazzle the soldier particularly amusing. At one point, Stanwyck has to pretend that she is the mother of an infant. The child is taken home by its real mother, and Greenstreet exclaims, "Do you realize what this baby means to my circulation?" *Variety* called *Christmas in Connecticut* "a laugh-paced farce."

Godfrey continued using war as a subject in an altered version of Philip Barry's play *The Animal Kingdom*, retitled *One More Tomorrow.* The director then started hitting his short-lived stride with *The Two Mrs. Carrolls* in 1947.

Held up for two years, *The Two Mrs. Carrolls* received widely mixed reviews upon release. The *Herald-Tribune*'s Howard Barnes called the tale of a psychopathic artist who paints his wives before murdering them "a violent and sometimes terrifying melodrama. . . . Peter Godfrey has directed the show with a properly mounting pace to a chilling climax." In the *Times*, Bosley Crowther called the production "as wretched a stew of picture-making as has been dished up in many a moon."

The Two Mrs. Carrolls is neither a brilliant chiller nor a contrived mystery, but rather a curious, yet typical Godfrey blend of those alternatives. There is little suspense, to be sure, and even the romance, marriage, and alienation of the couple (Humphrey Bogart and Barbara Stanwyck) fail to evoke sympathy or fear. It is as if the two are wrapped up in their own existence—Bogart with his psychosis, Stanwyck with her bewilderment and suspicion. If the screen had been split in half during their scenes together, with each in a different location, talking as if on a videophone, they couldn't seem more remote from each other and from the audience. Director Godfrey surrounds the distant figures in an aura

Humphrey Bogart and Barbara Stanwyck in The Two Mrs. Carrolls *(WB, 1947)*

of creaking boards, silences, shut doors, haunting paintings, and pulsating music, with Bogart's screen daughter the only vestige of warmth and sanity. The moment where Stanwyck moves through the house alone, on the strength of intermittent lighting and the sound of fear as footsteps cut through the silence, exemplifies Godfrey's ability to suffuse an old-style narrative with flourishes of Gothic terror.

Cry Wolf (1947), also starring Barbara Stanwyck, is likewise free of dependence on a hidden secret known to all but the film's leading lady. Errol Flynn co-stars as a staid doctor whose insane brother (Richard Basehart) marries Stanwyck, then disappears. She finds her husband on the grounds of the family's estate, and brother Flynn is forced to kill Basehart.

As in *The Two Mrs. Carrolls,* most of *Cry Wolf's* best moments come when Barbara Stanwyck searches the rambling house—for a clue to the screams in the night, for a talk with an unbalanced sister (Geraldine Brooks), for a peek inside Flynn's laboratory. The cast is uniformly excellent, despite some criticism of swashbuckling Flynn playing a soft-spoken, yet intense character in the somber film. *Cry Wolf* was termed by *Variety* "a fair melodrama" which "sags considerably before running its course."

Following two poor 1947 features, *Escape Me Never* and *That Hagen Girl,* Peter directed his finest film, an eerie adaptation of Wilkie Collins' classic Gothic novel, *The Woman in White* (1948). Once again set in a doom-drenched house, the nineteenth-century thriller concerns the scheme of Count Fosco (Sydney Greenstreet) to murder twin sisters (Eleanor Parker) and steal their fortune. Lurking at the edges of the frame are Fosco's tormented wife (Agnes Moorehead) and neurotic Frederick Fairlie (John Abbott), along with a pure pair of lovers (Alexis Smith and Gig Young).

When Young journeys to the house on foot at night, he catches a glimpse of a hauntingly beautiful woman, dressed in a white gown which drifts over her body as she spirits through the trees in the moonlight. Godfrey has thereby set the lightly mysterious tone of the film, where good, evil, and mental disorder mingle in a work far more complex than *The Two Mrs. Carrolls* and *Cry Wolf.*

The dinner scene is the subtlest evocation of evil in the director's three suspense films. Quick cuts from Fosco to the others at the table during the Count's verbal abuse of his wife are offset by the man's pet monkey Iago screeching in the background. Neurosis is capsulized in the introduction of Fairlie, cocooned in a world of silence, where the slightest noise is equal to a murderous scream. Disturbed Ann (Parker) sneaks in for a quiet visit with her sister, while the voices of Fosco and his partner in crime are sinisterly edged off-screen. Fosco's dramatic

Sydney Greenstreet and Alexis Smith in The Woman in White *(WB, 1948)*

Barbara Stanwyck, Geraldine Brooks, Errol Flynn, and Paul Davenport in Cry Wolf *(WB, 1947)*

death breaks the spell on the mansion and those who live in it.

"Meticulous production, excellent performances, and smooth direction," summed up *Variety*'s thoughts on *The Woman in White*. "Grotesquely archaic," asserted Howard Barnes in the *Herald-Tribune*. "Stilted speeches and indecisive direction on the part of Peter Godfrey keep the show swinging uneasily, between outright melodrama and a tale of country gentry." In the *Nation* James Agee was succinct: "The Wilkie Collins novel is given the studious, solid treatment ordinarily reserved for the ritual assassination of a Great Classic. This is not intended as a recommendation."

After the sporadically touching *The Decision of Christopher Blake* (1948), Godfrey directed eight more feature films, none of which rises above mediocrity. In 1950 Godfrey signed to direct a Grace Klein play, *Lily Henry*, starring Mae Henry, but withdrew from the production. Between film assignments, Peter kept busy in television, directing shows such as *This Is Our House* for Eddie Bracken Productions.

Peter's wife Renee died in 1966, and on March 4, 1970 the director followed her to the grave after a long illness. He is survived by three daughters—Barbara, Christina, and Jill.

Peter Godfrey was a supporting player in the lexicon of Hollywood directors, but for a time he proved that style could triumph over narrative, and that film technique was and is an art in itself.

The Films of Peter Godfrey

The Lone Wolf Spy Hunt (*Col., 1939*)
Unexpected Uncle (*RKO, 1941*)
Highway by Night (*RKO, 1942*)
Make Your Own Bed (*WB, 1944*)
Christmas in Connecticut (*WB, 1945*)
Hotel Berlin (*WB, 1945*)
One More Tomorrow (*WB, 1946*)
Cry Wolf (*WB, 1947*)
The Two Mrs. Carrolls (*WB, 1947*)
Escape Me Never (*WB, 1947*)
That Hagen Girl (*WB, 1947*)
The Woman in White (*WB, 1948*)

The Decision of Christopher Blake (*WB, 1948*)
The Girl from Jones Beach (*WB, 1949*)
One Last Fling (*WB, 1949*)
Barricade (*WB, 1950*)
The Great Jewel Robbery (*WB, 1950*)
He's a Cockeyed Wonder (*Col., 1950*)
One Big Affair (*UA, 1952*)
One Life (*20th, 1955*)
Please Murder Me (*Distributors Corp. of America, 1956*)

Linda Darnell and Edmund Goulding on the set of Everybody Does It *(20th, 1949)*

Lucille LaVerne and Conrad Nagel in Sun-Up *(MGM, 1925)*

9

Edmund Goulding

"Most of the people who have interested me are those who are in some kind of spot," Edmund Goulding said. "They were either beginning or desperately anxious." He continued, "The complacence of most successful players fails to interest me."

Edmund Goulding was a fine director of both women *and* men, and he had an uncanny sense of the camera's proper distance from an actor. He employed what was termed a "newsreel method" of direction. Unlike many filmmakers, Goulding talked to actors without the barest reference to camera placement, working only with the photographers in that area. Yet his filmic philosophy was ruled by the camera, albeit gently. "The camera must photograph players' thoughts in addition to the actors. The actor will, in fact, be working for the camera, rather than vice versa."

Throughout his thirty years in Hollywood, Goulding radiated a cool, professional, yet concerned presence on the set. The glories of *Grand Hotel, Dark Victory, The Razor's Edge,* and *Nightmare Alley,* to name four, are, at first glance, an erudite, ironic treatment of a pompous human condition in numbers one and two, accompanied by a soulful, prodding exploration of the psychological and social conflicts of the next pair. On second thought, the director's examinations are markedly similar in each case, varying primarily with the touch of different studios. A mainstay of the Goulding filmography is the great female performances, as Andrew Sarris has noted, from Greta Garbo to Bette Davis to Dorothy McGuire to Gene Tierney, down in the cast to Mary Astor, Anne Baxter, and others. They are ably abetted by males like the Barrymores, Tyrone Power, and Edmund Gwenn.

Edmund Goulding was born on March 30, 1891 in London, England. He received early stage training, and was an actor, writer, and director of plays on British stages until World War I. In 1915 he left the armed forces with an honorable discharge, the result of being twice wounded in action in France.

The talented young man immediately enrolled for private vocal study under the tutelage of Oscar Saenger in New York City. Edmund became an early favorite in English grand opera, with a repertoire of all the great baritone roles in standard opera. The critic from the *New York Dramatic Mirror* was at odds with the public on Goulding's performance. While admitting that Edmund projected a solid image with his stocky build fitted into a tweed suit, and that he had a broad accent that he used to its best advantage, the critic noted: "He was exceedingly nervous, his program of songs was badly selected, and the whole offering lacked distinctness." Yet the reviewer spotted something in the performer: "He has a rather likeable way with him, and a voice that sounds promising."

It was said in 1917 that Goulding gave up a three-year contract in *Kitty, Darlin'* (with Alice Nielsen) in London to re-enlist as an Army private, and during this hitch he drove trucks full of high explosives. Soon after the Armistice, multi-talented Edmund turned to novel-writing with *Fury*, a 120,000-word drama of the sea that he penned in five weeks. With Edgar Selwyn he then wrote *Dancing Mothers* (1924) starring Will Hays, and the show ran a year and a half on Broadway. According to *New York Evening Bulletin* critic Joseph R. Fleisler, *Dancing Mothers* was "a smart, modern comedy brilliantly acted, delicately staged, daringly written and with a finish that left the first night audience gasping."

In 1925 Goulding became a writer at MGM, and before the year was out he had scripted, directed, and produced his first film, *Sun Up*. Lucille La Verne and Conrad Nagel star in the melodrama of love and murder, which the *New York Times* called "a strong feature despite the amazing changes that have been wrought in transferring it [Lulu Vollmer's play] to the screen." Apparently the reviewer was distressed by Edmund's sensitive use of light, shadow, and camera placement: "His direction is for the most part smooth, although he loses time striving to obtain the usual bromidic photographic effects, which may be the silhouette of a woman's figure, unimpressive scenes of a mother and her son, or two hands trying to get hold of a door."

That year the director also proved a triple threat on Metro's *Sally, Irene and Mary*. In 1926 he wrote and directed *Paris*, after which he produced, directed, and wrote the story for *Women Love Diamonds*.

Love (MGM, 1928) was Goulding's first feature with Greta Garbo. The film, also starring John Gilbert, is an adaptation of Tolstoy's *Anna Karenina* which the director produced but didn't write (Louis B. Mayer

144

insisted on adding the awkward happy ending). The self-assured Edmund often found himself helping studio technicians with their jobs, even going so far as to model dresses by placing them in front of his body when the need arose. During the filming of *Love*, the 22-year-old Garbo couldn't find the right hairdresser. The director offered to style her hair just that once, but she was so pleased with the results that he found himself performing the chore every morning before the cameras rolled!

Early in 1928 Adolph Zukor sent Edmund to New York City to examine the Fox-Case Sound System. The director summed up his thoughts on the future of the talkie in a July 1928 article in the *National Board of Review Magazine*. He had little use for the first sound efforts: "Actually, they are but silent motion pictures accompanied by synchronized, but wholly mechanical and artificial sounding voices or instrumental music. Their novelty may be called the only element which invites attention to them." Goulding also synopsizes the coming sound filmmaker: "The new director will be more DeMaupassant than Dickens—terse, tense, succinct." Goulding proceeds to describe a number of elements which became staples of the sound film—a more natural, less stage-trained speaking voice and simple methods of skipping around time, as well as far-reaching camera functions and unlimited use of off-screen space.

In 1929 Goulding directed, produced, scripted, and even wrote a song for his first sound film, United Artists' *The Trespasser*. After several more efforts, including 1931s *Reaching for the Moon* (also UA), the director returned to MGM.

Edmund married Marjorie Violet Mose on November 28, 1931. Fading Metro star John Gilbert was his best man.

The director's second film under the new contract was the star-studded *Grand Hotel* (1932). The 105-minute extravaganza features Greta Garbo (ballerina), John Barrymore (jewel thief), Joan Crawford (stenographer), Lionel Barrymore (dying bourgeois), and Wallace Beery (tough businessman). The all-star cast excels in the drama of wit and manners at a luxury hotel where "nothing ever happens." Goulding observes the formal relationships between the classes in the film, yet manages to believably intermingle counts and clerks, royalty and robust commoners. The budding friendship between the doomed little man and the aging jewel thief beautifully illustrates novelist Vicki Baum's concept of leveling the social strata. Many things did indeed occur, even in the hallways of the grand hotel.

"It is a production thoroughly worthy of all the talk it has created," exclaimed Mordaunt Hall in his *New York Times* critique. "Edmund Goulding has done an excellent piece of work, but occasionally it seems as though he relies too much on close-ups."

145

Grand Hotel won an Oscar as the best picture of 1932, but Goulding didn't even get a nomination for his direction.

After a pair of fair Metro productions, Edmund signed a one-year contract with Warner Brothers. Until the director left the studio after *The Constant Nymph* in 1943, he escaped the harnessing seven-year deals which tied down most of his fellow contractees. Perhaps the combination of a good agent and an extremely gracious personality explains how Goulding operated at Warner Brothers with relative freedom. Producer Henry Blanke fondly reminisced about the director for author James R. Silke (in *Here's Looking at You, Kid):* "He was the most sensitive to the feelings of the performers; he could feel everything. He could tell how they were feeling before they got on the set."

Goulding's first Warner Brothers film was a remake of the early talkie *The Transgressor,* retitled *That Certain Woman* (1937). Bette Davis stars in Gloria Swanson's role of a gangster's widow who wants to break with the underworld. *Variety* called Goulding's Warner Brothers debut a "finely made picture which shoves Bette Davis a round or two higher as boxoffice lure."

Goulding was pleased with the studio's excellent production crew, and he commented favorably on the ability of cameraman Ernest Haller to make vital contributions to the camera set-ups of *That Certain Woman:* "A fine camera artist such as Haller does not resent this shifting of the usual order of things. On the contrary, he regards it as a challenge to his ingenuity, and he appreciates breaking away to a degree from the formal stiffness of the old conventions" (i.e., the director as God).

As Richard Kosarski notes in *Hollywood Directors: 1914-1940* (Oxford), "Goulding had an aversion to seeing his characters walk out of the edge of the frame, and whenever possible he had the cameras follow them until they literally disappeared from 'sight' through a doorway or behind an obstruction. While his camera crews often found this an absurdly theatrical form of staging, in reality it opened up vast areas of off-screen space and gave his pictures an extremely solid and naturalistic geography." When the director has Bette Davis exit through the door of Henry Fonda's office on camera (in *That Certain Woman),* it lends support to her vows to reform. The lens sweeps past Fonda and follows the determined Davis out of sight, as if in punctuation.

The Dawn Patrol (1938) is a fine reworking of Howard Hawks' 1930 film of the same name. Goulding lightened the hard relationship formerly shared by Richard Barthelmess, Douglas Fairbanks, Jr., and Neil Hamilton simply by casting Errol Flynn, David Niven, and Basil Rathbone in their places. Each of the trio was perfectly capable of parrying and thrusting witty verbiage in a comic script, and this inherent ability softens the doom-laden film. Edmund even made a personal request that the 28-year-old Niven be in the picture, a move remembered by the dapper, yet down-to-earth star.

The slightly old-fashioned anti-war production (though neither as melodramatic nor as ironic as its predecessor) nevertheless remains a fairly tense story of the World War I aviation officers who send young fliers to their deaths. Frank S. Nugent of the *New York Times* felt that the effort was "a thrilling, exciting, and heroic film—even though it is obviously crammed with shameless hokum, is erratically performed and is pretending (never successfully) to be a denunciation of the stupidity of war."

After another studio spent $50,000 for the rights to *Dark Victory*, a play by George Brewer, Jr. and Bertram Block, Warner Brothers acquired the property. Jack Warner made sure that the sensitive story was in the right hands, assigning Goulding and producer David Lewis to the film's staff. Both men had been significant forces in MGM's "women's" pictures of the early and mid-1930s.

Bette Davis gives a *tour de force* performance as spoiled heiress Judith Traherne. Suffering from headaches and dizziness, the rich country girl drives her station wagon to the office of Dr. Frederick Steele (George Brent), who diagnoses her brain tumor and advises immediate surgery to delay her terminal fate, which he conceals. After numerous boisterous exchanges, the two marry, and they move to a quaint New England residence where the doctor carries on medical research. While Steele is out of town, Judith begins to lose her sight. She realizes the truth, but hides the fact from her husband. Judith orders her friend Ann (Geraldine Fitzgerald) to leave, then drifts to the bedroom to die in peace.

Director Goulding had an unshakable conception of the film's narrative. "We kept love and death carefully separated in our story," he said at the time. A constantly shifting tone is certainly part of *Dark Victory*'s greatness. Casey Robinson's script is full of bitchy arguments, but Edmund alters moods quickly, from simple set pieces to comic, then bitter moments. All levels climax at the end and fade away when Judith is about to die. At that moment, she has come to terms with herself, and there is nothing left but the waiting.

One of the most effective moments in *Dark Victory* occurs in the garden. Judith is planting hyacinth bulbs with Ann. The sun slips behind a cloud, but Judith senses the warmth on her hand, and she panics.

Adding to the quality of the performances in the film must have been the respect that the stars felt for their director. One morning Edmund sensed that Bette Davis was going to have a bad day, and he only let her work for two hours. George Brent was appreciative of the Britisher's

Morton Lowater and Errol Flynn in The Dawn Patrol *(WB, 1938)*

Ferdinand Gottschalk and Greta Garbo in Grand Hotel *(MGM, 1932)*

Bette Davis and
Humphrey
Bogart in Dark
Victory (WB,
1939)

Herbert Marshall,
John Payne, Gene
Herbert Marshall,
John Payne,
Gene Tierney,
and Tyrone
Power in The
Razor's Edge
(20th, 1946)

intuition. "Ah, Goulding," Brent said with kindness. "I enjoyed working with him the most; an extremely sensitive man."

Dark Victory was nominated for an Academy Award as best picture, and Bette Davis' name adorned the ballot for top actress. The moving melodrama won spots on the Ten Best lists of the *New York Times* and *Film Daily*. Frank S. Nugent of the *Times* called Davis' acting "superb," and he commended the film as "one of the sensitive and haunting pictures of the season," adding, "Edmund Goulding's direction has fused it into a deeply moving unity." In the *New York Herald-Tribune*, Howard Barnes asserted: "*Dark Victory* on screen is all that it failed to be as a play . . . a haunting screen tragedy." *Dark Victory* was made into a three-hour telefilm in 1976, starring Elizabeth Montgomery and Anthony Hopkins (without benefit of Edmund's fine song).

Goulding followed *Dark Victory* with a solid series of "women's films," including *The Old Maid* (1939), *'Til We Meet Again* (1940—remake of Tay Garnett's 1932 *One Way Passage*), and *The Great Lie* (1941). In these works the director skillfully fuses melodramatic plots with a number of cynical supporting characters and comic players who add sparkle to humorous moments and thereby give the stories multi-level interest. Mary Astor was nominated for best supporting actress by the Academy for *The Great Lie*.

About this time the director was asked to define the essence of a great female screen personality. Clearly Edmund had become an expert at drawing fine work out of Bette Davis, Mary Astor, and Geraldine Fitzgerald at Warner Brothers. "It's something that theatre and picture people don't quite understand, but they have discovered it's a fact that the girl who oozes charm and personality in her daily life isn't apt to have much on the screen or in front of the camera." The statement seems particularly pertinent in Bette Davis' case. The star was not highly regarded early in her career because several studio bosses didn't think much of her face or personality. Conversely, consider the career of bubbling Fanny Brice, who never succeeded in Hollywood.

In 1939 Goulding suggested the formation of a Bureau of Propaganda in the U.S., similar to the one that had operated in England during World War I. "I hope we can get a leading newspaper publisher, a radio chieftain, a magazine owner, a ranking churchman, a movie producer, and a book publisher all to sit on the same committee," he stated, "talk over national problems and give their opinions to the public."

The public waited two years after *The Great Lie* for another Edmund Goulding film. *The Constant Nymph*, starring Charles Boyer (first given to Errol Flynn) and Joan Fontaine, was his next to last job at Warner Brothers. Boyer sympathetically etches the role of a composer who weds a socialite (Alexis Smith) but really loves a girl (Fontaine) who inspires him. On the set the director was helpful as usual with many details of character and costume. One actor balked at Edmund's step-by-step interpretation of a scene. "I'm not trying to show you how to do it," he assured the performer with the bruised ego. "I merely want to get over the point I'm driving at." Joan Fontaine testified that Goulding did just that. "You can get more from watching Eddie play a scene than you can from an hour discussing it."

"A bumpy screen tale with interplay of both draggy and interesting sequences," opined *Variety*. Conversely, the *New York Times* said: "Director Edmund Goulding deserves mention for telling a long story (about two hours) with a pace that rarely weakens." Joan Fontaine was nominated for an Oscar for her performance in *The Constant Nymph*.

In 1945 Edmund put $70,000 into a play he wrote and directed called *That Ryan Girl* (featuring Una O'Connor and Edmund Lowe). He lost the money. According to Wilella Waldorf of the *New York Post*, Goulding was "under the impression that while the films have been forging ahead all these years, the legitimate theatre has turned backward and is now rapidly approaching the turn of the century."

Two years earlier the director had signed with 20th Century-Fox, and soon afterward he remarked on the operation of the studio and its chief: "There are three dimensions, the creative, the interpretative, and the critical. The writer creates the script, the director interprets it line for line, and the producer criticizes. Zanuck doesn't ever want the writer to meet the director, except through the script."

Goulding's tour at Fox proved almost as rewarding as his seven years at Warner Brothers. *Claudia* (1943), *The Razor's Edge* (1946), *Nightmare Alley* (1947), *Mister 880* (1950), and *Teenage Rebel* (1956) are the best films of his final period.

Before switching to the above productions which balanced men and women better than those at Warner Brothers, where a Bette Davis or Mary Astor always outshone poor George Brent, Edmund did a tongue-in-cheek analysis of sex in the cinema: "The secret of sex in films and in life is the light or pianissimo touch on the keyboard of excitement." On women in sweaters: "In males it is like starting a motor with the accelerator pressed down to the floor. The impulse, intended to be powerful, makes a quick surge forward, chokes, and comes to a stop. Aside from the first momentary reactions the effort is opposite from the hoped for."

Claudia is a very clean, cute comedy starring Robert Young and Dorothy McGuire as newlyweds who face the comic but trying problems of married life with a sensible outlook. Goulding was particularly fond of his female star, calling Dorothy McGuire "the most talented actress I ever worked with." Considering that Bette Davis, Mary Astor, Geraldine Fitzgerald, and Miriam Hopkins all worked under Edmund during his Warner Brothers period, that's quite a statement.

After a brief return to Warner Brothers for an unsuccessful remake of *Of Human Bondage* in 1946, Goulding directed *The Razor's Edge,* a fine film starring Tyrone Power, Gene Tierney, Anne Baxter, John Payne, Herbert Marshall, Elsa Lanchester, and brilliant Clifton Webb as American blueblood Elliott Templeton. With superb ensemble acting, this adaptation of Somerset Maugham's mystic novel of the lost generation of the 1920s is full of zest and rarely bogs down in its philosophizing. *The Razor's Edge* is a heady brew of the passion, spirituality, and history of a set of Chicagoans who literally travel the four corners of the earth in search of self and money. Set against the backdrop of Alfred Newman's heavily melodic score, the film is at its most haunting in the sections where Power communes in India, and later when Power, Tierney, Payne, and Baxter rediscover each other in Paris. The seediness of Pigalle bistros is evidenced in full force in the scene where Baxter is reintroduced as a prostitute (her husband and baby died in a car crash years earlier). She slithers down crude steps, descending into a mass of arms, legs, torsos, cigarette smoke, dirty tables, and violence. After a drink, her pimp beckons, and Baxter returns to the deepest implications of the lower depths, disappearing into the crowd (but not out of the frame), tragically a part of it. Conversely, Power has "found himself" in India, discovering something in Fox's lush, painted backgrounds (which would have been even more unreal in color), and in the eyes of an ancient soothsayer.

The Razor's Edge received a wide range of response upon release. Howard Barnes of the *Herald-Tribune* claimed that the Fox film "has a dramatic depth which is rarely explored in Hollywood." However, the *Times'* Bosley Crowther disagreed: "It has aimed for a lofty exhibition of goodness within the soul of man and has shown little more than surface piety."

For her work in *The Razor's Edge,* Anne Baxter won an Academy Award as best supporting actress of 1946.

Nightmare Alley is considered by many to contain Tyrone Power's greatest performance. Featuring Joan Blondell, Coleen Grey, and Helen Walker, the film concerns an ambitious carnival worker (Power) who entangles a mindreader (Blondell) in a number of fraudulent schemes, including the blackmailing of a psychiatrist (Walker). This is undoubtedly Edmund Goulding's most bizarre film, but the director handles the twists as well as the performances of the women and Power with extreme finesse. As in many post-war crime films, *Nightmare Alley's* characters appear to vie for the role of villain, with Power succeeding one minute and Walker the next. A rather ironic refrain is the reference to the unseen geek in the carnival, the lowest spot in the circus hierarchy, and a spot that Power fills before his redemption.

In regard to *Nightmare Alley*, the *Nation's* James Agee wrote: "Two or three sharply comic and cynical scenes make it worth seeing."

Thereafter the director's films are less forceful, and certainly less full of spirituality, evil, and reformation. *Mister 880* is a case in point, dealing with an old man (Edmund Gwenn) who counterfeits a limited amount of money in order to pay his bills. Burt Lancaster is the treasury agent who has to track him down. The pleasant comedy-drama features Dorothy McGuire as a United Nations secretary, and her genuine charm offsets Lancaster's stolidity, while Gwenn steals the show from both of them. *We're Not Married* (1952) is a segmented comedy about a series of couples who discover they're exactly what the title says. The episodic quality tends to hurt the overall impact of the film, but, in this case, froth is froth, and nothing could have helped it be more than average.

Goulding's last notable film was *Teenage Rebel*, released in 1956. Ginger Rogers stars as a remarried mother who has to cope with a daughter spoiled (but not loved) by her ex-husband. The poorly titled film is a sensitive entry into the series of productions turned out in the 1950s which probe the relations of the generations. According to Bosley Crowther of the *Times, Teenage Rebel* is "another of 20th Century-Fox's unpretentious offerings in Cinemascope black and white." He added, "Mr. Goulding has paced the progression of ... movement ... with subtle skill."

Edmund Goulding died on Christmas Eve, 1959. His best qualities as a filmmaker were an insight into the potential of cinema, commercial applications, and, perhaps most important, the ability to make an actress feel so at ease that she lights up the screen with her reality.

The Films of Edmund Goulding

Sun Up *(MGM, 1925) (and producer, script)*

Sally, Irene and Mary *(MGM, 1925) (and producer, script)*

Paris *(MGM, 1926) (and script)*

Women Love Diamonds *(MGM, 1927) (and producer, story)*

Love *(MGM, 1928) (and producer)*

The Trespasser *(UA, 1929) (and producer, script, song)*

The Devil's Holiday *(Par., 1930) (and story, script, music)*

Paramount on Parade *(Par., 1930) (co-directed by Dorothy Arzner, Otto Brower, Victor Heerman, Edwin Knopf, Rowland V. Lee, Ernst Lubitsch, Lothar Mendes, Victor Schertzinger, A. Edward Sutherland)*

Reaching for the Moon *(UA, 1931) (and co-script)*

The Night Angel *(Par., 1931) (and script)*

Blondie of the Follies *(MGM, 1932)*

Grand Hotel *(MGM, 1932)*

Riptide *(MGM, 1934) (and script)*

The Flame Within *(MGM, 1935) (and script)*

That Certain Woman *(WB, 1937) (and script)*

The Dawn Patrol *(WB, 1938)*

White Banners *(WB, 1938)*

Dark Victory *(WB, 1939)*

The Old Maid *(WB, 1939)*

We Are Not Alone *(WB, 1939)*

'Til We Meet Again *(WB, 1940)*

The Great Lie *(WB, 1941)*

The Constant Nymph *(WB, 1943)*

Claudia *(20th, 1943)*

Forever and a Day *(RKO, 1943) (co-directed by Rene Clair, Cedric Hardwicke, Frank Lloyd, Victor Saville, Robert Stevenson, Herbert Wilcox) (and co-producer)*

Of Human Bondage *(WB, 1946)*

The Razor's Edge *(20th, 1946)*

Nightmare Alley *(20th, 1947)*

Everybody Does It *(20th, 1949)*

Mister 880 *(20th, 1950)*

We're Not Married *(20th, 1952)*

Down Among the Sheltering Palms *(20th, 1952)*

Teenage Rebel *(20th, 1956)*

Mardi Gras *(20th, 1958)*

Myrna Loy, Victor McGlaglen, and Robert Armstrong in A Girl in Every Port *(Fox, 1928)*

Tully Marshall, Gary Cooper, Barbara Stanwyck, and Howard Hawks on the set of Ball of Fire *(RKO, 1941)*

10

Howard Hawks

"Don't correct scenes which, in their very trip-ups, become more ingratiating and realistic—especially in comedy." This may be the key to Howard Hawks' success as an "eye-level" director: one who views film as a simple, direct art at its zenith when uncomplicated. He is definitely a man of film, not of letters or of the theatre. "Perhaps it is because I have had absolutely no stage training ... that I don't believe a vehicle should emerge letter-perfect as it is written."

Hawks' flexible attitude toward his projects has resulted in *Scarface, Twentieth Century, Bringing Up Baby, The Big Sleep, Red River, Rio Bravo,* and *El Dorado*—crime, comedy, and Western classics which are even more admired today than they were at the time of their respective releases. Howard Hawks was one of the first Hollywood-genre directors to be honored by French critics, as well as by that American bastion of auteurism, Andrew Sarris. In a way, Hawks' films have facilitated an appreciation of many of the men and women behind Hollywood cameras.

Howard Hawks was born to Helen and Frank Hawks on May 30, 1896 in Goshen, Indiana. A wealthy paper manufacturer, Hawks, Sr. fathered three boys who made a mark in the cinema. Besides Howard, younger brother Kenneth Hawks was a promising filmmaker until he died directing an air scene, and William became a successful producer.

In 1906 the Hawks family moved to California, where Howard attended elementary and high school in Pasadena. He later attended Phillips Exeter Academy and graduated from Cornell University with a degree in mechanical engineering. Before becoming an assistant prop man at Paramount in 1917, Howard was a crackerjack professional racing car driver, and in 1918 he won the U.S. Junior Tennis Championship. He served in the Army Air Corps in World War I, fought in France, and left the service in 1919 as a second lieutenant.

After the Armistice, Howard continued driving cars and started building airplanes. While in the property department at Paramount, the 21-year-old Hawks received an uncredited taste of directing *The Little Princess* (helmed by Marshall Neilan) starring Mary Pickford. In 1922 he was able to independently produce and direct short comedies, using money from an inheritance to finance the productions. Howard learned the value of a Hollywood dollar early. He put $3,000 into each production, which he in turn sold for twice the amount. Soon Howard was spending $20,000 and $30,000 per film, leading to $200,000 productions for Jesse Lasky and the Famous Players. He became a story supervisor, as well as title writer, finally emerging as one of the two chiefs of the production office. During these years Howard financed more than forty projects by Marshall Neilan, Allan Dwan, Allen Holumbar, and others. Then, seeing an opportunity to direct at MGM, Howard became the studio's story editor, but when nothing developed, he quit, and through the efforts of Sol Wurtzel, Fox's production head, he ultimately signed with Fox.

Wurtzel knew of Hawks' work for Lasky, and he developed a contract for the budding producer-writer-director which enabled Howard to direct seven films at Fox between 1926 and 1929. The first was *The Road to Glory*, which stars May McAvoy, Rockliffe Fellows, Leslie Fenton, and Ford Sterling. Resembling Hawks' 1936 film in name only, the silent story concerns a girl who renounces God and exists in seclusion after her father is killed and she is blinded in a car accident. The film is apparently workmanlike, but Wurtzel wanted much more from Hawks.

"Make something entertaining," the production head told his young director, and Hawks has been following that simple advice ever since. The secrets of Hawks' longevity in film are his economic know-how and a pulse on what the average moviegoer will enjoy. "Get the scene the hell over with as soon as possible," said the director. He does, and everyone from money-man to scholar to popcorn-mouthed child likes it.

In reaction to Wurtzel's directions, Howard wrote a story with a locale in the Garden of Eden. It was released as *Fig Leaves* in 1926. "It made back its money in the first theatre it played," recalled Howard.

According to Hawks, *Paid to Love* "was the beginning of a relationship I have used in a number of pictures. It's really a love story between two men." Some critics disagree, citing 1928's *A Girl in Every Port* to be Hawks' initial masculine romance, but there is apparently enough camaraderie in *Paid to Love* between an American banker and a crown prince to satisfy the director.

On the other hand, he didn't want to make *Fazil* (1928). "I'm not very fond of that picture. . . . It was a contractual thing, someone else's story, and I just shot it."

A Girl in Every Port was his own story about two sailors who independently play the game of *cherchez la femme*. Robert Armstrong as Bill seems to be a step ahead of his future buddy Spike, played by Victor McLaglen. Bill always leaves something of himself to his girl in every port, and Spike uses the little token, a locket with an anchor design, to trace the gob who blazes the trail of broken hearts. Later they will meet, fight, and then unite to defend themselves against the local police.

The charge of male chauvinism can probably be leveled more accurately against Hawks (as Pauline Kael did a few years back) than against any other Hollywood director. Yet Hawks' men of action are rarely misogynistic in the true sense of the word. More often they simply reflect the true intimacy shared by those who spend time together in restricted or isolated areas (headquarters in *The Dawn Patrol* and *Only Angels Have Wings*, the newsroom in *His Girl Friday*, etc.).

A Girl in Every Port is both misogynistic and close to a tender tale of two buddies. The "woman-hating" aspect of the film is embarrassing today, even though the female subject (Louise Brooks) of the contempt is demonstrably "no good."

Back in 1928, the only things that Spike and Bill were interested in were doing their job and having a good time, not necessarily in that order. Although Hawks makes little use of the professional lives of his characters (a trait in his sound films), he details the business of enjoyment while on shore leave. If a sailor wants girls and booze, he must be willing to pay for them in more ways than one. Spike and Bill must constantly contend with the police and other sailors who take a chauvinistic attitude toward their ships—their real sweethearts. The only time a symptom of Hawks' later affinity for illustrating professionals at work appears is during a scene where the boys are after the girls. Spike and Bill mistakenly come to an apartment occupied by a widow and her young son. When the mother is in another room, the son points to a picture of his father, a sailor who was "drownded" in the ocean. Even though the dead man was a stranger to them, they hide some money in the apartment and silently pay their respects to a lost comrade.

The Air Circus (1928) was Hawks' first aerial film. Co-directed by Lewis Seiler (who guided the production's occasional dialogue scenes), the film concerns two young men at flight school who learn what flying is all about through the efforts of a gorgeous aviatrix. "Very little story to it," said Hawks. "I directed it alone and then they wanted to incorporate some talking sequences and they brought a man out who they said was an authority on dialogue and he turned out to be a bur-lesque comedian.... And they generally botched up the picture."

However, the critics didn't agree. The *New York Times* called *The Air Circus* "a jolly, wholesome, and refreshingly human picture." They further stated that the two directors "have cooperated so well that the minute the picture starts with the two would-be fliers it captures the attention."

The director's first all-sound film was another sky story, *The Dawn Patrol* (1930), starring Richard Barthelmess, Douglas Fairbanks, Jr., and Neil Hamilton. All three at one time or another serve as commander of an ill-equipped, undermanned flight squadron. Hamilton is the first chief. He has quarreled off-screen with Barthelmess about a woman, and thus their relationship is strained. When Hamilton is promoted, Barthelmess takes over and is forced to send Fairbanks' younger brother on a fatal mission. Overwhelmed with guilt, Barthelmess takes Fairbanks' position on a flight and is himself killed. Fairbanks is thus left to assume the burden of leadership.

"The film maintains through a length that is somewhat great all its air of excitement that has suggested a melodrama," wrote the *New York Times* critic. More recently, Andrew Sarris declared,* "Hawks' treat-ment of the material is distinguished by his customary virtues: bare, clean, uncluttered technique, a stark story line entirely within the range of terse dialogue which states the situation and then withdraws when the moral conflict becomes implicit in its action, and, most important, a pervasive atmosphere of hopelessness captured with economy and incisiveness."

The Criminal Code (Col., 1931), set in prison, is most notable for some extremely black humor, another Hawks trademark. *The Crowd Roars* (WB, 1932), filmed from the director's original story, is a zesty if unspectacular film about racing.

Scarface: Shame of a Nation (UA, 1932), co-produced and directed by Hawks, is perhaps the oddest of the three major gangster films (the others are *Little Caesar* and *Public Enemy*) which emerged in the early 1930s. Howard told scriptwriter Ben Hecht, "I would like to do the Capone story as if they were the Borgias set down in Chicago." Hecht enthused over the unique concept and the script was finished in eleven days. "We made the brother-sister relationship clearly incestu-ous," the director commented. "But the censors misunderstood our intentions and objected to it because they thought the relationship be-tween them was too beautiful to be attributed to a gangster."

Films and Filming, July-August, 1962.

Several symbols in *Scarface* suggest the dictatorial urges of gangster Tony Camonte (Paul Muni) and the doom which awaits him and his intimate circle. A neon sign for Cook's Tours outside Camonte's luxurious penthouse flashes "The World Is Yours," and Hawks shows it at several vital intervals. Each time a man is killed in *Scarface*, an "x" appears somewhere in the shot. The marks are ingeniously incorporated, surfacing in an overhead fan, a shadow on the wall, even a "strike" mark in a bowling score. This last element may be the final illustration of Hawks' unhappy flirtation with Expressionism courtesy of Murnau's influence on Fox in the 1920s.

Sadly, Hawks' tough, perverted gangster yarn is rarely seen today, due to the entanglements of the estate of its producer, Howard Hughes. The film was shot in 1930, but it was held up for two years because of the millionaire. Therefore, few have recently caught a glimpse of Paul Muni's most sinister screen character, or George Raft's first really important role as Camonte's coin-tossing henchman. It was not to be the last conflict between the director and the iconoclastic producer.

"It is a stirring picture, efficiently directed and capably acted," insisted Mordaunt Hall of the *Times*. Andrew Sarris was more blatant in his praise: "*Scarface* is Hawks' greatest film, the bloodiest and most brutal of the early gangster films which embellished the American cinema of the early thirties."

In 1933 First National publicists announced that Hawks would direct Richard Barthelmess in *Shanghai Orchid,* to follow up the success of *Tiger Shark* the previous year, but the film was never made. Instead Howard spent part of two unhappy years at MGM, in which he directed only one film, *Today We Live* (1933). He also worked unbilled on *The Prizefighter and the Lady* (credited to W. S. Van Dyke) and *Viva Villa* (finished by Jack Conway). Howard indicated his displeasure during work on *Viva Villa* by shoving Louis B. Mayer and shouting that he would never direct at Metro again—and he never did.

Fortunately Hawks moved on to Columbia in 1934 to produce and direct one of the great comedies of the 1930s, *Twentieth Century*, starring John Barrymore and Carole Lombard. The film boosted Lombard to stardom, and was reportedly production in which she started to relax and become herself. On the first day of shooting, the 25-year-old actress was stiff and unnatural. Many had been known to wilt at the thought of working with the Great Profile. Either Hawks or Barrymore kicked Carole in the shins, and from that point on she engaged the matinee idol in a duel of wits, outbursts, and frenzied movements. It's a toss-up as to who is the greater ham in the film.

Howard Barnes of the *New York Herald-Tribune* lauded *Twentieth*

*Osgood Perkins
and Paul Muni
in* Scarface
(RKO, 1932)

*Carole Lombard
and John
Barrymore in a
publicity pose
for* Twentieth
Century
(Col., 1934)

Cary Grant,
Katharine
Hepburn, and
"Baby" in
Bringing Up
Baby (RKO,
1938)

Pat O'Brien,
James Cagney,
and June Travis
in Ceiling Zero
(First National,
1935)

Century as "an extremely funny comedy," while Hall of the *Times* exclaimed, "There is many a witty remark in this harum-scarum adventure."

Hawks doesn't think much of *Barbary Coast* (UA, 1935), a melodramatic fog-bound production starring Miriam Hopkins, Edward G. Robinson, and Joel McCrea, commenting: "As Ben Hecht said, 'Miss Hopkins came to the Barbary Coast and wandered around like a confused Goldwyn girl.'"

The director was back to aerial films again with the exceptional *Ceiling Zero* (WB, 1935). Based on Frank Wead's book (Wead himself was the subject of John Ford's biographical picture *Wings of Eagles* in 1957), the drama resembles *The Dawn Patrol*. The hazards of mail piloting are explored, as exemplified by a brash flier's (James Cagney) decision to undertake a dangerous mission after another has been killed while flying in his place. Hawks pulls a customary fast shuffle of comedy and drama on more than one occasion in this critical favorite. At one point, married Stu Erwin is something of a buffoon, but a moment later he assumes a heroic stance, while June Travis offers herself to Cagney to help him forget feelings of guilt about the dead pilot in a hard, non-melodramatic way.

Along with *Sergeant York, Ceiling Zero* received the finest reviews of any Hawks film. Otis Ferguson of the *New Republic* called it "the best of the airplane pictures," while the *London Daily Observer* labeled the production "undoubtedly one of the finest films ever to come out of Hollywood." "Grim and gripping," announced the *New York American*.

That same year Hawks left another major production. United Artist's *Come and Get It*, based on Edna Ferber's sprawling novel, was finished by William Wyler, and credited to both directors. Producer Sam Goldwyn insisted on using Ferber's original ending, the one he paid $100,000 to film, plus a $30,000 consultant fee to the author. Hawks wanted the novel altered, but he was overruled. However, he was able to console himself with such distractions as his 65-foot racing sloop "The Sea Hawk," his stable of thoroughbreds (like Raoul Walsh, Hawks is a horse lover), and his racing cars and motorcyles. Howard helped design the car which won the Indianapolis 500 in 1936.

Back behind the cameras, Hawks considered filming Goldwyn's *The Hurricane*, but the previous tension that had existed when he was at MGM may have eased him off the project, which was finally handled by his friend John Ford.

Two years later the next Howard Hawks film was released—the wacky *Bringing Up Baby* (RKO) which has since come to be regarded as a classic screwball farce. Katharine Hepburn makes a brilliant cinema comedy debut as a daffy heiress who plagues, pesters, and ultimately loves a bespectacled archaeology professor, brilliantly essayed by Cary Grant. The extended dinner scene where the pair look for Hepburn's dog, who has stolen one of the professor's brontosaurus bones, has to be seen to be believed. Featured here is a baby leopard who responds to the song "I Can't Give You Anything But Love." The romantic duo traipse through the Connecticut woods singing for the leopard and whistling for the dog, with Grant wearing Hepburn's bathrobe!

Some critics appreciated Hawks' admittedly bizarre and madcap sense of humor, but others remained dumbfounded. *Bringing Up Baby* "is funny from the word go," insisted Otis Ferguson in the *New Republic*. "A zany-ridden product of the goofy farce school," wrote *New York Times* critic Frank S. Nugent. *Time* magazine put the film "second only to last year's whimsical high spot, *The Awful Truth*." However, Howard Barnes of the *Herald-Tribune* found the comedy "an aggressively antic film farce" which is "mildly entertaining, but it tries so hard and so unsuccessfully to be hilarious that it deserves a lower rating in the overworked field of daffy farce."

The film *Plane No. 4* became *Only Angels Have Wings* (Col., 1939), Hawks' fourth aviation story and one of his fans' favorites. Cary Grant gives one of his most cynical performances as Geoff Carter, chief of a crew of mail pilots in Ecuador. Again the director picks up the narrative thread from *The Dawn Patrol*, stitched very closely to the pattern of *Ceiling Zero*, while Jean Arthur became the first of the tart, steamy, smart-mouthed women who appear often in Hawks' later films. Arthur's bitter arguments with Grant are also repeated in *To Have and Have Not*, *Red River*, and *Rio Bravo*. As in Howard's previous two aviation films, a repentant man, in this case Richard Barthelmess, causes the death of another and must himself die in the air.

Columbia announced that Hawks would produce and direct *The Cop from Hell's Kitchen* with Bruce Cabot, Jacqueline Wells, and Harry Carey, but the director instead adapted Hecht's and MacArthur's *The Front Page* for the studio in 1940. Howard called Ben Hecht and asked the author if he'd mind if the male reporter in the play and film, Hildy Parks, was changed to a female named Hildy Johnson. Hecht was delighted with Hawks' innovative approach to familiar material, and Columbia sought Jean Arthur for the role, since she had co-starred as a newspaperwoman in two great Frank Capra comedies of the era, *Mr. Deeds Goes to Town* and *Mr. Smith Goes to Washington*. Cary Grant then signed on for the part of editor Walter Burns, while Jean Arthur was dropped in favor of Irene Dunne, who was then replaced by Rosalind Russell.

The dizzying pace of *His Girl Friday* (1940) topped even *Bringing Up*

Baby. When Hawks was criticized for the persistent use of overlapping dialogue, he cracked, "Listen in on a cocktail party sometime." And that is exactly what the film is full of—bubbly, bitter, fast, and surface party conversation. Dizzier than Lewis Milestone's version of *The Front Page*, but not as technically dazzling, *His Girl Friday* treats the subject of impending execution as the funniest of funny ideas.

"Rosalind Russell and Cary Grant give such entertaining performances that nobody in the roaring audience seems to notice the tastelessness, to say the least, of playing hide-and-seek with a man condemned to death," the *Nation* critic acerbically commented. "Before it's over, you don't know whether you have been laughing or having your ears boxed," carped Frank S. Nugent in the *Times*. *His Girl Friday* "is not by any means as good as its photoplay prototype *The Front Page*, but it has stuck close enough to it still to be an engaging entertainment," was the comment of Howard Barnes of the *Herald-Tribune*.

In any case, instead of a salary, Hawks took fifteen percent of the box-office draw of *His Girl Friday*, and after nine weeks he had made $140,000. While working on *The Outlaw* for Howard Hughes, the director was reportedly pulling in $3,500 a week. "I made the introduction of Billy the Kid and Doc Holliday on location," Hawks recalled, "and then Hughes messed up the rest." One of the problems that the director and the producer had was the eternal one of money, but this time the classic positions were reversed. Hughes wanted to spend $1,500,000 on the production, but Hawks thought it could be better done for half. The result was that Hawks was removed from the project, Hughes took over the direction, finished *The Outlaw* in 1943, and then held up release of the film and Jane Russell's torrid body until 1946.

The Amazing Story of Sergeant York had its title shortened to *Sergeant York*, and it was released by Warner Brothers in July 1941. Based on several books about the Tennessee pacifist who became a World War I hero, the script by John Huston, Howard Koch, Abem Finkel, and Harry Chandlee was perfectly suited to the growing war sentiment in America. Its fortuitous opening in the year of Pearl Harbor helped make it Howard Hawks' most heralded success. "A good, native drama, inspiring in spots and full of life," stated Bosley Crowther in the *New York Times*.

Gary Cooper won an Oscar as well as the New York Film Critics award as best actor of 1941 for his sensitive portrayal of Sergeant Alvin York. The film made the Ten Best lists of the *New York Times* and *Film Daily* and was nominated by Academy members as best picture.

Although the film was an extremely topical affair, Andrew Sarris insists that age has not diminished its beauty and that it still is enhanced by the Hawksian "touch": "The film is completely Hawksian in its account of Alvin York's attempt to achieve the impossible in farming the hard, rocky soil of Tennessee, the temptations of liquor and violence, and the sudden conversion to the violation of all his moral convictions under the duress of the supreme disorder of war."

Some newspapers suggested that Howard had signed a three-year contract with Universal in 1942, but he made no films at that studio. Rather, he stayed with Warner Brothers for the fine war drama *Air Force* (1943), the fifth Hawks production to sprout wings. In a move similar to one he made twenty years later in *Red Line 7000*, Hawks used a cast of relative unknowns, aside from John Garfield, to portray his ethnic Air Force mix. Gig Young, Arthur Kennedy, John Ridgely, Charles Drake, and James Brown act the roles of Winocki, Weinberg, etc., men representing the best of the service in time of war, and the best of America.

Variety called *Air Force* "gripping, informative, entertaining, thrilling." Two decades later Andrew Sarris made a more reserved evaluation: "*Air Force*, one of the first World War II films, was easily the best until *They Were Expendable* (MGM, 1945).... The film is marred by its propagandist ending, which displays the complete obliteration (very exciting) of a Japanese task force by a squadron of bombers."

Next Howard produced *Corvette K-225* (Univ., 1943), but he left the direction to Richard Rosson. Hawks' next project, which he produced and directed, was *To Have and Have Not* (WB, 1944). An overrated film today, its script by Jules Furthman and William Faulkner was taken from a novel by Ernest Hemingway, a work that the author considered his worst. Howard, who was a friend of Hemingway, bet him that a good film could be produced out of the story of the world-sized problems of the owner of a fishing boat, but he was only partly right.

One of the main problems of *To Have and Have Not* is considered by many to be an asset. The celebrated exchanges between Humphrey Bogart and Lauren Bacall are simply too ritualistic and predictable. The feeling persists that they are playing a game but aren't quite sure of the nature of the opponent, each other, and the audience. Both characters appear to be much-traveled individuals who should be tired of the verbal foreplay that the director foists on them. The pair exist in similar molds, twenty years apart. Thus, the only sparks ignited are the legitimate kind which developed between Bogart and Bacall on the set of the production. There is nowhere for either screen person to move. There are no real sacrifices to be made, at least in their small circle.

The plot unwinds lethargically, and any interest in the stars cannot cloak the static quality of the action. Violence is limited, quickly executed, and poorly placed. When little occurs in the narrative, one must look to the story's characters to develop tension—and when there is no tension in a war film which attempts to cover the ground of its genre, there is little to recommend.

To Have and Have Not was fairly well received in the fall of 1944. Bosley Crowther of the *Times* noticed the hard-fought-for resemblance to Michael Curtiz's earlier (and superior) *Casablanca,* and he felt that Hawks' film had "a surprisingly comparable effect," while in his *New York Herald-Tribune* review Otis L. Guernsey, Jr. thought that the picture was "just what the public has ordered—one hundred minutes of Bogart-meets-girl with a dash of war added to give it a taste of danger." But Lauren Bacall got the best notices. According to *Variety,* "she's an arresting personality in whom Warners has what the scouts would call a find. She can slink, brother, and no fooling!"

That same year Hawks was scheduled to independently make *The Dark Page,* a newspaper yarn, but it wasn't until 1946 and *The Big Sleep* that another of his films hit the screen. Adapted by William Faulkner, Leigh Brackett, and Jules Furthman from Raymond Chandler's classic novel, *The Big Sleep* is deservedly considered one of the great detective films of the American screen. As Chandler's Philip Marlowe, Humphrey Bogart gives one of his greatest performances. His romantic interest is again Lauren Bacall, this time cast as a reticent, hard, and calculating woman, who toys with Marlowe's honesty and direct manner.

The film, however, is not nearly so direct. Screen writer Leigh Brackett, who has written other Hawks films such as *Rio Bravo, Hatari, El Dorado,* and *Rio Lobo,* recently recalled (in *Take One*) her first experience working with Howard: "Mr. Faulkner worked alone in his office. I worked alone in mine." They adapted alternate chapters of Chandler's novel. "I never saw his script, he never saw mine. Everything went in direct to Mr. Hawks, who was somewhere else. Beyond a couple of conferences, we never saw him. That is his way of working, and it has been known to drive good screenwriters up the wall. Most producers breathe constantly down a writer's neck. Howard Hawks sits down with you for a series of chats, giving you all his thoughts on what kind of story he wants, how it ought to go, etc., and then retires to Palm Springs and the golf course, leaving you to come up with a script the best way you can."

"It [the plot] didn't matter at all," Howard reminisced. "And I say neither the author, the writer, nor myself knew who had killed whom. It was all what made a good scene. I can't follow it. I saw some of it on television last night, and it had me thoroughly confused, because I hadn't seen it in twenty years."

The Big Sleep is composed of an intricate, unexplained series of brilliant scenes which exist on their own eye levels, and little else. The

Humphrey Bogart and Lauren Bacall in The Big Sleep *(WB, 1946)*

chemical balance between the actors in each scene is extremely attractive. Bogart and Bacall, Bogart and Dorothy Malone, Bogart and Elisha Cook, Jr., Bogart and John Ridgely, Bogart and Marsha Vickers, Bogart and Bob Steele, ad infinitum, are all relationships which function on an intimate level, whether the characters know it or not. Each pair define their own world. Bogart as detective Marlowe listens to everybody because he has to do the job of solving the case of the missing Sean Regan, and because he has to know the essence of those he contacts.

Not surprisingly, *The Big Sleep* received mixed reviews upon its release in August 1946. The *Tribune*'s Howard Barnes saw it as a "savage thriller," but Bosley Crowther of the *Times* considered it "a poisonous picture ... likely to leave you confused and dissatisfied." In the *Nation*, James Agee memorably evoked the film: "*The Big Sleep* is a violent, smoky cocktail shaken together from most of the printable misdemeanors and some that aren't—one of those Raymond Chandler specials which puts you, along with the cast, into a state of semi-amnesia through which tough action and reaction drum with something of the nonsensical solace of hard rain on a tin roof. Humphrey Bogart and several proficient minor players keep anchoring it to some sufficient kind of reality."

As Agee observed, the nonsensical nature of the narrative does not flaw *The Big Sleep*. Ironically, a similar silliness hurts, yet doesn't destroy Hawks' post-war comedies, including *I Was a Male War Bride* (20th, 1949), *Monkey Business* (20th, 1952), *Gentlemen Prefer Blondes* (20th, 1953), and *Man's Favorite Sport?* (Univ., 1964). The screwball quality of *Twentieth Century* and *Bringing Up Baby*, so right for the depressed, war-torn 1930s, had become archaic in the crisis-ridden, mostly non-violent frigid battles of the 1950s and early 1960s. In a world which constantly threatened to destroy itself, there was (and is) little room for Cary Grant to dress in women's clothing, or for Rock Hudson to be so childishly emasculated in *Man's Favorite Sport?*

Howard's first Western is one of the best ever made. *Red River* (UA, 1948), starring John Wayne, Montgomery Clift, and Joanne Dru, is about the cattle drive, the day-to-day existence of the men who moved the beef along the Chisholm Trail. A cattle boss (Wayne) adopts a boy (Clift as an adult), and together they fight stampedes, dust, aching bones, and the rawhide quality of their existence. A woman-as-destroyer (Dru) enters their lives and temporarily dislocates the males in a typically Hawksian manner. A big fight a la *The Spoilers* cleanses the men of their contempt for one another.

Red River is the first in a series of five Westerns directed by Hawks which commence as dramatic narratives featuring comic relief, and evolve into a more equal balance of comedy and drama, with laughs spinning from emotional situations. Although the lighter side is more prevalent in the later Westerns, *Red River* and *The Big Sky* certainly evidence some rather heavy whimsy.

At first John Wayne, the star of four of the five films (excluding *The Big Sky*), wasn't receptive to the director's dark humor. "I told John Wayne, 'Look, I've got an idea for a funny scene,'" Howard reminisced. "'You get your finger caught between a saddle horn and a rope, and it's mangled, and they say, "Well, that finger isn't going to be much use to you." And they get you drunk and they heat up an iron in the fire and sharpen a knife and cut off your finger.'" The Duke queried, "What kind of scene is that?" "It's supposed to be funny," Howard answered. "That isn't funny," Wayne said. So Hawks used the bit with Kirk Douglas in *The Big Sky*, and afterward John told the director, "If you say a funeral is funny, I'll do a funeral."

"*Red River*, as a comment on frontier courage, loyalty, and leadership, is a romantic, simple-minded mush, but an ingeniously lyrical film nonetheless," insisted Manny Farber. The *Herald-Tribune*'s Otis L. Guernsey, Jr. called Howard's first Western "a picturesque saga of the first cattle drive along the Chisholm Trail."

For the next decade Hawks directed enjoyable but mediocre comedies, including the lackluster *A Song Is Born* (RKO, 1948), a remake of Hawks' far superior *Ball of Fire* (RKO, 1941), produced and helped photographer Christian Nyby direct *The Thing* (RKO, 1951), contributed a segment to *O. Henry's Full House* (20th, 1952), and filmed *Land of the Pharaohs* (WB, 1955).

Land of the Pharaohs has been called "the most sensible film of its kind ever made" by Andrew Sarris. Built around the construction of a pyramid to immortalize a Pharaoh (Jack Hawkins), the William Faulkner-Harry Kurnitz-Harold Jack Bloom-scripted film is structured in two blocks of time. In this way, *Land of the Pharaohs*, like *Red River* before it, has a smoother narrative, one which concentrates on place and character without stopping every so often to span five or ten years.

"I didn't know how a Pharaoh talks," said Hawks. "And Faulkner didn't know.... None of us knew."

In 1956 Howard sued Warner Brothers for over a million dollars in expenses and lost profit when Gary Cooper refused to star in a proposed project, *Africa*. The conflict between the director and studio was settled, and Hawks went on to direct *Rio Bravo*, one of his finest films, which was released by Warner Brothers in 1959.

Rio Bravo's wordless beginning characterizes the relationship between the sheriff (John Wayne) and a drunken gunfighter (Dean Martin). Hawks employs the classic shot-counter shot, switching from

171

John Wayne in
Rio Bravo
(WB, 1959)

*John Wayne
and Walter
Brennan in*
Red River
(UA, 1948)

Robert Mitchum,
Arthur
Hunnicutt, and
John Wayne in
El Dorado
(Par., 1967)

John Wayne and
Jack Elam in
Rio Lobo
(National
General, 1970)

Wayne to Martin in the traditional Hollywood style (some say Hawks is *the* master of the simple technique).

Co-starring Walter Brennan, Ricky Nelson, and Angie Dickinson, the serio-comic Western is the first of Hawks' trilogy that also includes *El Dorado* (Par., 1967) and *Rio Lobo* (National General, 1970), the director's last film to date. Howard has said that *Rio Bravo* was made in reaction to *High Noon*, and the same can be said for the other films in the trilogy.

"I saw *High Noon* at about the same time I saw another Western picture, and we were talking about Western pictures and they asked me if I liked it and I said, 'Not particularly.' I didn't think a good sheriff would turn around and say, 'How good are you? Are you good enough to take the best man they've got?' And the fellow would probably say no, and he'd say, 'Well, then I'd just have to take care of you.' And that scene *was* in *Rio Bravo*."

In *Rio Bravo* there are many comic sequences between Wayne, Martin, Brennan, and Nelson, a number of which contain very violent or bitter moments. The final gun battle, where a family attempts to rescue one of its members from Wayne's prison, is tough, bloody, unsparing, yet comical.

As usual, this Howard Hawks film (since revered as a classic) received disparate reviews. "Well made but awfully familiar fare," carped A. H. Weiler in the *New York Times*. Paul V. Beckley applauded Hawks' filmmaking skill, writing in the *Herald-Tribune*: "The inventiveness that keeps this picture fresh and flavorsome ... ought to be a lesson in directorial ingenuity to be studied by some directors of Westerns." According to the *London Observer*, "The film starts with a fine burst of action, dwindles off, and long before the end becomes confused and repetitious."

Eight years later *El Dorado* received a somewhat better critical reception. "*El Dorado* is a Western that sticks to its guns by affirming the spirit of adventure instead of trampling it in the dust of a fashionable misanthropy. Humor and affirmation on the brink of despair are the poetic ingredients of a Hawksian Western," asserted the *Village Voice*'s Andrew Sarris. Ann Guarino of the New York *Daily News* gave the film three stars and admitted that it "isn't bad as far as old-fashioned Westerns go," while in the *New York Post* Archer Winstein deemed *El Dorado* "lively and far from finicky."

In *El Dorado*, John Wayne essays the role of a crippled gunfighter who helps the town sheriff (Robert Mitchum) get over his drunkenness and wipe out a band of outlaws. Mitchum assumes Dean Martin's part in *Rio Bravo*, James Caan takes Ricky Nelson's role, Arthur Hunnicut replaces Walter Brennan, and Charlene Holt acts a character similar to the one portrayed by Angie Dickinson. Even the lesser roles are repeated.

The same types emerge in 1970's mediocre *Rio Lobo*, starring Wayne, Jorge Rivero (Martin's role), Chris Mitchum (Nelson), Jack Elam (Brennan), and Jennifer O'Neill (Dickinson). *Rio Lobo* is a fair example of the long-held Hollywood dictum that one can't remake a great film. *Rio Bravo* is a great film, and *El Dorado* breaks the rule in its greatness, but Hawks couldn't make three great films in a row out of one basic script, even though that script was written and treated by Leigh Brackett in each case. *Rio Lobo* is tough, leathery, and uncompromising. It is also full of trite dialogue and inadequate performances. Jorge Rivero cannot compete with Dean Martin and Robert Mitchum from the earlier Westerns, and Jennifer O'Neill's mouth spurts so much corny dialogue that she hasn't got a chance against Charlene Holt, not to mention Angie Dickinson.

As many other veteran directors turned to European films and television to subsidize their careers in the midst of a corporate Hollywood, Hawks criticized overpriced actors for helping to ruin the studios. Four performers wanted the co-starring role in *Rio Lobo* at a fee of $150,000 instead of their usual $750,000. "There's just no work for people like them at their old prices, because the heavy losses suffered by retrenching studios has forced Hollywood to reappraise their value at the box office. They really aren't stars at all. Their agents oversold them, and now they're scared. But for the industry, in my opinion, it's a very healthy shakedown."

This attitude might have hindered the quality of the director's films during the 1960s, as Hawks became increasingly reliant on untested talent, performers who appeared in his films and then disappeared. In *Hatari* (Paramount, 1962), Hawks profitably guided one star, John Wayne, along with a series of experienced supporting performers, including Elsa Martinelli, Hardy Kruger, Red Buttons, and Gerard Blain. Conversely, *Man's Favorite Sport?*, *Rio Lobo*, and especially *Red Line 7000* (Par., 1965) suffer from a dearth of acting depth.

Howard's last film to date is *Rio Lobo*. During the past half-dozen years a crop of projects have received publicity, but nothing has materialized. In 1971 Hawks announced two film ideas—*Now, Mr. Gus*, "a crazy comedy about globetrotting oil snoopers," and *The Life of Ernest Hemingway*, to be produced by the director's production company, starring Burt Lancaster. The next year he considered remaking *A Girl in Every Port*, on the theory that "if a quarterback throws a touchdown pass, should he quit now because he's already done it? If it was good once, it can be good again." There was also talk of a four million dollar epic in Europe, and of Howard journeying to the Soviet Union to direct a film.

The films of Howard Hawks are still being heatedly debated by cinema specialists. Through his work Hawks has been called one of the first purveyors of modern moviemaking, a celluloid antique, a male chauvinist, a supporter of women's liberation, and on and on. Aside from frequent appearances on television, the director's creations can be seen in retrospectives such as the one at the Museum of Modern Art in New York in 1962, and another at the San Francisco Film Festival in 1972, among others. Howard Hawks was awarded a special Oscar in 1974, a belated but not too late recognition of a life of brilliance in the cinema.

The Films of Howard Hawks

The Little Princess *(Par., 1917) (not credited, directed by Marshall Neilan)*

The Road to Glory *(Fox, 1926) (and story)*

Fig Leaves *(Fox, 1926) (and story)*

The Cradle Snatchers *(Fox, 1927)*

Paid to Love *(Fox, 1927)*

A Girl in Every Port *(Fox, 1928) (and story)*

Fazil *(Fox, 1928)*

The Air Circus *(Fox, 1928) (co-directed by Lewis Seiler)*

Trent's Last Case *(Fox, 1929)*

The Dawn Patrol *(FN, 1930) (and co-script)*

The Criminal Code *(Col., 1931)*

The Crowd Roars *(WB, 1932) (and story)*

Scarface: Shame of a Nation *(UA, 1932) (and co-producer)*

Tiger Shark *(FN, 1932)*

Today We Live *(MGM, 1933) (and producer)*

The Prizefighter and the Lady *(MGM, 1933) (not credited, directed by W. S. Van Dyke)*

Viva Villa *(MGM, 1934) (not credited, co-directed by Jack Conway)*

Twentieth Century *(Col., 1934) (and producer)*

Barbary Coast *(UA, 1935)*

Ceiling Zero *(FN, 1935)*

The Road to Glory *(20th, 1936)*

Come and Get It *(UA, 1936) (co-directed by William Wyler)*

Bringing Up Baby *(Col., 1938) (and producer)*

Only Angels Have Wings *(Col., 1939) (and producer, story)*

His Girl Friday *(Col., 1940) (and producer)*

Sergeant York *(WB, 1941)*

Ball of Fire *(RKO, 1941)*

Air Force *(WB, 1943)*

The Outlaw *(RKO, 1943) (uncredited, directed by Howard Hughes)*

To Have and Have Not *(WB, 1944) (and producer)*

The Big Sleep *(WB, 1946) (and producer)*

Red River *(UA, 1948) (and producer)*

A Song Is Born *(RKO, 1948)*

I Was a Male War Bride *(20th, 1949)*

The Thing *(RKO, 1951) (not credited, co-directed by Christian Nyby)*

The Big Sky *(RKO, 1952) (and producer)*

O. Henry's Full House *(episode: The Ransom of Red Chief) (20th, 1952)*

Monkey Business *(20th, 1952)*

Gentlemen Prefer Blondes *(20th, 1953)*

Land of the Pharaohs *(WB, 1955) (and producer)*

Rio Bravo *(WB, 1959) (and producer)*

Hatari *(Par., 1962) (and producer)*

Man's Favorite Sport? *(Univ., 1964) (and producer)*

Red Line 7000 *(Par., 1965) (and producer, co-script)*

El Dorado *(Par., 1967) (also producer)*

Rio Lobo *(National General, 1970) (and producer)*

John Huston in 1975

11

John Huston

"What attracts me is adventure, and adventure is usually all-male," said the lanky director whose life has been as varied and exciting as his films. "If there's a pattern to my work," John Huston mused, "it's that I haven't made any two pictures alike. I get bored too quickly."

While Huston always seems to be off on another adventure, constant movement doesn't prevent commitment. When accused of being a fickle director whose irresponsible rampaging has ruined more than one potentially good film, Huston will retort, "No one ever really has a final cut, even when you're a producer. Somebody else always owns the picture, and there's always somebody ready to take it away from you and screw it up."

Although Huston stands fast on his integrity as a filmmaker, he realizes that his films are difficult to type. In an age of the *auteur*—a director with a visible theme and cinema style—some critics have misread John's flexibility as apathy. "That is not to say variety is to be preferred," the director insisted. "I think, as a matter of fact, it tends to throw people, and I think it's awfully difficult for an audience to know what to expect from me. I don't stand for anything in particular."

That man who doesn't stand for anything has directed *The Maltese Falcon, The Treasure of the Sierra Madre, The Asphalt Jungle, The Red Badge of Courage, The African Queen, Moby Dick, The Misfits*, and *Fat City*, films which exude a vibrant masculine air, sometimes colored by greed, introspection, women, fate, or dreams—films which talk of man from the top of his head to the bottom of his feet, and everything in between, inside and out. Huston's early cinema males are framed in action, while the later ones are encased in thought or marked by the inability to succeed or even act. His most recent film, *The Man Who*

179

Would Be King, combines action and dreams—what two men would like to do, and what they really do.

One of Huston's friends, the late James Agee, conceived a marvelous word-picture of the director. "He roughly suggests a jerked-venison version of his father, or a highly intelligent cowboy. A little over six feet tall, quite lean, he carries himself in a perpetual gangling-graceful slouch. The forehead is monkeyishly puckered, the ears look as clipped as a show dog's; the eyes, too, are curiously animal, an opaque red-brown. The nose was broken in the prize ring. The mouth is large, mobile, and gap toothed. The voice which comes out of the leatheriness is surprisingly nice, gentle, and cultivated. The vocabulary ranges with the careless ease of a mountain goat between words of eight syllables and of four letters."

John Marcellus Huston was born to Rhea (Gore) and Walter Huston on August 5, 1906 in the little town of Nevada, Missouri. Rhea, a former journalist, persuaded her new husband to leave the acting profession shortly after their marriage in 1905. After some travel, Walter obtained work at a power and light company which John's maternal grandfather had reputedly won in a poker game. As the director recalled, "My father's roadshow had gone bust, so he took the job. One night there was a fire, and he overheated the boilers to get more pressure for the horses. The plant blew up and half the town burned down. We left that night for Weatherford, Texas."

By 1909 Walter Huston had become a moderately successful engineer, but his desire to return to the theatrical boards was increasing. He finally yielded to temptation and in 1914 the Hustons were divorced. As a result John spent his formative years journeying between parents. Walter soon married a variety actress named Bayonne Whipple, and Rhea resumed her newspaper career. Young John traveled with his father and stepmother across America as they fulfilled their theatrical engagements. John in fact made his acting debut at the age of three as a rather underdeveloped Uncle Sam in one of his father's shows.

Despite a rugged existence, or perhaps because of it, John was a sickly youngster. In 1918 he entered a California military school, but his health was so delicate that doctors feared for his life. At that point, John Huston took a giant leap toward the man he was to become. Paralyzed by youthful timidity, he remembered, "I haven't the slightest doubt that if things had gone on like that, I'd have died inside a few more months." To toughen himself, the future adventurer crawled out of his window at night to swim in a nearby stream. "The first few times, it scared the living hell out of me, but I realized—instinctively anyhow—it was exactly fear I had to get over."

If John inherited a passion for the arts from his father, his love of gambling and spur-of-the-moment flings came from his mother. Once she and her son pooled $20 for a 100-to-1 shot at the racetrack, and the horse won! It was that spirit which made Huston quit Los Angeles' Lincoln High School to become a prize fighter. Within a short time he held the title of Pacific Coast amateur lightweight boxing champion. The director's won-lost record was a fine 23-2. "I was a pretty good boxer," he said. "There was a time in the ring when for five minutes I dreamed of being champ."

Soon that dream withered and another entered his head. He moved to New York to be with his father, then winning acclaim in Eugene O'Neill's *Desire Under the Elms*. In 1925 John acted a lead role in Sherwood Anderson's *Triumph of the Egg*, produced in Greenwich Village. Other parts in shows such as *Ruint* and *Adam Solitaire* did little to keep the restless soul harnessed in the theatre. His mother got him a job as a cub reporter on the *New York Graphic,* but the job was short-lived. "I was the world's lousiest reporter," Huston admitted.

From New York, John tore through the rest of the world. He served in the Mexican cavalry. He was an artist who slept on benches in London and Paris. He wrote short stories for the *American Mercury* about his experiences. "I was just having a very good time," proclaimed John. He even tried marriage. High school sweethearts John and Dorothy Harvey were wed in 1926, but the bond was dissolved a few months later.

In 1929 John wrote "a puppet play with music," called *Frankie and Johnny.* It was produced in New York by Ruth Squires, with a score written by future executive and actor Sam Jaffe. The next year, Boni and Liveright published the play in book form, which convinced Huston that he could earn a living as a writer.

At that time Walter Huston was working toward great performances in *Abraham Lincoln, Dodsworth,* and other films by acting in two-reel talkies at Paramount's Long Island studio. When Walter went to Hollywood, he took John with him. The younger Huston gratefully left a failed career as an opera singer as well as the whole New York theatre to become a $150 a week screen writer for Sam Goldwyn. After six months John was fired, without having done any writing.

Universal contracted Walter for two films, and John followed close behind. The father starred in *A House Divided* in 1931, directed by William Wyler. The son wrote additional dialogue for the script by John Clymer and Dale Van Emery. John also contributed words to Robert Florey's atmospheric reworking of Poe's *Murders in the Rue Morgue,* starring Bela Lugosi. Yet he wasn't happy as a scenarist. "I served two terms as a writer in Hollywood," the director reminisced. "The first time I went out—in the early thirties—I wasn't at all successful, and you

181

know, really, that was the day of the hack."

Warner Brothers' producer Henry Blanke was one of John's early de-fenders, but he had no illusions about the young man's aimlessness. "Just a drunken boy, helplessly immature," he asserted. "You'd see him at every party, wearing bangs, with a monkey on his shoulder. Charming. Very talented but without an ounce of discipline in his make-up."

The wild but talented Huston then turned back to theatre. He won the title role in the WPA's production of *Abe Lincoln in Illinois*, and he traveled across America acting in that show and others in the mid-1930s. John married Leslie Black during this period, and it is be-lieved that she toned down her husband and helped him to focus his career.

The new John Huston was signed to a writing contract by Warner Brothers in 1937, and this time he didn't languish (no employees at War-ner Brothers were ever without some work to do—unless they were on suspension). Yet producer Blanke spent many hours persuading Jack Warner not to fire the writer who was rarely on time and more often unruly, and his belief in the young man soon was justified. Over the years 1937-41 Huston co-scripted the solid to classic films *Jezebel*, *The Amazing Dr. Clitterhouse* (both 1938), *Juarez* (1939), *Dr. Ehrlich's Magic Bullet* (1940), *Sergeant York*, and *High Sierra* (both 1941).

During this time John's interest in directing, possibly first aroused after watching Wyler guide the senior Huston in *A House Divided*, grew to the point where he bargained for a chance to join the ranks with Curtiz, Dieterle, Bacon, and the rest. Jack Warner was planning to make a series of low-budget films with fresh talent, and he promised Huston a directorial assignment if he and W. R. Burnett wrote a good script for Burnett's novel *High Sierra*. Under Raoul Walsh's direction, *High Sierra* became a classic, and Huston thereby won the right to direct.

The successful scenarist had long wanted to film Dashiell Ham-mett's detective novel *The Maltese Falcon*, feeling certain that he could improve upon mediocre 1931 and 1936 efforts. He adapted the novel, retaining much of Hammett's fresh, crackling dialogue, and shot the film, budgeted at $300,000, in about two months. As detective Sam Spade in Huston's classic crime film, Humphrey Bogart confirmed the star status he had achieved in *High Sierra*. *The Maltese Falcon* is con-sidered by some film historians to be the first *film noir*—a series of productions which explored the psychology of evil and encompassed many genres after World War II. Bogart and fellow cast members look as if they were born for the roles. Mary Astor (the conniving Brigid O'Shaunessy), Peter Lorre (effeminate Joel Cairo), Sydney Greenstreet (the charmingly evil Casper Gutman), and Elisha Cook, Jr. (demented gunman Wilbur) all help Huston breath life into Hammett's fiction, a task that earlier versions failed to complete.

Writing in *Life* magazine, James Agee called *The Maltese Falcon* "the best private eye melodrama ever made," while Bosley Crowther of the *New York Times* labeled it "the best mystery of the year," and he prophesized: "Young Mr. Huston gives promise of becoming one of the smartest directors in the field." The *New York Herald-Tribune* was also lavish in the praise, asserting: "John Huston and Dashiell Hammett are both to be congratulated for *The Maltese Falcon*."

Thus it was probably with bewilderment that Hollywood waved good-bye to John Huston, as the hottest director in town left to write a play with scenarist Howard Koch about the United Nations called *Time to Come*. The show lasted less than two months on Broadway, but it won the New York Drama Critics Circle Award as the best play of 1941-42.

John's second film was a solid although unspectacular melodrama, *In This Our Life*, showcasing the considerable talents of Bette Davis. The most memorable aspects of the 1942 film are the vague racial exploration, still a taboo despite LeRoy's *They Won't Forget* in 1937, and the hint of incest courtesy of the Davis character and her uncle, essayed by Charles Coburn. The production was hurt by Huston's failing marriage and reported affair with co-star Olivia de Havilland. Crowther of the *Times* rightfully termed the production "neither a pleasant nor an edifying film."

Across the Pacific (also 1942) is a cross-breeding of Huston's first two films. It contains a mildly suspenseful plot, but the mechanics of the mystery are embroiled in melodrama derived from the protagonist's supposed sympathy for the Japanese cause. As such, the film is enjoyable, but hardly intriguing.

The director had to leave the production before the shooting was completed, and, playful devil that he is, he wrote an unfilmed ending which featured star Humphrey Bogart tied up in a room with Japanese gunmen surrounding him, leaving it up to director Vincent Sherman to extricate Bogart and Warner Brothers from the cliff-hanger with a shred of dignity. Sherman did so, but just barely.

Along with the ending of *Across the Pacific*, plans to film father Walter as Captain Ahab in *Moby Dick* had to be put aside when Lieutenant John Huston donned the uniform of the U.S. Signal Corps. The director shot his first war documentary, *Report from the Aleutians*, in 1942. Six cameramen accompanied him to Adak Island, where much of the footage was taken. Huston and crew flew bomber raids and narrowly missed being gunned down over enemy territory on a number of occasions. However, a proposed film of North Africa had to be dropped when the war zones became too frenetic for a film crew.

The Battle of San Pietro is considered by many to be the finest war documentary ever made. Huston's film, originally one hundred minutes long, contains a series of grim scenes of wounded and maimed American soldiers that were considered too strong for civilians' stomachs. Director and crew shot their record of GIs in Italy on actual battlefields, and Huston mailed the film to Washington for developing. It was months before the director edited or even viewed the material. The version seen in stateside theatres in early 1944 was trimmed to fifty minutes, yet it was, and still is, a powerful record of the fighting and the dying and the feeling of World War II.

In 1945 John Huston left the service with the rank of major, and by the end of the year he had divorced his wife Leslie. Before resuming his Hollywood career, he directed another war documentary, this time about the effects of battle on hospitalized GIs. Shot at the Mason General Hospital on Long Island, New York, *Let There Be Light* is another cinematic document of the destructive impact of war on the minds and bodies of American soldiers. Hidden cameras were used to film interviews with men who had been beaten, scarred, driven half-insane by mortar fire, and cut into pieces. In fact, *Let There Be Light* was so devastating that the Army decided not to release it at all. Huston was immensely disappointed, as he considered the documentary to be among his best works.

Back in Hollywood, Huston polished a script that he had written with Howard Koch before the war. Entitled *Three Strangers*, it was intended as a successor to *The Maltese Falcon*, but when it was filmed in 1946, its director was Jean Negulesco (whom Huston replaced on *The Maltese Falcon*), and its stars were Peter Lorre, Geraldine Fitzgerald, and Sydney Greenstreet, instead of the original cast of Bogart, Mary Astor, and Greenstreet. Director Negulesco made an excellent film of the moody Huston-Koch story of three people whose lives are complicated by a sweepstakes ticket. Huston also planned to direct his adaptation of Hemingway's *The Killers*, but after a disagreement with producer Mark Hellinger, Robert Siodmak was assigned to guide the 1946 Universal film.

Even then, Huston's post-war frustration wasn't over. He and Anthony Veiller completed a script from Victor Travas' story *The Stranger*, about the hunt for a Nazi war criminal in a Connecticut college town. However, producer Sam Spiegel wanted Orson Welles to play the Nazi, and since he was afraid that the *enfant terrible* wouldn't consent to star unless he was also permitted to direct, Huston was asked to step aside.

John retreated to Broadway again, this time to direct Jean-Paul

Sartre's existentialist play *No Exit*. A surrealistic study of three people locked inside hell as represented by a single room, the show was a critical triumph for both Sartre and Huston, but it closed in a month. *No Exit* was named the best foreign play of the year by New York drama critics.

Perhaps refreshened by adulation, Huston started work on a novel on which he had taken an option back in 1942—B. Traven's *The Treasure of the Sierra Madre*. Henry Blanke protected the property for the director during the war, and he persuaded Jack Warner to give John another contract. The time of Traven's story is the 1920s, the place, Mexico, the people, Fred C. Dobbs (Humphrey Bogart), Howard (Walter Huston), and Curtin (Tim Holt). The three drifters set out to mine riches from the Sierra Madre hills. After weeks of digging dirt and cracking rock, they find gold, but their camaraderie is lost in the glint of all that wealth. Paranoia and greed strangle any remaining friendship, and the feeling persists that the partners are just waiting for each other to die, any way at all. Howard is left behind to care for ailing Indians, while Dobbs and Curtin head for town. The solitude of the wilderness compounds their mutual mistrust. At night, with only the underbrush and the sounds of crickets between them, a half-crazed Dobbs shoots Curtin. Shortly after Dobbs is confronted by Mexican bandits. He sees their reflection in the water, and he knows he's going to die. They play games—"We have no badges," the laughing leader of the outlaws tells Dobbs. The torment of the man melted by fear is finally ended with his quick death, but the bandits mistakenly scatter the gold dust on the trail. Curtin is later found alive, and he and Howard ride off in different directions.

The most telling image of the film comes with the return of the gold dust to the ground. The formerly bulky bags are now slapping along the dry dirt, rolling with the wind and the mesquite bushes, and Curtin and Howard have to laugh at it all. For the first time in a John Huston film, the masculine characters are defeated—defeated by themselves. A cloud will always be hovering to muddy masculine endeavors in Huston's later films.

The Treasure of the Sierra Madre was voted the best picture of 1948 by the New York film critics, and Huston was named best director. The film made the Ten Best lists of the *New York Times*, the *National Board of Review*, and *Film Daily*. It won three major Academy Awards —best director, best screenplay, and best supporting actor (Walter Huston). "Trenchant and fascinating," insisted Bosley Crowther in the *New York Times*, who also called it "a most vivid and exciting action display." However, as always, there were critics. "It is not quite a completely satisfying picture," lectured James Agee of the *Nation*, "but on the strength of it I have no doubt at all that Huston, next only to Chaplin,

Lee Patrick and Humphrey Bogart in a publicity pose for The Maltese Falcon *(WB, 1941)*

Tim Holt, Walter Huston, and Humphrey Bogart in The Treasure of the Sierra Madre *(WB, 1948)*

is the most talented man working in American pictures, and that this is one of the movie talents in the world which is most excitingly capable of still further growth. *The Treasure* is one of the very few movies made since 1927 which I am sure will stand up in the memory and esteem of qualified people alongside the best of the silent movies."

Shortly after his divorce from Leslie Black Huston, John married actress Evelyn Keyes. After a short courtship, the director decided to literally sweep Evelyn off her feet. That night he borrowed money from a friend, sped back to his house to retrieve a wedding ring a guest had left in his swimming pool, hired a plane, and picked up his bride-to-be. They flew to Las Vegas to be married and then settled down on a 480-acre ranch in Tarzana, California, and adopted a Mexican boy, Pablo Alberran, who had a bit part in *The Treasure of the Sierra Madre*. Huston blueprinted the house personally, decorating it with many paintings and pre-Columbian art.

In 1949 John was the spokesman for a Hollywood group formed to defend film figures against the slurs of the House Committee on Un-American Activities. When Huston was given the "One World Award" at Manhattan's Plaza Hotel on May 11, 1949, many of the four hundred distinguished guests failed to attend, perhaps in reaction to Huston's controversial and courageous stand. (Three years later he would leave the United States because of his unhappiness with the United States in the McCarthy era, in order to settle in his beloved Ireland.)

During the next few years Huston was busy turning out some of his finest films. A solid version of Maxwell Anderson's talky play *Key Largo* (WB, 1948) was followed by the confused *We Were Strangers* (Col., 1949), the brilliant *The Asphalt Jungle* (MGM, 1950), *The Red Badge of Courage* (MGM, 1951), *The African Queen* (UA, 1951), and *Moulin Rouge* (UA, 1952). However, Warner Brothers was reluctant to let him film such novels as Melville's *Moby Dick*, Dostoevski's *The Idiot*, and Dreiser's *Jennie Gerhardt*.

In 1949 Huston signed a three-picture deal with a rejuvenated MGM as a writer-director. During the previous year Dore Schary had become Vice-President in Charge of Production at MGM, and he believed that in addition to the well-mounted fluff it had been making for a quarter of a century, the studio should produce gritty, realistic films such as *Battleground* and adapt literary classics.

However, MGM wanted proof that Huston was box-office, and so he wasn't allowed to direct *The Red Badge of Courage* until he had cranked out a popular success. He started work on *Quo Vadis*, starring Gregory Peck, but lengthy delays forced him off the project. Mervyn LeRoy took over the direction, and Peck was replaced by Robert Taylor.

187

The Asphalt Jungle was the made-to-order hit, and in the making it became a crime classic as well. Huston and Ben Maddow delivered a brilliant translation of W. R. Burnett's novel to the screen, the third time that the director retained the spirit of an author's words on film. The simple plot concerns a selection of men picked to engineer a million dollar jewel heist. An aging ex-con named Doc Reidenschneider (Sam Jaffe) works out the mechanics of the robbery, and the scheme is financed by a shady lawyer (Louis Calhern). A hard-drinking criminal (Sterling Hayden) and several others are enlisted to execute the plans, and the theft is successfully accomplished. The thieves escape with the jewels, only to be tracked down, one at a time, by a thoroughly efficient police force. As in *The Treasure of the Sierra Madre*, the men beat themselves: each criminal is caught because of a particular character flaw. The final shot of the film frames the boozing hood dead in the pasture, being inspected by one of the horses which was to be part of his dream ranch.

"Not since *Public Enemy* has there been so savage a screen account of underworld activities," wrote *New York Herald-Tribune* critic Howard Barnes. Bosley Crowther of the *Times* was both fascinated and repelled by the film, asserting that John Huston's direction, "in brilliantly naturalistic style, gives such an electrifying picture of the whole vicious circle of a crime—such an absorbing illustration of the various characters involved, their loyalties and duplicities, and of the minutiae of crime technique—that one finds it hard to tag the item of repulsive exhibition in itself. Yet that is our inevitable judgment of the film."

By this time Huston's salary was reportedly anywhere from $3,000 a week to $500,000 per film. John found the atmosphere at MGM to be much more relaxing than the high pressure zone at Warner Brothers, but he remained a controversial figure wherever he went. Much to Louis B. Mayer's displeasure, plans were made to film *The Red Badge of Courage*. Dore Schary and producer Gottfried Reinhardt wholeheartedly endorsed the project. Yet all the enthusiasm in the world couldn't stave off the myriad problems faced by all those connected with the film. The entanglements were so multi-faceted that Lillian Ross wrote an account of the production from drawing board to finished film in the *New Yorker* magazine, and that account was later issued in book form.

Huston used faces in *The Red Badge of Courage*, not stars. The most decorated soldier in World War II, Audie Murphy, brilliantly etches the Union recruit who deserts in time of battle but returns to become a hero. Cartoonist Bill Mauldin *is* the Loud Soldier, Royal Dano evokes much sympathy as the Tattered Man, and John Dierkes looks right as the Tall Soldier. In other words, the director's casting genius is once more confirmed.

Sterling Hayden and Jean Hagen in a publicity pose for The Asphalt Jungle *(MGM, 1950)*

The re-creation of a Civil War ambience in general, and the battle scenes in particular, benefit greatly from a concentration on the mechanics of nineteenth-century war and their effect on non-professional soldiers, rather than the suspense and melodrama of violence. Although much of the footage, including a reportedly touching bit with Huston himself, was cut, and a narration by James Whitmore added, MGM wasn't confident enough in its product to wage an all-out publicity campaign.

However, the critics were mostly congratulatory, and the film has grown in stature over the years. Otis L. Guernsey, Jr. of the *New York Herald-Tribune* declared that *The Red Badge of Courage* "is the kind of superior film one would expect from a John Huston writing-directing job." On the other hand, *Variety* may have echoed the popular sentiment of the time when it asserted: "This is a curiously moody, arty study of the psychological birth of a fighting man from a frightened boy."

Huston could not supervise the editing of *The Red Badge of Courage* because he was working with James Agee on the script of *The African Queen,* based on C. S. Forester's novel. Agee later called the director's leaving of the cutting of such an obviously personal film to others "a startling irresponsibility in so good an artist." Huston's retort was probably something to the effect that since he shot such a limited amount of footage, his films could only be edited in a certain way, no matter who handled the job.

The African Queen is one of Huston's best works, a sardonic comedy laced with adventure and romance. The main characters make an unlikely couple—a prim British missionary (Katharine Hepburn) and the salty Canadian operator of a thirty-foot boat (Humphrey Bogart). Set in World War I Africa, the story recounts the flight of the missionary after the Germans attack her village. The boat "African Queen" is the only means of possible escape, and aside from personal friction, the missionary creates more trouble by planning to destroy a German gunboat.

"The first few days Kate played an austere, bitter woman, armored, bristling," Huston recalled. "It wasn't coming off right, so one day I said, 'Play her like a lady, Kate.' She said, 'Whom do you suggest?' and I said 'Eleanor Roosevelt!' And from then on she was totally different." Shot in ten weeks in the Belgian Congo, with a few interiors taken at a London studio, *The African Queen* was released at the end of 1951 to good critical and box-office reception. Huston was nominated for writing and directing Oscars, while Bogart was voted the best actor award over Marlon Brando (for *Streetcar*), much to the surprise of the Hollywood experts.

The African Queen, which was Huston's first film in color, was called "a slick job of movie hoodwinking with a thoroughly plausible romance" by Crowther of the *Times*. "It plays a full orchestra of movie effects," declared the *Tribune*'s Otis L. Guernsey, Jr., adding: "It ranges from intimacy to spectacle in a thoroughly enjoyable show."

Filmed in Paris during the summer of 1952, *Moulin Rouge* was the second of Huston's three films for United Artists. This romanticized treatment of the life of artist Toulouse-Lautrec is literally one of the most colorful films ever made. Writing in *Esquire*, John stated his premise for the biography: "The idea has been to make *Moulin Rouge* look as though Lautrec directed it himself." All the hues and colors in the palette go whizzing by in the Parisian streets, country homes, and cabarets of the late 19th century. Dancing girls in reds and blues, against a misty brown-gold backdrop, flourish their silks and feathers in the face and soul of a dwarfed painter who could recreate their essence on canvas, yet never possess them physically. Special color filters and lighting facilitate the rebirth of Lautrec's Paris on screen, as well as the painter's canvases.

It is the spiraling tragedy of Lautrec's (Jose Ferrer) life which bounces around the rainbow framework. The cruel prostitute (Colette Marchand) to whom he gave his love and the young woman (Suzanne Flon) who befriended the artist motivate the narrative, from the crippling-fall in the home of his father to the death-fall in the dingy saloon.

Brilliant work by Ferrer, fine support by Marchand and Flon, and the airy conviviality of Zsa Zsa Gabor cap the film, dubbed "one of the great films of this or any year" by *Cue* magazine. However, the *New Yorker* came closer to the view that history has assumed of Huston's biographical film when it stated: "While the physical attributes of *Moulin Rouge* are uniformly satisfactory, it is possible that the drama accompanying the sets isn't quite so stimulating." Nevertheless, the public made *Moulin Rouge* one of the big hits of 1953, and the film and its director won Oscar nominations.

By 1952 Huston and his new wife, dancer-model Ricki Soma, and their children Pablo and Tony moved to the director's dream country, Ireland. The family lived in a rented estate in County Kildare, which served as their home between productions. In 1964 John became a citizen of Ireland.

Even so, he was busy in the United States. It took quite a while to untangle *Beat the Devil* (UA, 1954), and some critics allege that it has yet to be done. "We went into that film without a script," Huston confessed. "We found ourselves in a situation and decided to box our way out of it."

Humphrey Bogart had taken an option on James Helvick's novel and

Bill Mauldin and Audie Murphy in The Red Badge of Courage *(MGM, 1951)*

Katharine Hepburn and Humphrey Bogart in The African Queen *(UA, 1951)*

Humphrey Bogart and Jennifer Jones in a publicity pose for Beat the Devil *(UA, 1954)*

Audie Murphy and Burt Lancaster in The Unforgiven *(UA, 1960)*

asked Huston to direct. Starring as an adventurer who is enticed by four criminals into buying some fraudulent uranium property in British East Africa, Bogart hoped to rekindle the smoldering fires of *The Maltese Falcon*. The first script for *Beat the Devil*, written by Huston, Anthony Veiller, and Peter Viertel, was rejected by the star. Somehow John convinced Bogart to let Truman Capote help out on the rewrite, and the result was a decided parody on the film that the actor had originally envisioned. An improvisatory aura imbues *Beat the Devil*. "Kind of a shell game, with the operator sometimes forgetting under which shell the black ball is hidden," cracked Guernsey of the *Tribune*.

With the new regime coming to Warner Brothers, Huston was finally allowed to bring his dream project *Moby Dick* into reality. Sadly his father Walter had died in 1950, so a search was initiated for an actor to play Ahab. Although the director had the good fortune of proposing the Melville project when epics were in vogue, Warner Brothers insisted on a star for the role of Ahab, the impassioned man with a mission. The studio suggested Gregory Peck, and Huston consented. The supporting cast of Richard Basehart (Ishmael), Leo Genn (Starbuck), and Orson Welles (Father Mapple) was hand-picked by Huston, along with Harry Andrews, James Robertson Justice, Bernard Miles, and Seamus Kelly (as seamen), and an inexperienced Austrian actor named Friedrich Ledebur for the role of the tattooed Queequeg.

The director hired science fiction writer Ray Bradbury to co-script the project, and in the fall of 1953 Bradbury journeyed to Ireland to fulfill that assignment. Of *Moby Dick* the author said, "Now there is a film of which I am immensely proud."

Huston and Anthony Veiller had worked on an adaptation, but Bradbury wrote an entire script on his own. At the time of *Moby Dick*'s release, controversy developed over the proper billing of the writing credits, and today Bradbury's name is listed over Huston's.

Wherever the truth lies, Huston took a finished script and transformed an Irish seaport town of Youghal into New Bedford, Massachusetts. The sea scenes were shot all over the world, sometimes at great peril to cast and crew, as well as to the studio-built Pequod. Waters off the Azores, Portugal, the Canary Islands, and Wales became part of *Moby Dick*. The winter of 1953-54 was so hazardous that the Pequod had to be dismantled three times for fear that it would get lost at sea. There were no rear projection screens, back-lot lakes, or any other faking of the natural creations in *Moby Dick*, except for some model whales composed of latex, wood, and steel. Huston incorporated real mammals more than once, but at the end when Ahab goes to his doom strapped to the white whale, actor Peck was fastened to a large cylinder in a London studio.

194

Moby Dick cost $5,000,000. The production faced delays which added eight months to the shooting schedule, but John Huston spared no emotional, physical, or economic expense in filming Melville's masterpiece. Yet the director wasn't so in awe of his material that he was afraid to change a single word. "For dramatic purposes, we had to make some changes in Melville's construction," John said at the time. "But most difficult of all was putting into dialogue the basic conflict between Starbuck and Ahab." Perhaps part of the problem lay in Huston's periodic sojourns into the character of Captain Ahab. The director has said he "becomes" the characters he guides, but Melville's obsessed sea captain might have touched John too deeply. "Huston was more Ahab himself than any actor could be," stated Gregory Peck. "His intense desire to make this picture without any compromises is certainly comparable to Ahab's relentless quest to kill the whale. Huston was always up in the prow of one of the boats with the harpoon."

To achieve the suppressed sepia tone of the film, photographer Oswald Morris (who shot *Moulin Rouge*) used two sets of negatives, one technicolor, one black and white. Superimposed and printed, the effect resembles old whaling pictures. A decade later Huston tried a similar process in *Reflections in a Golden Eye*.

The brilliant film, which commenced with the words "Call me Ishmael," received mixed reviews from critics, and was weak at the box office. "Beneath a mortal tale, Huston has dared to hunt its immortal meanings, and he has found them. *Moby Dick* is a monument to his genius and his integrity," proclaimed William K. Zinnsser in the *New York Herald-Tribune*, while Crowther of the *Times* deigned it "one of the great motion pictures of our times." However, C. A. Lejeune's analysis in the *London Observer* was less passionately enthusiastic: "Huston's direction employs an interesting pattern of alternating sequences of feverish activity and doldrum calm." According to the *New Yorker*, *Moby Dick* is "a fine, elementary job that misses the mystical Melville by several nautical miles but affords us an almost completely satisfactory tour of the boundary main." *Variety* had the most down-to-earth comment of all: "Essentially it's a 'chase' picture with all the inherent interest thereby implied and yet not escaping the quality of sameness and repetitiousness which often dulls the chase formula."

The New York film critics named John Huston the best director of the year for *Moby Dick*, and the National Board of Review honored him in the same fashion. Yet John wasn't satisfied with the film's overall reception: "Well, you know, I think the idea of *Moby Dick* was never really recognized by the critics, at least never dwelt on. And that is that the whole thing is blasphemy. Melville hated God! I never saw Ahab as a ranting madman, but rather as a profound figure, a dedicated blasphemer. Peck furnished a kind of nobility, a heroic stature, O'Neill-esque. But the role didn't coincide with people's ideas about Peck, just as it didn't coincide with their ideas about Ahab."

John was so impressed with Peck's acting (his performance in *Moby Dick* has come to be respected by many) that he planned to star him in a version of Melville's first novel, *Typee*, but the proposed budget put an end to that project before it began. Huston's next three films, *Heaven Knows, Mr. Allison* (20th, 1957), *The Barbarian and the Geisha*, and *The Roots of Heaven* (both 20th, 1958) are certainly among his lesser efforts, although the first received an Oscar nomination for best script.

Heaven Knows, Mr. Allison is something of an attempt to duplicate the success of *The African Queen*. Robert Mitchum and Deborah Kerr do create sparks as a soldier and a nun, respectively, but the script is simply too rambling to command complete attention.

Originally called *The Townsend Harris Story*, *The Barbarian and the Geisha* concerns the fictitious romance of America's first ambassador to Japan and the titled geisha. John Wayne is absurd as Harris, embroiled in the intrigues of an Occidental-Oriental romance. Studio interference hurt a potentially fascinating historical pageant by insisting on the melodramatic emphasis.

The Roots of Heaven, personally supervised by Darryl F. Zanuck, fared no better. This last film under Huston's contract at Fox is about the efforts of a dentist (Trevor Howard) to save an African game preserve. The film is most memorable for its awful production circumstances, one of which was 138-degree heat. "Well, we had pretty close to 100% incidence of casualties," Huston recalled. "Malaria, heat, dysentery. But as long as nobody gets killed, it's okay. I'm pleased to say that I've never lost an actor." In *The Roots of Heaven*, he squandered what might have been a provocative story in the vague motivations of the dentist, and he failed to capture the cohesive appeal of the Army deserter (Errol Flynn), the prostitute (Juliette Greco), and the news photographer (Eddie Albert).

That year the director reportedly negotiated a five-film deal with Seven Arts Productions, the first of which was to have been a version of *Lysistrata*. The contract apparently failed to materialize, and in 1959 Huston signed with Hecht-Hill-Lancaster to film *The Unforgiven*, his first period Western.

Shooting commenced in February 1960 near Durango, Mexico. With a script by Ben Maddow which reflects not only racial and religious tension, but the whole range of cultural values in the nineteenth-century American West, *The Unforgiven* is a stark, at times mystical investigation into those qualities. There seems to be a kind of tension in every scene—between the family members, between man and woman, between white man and red man, between righteous lunacy and immoral sanity.

As was by then habitual with a Huston production, *The Unforgiven* had its share of production problems. The main delay was the month lost when Audrey Hepburn fell off a horse, which jacked up the budget of the $4,500,000 film by another million. In addition, the expected hazards of shooting on location in a remote area had to be overcome.

The stars of this John Huston Western are Burt Lancaster, Audrey Hepburn, Audie Murphy, John Saxon, Charles Bickford, and Lillian Gish as Mrs. Zachary. The latter part was first offered to Bette Davis, who rejected it because she couldn't see herself as Burt Lancaster's mother.

The Unforgiven received many good reviews upon its release in the spring of 1960. "It may not rank with the greatest of the Huston pictures," wrote Archer Winstein in the *New York Post*, but "considered from every angle . . . for what it tries to do, *The Unforgiven* is a very perfect work." *Time* magazine described it as a "massive and masterful attempt to gild the oat."

Playwright Arthur Miller wrote his first film script as a vehicle for his wife Marilyn Monroe. A philosophical tale of disillusionment and aimlessness, *The Misfits* was supposed to establish Marilyn as a dramatic actress, thus liberating her from a decade of steamy cheesecake roles in sexy comedies. The film was to be produced by Seven Arts and released through United Artists, and all concerned wanted John to direct it, especially Monroe who had received her first important role in Huston's *The Asphalt Jungle*. Clark Gable eagerly accepted the role of middle-aged cowboy Gay Langland, feeling that it would be his meatiest part in years. He too liked the director. Montgomery Clift and Eli Wallach signed on as co-stars of this modern Western.

The Misfits is literally about four people who don't fit into society. A divorcée (Monroe) meets cowboy Langland (Gable), who is getting too old for his job. They decide to live together. A former rodeo star (Clift) and an unemployed mechanic (Wallach) join in the drifting. Huston's masculine images are stripped of their former glory, existing only on a gruff exterior which fails to cloak what has been lost. Eventually the men agree to round up wild mustangs for a dog food manufacturer. Scenes of the trio and Monroe speeding across the prairie in a beaten-up truck, raising a hurricane of dust while attempting to rope the stallions, are the strongest evocations of lost souls wandering in time.

The director's primary problem in *The Misfits* was Marilyn Monroe. It was said that her marriage to Miller was dissolving, and she halted the production many times by failing to show up. Huston was always

kind, and he later referred to the tragic performer as a "complete amateur who was ... wonderful." But costs spiraled, and *The Misfits* was
bound to lose money due to its $4,000,000 budget. Called "the most
expensive black-and-white film ever made," it also had the distinction
of being the second Huston film to become the subject of a book (by
James Goode).

"Despite undeniable brilliance, the picture does not stand as top-
grade work from either Miller or Huston," insisted the *New York Post*.
It "just doesn't come off," wrote Bosley Crowther in the *Times*. Yet
Crowther admitted that Huston's direction was "dynamic, inventive,
and colorful."

Seen from a distance of almost twenty years, *The Misfits* transcends
its divergent contributors to become a masterful exploration of the
angst and corruption of decent people who have to compromise their
ideals in order to survive. It is at once a symbol of the downbeat course
that the director's men will tend to follow in the future, and a prophecy
of the films that would be produced in the 1960s and 1970s on alienation
in America.

Freud (1962) and *The List of Adrian Messenger* (1963) were both
filmed for Universal. Huston co-scripted his biographical study of the
father of modern psychoanalysis and retained Montgomery Clift from
The Misfits for the title role. The film spans only 1885-90, the five
crucial years in which Freud's main theories evolved. Susannah York
sensitively portrays a difficult compilation of a number of the psychiatrist's real patients, Susan Kohner has the role of Freud's wife, and
Larry Parks, the blacklisted actor who won fame in *The Jolson Story*,
makes a fine comeback as a doctor who encourages Freud's early
experiments.

Generally a solid biography which concerns itself with the progression of Freud's investigation into the human psyche, the black-and-
white film's highlights are four harrowing dream sequences. Hard-
hitting surrealistic visions of fact and psychosis, they are as effective
in their way as the can-can sequences in *Moulin Rouge* and the gritty,
almost non-dramatic battles of *The Red Badge of Courage*. Nevertheless *Freud* wasn't a moneymaker, and a title change to *The Secret Passion* only succeeded in distorting the image of a fine film. Critics were
generally enthusiastic, and the film was nominated for several awards.

The List of Adrian Messenger, something of a spoof along the lines
of *Beat the Devil*, is a complete failure. Composed of an inane series of
guest appearances by stars incognito, with little humor and less
suspense, it stars George C. Scott and Dana Wynter, with appearances
by Kirk Douglas, Frank Sinatra, Tony Curtis, Burt Lancaster, Robert
Mitchum, and the director himself. Some reviews were kind. Many
more weren't.

In 1963 John Huston appeared for the first time in a major acting role in a motion picture, *The Cardinal,* and there was talk of a supporting Oscar for the director's fine portrayal of leathery Cardinal Glennon in Otto Preminger's rambling epic, in which the title role was essayed by Tom Tryon.

After that, John directed Tennessee Williams' *The Night of the Iguana* (MGM, 1964). A number of critics consider this adaptation by Huston and Anthony Veiller of one of the playwright's lesser works to be superior to the original. Solid performances by Richard Burton, Ava Gardner, and Deborah Kerr, along with good support by Sue Lyon, Grayson Hall, and Cyril Delevanti, make *The Night of the Iguana* a commendable if not outstanding film in Huston's oeuvre. Shot in extreme discomfort for three months in the Mexican west coast village of Puerto Vallarta, the cast and crew "got along famously," according to the director. Since there was so much star power in the film, Huston gave each cast member a derringer with the names of the other actors on the bullets. Waving one of the weapons probably broke the tension on a number of sticky occasions.

There was speculation that John would direct *This Property Is Condemned* (eventually turned out by Sydney Pollack in 1966), but his next film was the spotty epic *The Bible* (20th, 1966). "I accepted *The Bible* because I felt it could be a picture of beauty, dignity, simplicity, and fascination. I've never before been so gripped, so completely immersed in any other film," the director said at the time.

Others failed to generate Huston's enthusiasm. Cinema scholar Andrew Sarris even called the director's whole career into question on the basis of *The Bible.* "Huston's career since the war has raised disturbing questions about freedom and discipline in the cinema," he wrote in *Interviews with Film Directors* (Avon). "That is to say, that in a quarter of a century of alleged liberation, John Huston has progressed from *The Maltese Falcon* to *The Bible.*"

Huston spent a year of his life shooting *The Bible* in Italy and North Africa. Originally producer Dino De Laurentiis envisioned a number of films based on the Old Testament, to be directed by Orson Welles, Robert Bresson, Federico Fellini, and Huston. An all-star cast, including George C. Scott, Peter O'Toole, Ava Gardner, Michael Parks, and Franco Nero, attempts to bring cinema life to the first twenty-two chapters of Genesis, but it succeeds only occasionally in lifting the spirit of the great book onto film. An outstanding sequence is the creation of Adam, yet regrettably too much of the narrative is bogged down in clichés of the epic.

Judith Crist of the *New York World-Journal-Tribune* gave a particularly scathing critique: "What there is not is a sense of the power and the

199

glory of the source—a sense that cannot be conveyed by thunder and lightning and an off-screen voice. Reverence—and awe—are not enough. The movie doesn't quite come up to the book." On the other side, Kate Carroll of the *New York Daily News* awarded *The Bible* the newspaper's top rank of four stars, and she exclaimed: "The film is stupendous in its poetic images of the creation of the earth ... might be called Chapter I in the De Laurentiis-Huston film of the Good Book."

Casino Royale (Col., 1967) is such a poverty-stricken super-spy extravaganza that the less said about it the better. Huston co-directed with Val Guest, Ken Hughes, Joseph McGrath, and Robert Parrish, and he acted in a cute segment, but overall the film is a dismal failure.

The vaguely implied homosexuality in *The Maltese Falcon* is heavily obvious in Huston's excellent adaptation of Carson McCullers' 1941 novel *Reflections in a Golden Eye* (WB-Seven Arts, 1967). Produced in Rome at the insistence of star Elizabeth Taylor, the film is set on an Army post in Georgia of the late 1940s. Elizabeth is married to a major (Marlon Brando, replacing the recently deceased Montgomery Clift) who lusts after a young soldier. The wife in turn has an affair with another officer (Brian Keith). Keith himself is wed to a neurotic woman (Julie Harris) who keeps company with their effeminate houseboy.

John added a distinct look to the script by Chapman Mortimer and Gladys Hill. Although the film was shot in color, it possessed a sepia tone similar to that seen in *Moby Dick*. The color was dissipated considerably, with only touches of gold, red, and pink surrounded by images which almost look black and white. This very explicit and tense narrative did not find favor with the public, and in an effort to give the production something of a whitewashing, all sepia prints were removed from distribution and replaced by normal technicolor copies.

Despite a uniformly excellent cast and a violent finish which features a rapidly moving camera picking up clumps of an hysterical Taylor and stunned Brando reacting to a spectacular murder, *Reflections in a Golden Eye* received disparate reviews. The *New York Post*'s Archer Winstein thought the production "a picture of superlative perform-ances, occasional marvel, and psychopathic sexualis," while Bosley Crowther delivered one of his more iconoclastic reviews in the *Times*: "Hell hath no fury like a homosexual scorned. This is the commonplace conclusion that is melodramatically reached after a detailed and devastating study of officer life on an American Army base." "Where Huston falters is the atmosphere he provides for the actor," carped Andrew Sarris in the *Village Voice*. "Huston overdirects *Reflections* for the sake of a mass audience in which he has little confidence."

In the next few years John appeared in such films as *Candy* (Cine-rama Releasing Corp., 1968), *De Sade* (AI, 1969), *Myra Breckinridge*

(20th, 1970), and *The Bridge to the Jungle* (UA, 1970) scattered between directing *Sinful Davey* (UA, 1969), *A Walk with Love and Death* (20th, 1969), and *The Kremlin Letter* (20th, 1970). He started work on *The Madwoman of Chaillot* (WB-Seven Arts, 1969), but he was replaced (by Bryan Forbes) when he disagreed with producer Ely Landau's decision to modernize the story.

During this period Huston's critical reputation took a plunge. Of his three films of that time, only *The Kremlin Letter* is a quality production, and its reviews were uniformly negative. *Films in Review* condemned it as "drivel made incomprehensible." Said John, "I didn't see how in the world it could make me anything but rich beyond calculation and nobody went to see it."

A tough, intricate espionage film, *The Kremlin Letter* is loaded with characters who kill without personal or patriotic motive. Friendship, loyalty, nationalism, and even sexuality are debunked. The director appears to contradict everything he promoted in earlier films. Group immorality is rampant, and there isn't a truly sympathetic character in sight. The basic plot revolves around a curious company of American agents sent to Moscow to recover a vital document whose revelation could lead to war with China. Shot in Mexico, New York, and Finland (the last substituting for Moscow), *The Kremlin Letter*'s huge cast includes Max Von Sydow, Richard Boone, Bibi Anderson, and George Sanders, who does a particularly perverted scene in drag.

John's response to the bad press that his films received was typically strong: "American film criticism is about the worst in the world, especially the New York enclave and especially the magazines." When he wasn't annoyed at film critics, the director was off hunting wild boar, stags, and chamois in Austria and Bavaria, as well as planning to make a film in the United States for the first time since 1960.

Fat City (Col., 1972) was that film. Starring Stacy Keach and Jeff Bridges, this depressing but vividly real and powerful narrative of a washed-up boxer Billy (Keach) who befriends rising middleweight Ernie (Bridges) is one of John Huston's finest films. Scenes of the men in cheap diners and hallways, fighting in the ring, and laboring in fields look so authentic that they virtually drip with sweat and the smell of farm dirt. In the diner, one can almost feel the crushed cigarettes on the floor or wet a finger and wipe coffee stains from the counter.

It is the dashed American dream that Huston speaks of in *Fat City*. Like *The Misfits*, it is a slowly paced, almost anti-climactic production. The story revolves around Billy, a man who never made it in the sports field. Sports itself is an institution which allows grown men to act like boys, and if one can't even succeed as a boy, how can a man develop? That's what *Fat City* seems to ask. Billy and Ernie sit in an

Clark Gable and Marilyn Monroe in The Misfits *(UA, 1961)*

Brian Keith and Elizabeth Taylor in Reflections in a Golden Eye *(MGM, 1967)*

Stacy Keach and Jeff Bridges in Fat City *(Col., 1972)*

Michael Caine, Christopher Plummer, and Sean Connery in The Man Who Would Be King *(Allied Artists, 1976)*

all-night cafeteria and live the question. An elderly Chinese man slowly prepares coffee for the pair. His wrinkled face appears to contain the history of the world, but no answers. "How would you like to wake up in the morning and be him?" asks Billy.

The director's admiration for the men in *Fat City* is evident in the film. "Certainly it's a downbeat film," he readily admitted. "But rather than being downbeat, a word I don't like, I feel an admiration for the valor of these people who, ever so briefly, look life in the teeth and then have the drive to go on kidding themselves."

"*Fat City* is a classic," proclaimed Archer Winstein of the *Post*. "*Fat City* recaptures the truths and compassions of such Huston works as *The Maltese Falcon* and *The African Queen*," insisted *New York* magazine critic Judith Crist. In the *New York Times*, Vincent Canby viewed *Fat City* as "a film that indulges his [Huston] old affection for misfits and strays, but with a mellow difference that is the particular contribution of novelist [Leonard] Gardner. *Fat City* is sad, but it's also extremely funny."

The only thing that *The Life and Times of Judge Roy Bean* (National General, 1973) has in common with its predecessor is extreme subjectivity. Dealing with myths as an abstraction of history, the film purports to trace the existence of Bean—"the only law west of the Pecos," according to the old teleseries blurb. *Bean* suffers from the same episodic build-up that makes *The List of Adrian Messenger* a tangled affair. Huston's second period Western, starring Paul Newman, Victoria Principal, and a host of star cameos, it has a realistic flavor which only serves as a backdrop for the guest shots. While the film is often amusing, and toward the end quite touching, it must rank as a lesser Huston effort.

"Perhaps my greatest contribution has been that of keeping certain films from being out-and-out disgraces, of turning them into mediocrities instead," Huston told Jim Watters of the *New York Times*. "Take *The Mackintosh Man*, for example. We all needed money—Paul Newman, John Foreman, and I." Here the director sums up his feeling about the modest Warner Brothers 1973 espionage film, and speaks for his audience as well. *The Mackintosh Man* had but a brief run in major theatres, and was given surprisingly sparse critical attention, despite the high-powered star and director. Ironically, Andrew Sarris thought that the work was good enough to warrant a re-evaluation of Huston's filmography.

"I think it's one of the greatest adventure stories ever written," said John Huston of *The Man Who Would Be King*. "And it has excitement, color, spectacle, and humor. It also has some spiritual meaning, which becomes clear toward the end of the story. It is, too, a wonderful story of the warm relationship between two men—two tough and like-able rogues who were loyal to each other and to their ideals. Now that it's become a motion picture, one of my cinematic ambitions is finally coming to fruition and I'm very happy indeed."

John Huston had to wait twenty years before filming Rudyard Kip-ling's story *The Man Who Would Be King* (AA, 1976). In the 1950s Gable and Bogart were slated to play Kipling's endearing rogues who almost make off with the wealth of a remote native nation, but Bogie died. The second attempt to film the tale was halted by Gable's death.

As the United States reveled in the Bicentennial, it was appropriate that Huston's wish to put this tale of British colonial India on screen became a reality. The brash partners with the bold plans in *The Man Who Would Be King*, in spite of British origins, are fitting reflections of the aggressive American spirit that was being celebrated. The film itself is a wonderful paean to the classic Hollywood adventure film which interspersed humor without parody amid swashbuckling swordplay.

Sean Connery and Michael Caine play the roles originally designated for Gable and Bogart. Huston's casting genius sparks the already ani-mated masculine narrative he adapted with Gladys Hill. Connery and Caine almost leap out of the screen and harken one back to memories of a grandfather telling stories of the days when adventurers like these really gave the world a shot in the arm, even while breaking the law, and times were simpler, and men were willing to face up to the conse-quences of their actions.

"Not in a very long while has Mr. Huston, who wrote the screenplay with Gladys Hill and also directed the film, been so successfully light-hearted and so consistently in command of his subject," asserted Canby of the *New York Times*. According to the *New Yorker*'s Pauline Kael, Huston's adaptation was "an exhilaratingly farfetched adventure fantasy about two roughneck con men."

Recently Huston stated, "I think I've made only three good films in the last decade: *Reflections in a Golden Eye, Fat City,* and *The Man Who Would Be King*. And they are not remotely similar."

At this writing, John Huston and his present collaborator Gladys Hill are busy with a screenplay of Hemingway's *Across the River and into the Trees*. "The book, which was largely a disaster," opined the direc-tor, "is a dialogue between a colonel who is dying and a very young Ital-ian girl. Papa was very dejected by the reception of the book and I've got correspondence from him which was written when he was so down about it. I know the background, a lot of the personal things. He really exposes himself in the book, and it is hard to draw the line between Hemingway and the old colonel."

Today Huston can be considered the grandfather of the American cinema, circa 1976. His brilliant career is longer than any other director working regularly in American film today. From the tough films of the 1940s, through the literary adaptations of the 1950s, the soul-searching productions of the 1960s, and the potpourri of the 1970s, John Huston is a man's director in a world where adventure's the thing, but adventure often filled with spiritual awareness.

The Films of John Huston

The Maltese Falcon *(WB, 1941) (and script)*

In This Our Life *(WB, 1942) (and co-script)*

Across the Pacific *(WB, 1942)*

Report from the Aleutians *(documentary, 1942)*

The Battle of San Pietro *(documentary, 1944)*

Let There Be Light *(documentary, 1945)*

The Treasure of the Sierra Madre *(WB, 1948) (and script, actor)*

Key Largo *(WB, 1948) (and co-script)*

We Were Strangers *(Col., 1949) (and co-script)*

The Asphalt Jungle *(MGM, 1950) (and co-script)*

The Red Badge of Courage *(MGM, 1951) (and script)*

The African Queen *(UA, 1951) (and co-script)*

Moulin Rouge *(UA, 1952) (and producer, script)*

Beat the Devil *(UA, 1954) (and co-script)*

Moby Dick *(WB, 1956) (and co-producer, co-script)*

Heaven Knows, Mr. Allison *(20th, 1957) (and co-script)*

The Barbarian and the Geisha *(20th, 1958)*

The Roots of Heaven *(20th, 1958)*

The Unforgiven *(UA, 1960)*

The Misfits *(UA, 1961)*

Freud *(Univ., 1962) (and co-script)*

The List of Adrian Messenger *(Univ., 1963)*

The Night of the Iguana *(MGM, 1964) (and producer, co-script)*

The Bible *(20th, 1966) (and narrator, actor)*

Casino Royale *(Col., 1967) (co-directed by Val Guest, Ken Hughes, Joseph McGrath, Robert Parrish) (and actor)*

Reflections in a Golden Eye *(WB-Seven Arts, 1967)*

Sinful Davey *(UA, 1969)*

The Madwoman of Chaillot *(WB-Seven Arts, 1969) (replaced by Bryan Forbes)*

A Walk with Love and Death *(20th, 1969) (and co-producer)*

The Kremlin Letter *(20th, 1970) (and co-script)*

The Last Run *(RMG, 1971) (replaced by Richard Fleischer)*

Fat City *(Col., 1972) (and co-producer)*

The Life and Times of Judge Roy Bean *(National General, 1973) (and actor)*

The Mackintosh Man *(WB, 1973)*

The Man Who Would Be King *(AA, 1976) (and co-producer, co-script)*

Across the River and into the Trees *(1977) (co-script)*

William Keighley and the Mauch Twins on the set of The Prince and the Pauper *(WB, 1937)*

Maxine Doyle, Glen Boles, Guy Kibbee, and Aline MacMahon in Babbitt *(First National, 1934)*

12

William Keighley

"The basic principle of good screen fare is the same as the basic principle of the solar system," quipped William Keighley. "No matter what kind of stars you're dealing with, you must observe the natural law of attraction and repellance. That's why co-starring is so sound. Two stars reacting to each other. That's the first element of dramatic interest."

Although Keighley spent thirty years in the theatre before directing his first film, he was well aware that actors do not the cinema make. "Motion picture means 'move,'" he pointed out quite clearly. "And if you don't move, the audience moves out on you."

Many of Bill's thirty-seven films sparkle with actors' energy and flow in the best Warner Brothers tradition. Keighley's finest efforts, *G-Men*, *The Green Pastures*, *Bullets or Ballots*, *The Prince and the Pauper*, and *Torrid Zone*, signify Jack Warner's adaptable production crew at its height and reflect the light vein running through even the most serious subjects filmed by the director.

William Keighley was born on August 4, 1889 or 1893 in Philadelphia, Pennsylvania, the son of William Jackson and Mary (Hauser) Keighley (the name "Keighley" means "cow pasture" in German). Young Bill was educated at the Philadelphia Northeast Manual Training School (one of the first in the country), and then sailed to the Alliance Francaise in Paris.

It is claimed that by 1905, 12- or 16-year-old Bill had won acceptance into Ben Greet's Shakespeare Repertory Company and acted thirty-two roles in thirteen plays during his first four months of membership. The youthful sophisticate (he was much traveled by then) did one-night stands in every state except Rhode Island and Florida. Before long, Bill struck out on his own, selling modern drama to the Chautauqua Circuit for the first time and performing with his own company. In 1915 Keighley made his first appearance in New York, in *Inside the Lines*. He also acted in *Just Suppose*, opposite 22-year-old Leslie Howard who was making his New York debut in the play. During the 1920s he performed with many of the theatre greats of the day. Among others, Keighley shared a stage with John Barrymore (in *Richard III*) and sister Ethel (in *Romeo and Juliet*). The *Toronto Blade* commended Bill for his "outstanding performance" as Paris in the latter classic.

Keighley spent the 1924-25 season in Paris, studying French literature and drama. Back in New York, he became the associate director of Charles Hopkins' theatre, working on a number of box-office hits, including *The Perfect Alibi*. After a jaunt in London, Bill guided James Cagney and Joan Blondell in *Penny Arcade*.

A 1930 vacation to the West Coast turned into a six-year stay directing plays, including *Grand Hotel* and *Elizabeth the Queen* at the Belasco Theatre in Los Angeles. Bill's fluent French enabled him to translate as well as direct *Cyrano de Bergerac*, starring Richard Bennett, and to modernize *Camille* for Jane Cowl.

In 1932 Keighley became associated with Warner Brothers-First National, and the relationship lasted until the end of the director's career. He assisted William Dieterle on *Jewel Robbery* and *Scarlet Dawn*, as well as Michael Curtiz on *The Cabin in the Cotton*. Bill also served as dialogue director for Lloyd Bacon's *The Picture Snatcher* in 1933. During this time he co-directed two productions with Howard Bretherton, *The Match King* (1932) and *Ladies They Talk About* (1933).

Easy to Love (1934) was Bill's first solo flight as a director, and he soon defined his approach to film: "Instead of a palette of colors and brushes, I have a story and a group of players to paint my picture with." He brushed some pretty pictures with star Genevieve Tobin on the set of the production. They were married on September 19, 1938, eloping to Las Vegas. The marriage is strong to this day. The Keighleys then moved into a three and a half acre home in Beverly Hills, decorating their walls with modern paintings.

"Bright, strenuous, and thinnish in equal proportions," wrote Frank S. Nugent in the *New York Times* of *Easy to Love*. Co-starring Adolphe Menjou and Mary Astor, the light plot revolves around a cheating husband who is cuckolded by his wife.

That year, after Bill worked with friend Joan Blondell in *Kansas City Princess*, he directed one of his better films, *Babbitt*. Adapted from the Sinclair Lewis story of life in a small Midwestern town, the tale stars Guy Kibbee in the title role, supported by Aline MacMahon, Claire Dodd, and Alan Hale. The director shows his penchant for illustrating Americana for the first time in *Babbitt*, a trait carried over to *Four*

Mothers (1941) and *George Washington Slept Here* (1942). André Sennwald of the *Times* labeled *Babbitt* "a skillfully managed motion picture ... an enjoyable entertainment."

Bill's next series of films basically divide into three groups—crime, melodrama, and musical. The first section is strongest, containing *G-Men* (1935) and *Bullets or Ballots* (1936).

G-Men reunited Keighley with James Cagney, and the pair made the most of the association. The outcry of Hollywood censors against the "glorification" of gangsters in the early products of Warner Brothers and other studios brought a modification in emphasis, if not violence. *G-Men* has Cagney portraying a lawyer who went through school on a crime boss' scholarship. He joins the government men after an unarmed friend is killed subduing a criminal. There are several fierce gun battles in the film, which is a well-cut and fast-paced production. The fighting is brutal—in fact more so than in many of the pre-Will Hays Code films. When Cagney's benefactor quits the rackets, he is disposed of in a chilling way.

"Not since *The Public Enemy* startled film-goers with its stark and brutal reconstruction of gangster activities has there come so compelling a photoplay of the underworld as *G-Men*," wrote *Herald-Tribune* critic Howard Barnes. "That he has been able to weld these disparate elements into a gripping fast-moving melodrama is something of an achievement on the part of William Keighley, the director." André Sennwald of the *Times* disagreed: "At ninety minutes it seems overlong and it is handicapped by the tiresome Cagney formula." Yet even he admitted that "*G-Men*, despite its flaws, is a superior melodrama."

In 1949 *G-Men* was reissued with a tacked-on prologue, explaining how the film instructs new recruits on the mechanics and craft of tracking down criminals. It was certainly a forerunner of the semi-documentary crime thrillers that dominated the genre in the late 1940s.

Even *Bullets or Ballots* reflects newspaper headlines, since it was adapted from the real-life exploits of journalist Martin Mooney. Somewhat reminiscent of the *March of Time* series is the opening which features the stentorian tones of a narrator, while the camera catches a spinning globe. Edward G. Robinson gives a hard-hitting portrayal of Mooney, and co-stars Joan Blondell, Humphrey Bogart, Frank McHugh, and Barton MacLane provide able support. Robinson's slow death is a particularly dramatic development in this production that features a "crisp, cohesive, and fast-moving script" (by Seton Miller), according to Nugent of the *Times*.

Stars Over Broadway (1935) and *The Green Pastures* (1936) are Bill's somewhat unusual contribtuions to Warner Brothers' musical cycle. The first film, co-directed by Busby Berkeley, was awarded three stars by the New York *Daily News*. This frequently funny parody of grand opera stars Pat O'Brien, Jane Froman, Jean Muir, Frank Fay, and Marie Wilson. *The Green Pastures,* co-directed by Marc Connelly, from Connelly's own theatre fantasy of the black view of the Bible, is a classic if occasionally embarrassing film. In its day, *Variety* labeled it "a simple, enchanting, audience-captivating cinematic fable." *The Green Pastures* did provide black actor Rex Ingram with one of his few excellent cinema roles, and it skillfully merges wood-and-paint theatrical backgrounds with lush outdoor scenes.

After achieving a solid track record with critics and audiences, Keighley was awarded direction of *The Prince and the Pauper* (1937), the studio's adaptation of Mark Twain's tale of two look-alike boys who switch lives in sixteenth-century England. "I worked with the screen's two most unusual actors in that production," said Keighley in recounting how he directed the 12-year-old twins Billy and Bobby Mauch. "It gave me the uncanny feeling of seeing double when I directed them."

The Warner Brothers production crew did a fine job recreating the England of the Middle Ages, and although Keighley himself only termed the film "all right," *The Prince and the Pauper* was well received. "The novel and the screen have been bridged so gracefully we cannot resist saying that Twain and the movies have met," joked Frank Nugent of the *Times*. Barnes of the *Tribune* commended Keighley's "handsome treatment" of the subject.

As is customary for a Warner Brothers production, the fine period film manages to explore the plight of the poor as it entertains. Director Keighley never lets the script languish in cynicism or sadness, but retains the playful spirit of Mark Twain and puts on celluloid the great writer's caustic, penetrating wit.

Bill was particularly successful in pulling believable performances from the Mauch twins. His sense of humor and easy-going style camouflaged a consummate professional who knew how to motivate performers as well as the camera. Keighley reportedly never raised his voice on the set. "It would be embarrassing if anybody but the actors heard me," he explained. Instead he often calmed a situation by replying to questions in French, bewildering his associates before translating in English. Whenever a scene was being shot, Keighley isolated himself from everything but the action in front of the lights, crouching somewhere near the camera, whispering the lines with the actors.

Bill Keighley started directing *The Adventures of Robin Hood* in 1938. It was the studio's most expensive production up to that time, and cameramen shot much of the film on location in the new three-color outdoor technique. The cameras featured three rolls of film, one each in red, blue, and yellow, and were so expensive that they had to be rented at high fees from the Technicolor people. After eight weeks of shooting, producer Henry Blanke decided that Keighley's approach to the English legend was too light, so Michael Curtiz took over the direction, reshot much of Bill's footage, and finished the film.

Although removed from *Robin Hood*, Keighley remained a favorite at Warner Brothers, and he continued directing well-liked productions. He seemed to be tuned in to the taste of the public—and Jack Warner loved that wavelength. The mogul paid Bill $1,750 a week to remain at the studio. In the late 1930s the director asserted that he would rather "serve the great masses who actually do know good entertainment when they get it." Ironically, Keighley didn't look much like one of the masses in his dapper, expensive wardrobe that inspired James Silke (in *Here's Looking at You, Kid*) to describe him as a "cut-out of a Lord and Taylor ad." The slightly chunky director of average height, soft features, and thinning hairline even maintained a sophisticated look on location for *The Adventures of Robin Hood* in his elegant brown shirt, matching pants, and sharp hip boots.

Keighley continued to entertain the public with *Brother Rat* (1938), *Each Dawn I Die* (1939), *The Fighting 69th, Torrid Zone, No Time for Comedy* (all 1940), *Four Mothers, The Bride Came C.O.D.* (both 1941), *The Man Who Came to Dinner*, and *George Washington Slept Here* (both 1942). These films represent the apex of the director's career. He switched from comedy to action drama with a facile hand, only slipping slightly in *Four Mothers* and *The Bride Came C.O.D.*

Brother Rat, based on the smash stage show, stars Ronald Reagan, Priscilla Lane, Jane Wyman, and Wayne Morris and introduces Eddie Albert in a comedy set at the Virginia Military Institute. It's a little creaky today, but still enjoyable. *Brother Rat* inspired a sequel, *Brother Rat and the Baby*, and was remade in 1950 as *About Face*.

Each Dawn I Die benefits from Keighley's refusal to surrender to the melodramatic turns in an improbable plot. James Cagney plays a reporter sent to prison on a frame-up. He eventually escapes with the help of a convict (George Raft), a character who reforms, yet the picture avoids the usual sentimental gestures in favor of the movement of action. The shoot-out at the prison is patterned somewhat after the large gun battle in *G-Men* and is equally brutal. Cagney's emoting is at its height in the scene where the prison conditions wear him down to the point of nervous collapse. The scene is a prophecy of the searing headaches that the actor brilliantly evokes as psychotic Cody Jarrett in *White Heat* (1949). "I'm gonna get outta here if I have to kill every screw in the joint," screams wrongly convicted Cagney to the warden.

The Fighting 69th is a solid tribute to that World War I battalion, and the film overcomes a hackneyed though action-filled script through en-

Russell Hopton, James Cagney, Edward Pawley, and Barton Maclane in G-Men *(WB, 1935)*

Rex Ingram in The Green Pastures *(WB, 1936)*

*Ann Sheridan,
James Cagney,
and Helen Vinson
in* Torrid Zone
(WB, 1940)

*Harry Cording,
James Cagney,
Jane Bryan,
Louis Jean
Heydt, and
John Ridgely
in* Each Dawn I
Die *(WB, 1939)*

thusiastic performances by all, including James Cagney, Pat O'Brien, and the Warner Brothers stock company. Particularly memorable is the final battle sequence in which O'Brien (playing a priest, of course) stirs Cagney into rejoining his troops. As the bombs blast, shaking the foundation of the rebellious soldier's lonely prison cell, with dirt flying through the air in clumps, the priest extols the hard, dirty but glorious task of warring for one's country. Cagney ultimately picks through the wreckage and once more becomes a member of the fighting group. The film succeeds because Keighley and the writers keep the rhetoric within the framework of the action. Consequently, *The Fighting 69th* proved to be a stirring call to proclaim love for country at a time when America was deeply divided about the world crisis.

Torrid Zone is one of the top hard-boiled comedy dramas of pre-war Hollywood. The film is set in a South American locale (a realistically designed studio backlot) replete with banana plantations, jungles, a steamy seaport, bugs, white suits, sweat, wisecracks, violence, and week-old beards. The sparkling Richard Macaulay-Jerry Wald script revolves around the Baldwin Fruit Company operated by Steve Case (Pat O'Brien), run by Nick Butler (James Cagney), disrupted by singer Lee Donley (Ann Sheridan), and pillaged by the bandit Rosario (George Tobias).

Rarely in Hollywood history has dialogue jumped so much as in the Mark Hellinger-produced celluloid dynamo. Snappy patter streams from the tongues of Cagney, O'Brien, Sheridan, Tobias, and Helen Vinson (wife of a Baldwin employee and former flame of Cagney). It took Keighley forty-one days to film a script loaded with verbal jewels. Upon Sheridan's arrival at the plantation (after O'Brien tries to throw her out of the country as an undesirable alien), Vinson disdainfully promises to help find her lodging at the plantation house. "Don't strain yourself," cracks Sheridan. "I can always sleep in a tree." "Heredity," retorts Vinson. Then she indicates a rather "cozy" room: "I'm sorry, this is the best we can do. We're very cramped." "I wouldn't be surprised," says Sheridan.

As if in Hecht-MacArthur terrain, *Torrid Zone* deftly blends the comic and the deadly serious, particularly visible in the character of bandito Rosario. Just the casting of funny player Tobias indicates Keighley's light touch. The early jail scenes featuring the blossoming friendship of Lee and Rosario are typical. They play cards together, joke, and perspire as one. She is touched when he escapes the firing squad, shouting: "Hurray for our side." The talkative not-so-bad guy leaves her a ring in remembrance of their chance meeting.

"Many people thought the teaming of James Cagney, Pat O'Brien, and Ann Sheridan was ample justification for entitling this picture *Torrid*

Zone," reported the *Brooklyn Daily Eagle*. "But the title comes from the locale of the production, rather than from the fiery quality of the stars." *Variety* labeled the production "fast-moving entertainment."

"A lively and wistful comedy for which everyone should do well to find the time," wrote the *New York Times'* Bosley Crowther of *No Time for Comedy*, starring James Stewart, Rosalind Russell, and Bill's wife Genevieve Tobin. The film is a bit stagey compared to other studio offerings of the period, but the sparring between Stewart and Russell remains effective, as does the constantly moving narrative.

The Bride Came C.O.D. is extremely reminiscent of Frank Capra's *It Happened One Night* (1934). Keighley and company create a workman-like version of the earlier classic, this time starring James Cagney as a pilot who kidnaps an heiress (Bette Davis) at her father's request, only to fall in love with the spoiled girl himself. The film is loosely structured, hanging together for an excessive time on a thin string from which numerous unrelated bits dangle like charms, some tantalizing, others not. The unattached moments are often funny, and very American, but nevertheless they serve to mire the narrative in irrelevance. The best line in the film comes during the scene in which Cagney convinces his captive that there are no signs of new faces, food, or rescue. After having a nice sandwich on the sly, he tenderly kisses her lips. Davis stops mid-smooch and screams, "Mustard!"*

Although *The Man Who Came to Dinner* earned a spot on *Film Daily*'s Ten Best list, it received widely mixed notices. "In direction, it is often a case of overemphasis," carped Otis Ferguson in the *New Republic*—"big takes, exaggeration, confusion, too much noise." On the positive side, the *Times'* Bosley Crowther called *The Man Who Came to Dinner* "the niftiest comedy of the year . . . the most vicious but hilarious cat-clawing exhibition ever put on screen."

Monte Woolley is undeniably brilliant as the famous author who must live with an Ohio family. Ann Sheridan, Jimmy Durante, Billie Burke, and others are marvelous too, but Bette Davis seems wasted in this Warner Brothers adaptation of the hit play by George S. Kaufman and Moss Hart.

George Washington Slept Here was Keighley's last Hollywood film until *Honeymoon* in 1947. A modest tale of a city couple who buy a home, it was embellished by Bill with his insight into folksy people and their particular brand of humor.

The Keighleys took a rather dangerous world tour in 1939, and were in

---

*Asked recently about the film, the star retorted, "Who directed *The Bride Came C.O.D.?* An awful film, a dreadful man."

217

Mexico when the Japanese bombed Pearl Harbor on December 7, 1941. Shortly before the war, Bill was involved in a number of projects that were never produced, or at least not with his name on them. He started directing *Captains of the Clouds*, which would have been his seventh film with James Cagney, but left in favor of Michael Curtiz. Among others, Warner Brothers discussed the shelved properties *Iron Cavalry* (again with Cagney) and *For the Rich They Sing* with the director, but nothing developed. Somewhat compensating for those disappointments was his appointment as a Professor of Cinema at the University of Southern California in 1940.

In 1942 Keighley enlisted in the Air Force with the rank of lieutenant colonel, serving in the motion picture division until 1945 and rising to the rank of full colonel. One of his tasks was creating simulated bomber raids for the benefit of American fliers. Bill also made a full-length documentary on the Eighth Air Force bomber command, called *Target for Today*, that was seen stateside in the *March of Time* series. *Target for Today* had the distinction of being the first film chosen by the U.S. Archives for its library.

After the war, Bill became the director and host of CBS' *Lux Radio Theatre*, replacing Cecil B. DeMille. *Newsweek* commented that Keighley "has the poised dignity that was a great DeMille asset."

William Keighley directed only five more films. *The Street with No Name* (20th, 1948) and *The Master of Ballantre* (WB, 1953) are the best of the group. Unlike many fellow Warner Brothers contractees, Keighley finished his career with the studio which gave him his first chance to direct motion pictures.

The Street with No Name is a solid example of the gritty, semidocumentary style that the crime film embraced after the war. The production, based on an actual FBI case regarding the uncovering of the leader of an urban mob, benefits greatly from sympathetic performances by many of the supporting players, as well as from a subdued approach to details of government investigation. Unlike such movies as *The House on 92nd Street* or *He Walked by Night*, Keighley's *film noir* doesn't treat the routine of law enforcement in a monolithic manner. His people are something more than cogs in a well-oiled machine.

The Master of Ballantre is virtually the last hurrah for the Warner Brothers swashbuckler. Adapted from Robert Louis Stevenson's story, the film stars Errol Flynn as a member of the Scottish royalty pulled into a plot to have Bonnie Prince Charlie rule Great Britain. On-location production in England adds much color to the commendable 89-minute costume drama.

"With plenty of good, old-fashioned muscularity crowding a highly pictorial Technicolor frame, at least three-fourths of *The Master of Bal-*

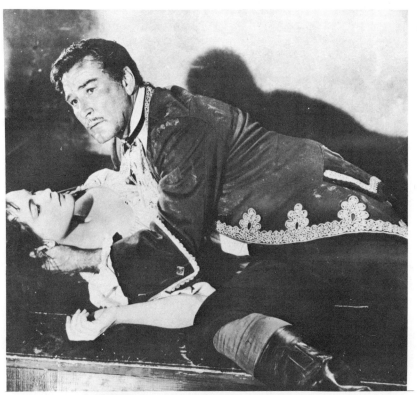

Yvonne Furneaux and Errol Flynn in The Master of Ballantre *(WB, 1953)*

Mark Stevens, John McIntire, and Lloyd Nolan in The Street with No Name *(20th, 1948)*

lantre makes a rousing, spectacular outlet for a pair of estimable adventurers," wrote Howard Thompson in the *New York Times*.

Based on *The Master of Ballantre*, it can be assumed that Keighley could have directed some of the Warner Brothers adventures of the 1930s and 1940s with a uniquely light, distinguished hand, thus providing a fine contrast for Michael Curtiz's lusty pictorialism.

Shortly after *The Master of Ballantre* was completed, Keighley left Hollywood. In 1957 he and his wife journeyed to Paris to study at the Sorbonne. They both vowed not to speak English for a full year, and with Bill's fluent French, the promise was assuredly kept.

Throughout the years the Keighleys lived in various hotels as well as homes in Europe and New York. Once a friend asked him, "With your money, why don't you live in a house?" Bill smiled and raised his hand. "Because of these three buttons," he replied, pointing to buzzers for a waiter, maid, and porter.

The films of William Keighley are marked with a light, good natured, witty touch that has occasionally caused him to be called an American Lubitsch. Keighley often managed to expose the underside of even his toughest characters and situations without sinking to melodramatics or bizarre motivations.

The Films of William Keighley

The Match King *(FN, 1932) (co-directed by Howard Bretherton)*

Ladies They Talk About *(WB, 1933) (co-directed by Howard Bretherton)*

Easy to Love *(WB, 1934)*

Journal of a Crime *(FN, 1934)*

Dr. Monica *(WB, 1934)*

Big-Hearted Herbert *(WB, 1934)*

Kansas City Princess *(WB, 1934)*

Babbitt *(FN, 1934)*

The Right to Live *(WB, 1935)*

G-Men *(WB, 1935)*

Mary Jane's Pa *(FN, 1935)*

Special Agent *(WB, 1935)*

Stars Over Broadway *(WB, 1935) (choreographed by Busby Berkeley)*

The Singing Kid *(FN, 1936)*

The Green Pastures *(WB, 1936) (co-directed by Marc Connelly)*

Bullets or Ballots *(FN, 1936)*

God's Country and the Woman *(WB, 1936)*

The Prince and the Pauper *(WB, 1937)*

Varsity Show *(WB, 1937) (choreographed by Busby Berkeley)*

The Adventures of Robin Hood *(WB, 1938) (replaced by Michael Curtiz)*

Valley of the Giants *(WB, 1938)*

The Secrets of an Actress *(WB, 1938)*

Brother Rat *(WB, 1938)*

Yes, My Darling Daughter *(WB, 1939)*

Each Dawn I Die *(WB, 1939)*

The Fighting 69th *(WB, 1940)*

Torrid Zone *(WB, 1940)*

No Time for Comedy *(WB, 1940)*

Four Mothers *(WB, 1941)*

The Bride Came C.O.D. *(WB, 1941)*

Captains of the Clouds *(WB, 1941) (replaced by Michael Curtiz)*

The Man Who Came to Dinner *(WB, 1942)*

George Washington Slept Here *(WB, 1942)*

Target for Today *(documentary, 1945)*

Honeymoon *(RKO, 1947)*

The Street with No Name *(20th, 1948)*

Rocky Mountain *(WB, 1950)*

Close to My Heart *(WB, 1951) (and script)*

The Master of Ballantre *(WB, 1953)*

13

Mervyn LeRoy

"Don't improve the story into a flop," advised Mervyn LeRoy whenever an eager writer, producer, or director sought to tamper with the very qualities in a novel, play, or story which made it cinematic material in the first place. LeRoy knew what he was talking about. Out of seventy-five films directed over the past half-century, not one was a complete artistic and popular failure. "No, I never had a real flop," he wrote in his autobiography. "I've had a few that I didn't particularly like and that didn't make too much money, and quite a few that the critics didn't like. There has never been one, however, that the public hated enough so that it lost money."

Perhaps the director himself best explains a talent for producing films with mass appeal alongside enduring social classics like *Little Caesar, I Am a Fugitive from a Chain Gang*, and *They Won't Forget.* "I saw life in the raw [as a boy] in the streets of San Francisco. I met the cops and the whores and the reporters and the bartenders and the Chinese and the fishermen and the shopkeepers. I knew them all, knew how they thought and how they loved and how they hated. When it came time for me to make motion pictures, I made movies that were real, because I knew at first hand how people behaved." That encompassed a wide variety of people, most of whom constantly turned up in Warner Brothers films of the 1930s and 1940s.

Mervyn LeRoy was born on October 15, 1900, the son of Edna and Harry LeRoy of San Francisco. The elder LeRoy ran a successful department store called "The Fair," and his mother maintained a love for vaudeville. Looking back on his parents, Mervyn wrote: "I inherited a love of show business from my mother and an outgoing personality from my father." That outgoing personality was an aggressive business personality, it might be added. The combination of qualities allowed him to take advantage of many theatrical and film offers in his younger days which catapulted him to a $1,000 a week job as director at the age of 28.

Ironically, one of LeRoy's most significant early influences was the San Francisco earthquake. On the morning of April 18, 1906 Mervyn was sleeping in his father's solid stone house on 62 Geary Street when his whole world literally began collapsing. Harry LeRoy grabbed his son, and together the pair pushed past the rubble which minutes earlier had been their home. Later in the day Mr. LeRoy found his store all over the ground, indistinguishable from crumpled neighboring structures. If "The Fair" had continued to prosper, Mervyn reasoned that he probably would have gone into the business and never let his interest in vaudeville and theatre grow beyond the boundaries of the amateur production.

The years 1905-06 were not happy ones for either male LeRoy, for aside from the tragedy of the earthquake, Edna LeRoy had left her husband the year before in order to live with a San Francisco newspaperman named Percy Temple. By 1912 Mervyn decided to supplement his father's income by selling newspapers. Although he had made his stage "debut" at the age of six months in a West Coast production of *The Squaw Man* (by being in the right place at the right time with his mother) and had spent several enjoyable weeks in 1910 making a "photoplay" of Jules Verne's *Twenty Thousand Leagues under the Sea* with friends, he had no intention of carving a career in show business—until about 1914, that is.

Mervyn sold papers near the Alcazar Theatre in San Francisco. One evening Theodore Roberts, an actor who would shortly become one of the first cinema stars, passed by the newsboy, and on an impulse he offered Mervyn a job in a new play he was rehearsing called *Barbara Frietchie*. Hired at $3.50 a week, the teenager thought that the notion was absurd—and even more so after his salary was raised to $5.00 a week when he fell out of a tree. It was all by accident, of course. The young actor was supposed to speak his line from a branch, and one night he simply toppled out of the tree. The audience roared, and the stage manager offered him a raise if he agreed to take the tumble every night.

After the play closed, Mervyn resumed his paper-selling career, but he couldn't eliminate his memories of the theatre, the acting, the audiences, and the generous salaries. Nor did selling papers help, for he would frequently come upon Charlie Chaplin filming one of his early comedy shorts. Since the productions were extremely economical, the Little Tramp could often be spotted bewildering people in public with his cinema antics. Mervyn even started to imitate Chaplin in front of a mirror, and soon he was entering talent contests in local theatres. He then formed an act, featuring himself as "The Singing Newsboy." His show stopper was "'Twas Only an Irishman's Dream," which he sang without benefit of an Irish costume.

After his father's death in 1915, Mervyn moved to Oakland to live with his mother and stepfather, but in 1916 the restless young man met another amateur talent called Clyde Cooper. Cooper played the piano, and they decided to team up. Calling themselves "Two Kids and a Piano," the pair played vaudeville circuits for several years. The act broke up when Cooper's father died and Clyde returned to San Francisco to run the family motel.

LeRoy remained in vaudeville until the early 1920s, finally quitting his troupe in New York City when success seemed to be nothing but an elusive dream. However, in the LeRoy tradition, this misfortune became very fortunate indeed. Sitting around the National Vaudeville Artists Club with other unemployed performers, LeRoy claims to have been chosen for a role in the serial *The Perils of Pauline*. If the director's memory of the basic time (1920s) is correct, he is mistaken about the serial, which was shot in 1914.

In any case, at one point in his life he participated in the filming of a daredevil action film possibly starring Pearl White. "As I waited for my scene, that day in Fort Lee," he later wrote, "I watched them making *The Perils of Pauline*, and it was thoroughly intriguing. The idea of motion pictures as a career, that idea that had been slowly growing in the back of my mind, surfaced that day." The problem was breaking in on more solid footing than a day's work as an actor. He thought of his cousin, Jesse Lasky, who with a glove salesman named Sam Goldfish (later changed to Goldwyn) had started the Jesse L. Lasky Feature Play Company, with the help of 32-year-old Cecil B. DeMille, then an unsuccessful playwright. Under Lasky's aegis, DeMille started shooting one of the earliest feature films in Hollywood, *The Squaw Man*, on December 29, 1913.

A decade later, when Mervyn decided to make the cinema his career, Lasky's company had become Famous Players-Lasky, after a merger with Adolph Zukor's Famous Players. The young ex-vaudevillian entered his cousin's Manhattan office and asked for a job in Hollywood. Lasky wrote a name on a piece of paper, and Mervyn LeRoy was on his way. He arrived in the fall of 1923 and started work in the wardrobe department of Famous Players. Soon tiring of the ignoble position, and afraid that he'd never get to be a movie director, Mervyn talked Lasky into getting him a position in the lab.

For months he dipped film into various dyes, getting so "colorful" that his friends took to quipping "Here comes the rainbow" when young

LeRoy came their way. Yet the position led to the director's chair, in a way. One day director William DeMille was discussing a problem with two lab supervisors. The older brother of Cecil B. couldn't get moonlight to reflect properly on water. That night Mervyn stayed late. "Somewhere, I got a big wooden box about twelve feet square, painted the inside black, and lined it with tar paper. Then I filled it with distilled water from Jesse's office—he only drank distilled water. I got a spotlight and carefully set it up so its lights played along the surface of the water in the box. I took one of the studio's Pathé cameras, found a supply of raw film, and shot some five thousand feet of my pseudo-moonlight-on-the-water."

For that bit of ingenuity, Mervyn was promoted to assistant cameraman. As he recalled in his autobiography *Mervyn LeRoy: Take One* (Hawthorn Books): "All I can remember of my days as an assistant cameraman is aching legs and back and arms, and cut and bleeding shoulders from where the tripod dug into my flesh as I lugged it around." LeRoy's endurance was more than rewarded when he was assigned to direct First National's *Peg o' My Heart,* to star his new friend, Colleen Moore. However, due to problems with the star and her movie executive husband John McCormick, the project was canceled.

In 1927 Mervyn LeRoy directed *No Place to Go* for First National. Finding the property himself in the stacks of materials that the ambitious young man always read, Mervyn threw himself into the production of the film. The director told me recently, "I always worked with the writers on the scripts, although I never wrote the scripts myself. You cannot start a motion picture without having it first on paper. After all, Shakespeare agrees with me—the play is the thing." Although LeRoy is modest about his debut as a director, he did say, "It wasn't particularly original but it had an honest situation (a bickering married couple), characters who were real and believable, and, most important, a quality I always strove for in my films—the quality that goes by the corny descriptive name of 'heart.' Heart is difficult to define, but the audience knows when it's there and misses it when it's not. *No Place to Go* had it."

Harold Teen (First National, 1928) was LeRoy's first hit as director. Arthur Lake and Alice White star in this dated tale of teenage amors. Along with the title character, LeRoy had problems with his female star: "She was hard to direct, primarily because she was never much of an actress. Somehow, I was able to get pretty good work out of her." That "somehow" was a reflection of Mervyn's early experience with many types of people. The director could adapt his handling of actors to suit a certain situation and take advantage of deficiencies or mistakes, as he did notably in *I Am a Fugitive from a Chain Gang.*

226

Critics weren't ecstatic about *Harold Teen*, as exemplified by the *New York Times* reviewer who philosophized that the production "may not be a feature of any depth or one to stimulate higher minds, but, curiously enough, it is far from disappointing."

The critique may very well hold a clue to Mervyn LeRoy's longevity as a director. His films maintain a solid middle ground in the American cinema. There are no idealist biographical works, no propaganda films, and no "preaching," not even in his socially conscious films of the 1930s. "I made *I Am a Fugitive from a Chain Gang*," the director asserted, "because it was a great story. The same goes for *Little Caesar, Five Star Final*, and *They Won't Forget*."

By the end of 1928 Mervyn LeRoy was making $1,000 a week. He was, to put it mildly, wild about his professional *and* social life. Always known as a snappy dresser, Mervyn could be seen speeding along Hollywood streets in his roadster, perhaps with German starlet Marlene Dietrich or Betty Compson sitting close beside him.

And things were getting better! While America plunged into the Depression of 1929, LeRoy busied himself with four First National Productions, *Naughty Baby* (his first sound film), *Hot Stuff* (with newcomer James Cagney), *Little Johhny Jones*, and *Broadway Babies* (a gangster melodrama with a pre-Berkeley, unpretentiously effective musical background).

Little Caesar came shortly thereafter and proved to be the turning point in LeRoy's career. A voluminous reader, he eagerly agreed when Jack Warner suggested that he study a manuscript submitted by W. R. Burnett. The director had a dinner date that night, but by the next morning he had finished Burnett's tough, unrelenting, and spare tale of the rise and fall of gangster Caesar Enrico Bandello. He was determined to film it, but Jack Warner didn't share LeRoy's enthusiasm, and other people on the lot were similarly unimpressed.

In addition, there was a conflict within the studio over what was the proper screen fare for bankrupt audiences. There were those who spoke of escapism, citing that current American life was too sad to film, and certainly not box-office. Others, including Jack Warner's associate Darryl F. Zanuck, felt that the time was right for a change from the romanticism of the silent screen. They wanted a new image to fit the new talking image.

Someone finally convinced Jack Warner to buy the property. Hal Wallis was assigned to produce the film, with LeRoy directing. It was agreed that experienced stage actor Edward G. Robinson should play the title role, and he accepted without hesitation. Warner contractee Glenda Farrell won the part of the gun moll. The character of dancer Joe Masara proved difficult to cast. Warner favored Douglas Fairbanks,

Jr., but LeRoy thought that the son of the cinema swashbuckler was too sophisticated for the part of a boy who emerges from the gutter along with Rico. The director finally thought he had found his Masara one night at the Majestic Theatre in Los Angeles, acting in a play called *The Last Mile*. It was Clark Gable.

Tested for the role, Gable was found unsuitable by Warner and Zanuck. Enraged, Zanuck shouted at LeRoy: "What the hell have you done, Mervyn? I'll tell you what you've done—you've just thrown away five hundred bucks on a test. Didn't you see the size of that guy's ears?" That ended the discussion, and soon after Gable became a star at MGM.

The unqualified success of *Little Caesar* lifted LeRoy's salary by $1,000 a week, but the director had earned it. He became involved with the production day and night, as the script was rewritten several times. Both LeRoy and Robinson agreed that the film should be faithful to the book, focusing on Bandello's character, his success, and his ultimate failure, and not on sheer violence. The project cost $700,000, ten times the budget of LeRoy's directorial debut with *No Place to Go*.

To this day, the director believes that Chicago mobsters sent observers to report back on the filming of *Little Caesar*. (The gangsters had good reason to worry, since the Warner Brothers exposés of criminal methods in a series of films led to the end of more than one gangland overlord's career.) Anyone unnerved by the presence of real-life gunmen may have been calmed by Mervyn's sense of humor and his ability to cope with any problem. Less critical in real life but crucial to the success of *Little Caesar* was Edward G. Robinson's ability to make audiences believe him as Bandello. A triggerman who blinks every time he fires a gun isn't likely to arouse much fear, yet the extremely gentle actor couldn't break himself of the habit, and neither could his director. LeRoy finally solved the problem when he would tape Robinson's eyelids open before filming the actor shooting a gun. Consequently Robinson's Caesar is consistently terrifying and fearless until his timely end.

As was the case with the soon to be produced *Public Enemy*, *Little Caesar* hypnotized audiences with subtly-evoked violence. A shadow or other symbol of death is much more effective than a falling body. One such instance is accomplished with but two shots and a bit of dialogue. Bandello admires a fellow mobster's diamond stickpin and snorts, "That's a nice pin. I'm gonna have one like it some day." The next shot is of the pin, but the camera pulls back to reveal it being worn by Rico.

Little Caesar was received enthusiastically by the critics, and it electrified audiences. In the *New York Times* Mordaunt Hall wrote that the film "would rank as just one more gangster film except for two things. One is the excellence of Mr. Burnett's credible and compact story. The other is Edward G. Robinson's wonderfully effective performance." Years later film historian Lewis Jacobs put LeRoy's classic gangster film in perspective: "*Little Caesar* realistically and uncompromisingly depicted the rise and fall of the egoist through aggressiveness, ruthlessness, and organized large-scale racketeering."

Continuing in the new Warner Brothers mold of filming socially conscious, hard-hitting action dramas, LeRoy directed an exposé of yellow journalism entitled *Five Star Final* (1931). The screenplay by Byron Morgan and Robert Lord is based on the autobiographical play by Louis Weitzenkorn, and the successful pairing of Mervyn LeRoy and Edward G. Robinson continued in the topical story. Robinson is the editor of a sensationalist rag who at first goes along with his bosses' idea to reprint the particulars of an old murder as a publicity stunt. The tragic complications which arise contain the film's only maudlin sequences. At this point, editor Robinson turns from wrecking human lives to write a searing attack on journalists who seek to exploit the public.

Named as one of the Ten Best of the year by *Film Daily, Five Star Final* was nominated for an Academy Award and benefited from excellent worldwide reviews. The *London Times* called the production "even better than most of its type," and there was a deluge of newspaper movies after the success of *The Front Page* in 1931. *Variety* insisted that *Five Star Final* had "all the elements to make a hit attraction."

If there has to be only one film that Mervyn LeRoy is remembered for, it should be *I Am a Fugitive from a Chain Gang*. This classic production of a man on the run from the law, but not from justice, is another story that Warner Brothers took from the daily journals. In this case, the film made quite a few blockbusting headlines of its own.

An escaped convict named Robert Burns brought Warner Brothers a story co-authored with his clergyman brother in order to stir up support for his case. The tale of life on a Georgia chain gang was harsh and uncompromising, but totally realistic, and it was exactly what Jack Warner wanted. Playwright Sheridan Gibney spent many nervous hours with escapee Burns fashioning a screenplay from the story. The man had already broken out of prison once, and he had been dragged back in chains. Now, after several years of hiding out, Burns had learned to look for his pursuers at every sudden noise that sounded like a police siren or gunshot. Once he grabbed his hat and ran into the street upon hearing a loud siren. The sharp sound had come from the next lot, where a crime film was in production. It was a nervous time for Gibney and everyone else at the studio, since Burns was terrified at the thought of any publicity of his stay in Hollywood reaching the Georgia prison, even though he couldn't be legally extradited from California.

With the script completed, LeRoy was assigned to direct, and Paul Muni was chosen to star as Burns, renamed Jim Allen. Again Mervyn illustrated the brutal core of his story without shooting large doses of graphic violence. When a convict is whipped, the main sound heard is that of screaming, while the images portrayed are the shadow of a whip thrashing a back and the men's horrified faces. When Jim Allen persuades a muscular black inmate to smash his leg irons with a sledge hammer, the main sound heard is that of the chains cracking, while the images portrayed are the descending hammer and the agony on Muni's face.

In this film LeRoy took advantage of one of the major flukes in the history of American film production. Sheridan Gibney's final scene is between Allen, who has become a dirty, ragged drifter, and his girlfriend. Shot in an alley in downtown Los Angeles, the girl asks a nervous Allen, "How do you live?" He replies pathetically, but with a hint of cunning, "I steal." As the lines are spoken, the screen grows gradually darker, and the image becomes black at Muni's answer—the result of a fuse blowing out on a klieg light. "It was an accident," LeRoy later wrote, "but I immediately recognized it as an accident that worked. ... Eventually, after some experimentation, I decided that a sudden blackout wasn't as effective as a gradual dimming of the lights, and that's the way it was done."

The way Mervyn LeRoy did it made screen history, and *I Am a Fugitive from a Chain Gang* won rave reviews and a host of awards. *Film Daily* named the exposé of prison conditions among the best efforts of the year. It drew, along with another studio production, *42nd Street*, ballots as best picture in Academy Award polling, and Paul Muni was considered for an Oscar for his harrowing portrayal of escaped convict Jim Allen.

Film critics were full of praise. "It is a motion picture which not only approaches greatness but captures greatness without a struggle," wrote a reviewer in the *Brooklyn Daily Eagle*. In its usual taut way, *Variety* deemed the film "a picture with guts," and the *New York Sun*'s John S. Cohen, Jr. praised the "tragic and powerful tale of a man unjustly sent to the chain gang of a southern state."

That particular southern state, Georgia, was uniformly displeased with *I Am a Fugitive from a Chain Gang* and anyone connected with the production. The Warner brothers and LeRoy were warned not to cross the boundaries into Georgia, and the studio was slapped with a libel suit by the state. In addition, two of Georgia's prison wardens instituted court actions of their own for various sums up to a million dollars.

Even Reverend Vincent G. Burns became embroiled in American jurisprudence over *I Am a Fugitive from a Chain Gang*. In 1938 he sued his brother Robert for claiming all the money received from the original story of the production.

Robert Burns officially stayed a fugitive until 1945 when the state of Georgia erased his crime from the books. However, he died in 1955 without having received a pardon because he had admitted his guilt.

However ironic the fate of the subject and co-author of *I Am a Fugitive from a Chain Gang*, the film forced Georgia officials to remove the chains from their prisoners, and widespread reform was initiated. Thus the cinema as social document had truly triumphed, and in this case it had told a good story as well.

The next year Mervyn switched to a lighter subject for his next major production, *Gold Diggers of 1933*. His instinct told him that it was time for a variation on the many steamy, topical action dramas that Warner Brothers had been turning out at a factory rate. With choreographer Busby Berkeley, LeRoy created a snappy successor to Lloyd Bacon's and Berkeley's *42nd Street*. One of the production numbers of LeRoy's musical, the "Forgotten Man" sequence, is a brilliant surrealistic view of the Depression in the world of the Jim Allens, the men and women whom the well-to-do did not want to see. Writing in the *New York Times*, Mordaunt Hall applauded the "imaginatively staged and breezy show ... the excellent camera work and artistry of the scenic effects."

Changing his stride a bit more from topical films, LeRoy talked Jack Warner into letting him direct Hervey Allen's hefty best-seller, *Anthony Adverse*. This rambling tale of the education of the title character contained LeRoy's first battle with the censors. The Joseph Breen Office, which received copies of all scripts under the new Will Hays Morality Code, eliminated forty pages from the original adaptation. One of those scenes contained a naked boy, but the director appeased them by filming the child in an extreme long shot.

Although it was felt that *Anthony Adverse* might offend the Catholic Church, the Breen Office allowed LeRoy the privilege of shooting the film his own way, with the understanding that any material deemed unviewable would be scissored out. When the director screened the film for Joe Breen, the tension was almost unbearable, but *Anthony Adverse* passed the test. It was nominated for an Oscar as best picture of the year, and even the Catholic Church loved it.

However, the critics weren't as pleased. Frank S. Nugent of the *New York Times* called the film version of the 1,224-page novel "a bulky, rambling, and indecisive photoplay which has not merely taken liberties with the letter of the original but with its spirit." Howard Barnes was kinder in the *New York Herald-Tribune*. He called the film

Edward G. Robinson and Joan Blondell in Five Star Final *(First National, 1931)*

Paul Muni and Noel Francis in I Am a Fugitive from a Chain Gang *(WB, 1932)*

Robert Taylor and Vivian Leigh in a publicity pose for Waterloo Bridge *(MGM, 1940)*

Claude Rains and E. Alyn Warren in They Won't Forget *(WB, 1937)*

starring Fredric March and Olivia de Havilland "colossal." "What dramatic unity the screen *Anthony Adverse* has," Barnes continued, "is derived from the crafty but not altogether effective reworking of the original story." However, the reviewer enjoyed LeRoy's "canny sense of pictorial values."

Early in 1936 Jack Warner asked LeRoy to read a novel by Ward Greene called *Drums in the Deep South*. A powerful story of a Jewish man unjustly lynched for the rape and murder of a teenage girl, it was based on the Leo Frank case of 1912, which was one of the few trials to end in the execution of a white man on the word of a black man.

LeRoy turned it into a spine-tingling exploration of the exploitation of the poor and oppressed by the powerful. His first step was to change the title of the book to *They Won't Forget*. Twenty-seven-year-old screenwriter Robert Rossen handed the director a brilliant script which had all the surging melodrama and very real characters that animated Green's book. Claude Rains plays the crafty prosecutor, supported by Edward Norris and Gloria Dickson as the victim and his wife. When a search was instigated for the small but pivotal role of the voluptuous teenage girl, LeRoy found 15-year-old Lana Turner on the studio lot wearing a modest blue cotton dress, and not in Schwab's drugstore as legend insists. Not wanting to have Turner become a star at another studio à la Gable, LeRoy signed her to a personal contract, and she only moved on to MGM when he went there.

They Won't Forget (1937) is perhaps the first and foremost Hollywood film about racism, and it contains one of the earliest evocations of a dignified black man on screen. In the role of the school janitor, who is the first to be accused of murdering the white girl, Clinton Roseman is properly fearful of white authority, but he nevertheless maintains his plea of innocence and implicates the Jewish school teacher.

Otis Ferguson of the *New Republic* capsulized liberal sentiment about *They Won't Forget* by writing: "In content and in uncompromising treatment this film is just the blood-and-guts sort of thing we've been hollering for." Nugent of the *Times* called LeRoy's classic "a brilliant sociological drama and a trenchant film editorial against intolerance and hatred." The *Tribune*'s Howard Barnes echoed the praise, asserting that the film was "a challenging indictment of bigotry and mob violence."

Like *I Am a Fugitive from a Chain Gang*, *They Won't Forget* ends on a heartbreaking note, this time extremely ironic. A reporter (Allyn Joslyn) asks the prosecutor (Rains), "Now that it's over, Andy, I wonder if he really did it." The prosecutor looks out his window and muses, "I wonder."

Toward the end of the 1930s Mervyn LeRoy started seriously thinking of moving from Warner Brothers to MGM. He was producing as well as directing films by then, and in fact had just produced *The Great Garrick* (1937) directed by James Whale. Earlier Louis B. Mayer had borrowed LeRoy's services to direct *Tugboat Annie* (1933) starring Marie Dressler and Wallace Beery, and he had been after Mervyn ever since to join Metro's roster of filmmakers, and later to take over the role left vacant by Irving Thalberg's death, that of supervisor of production. Unlike many of his contemporaries, for instance fellow director William Wellman, LeRoy liked the dictatorial Mayer. The two had a genuine feel for the sentimental in life to bind them together.

Mayer paid the director the then astronomical salary of $6,000 a week, twice the money doled out by the frugal Warner Brothers studio. Certainly the economic issue figured in LeRoy's switch, but two other factors may have been significant. First, although Warner Brothers was an enormously profitable organization by the late 1930s, as witnessed by expensive productions such as the Errol Flynn Westerns and swashbucklers directed by Michael Curtiz, the later biographies, and even the more modestly budgeted *They Won't Forget*, the brothers apparently remembered leaner days, and the salaries of men and women who made the movies weren't generally commensurate with those paid by other top studios. Second, MGM had a tradition of spending more time on its productions. A director with a string of successes the length of LeRoy's was in a position to demand the best possible conditions for motion picture production. True, the Warner Brothers budgets were getting better, but change had always meant growth in the career of Mervyn LeRoy.

Mayer put one condition on LeRoy's huge salary—it had to be kept secret. Even so, news that the director-producer was, in his words, "making more than anybody else in town had ever gotten" somehow spread all over Hollywood. Consequently the unhappy Mayer had to account for the salaries of all his top executives, as ordered by a suit initiated by Metro's parent company, Loew's.

For the first time in his life, Mervyn LeRoy felt really secure. He was able to buy a fine home for his mother and stepfather in Hollywood, and also to pursue a formerly forbidden interest in buying fine works of art.* Yet he wasn't happy. Mayer had plunked him behind a desk and expected him to stay there. About a year after he started to play executive at Metro, LeRoy asked to be allowed to direct again, even

---

*He had been married to Doris Warner (daughter of Harry) for three good years. They had a baby son, Warner, and daughter Linda arrived during that successful year of 1938.

235

offering to take a cut in salary. After some discussion, Louis B. sadly accepted Mervyn's desire to change from the executive suite to the director's chair.

During his short span as a major executive at MGM, LeRoy produced the classic *The Wizard of Oz*, directed by Victor Fleming. The film cost over $3,000,000 by the time it was finished in 1938. An entire town, consisting of one hundred and twenty-two buildings, was masterminded by Cedric Gibbons under LeRoy's supervision. The sixty-five sets would have spanned twenty-five acres of Metro's back lot if they had been erected all at once. "I'm very proud of *The Wizard of Oz*," the director said in his autobiography. "I think it will live long after I'm gone."

The first film Mervyn directed at MGM under his new contract was the fine *Waterloo Bridge* (1940), starring Robert Taylor and Vivien Leigh. Produced by another former director, Sydney Franklin, the film is based on Robert Sherwood's dewey-eyed play, adapted by Samuel Bierman. Since the locale of almost the entire film is foggy London, it was necessary to endure the unpleasant odor of the Metro substitute for mist. However the untouchable cloak served to hide suggestions of sets (shades of Warner Brothers) which would have had to be completed had they been in clear view.

One of the problems of Bierman's script involved a pivotal scene in a nightclub. It was well written, yet it didn't sound right on film, and no one could figure out why. "At four in the afternoon, after some hours of fruitless fiddling with the scene, I told everybody to go home," the director recalled. "I sat there, in that make-believe nightclub, with just one small light to give me illumination. Over and over, I read the scene, read the words that Sam, Sydney, and I had labored to get right. I was still there at two in the morning, when suddenly the answer came to me. 'No dialogue!' I said, aloud. 'No dialogue at all!'" That's how the scene was played. LeRoy starts with a long shot of Taylor and Leigh dancing to an orchestra playing "Auld Lang Syne." The camera then cuts to the orchestra, with each musician extinguishing a fire on the candle in front of him, then to a close-up of the lovers, and then back to the orchestra.

Bosley Crowther of the *New York Times* said that *Waterloo Bridge* "spans a dream-world of sentiment," adding: "Mervyn LeRoy has directed the picture with an emphasis on romantic close-ups, has given it ironic overtone through a tie-up at the beginning and end with the present-day in England and has provided one super sequence—a dance by the two lovers in the candlelit cabaret the night before his departure for the front—which will live in tender memory." Barnes of the *New York Herald-Tribune* felt that the production "has been staged with imagination and a fine feeling for mood by Mervyn LeRoy."

Next came *Blossoms in the Dust* (1941). Along with *I Am a Fugitive from a Chain Gang*, LeRoy feels that this Metro production accurately reflects how Americans look at the downtrodden. In the earlier film the subject was convicts; here it is orphans. Greer Garson, in the role of Mrs. Gladney, the head of a Texas home for homeless children, is teamed with Walter Pidgeon for the first time in this touching tale. From there the pair went on to make the unforgettable *Mrs. Miniver*.

Acknowledged to be a heart-render, *Blossoms in the Dust* was received cordially by critics. Bosley Crowther of the *Times* wrote, "As pure inspirational drama with a pleasant flavor of romance, *Blossoms in the Dust* should reach a great many hearts."

Perhaps LeRoy's greatest non-Warner Brothers film is the romantic *Random Harvest* (1942). This time Greer Garson acts with Ronald Colman and, according to the director, "between the two of them, the English language was never spoken more beautifully on film." Adapted from James Hilton's best seller, LeRoy's film so pleased the author that he insisted on speaking the narration which opened the production.

Critical reception to *Random Harvest* was mixed. The *New York Herald-Tribune* felt that it was "fascinating and sentimentally appealing," but James Agee of the *Nation* was blunt, as usual: "I would like ... to recommend *Random Harvest* to those who can stay interested in Ronald Colman's amnesia for two hours and who could with pleasure eat a bowl of Yardley's shaving soap for breakfast."

Despite unfriendly critiques, *Random Harvest* strikes one now as a poignant, and, yes, sentimental tale of the love between a man and a woman overcoming what is literally the greatest and most contrived of boundaries: one lover doesn't *recognize* the other. Adding to the acceptance of the situation are the sympathetic performances by the leads, along with LeRoy's subtle cinematography, full of little touches such as symbols of the passing of time—autumn leaves dissolving to winter snow framed through a window.

Since Warner Brothers did very few fine biographies in the 1940s, it was ironically appropriate that Mervyn LeRoy should direct the biographical *Blossoms in the Dust* in 1941, and then follow it up two years later with *Madame Curie*, the story of Eve and Pierre Curie, the discoverers of radium. LeRoy's romanticized biographical picture is among his personal favorites of the films he directed. According to the *Times'* Bosley Crowther, "The sweetness and light which sometimes creeps in is, indeed, the only excessive quality in a film which is generally exalting and a fine stimulation for the heart." On the other hand, the *Nation's* James Agee damned the production with faint praise: "*Madame Curie* enlists an unusual amount of competence, patience, and commercialized sincerity in the production, which rather saddens than angers or pleases me, of the screen equivalent to *Harper's* Prize 'literature': safe, smooth, respectable, an epitome of all that the bourgeois likes what he calls his art to be."

However, Agee was friendlier toward *Thirty Seconds Over Tokyo*, LeRoy's first war film, which was released by Metro in 1944. "*Thirty Seconds Over Tokyo* is in some respects the pleasantest of current surprises: a big-studio, big-scale film, free of artistic pretension, it is transformed by its not very imaginative but very dogged sincerity into something forceful, simple, and thoroughly sympathetic in spite of all its big-studio, big-scale habits."

Starring Van Johnson, Robert Walker, and Phyllis Thaxter, with an appearance by Spencer Tracy as General Jimmy Doolittle who masterminded the bombing raids over Japan, *Thirty Seconds Over Tokyo* benefits from LeRoy's meticulous concern with keeping his characters real. There may be a dash of heroics in the film, but mostly it's about the actions of young Air Force men in war. The most touching scene in the film takes place when a group of flyers crash-land in enemy territory. Their fear is immediate, and LeRoy ends the scene with the inexperienced warriors huddled in a mass, then pulls the camera back to frame their fright and tears.

In 1945 LeRoy moved to RKO to co-produce, with Frank Ross, an Academy Award-winning short called *The House I Live In*, starring Frank Sinatra. Directed by Axel Stordahl, this sentimental comment on the evils of prejudice capped LeRoy's career as a maker of social films.

After the war the film industry underwent mighty changes. New production heads replaced the old, television ushered in fresh, strong competition, and union demands skyrocketed. Government anti-trust suits soon broke MGM from its parent company, Loew's, and the studio never regained its former glory. Between 1946-48, not one Academy Award sat on Metro's mantlepiece, an unheard of phenomenon for a studio which had "more stars than there are in heaven." The early 1940s saw many MGM greats such as Greta Garbo, Norma Shearer, Jeanette MacDonald, Joan Crawford, and Rosalind Russell exit the gates of the studio where their star power was the brightest. In 1948 Dore Schary was appointed Vice-President in Charge of Production (essentially the position held by Thalberg, and briefly by LeRoy), and Louis B. Mayer was on his way to retirement.

Mervyn didn't get along with Schary, and he left Metro in 1954, only two years before the executive.* The director's work during this period

---

*LeRoy's life had changed too. Three years after divorcing his wife Doris in 1943, he married Kitty Spiegel.

is not his best by any means. The top efforts, aside from the costly *Quo Vadis* (1950), are *Any Number Can Win* and *East Side, West Side* (both 1949), solid productions, but not up to his peak at Warner Brothers.

Quo Vadis finally cost MGM approximately $12,000,000, standing as one of the most expensive films produced up to that time. John Huston started the project, but he bowed out after $2,000,000 had been spent. Anthony Mann helmed the huge production for a while, but LeRoy took over and stayed in Rome for fourteen months, actually shooting in seven. The film stars Robert Taylor (about to go on a binge of costume spectacles), Deborah Kerr, Leo Genn, and Peter Ustinov.

The film which eventually made $12,500,000 in domestic box-office rentals was given a cool reception by critics. The following remarks are of the type that films with the perpetual "cast of thousands" would receive for the next fifteen years. *Variety* determined: "*Quo Vadis* is a blockbuster. No two ways about its economic horizons." The *Times'* Bosley Crowther very unprophetically predicted that the production "could be ... the last of a cinematic species, the *super* super colossal film." Crowther also warned that the film "was not made for the overly sensitive or discriminating."

In 1954 LeRoy gave up a $6,000 a week salary at MGM to return to Warner Brothers. Although he failed to maintain his former standards at the studio, the director did turn out a fine version of the Broadway hit *Mister Roberts*, taking over for the ailing John Ford. Although LeRoy directed about 90 percent of the film, he insisted that Ford be listed as co-director. He also didn't like the finished script, so he shaped the production of *Mister Roberts* to a more accurate reflection of the play. One of the changes he made was to switch William Powell's character from the drunk that Ford envisioned to the original, sober Navy man.

From *Rose Marie* in 1954, to 1965's *Moment to Moment*, the director served as producer to all his films in between, except for *Mister Roberts, Toward the Unknown* in 1956, *Wake Me When It's Over* in 1960, and *Moment to Moment,* a total of ten productions. The last film Mervyn LeRoy has directed any part of is *The Green Berets* in 1968, where he helped out old friend John Wayne.

Veteran director Mervyn LeRoy, like many of his contemporaries, had little use for the Hollywood which emerged for keeps in the 1960s. When the Kinney Company bought Warner Brothers, it signaled the end of Mervyn's career at the studio. He was supposed to direct a project called *Thirteen Clocks,* but Kinney's canceled it. Another production, *Downstairs at Ramsey's,* has yet to be filmed.

The director left the new Warner Brothers a sad man. "I turned away quickly," he lamented in his autobiography. "Nowadays movies aren't made by great creative minds," LeRoy said, echoing the sentiments of

Ronald Colman and Greer Garson in Random Harvest *(MGM, 1942)*

Robert Walter, Van Johnson, and Spencer Tracy in Thirty Seconds Over Tokyo *(MGM, 1944)*

Jean Seberg,
Arthur Hill,
and Peter
Robbins in
Moment to
Moment
(Universal,
1965)

Robert Taylor in
Quo Vadis
(MGM, 1950)

many Hollywood vets, "but by a cartel of businessmen on the one hand and a haphazard group of youth and undisciplined rookies on the other."

For a time he was interested in filming Pierre Boulle's science fiction novel *Planet of the Apes,* but he didn't want to risk his own money. However, while other properties come and go, movie-goers haven't forgotten the films of Mervyn LeRoy. In 1970 a season's retrospect of his work was held at the British Film Institute, and in 1976 the director who never made a complete flop received the Irving Thalberg Award, presented to "creative producers." LeRoy was and can still be just that.

In 1975 the busy Mervyn was elected to the board of Mego International, an Annex firm, but he has a strong desire to get behind the cameras again. Recently, Mervyn LeRoy advised me, "I have just taken an option on a few new books and I am still working on the Western *Cowboys and Indians.* I hope to make it someday." The last-mentioned would star Cary Grant and John Wayne, the former as a English lord who comes to the American West to be a cowboy, the latter as a cowboy who does the opposite. If it is ever filmed, it is certain that Mervyn LeRoy will not "improve the story into a flop."

The Films of Mervyn LeRoy

No Place to Go *(FN, 1927)*
Harold Teen *(FN, 1928)*
Flying Romeos *(FN, 1928)*
Oh Kay! *(FN, 1928)*
Naughty Baby *(FN, 1929)*
Hot Stuff *(FN, 1929)*
Little Johnny Jones *(FN, 1929)*
Broadway Babies *(FN, 1929)*
Playing Around *(FN, 1930)*
Numbered Men *(FN, 1930)*
Little Caesar *(FN, 1930)*
Showgirl in Hollywood *(FN, 1930)*
Top Speed *(FN, 1930)*
Gentleman's Fate *(FN, 1931)*
Too Young to Marry *(WB, 1931)*
Broad-Minded *(FN, 1931)*

Local Boy Makes Good *(FN, 1931)*
Five Star Final *(FN, 1931)*
Tonight or Never *(UA, 1931)*
High Pressure *(WB, 1932)*
Two Seconds *(FN, 1932)*
Heart of New York *(WB, 1932)*
Big City Blues *(WB, 1932)*
Three on a Match *(FN, 1932)*
I Am a Fugitive from a Chain Gang *(WB, 1932)*
Gold Diggers of 1933 *(choreography by Busby Berkeley)*
Tugboat Annie *(MGM, 1933)*
Hard to Handle *(WB, 1933)*
Elmer the Great *(FN, 1933)*
The World Changes *(FN, 1933)*

Hi, Nellie *(WB, 1934)*
Heat Lightning *(WB, 1934)*
Happiness Ahead *(FN, 1934)*
Sweet Adeline *(WB, 1935)*
Oil for the Lamps of China *(WB, 1935)*
Page Miss Glory *(WB, 1935)*
I Found Stella Parish *(FN, 1935)*
Three Men on a Horse *(FN, 1936)*
Anthony Adverse *(WB, 1936)*
The King and the Chorus Girl *(WB, 1937)*
They Won't Forget *(WB, 1937)*
Fools for Scandal *(WB, 1938)*
Waterloo Bridge *(MGM, 1940)*
Escape *(MGM, 1940)*
Blossoms in the Dust *(MGM, 1941)*
Johnny Eager *(MGM, 1941)*
Unholy Partners *(MGM, 1941)*
Random Harvest *(MGM, 1942)*
Madame Curie *(MGM, 1943)*
Thirty Seconds Over Tokyo *(MGM, 1944)*
Without Reservations *(RKO, 1946)*
Desire Me *(MGM, 1947) (co-directed by George Cukor, both uncredited)*
Homecoming *(MGM, 1948)*
Little Women *(MGM, 1949) (also producer)*
Any Number Can Play *(MGM, 1949)*
East Side, West Side *(MGM, 1949)*
Quo Vadis *(MGM, 1950) (replaced John Huston and Anthony Mann)*

Lovely to Look At *(MGM, 1952)*
Million Dollar Mermaid *(MGM, 1952) (choreography by Busby Berkeley)*
Latin Lovers *(MGM, 1952)*
Rose Marie *(MGM, 1954) (choreography by Busby Berkeley) (and producer)*
Mister Roberts *(WB, 1955) (replaced John Ford)*
Strange Lady in Town *(WB, 1955) (and producer)*
The Bad Seed *(WB, 1956) (and producer)*
Toward the Unknown *(WB, 1956)*
No Time for Sergeants *(WB, 1957) (also producer)*
Home Before Dark *(WB, 1958) (and producer)*
The FBI Story *(WB, 1959) (and producer)*
Wake Me When It's Over *(20th, 1960)*
The Devil at Four O'Clock *(Col., 1961) (and co-producer)*
A Majority of One *(WB, 1961) (and producer)*
Gypsy *(WB, 1962) (and producer)*
Mary, Mary *(WB, 1963) (and producer)*
Moment to Moment *(Univ., 1965)*
The Green Berets *(WB-Seven Arts, 1968) (with Ray Kellogg, both uncredited, directed by John Wayne)*

*Anatole Litvak
in the sixties*

*Charles Boyer
and Claudette
Colbert in
Tovarich (WB,
1937)*

Anatole Litvak

"It may seem reckless of me to try to direct grim and cruel subjects which unfold at the lower depths of life when such subjects have already been treated with great technique by directors of great talents," Anatole Litvak said in regard to *Coeur de Lilas* in 1932. "My cast speaks only when it's necessary for the drama, and words are not the only sound effects. We use street noises and the sounds of motor cars.... It is necessary nowadays to remember that sounds are another support for the film's images, heightening their pictorial values, underscoring their visual beauty."

More than any other director in the American cinema, Anatole Litvak was fascinated by the shattering of empires, the destruction of ways of life, the decimation of the worlds of idealistic lovers, and, above all, the tarnishing of innocence. He found the lower depths in even the most socially prominent atmosphere. Rarely do institutions or persons totally recover in Litvak's films. The best they can do is cope.

It is not surprising that Litvak's work should be imbued with disruption, inasmuch as he grew up in a society which had already started collapsing when he was born, and by the time the boy reached mid-adolescence his world was gone. Michael Anatole Litvak was brought into life on May 10, 1902 in Kiev, Russia. Little is known of his background, as the director remained reluctant to discuss his early life, and he rarely made reference to his career in film and theatre in the Soviet Union.

Three years after Anatole, or "Tola" to his friends, was born, the revolution of 1905 cracked the divine aura of the Czar's empire. Dissidents were violently repressed, but the overthrow which had been planned for decades would not be stopped. Litvak grew up in a country of bloody pogroms, persecutions, an indifferent royalty, and a burgeoning, callous bureaucracy.

Litvak's family moved to St. Petersburg (now Leningrad) while he was very young, and he gained admission to the University of St. Petersburg at the age of 14 in 1916. Five years later Litvak graduated from the school, whose name had been changed to the University of Leningrad, with a Ph.D. in philosophy.

While he was being introduced to academics at the university in 1916, Litvak made his acting debut in avant-garde theatre in St. Petersburg. He also journeyed to Moscow to study with Meyerhold and Eugen Vagtangov, himself a former pupil of Stanislavski. After obtaining his Ph.D., Anatole became active in a small Leningrad theatre, and he soon entered the State School of Theatre. A year later he was directing productions as well as acting.

Like so many other institutions in the new Union of Soviet Socialist Republics, Litvak's theatre was expanding beyond all control, so the young man grew disenchanted. "I would have stayed at the little theater," he recalled years later, "had it not been transformed into an immense place absolutely unsuited for being an experimental theater. It was at that time that I chose cinema."

In 1923 Anatole Litvak directed his first film, a short entitled *Tatiana*, which the director said is "a film about kids." This and an anti-West comedy, *Hearts and Dollars* starring the noted performer Petrov, were both produced by Nordkino Studios. The latter film was released in France as *Le Coeur*. Enigmatic Anatole once revealed that he was involved in about "ten silent films," but it is unclear as to his extent of participation in the projects, and which were Soviet, German, and French. He may have assisted the director on three of the productions and been set director on nine others. It is known, however, that Litvak co-authored the script of director K. Derszhavin's *Samii Yunii Pioner (A Very Young Pioneer)* with Derszhavin. The feature was filmed in 1924 and released early the next year. Writing in *Films in Review*, Jack Edmund Nolan stated, "It's a comedy about a teenage, anti-West activist who, during the '19-20 civil war, fights White Russians and their allies, especially German ones."

By 1925 Litvak had left the Soviet Union to study filmmaking procedures in the sophisticated Ufa film studio in Germany. He may have gone to Paris beforehand, but that is uncertain. The director learned something about editing while working with G. W. Pabst on *Die Freudlose Gasse (The Joyless Street)*, and until 1929 he assisted expatriate Russian director Nicholas Alexander Volkoff, often commuting between Paris, the home of many White Russians, and Berlin, where Volkoff shot Ufa productions. Other notable Russian theatre and film people who fled the Communists were the actor Ivan Moszhukin (the performer who helped demonstrate the classic Kuleshov Effect in editing—a prime theory in Soviet filmmaking before Stalin), directors Jacob Protozanov and Viktor Tourjansky (later a top director in Nazi Germany), the puppet director Ladislas Starevitch, and the producer Ermoliev.

Casanova, starring Ivan Moszhukin, was one of the more important productions Litvak was involved in, along with 1928's *Sheherazade* (released in the U.S. as *Secrets of the Orient*), which, according to Jack Nolan, "utilized indirect lighting, and had enormous sets, most of which were burned up for fire sequences." *The White Devil*, Volkoff's adaptation of Tolstoy's tale of the legendary Hadji Murat, started out as a silent production in 1929. But by then sound had swept over Europe, and Litvak was assigned to include dialogue and music in an otherwise soundless production.

It was the talking film which brought Anatole Litvak out of Volkoff's shadow. He had had several years of theatrical experience, training with Meyerhold (one of the giants of Soviet theatre), and he spoke German, French, and a bit of English, in addition to his native Russian. Since films of the early sound era were occasionally produced in more than a half-dozen language versions, his talents were highly marketable.

Dolly Macht Karriere (1930), starring Dolly Haas (director John Brahm's wife), was Litvak's first full-length film as a director. A light production full of music, the film was a box-office winner but was clearly not of the caliber that would bring Litvak notoriety in his Hollywood films.

The next year Anatole directed and co-scripted *Nie Wieder Liebe*, and he filmed the French version as well. Assisting Litvak on the French film was 28-year-old Max Ophuls, and the large cast included Lillian Harvey, Felix Bressart, and Margo Lion.

Litvak's first crime film was the French *Coeur de Lilas*. Released in 1932, the tough gangster yarn stars Jean Gabin. Litvak wrote the script from a play by Tristan Bernard, and it was the first of his films that he seemed to like. *Coeur de Lilas* was a big success.

Consequently the director's name became better known in Berlin. For the next few years Anatole continued shooting films in France and Germany—as many as three language versions of a production at once. He reportedly filmed, or at least "supervised," *La Chanson d'une Nuit*, possibly directed by Henri Georges Clouzot, another filmmaker with an appetite for the sordid and corrupt. Not long after that Litvak went to England to direct Gaumont-British's *Sleeping Car*, starring matinee idol Ivor Novello.

Litvak's films of the period were either melodramas, comedies, or musicals. He often wrote his own scripts, and his reputation rose slowly. The last film he made before *Mayerling* (1936), the production which brought him to Hollywood, was the fascinating *L'Equipage* (*Flight into Darkness*) (1935).

L'Equipage stars Charles Vanel as a heroic pilot, with Annabella essaying his adulterous wife, and 23-year-old Jean-Pierre Aumont playing the aspiring flier who sets his sights on Annabella. *L'Equipage* features an exciting 20-minute aerial battle cut to the strains of Arthur Honegger, similar in style to the four-minute sequence in the later *City for Conquest*, which shows Arthur Kennedy conducting an orchestra without a single word passing from the counter-shots of the audience. *L'Equipage* was labeled "a gripping, human story, beautifully told," by *Variety*, which added: "Camera work and direction are outstanding."

Mayerling is the film that French audiences associate with the name Anatole Litvak. It is a fine version of the passionate love affair between Austria's Archduke Rudolph and Maria Vetsera, which ended in the suicide of both lovers. Starring Charles Boyer and Danielle Darrieux, the film depicts the Austro-Hungarian empire in its glory, despite the scurrilous royal characters that Litvak etches to counteract the lush vision of the world that used to be.

The director's filmmaking style was at its zenith here, full of dissolves and sweeping camera movements. "I like to cut as little as possible," Litvak once said. The Russian's form may have influenced Max Ophuls who had assisted him in making *Nie Wieder Liebe* several years earlier (Litvak borrowed a poignant, drifting shot from Ophuls fifteen years later).

Variety scoffed at *Mayerling* which had been shot in five weeks: "They had to rush his [Boyer's] scenes so frantically in order to enable him to get back to Hollywood on time, it's a wonder the picture is over quickie standards." However, the journal felt that the romantic vehicle "gives French class to an ideal boy-meets-girl story, good for youngsters of all ages."

Flown to Hollywood thereafter, it took some time for Anatole to find the right project. He was to film *The Garden of Allah* for Walter Wanger, but he came to dislike the project. There was talk that he would direct Claudette Colbert in his own script of *Joan of Arc* at RKO, and publicists announced that he would do a version of *Phantom of the Opera* for Universal, but nothing happened. Meanwhile, Columbia planned to have the Russian direct *Wuthering Heights* with Charles Boyer and Sylvia Sydney, but that was another derailed project.

In 1937 Litvak remade his own *L'Equipage* as *The Woman I Love*, with Paul Muni and Miriam Hopkins taking the Vanel-Annabella roles. The film wasn't very successful, but it enabled Anatole to meet his first wife, Miriam Hopkins, whom the director married on September 4, 1937. The bond lasted until September 11, 1939.

During this time, France gave Anatole Litvak an award for his contributions to the French cinema, and soon thereafter the Russian was assigned to the project which helped to establish his fine reputation in Hollywood. Warner Brothers was planning a version of Robert Sherwood's play *Tovarich*. With the plot revolving around two White Russians (Charles Boyer and Claudette Colbert) who flee to Paris and become servants in the house of a wealthy but not too bright banker, the film was well-suited to Anatole.

One of Litvak's first actions was to put back several scenes in the script which Sherwood had cut from *his* adaptation of Jacques Deval's comedy. Litvak, who has often been compared to Lubitsch for a similar European outlook and an early reputation for filming royalty and pageantry, also sought a more gracious brand of comedy here. "Filming a comedy is not the most amusing job in the world," Litvak remarked with a stern face. "Throwing a custard pie is an act that generates its own tempo. But your fragile, sophisticated comedy—ah, that's something else again."

A lesson in patience and ingenuity was learned by all during the filming of the Bastille Day celebration in *Tovarich*. Three hundred extras were milling around a real street when fog drifted in to prevent further filming. Litvak moved a process screen rooftop to a sound stage, but he couldn't achieve the proper camera angles at the new location. Special effects man Byron Haskins finally came to the rescue with a mirror borrowed from the set of the musical *Wunderbar*. Litvak and Haskins set up a 75-foot cloth tunnel. At one end a rear projection machine was placed, focused on the glass at the other end. The mirror was tilted to reflect on the screen erected at the edge of the roof set. The camera on the roof ridge filmed the necessary shot of Boyer and Colbert on the rooftop as they gazed down in bewilderment at the celebration in the street.

Tovarich was accorded a mixed reception by the critics. Frank S. Nugent of the *New York Times* called Litvak's serio-comedy "neither high comedy nor low but something in a pleasant middle ground." However, other reviewers weren't as kind. *Variety* deemed *Tovarich* "something less than superlative, lacking the keen polish of Gilbert Miller's stage presentation." "A series of photographed stage scenes," complained Howard Barnes in the *New York Herald-Tribune*, although he did admit that "Anatole Litvak has staged the offering handsomely and tastefully."

Litvak worked on *The Roaring Twenties* for two days in 1939 as a favor to Hal Wallis, but Raoul Walsh directed the final version of the gangster film. "I hated it," Anatole later admitted. He was also supposed to film a version of Somerset Maugham's *Villa on the Hill* that year, but the production never materialized.

Confessions of a Nazi Spy was Litvak's next big project. How the daring film exploration of pre-war Nazi activity in America evolved is a matter of controversy. Litvak himself insisted that the idea was his, stating: "There was a period at Warner Brothers which was very interesting.... This was the moment when I did *Confessions of a Nazi Spy*, which I brought to Warners and which was entirely my idea. They were brave enough to let me do it."

In his book *Warner Brothers* (Scribner's), Charles Higham tells a different story. Somehow in 1938 Jack Warner discovered that the FBI had a number of Nazi spies under surveillance in the East. With President Roosevelt's blessing (FDR was a personal friend of the mogul's), Warner secretly contacted contract writer Milton Krims and instructed him to travel to New York to work with FBI agent Leon Turrou. Turrou had attended rallies of the German-American Bund, and he possessed a wealth of information which Krims put to good use in his screenplay. The writer obtained a complete transcript of the trials of several spies and created a fact-based script which he envisioned as a realistic, yet subtle Warner Brothers production.

When Litvak was brought into the project, he and Krims were immediately at odds. The director wanted to open the film with scenes of Nazi atrocities (such graphic footage didn't find its way into a Hollywood film until Welles' *The Stranger* in 1946), and he also decided to melodramatize the plot. As the production continued, many associated with it received threatening letters, and in fact the German consul in Los Angeles attempted to have the shooting stopped. When *Confessions of a Nazi Spy* was released, the German-American Bund sued Warner Brothers for $500,000 for defamation. The suit was dropped when former organization head Fritz Kuhn was brought to trial for embezzling the group's funds.

Confessions of a Nazi Spy stands today as a solid suspense film with good production values. While its dated message has tarnished the film's impact somewhat, the work still serves as a symbol of the studio's courage in producing stories which attacked bigotry, oppression, and poverty all over the globe.

All This and Heaven Too (1940) reunited Litvak with Charles Boyer, and also with Paris. Scripted by Casey Robinson from Rachel Lyman Field's novel, and loosely based on the murder of the Duchess de Praslin in 1847, the film is a long (140 minutes) melodrama of a sacrificing governess, brilliantly etched by Bette Davis. In love with her boss (Boyer), the governess suffers in silence for years, but he is unable to free himself from his neurotic wife.

In that same year Litvak moved once more to a social film, *City for Conquest*. Originally titled *The World Moves On*, John Wexley's hard yet heartrending script tells the story of a boxer (James Cagney) who is blinded by a corrupt fighter and reduced to vending newspapers on the street. Ann Sheridan co-stars as his ambitious girl friend, with able support from Arthur Kennedy as Cagney's screen brother, a boy from the slums with the dream of writing a symphony.

City for Conquest pleased some reviewers of the day, but not star James Cagney. Said Cagney, "I trained as though I were going into a ten-rounder . . . and then I saw it cut. . . . The editing took an awful lot of the sound, solid substance out of it." Bosley Crowther of the *New York Times* agreed with Cagney, asserting that the film is "unevenly paced, mounts slowly to a sizzling prizefight sequence, which comes somewhere about the middle, then sags off to a long-drawn, agonized finish." However, the *New York Herald-Tribune*'s Howard Barnes disagreed, praising the film for having "a vivid portrayal and a terrific tempo," and adding that Anatole Litvak "has staged a corny script with such pace and flavor that it seems a lot more substantial than it actually is." In its usual clipped style, *Variety* remarked: "Ably scripted and deftly directed . . . carries plenty of dramatic punch."

Ginger Rogers was originally sought for the female lead in *City for Conquest*, but Sylvia Sydney won the role. Then as production began she dropped out in favor of Ann Sheridan. As Cagney stated, the film emerged from the editing room considerably different from Wexley's script, with the female lead difficulties seemingly symbolic of the constant changes that the production underwent before its release. An onstage narrator like the one used in *Our Town* was adapted for the story, in the person of Frank Craven, but he was finally eliminated, apparently, along with much of the story. Seeing the film today, it is difficult to imagine that an old man sitting on a curb philosophizing could be anything but a detriment to the progression and impact of the narrative. One clearly understands the younger brother's "Symphony of a Great City" to be a symbol of the lives of the characters in the film. There's no need to have anyone look in the camera and say it.

An American citizen since 1938, Litvak was eager to help the Allied cause in World War II. After directing *This Above All* (1942) for Fox, he joined the Special Services Film Unit of the U.S. Army. A short time spent photographing North American landings was followed by work with Frank Capra on the *Why We Fight* series, mainly constructed at Fox. Litvak co-produced and co-directed four of the nine entries, and the last one, *The Battle of Russia*, he directed himself. In all the films, fiction footage is ably combined with documentary material, a skill that Anatole learned early in his career. *The Battle of Russia* was the only American war documentary that Stalin allowed Soviet audiences to view. Archer Winstein of the *New York Post* felt that Litvak's documentary was "a film as fascinating as it is educationally valuable."

Edward G. Robinson in Confessions of a Nazi Spy *(WB, 1939)*

Ann Sheridan, Frank McHugh, James Cagney, and Anthony Quinn in City for Conquest *(WB, 1940)*

Oskar Werner (second from left) and Hildegarde Neff in Decision Before Dawn *(20th, 1951)*

Donald Pleasance, Peter O'Toole, John Gregson, and Omar Shariff in The Night of the Generals *(Col., 1967)*

After the war Litvak didn't return to Warner Brothers. Studio head Jack Warner was looking to dispense with some of his high-priced talent, and the war provided a perfect interlude to bring in new faces. As a result, Anatole free-lanced for the rest of his career, never staying at one studio too long. The director was involved as either producer or co-producer on most of his last thirteen films, sometimes taking a credited hand at writing the scripts.

Litvak was briefly committed to film a Herbert J. Biberman screenplay called *New Orleans*, about black jazz musicians, but he withdrew in favor of Arthur Lubin. *The Long Night* (RKO, 1947), a lackluster remake of Carne's *Le Jour se Leve*, and *Sorry, Wrong Number* (Par., 1948), a version of Lucille Fletcher's radio drama featuring a number of added flashbacks (one of Litvak's trademarks), followed before one of his best films of the 1940s, *The Snake Pit* (20th, 1948).

"People said I was as crazy as the woman in the book when I bought the story," Anatole recalled. It took some doing for him to persuade Fox studio chief Darryl F. Zanuck to approve the production of Mary Jane Ward's novel of a woman committed to a mental institution. Although the director spent four important years at Warner Brothers, he stated, "I'd say my best experience was with Zanuck at Fox."

Starring Olivia de Havilland as the inmate, *The Snake Pit* was nominated for an Academy Award and selected as one of the year's Ten Best films by the National Board of Review. "I'm proud of *The Snake Pit*," Litvak declared.

The director didn't see another film with his signature on the screen until *Decision Before Dawn* in 1951. Initially titled *The Steeper Cliff*, it was his first European film in fifteen years. Litvak considers this powerful narrative of Nazi prisoners of war deciding to spy on Hitler to be "*the* important post-war film I've done." Some film specialists consider it his finest film, period.

Decision Before Dawn was shot in the realist tradition that one suspects writer Milton Krims wished the director had used in *Confessions of a Nazi Spy* a dozen years earlier. In this case, Litvak's simple lighting and raw footage of Allied and Axis camps are perfectly suited to the sense of destruction that the crumbling German empire evoked. Oskar Werner breathes life into the role of "Happy," the German soldier executed for infiltrating Nazi lines.

Otis L. Guernsey, Jr. of the *New York Herald-Tribune* enthusiastically stated: "Taut as a bow string and visually interesting in every scene, it is a first-rate spy story of the modern realistic school." *Variety* declared that Litvak "has given the picture a strong feeling of reality through a semi-documentary treatment." *Decision Before Dawn* was nominated for an Oscar, and also won a place on the National Board of Review's Ten Best list.

Anatole married French model Sophie Bourdeen on September 2, 1951, and his next film wasn't finished until 1953. *Act of Love*, taken from Alfred Hayes' novel *The Girl on the Via Flamina*, was financed, produced, directed, and co-written by Anatole Litvak. Originally set in Italy, the director changed the locale of the love story to his beloved Paris, and he borrowed a lush camera movement from a former assistant, Max Ophuls. Ophuls ended his 1932 *Libeleli* with a romantic, flowing examination of the apartment where the doomed lovers hoped to meet. In Litvak's film, the American GI (Kirk Douglas) returns to the little room, and the fluid caressing is repeated by the camera. It is a beautiful ending. Yet the director was disappointed at the overall results. "[It] was a story that didn't work out as well as I thought it would."

Anastasia (20th, 1956) is another one of Litvak's finest films. A defrocked Czarist general (Yul Brynner) attempts to swindle a royal fortune from surviving Romanoffs in Paris by convincing them that a girl he has found in the streets (Ingrid Bergman) is the real Anastasia, the youngest daughter of Czar Nicholas, who was believed to have been killed with her family. The director's main problem during the shooting was Ingrid Bergman: "She was a lot of trouble in the first week for all of us, particularly for me, until I was able to prove to her I really did know what I was doing."

He certainly did. The type of story, the characters, the setting, and the underlying Litvak theme were all there. The destroyed empire and the tarnishing of innocence are the strongest narrative elements in *Anastasia*.

Bosley Crowther wrote in the *Times:* "The color production is splendid, and the musical score is very good. Put this one in a class with *Mayerling*." However, the *Christian Science Monitor* proclaimed, "Romance wins the day. . . . As a result, the taut little melodrama, with its histrionically effective scenes, sacrifices a good deal of the essential excitement which was its chief justification on stage."

Litvak didn't like the original play by Marcelle Maureth that had been adapted by Guy Bolton. In his judgment it lacked substance and the ending was contrived. Therefore, he made the appropriate changes.

Next came the grandiose NBC-TV color version of *Mayerling* in 1957, starring Audrey Hepburn and Mel Ferrer as the lovers. It was reported in the trade papers that Hepburn's husband, Ferrer, had been acting as his wife's Svengali throughout the production. "If he directed her through three weeks of rehearsals, I didn't notice it," the director retorted. "And I think I would have."

The production cost $620,000, more than any television show up to that time. Despite the budget, the TV *Mayerling* was considered to be static, with the *New York Times'* Jack Gould snorting, "$620,000 isn't everything."

Throughout the 1950s and early 1960s Litvak directed three mediocre films—*The Journey, Goodbye Again,* and *Five Miles to Midnight.* He was then taken off *A Shot in the Dark* (replaced by Blake Edwards) before making one more memorable cinematic impression in the psychological war film, *The Night of the Generals.*

Released by Columbia in 1967, the eerie story concerns a psychotic Nazi general (Peter O'Toole) who smashes a plot against Hitler and goes on a murderous rampage all his own. Explaining why he had waited four years to shoot another film, the director explained, "I decided I would like to wait and see if I could get a subject that would be the star of the project instead of the stars themselves."

He certainly got what he wanted. The narrative takes many twists, yet emerges as a powerful tale of Nazi egomania, lust, and retribution. *The Night of the Generals* possesses a uniformly somber look. "We are trying to make a color picture, eliminating color as much as we possibly can," Litvak said at the time. Substituting for color values is the grotesque make-up applied to some of the actors, especially O'Toole. His pancake and age lines are extremely theatrical, offering his demented character as a sort of mythically evil man, decidedly a myth of the twentieth century. Yet this myth was on the whole horrifyingly real.

A number of critics didn't care for the results. Richard Schickel of *Life* magazine wrote, "The death of the movie must . . . be attributed to Anatole Litvak, who did not so much direct it as administer to it a brutal succession of coups de grace."

Litvak's last film was the bland *The Lady in the Car with Glasses and a Gun*, released by Columbia in 1971. Seven years earlier the director had bought the rights to Rolf Hochhuth's controversial play, *The Deputy*, which criticized Pope Pius XII for not taking firmer action against the Nazi persecution of the Jews. Unfortunately Litvak didn't live to direct what might have been a fascinating film on a subject he knew well.

The Litvaks lived in France in the 1970s, which is where Anatole died on December 15, 1974 after several weeks of care at a hospital in suburban Neville. His will left an estate valued at $750,000 to his wife Sophie. Director Anatole Litvak also left behind a series of fascinating explorations of decaying worlds, love, and fast-fading idealism. A retrospective of his films is certainly in order.

The Films of Anatole Litvak

Dolly Macht Karriere *(German, 1930)*

Nie Wieder Liebe *(German, 1931, and French version) (and co-script)*

Coeur de Lilas *(French, 1932)*

Das Lied einer Nacht *(German, 1932) (French version:* La Chanson d'une Nuit*) (British version:* Tell Me Tonight*)*

Sleeping Car *(Gaumont-British, 1933)*

Cette Vieille Canaille *(French, 1933)*

Mademoiselle Docteur *(French, 1934) (co-directed by G. W. Pabst)*

L'Equipage (Flight into Darkness) *(French, 1935) (and co-script)*

Mayerling *(French, 1936)*

The Woman I Love *(RKO, 1937)*

Tovarich *(WB, 1937)*

The Amazing Dr. Clitterhouse *(WB, 1938) (and co-producer)*

The Sisters *(WB, 1938)*

Confessions of a Nazi Spy *(WB, 1939)*

The Roaring Twenties *(WB, 1939) (replaced by Raoul Walsh)*

Castle on the Hudson *(WB, 1940)*

City for Conquest *(WB, 1940)*

All This and Heaven Too *(WB, 1940)*

One Foot in Heaven *(WB, 1941) (replaced by Irving Rapper)*

Out of the Fog *(WB, 1941)*

Blues in the Night *(WB, 1941)*

This Above All *(20th, 1942)*

The Nazis Strike *(U.S. Government, 1942) (co-directed by Frank Capra)*

Divide and Conquer *(U.S. Government, 1942) (co-directed by Frank Capra)*

The Battle of Russia *(20th, 1943)*

The Battle of China *(U.S. Government, 1943) (co-directed by Frank Capra)*

War Comes to America *(RKO, 1945) (and co-script)*

The Long Night *(RKO, 1947) (and co-producer)*

Sorry, Wrong Number *(Par., 1948) (and co-producer)*

The Snake Pit *(20th, 1948) (and co-producer)*

Decision Before Dawn *(20th, 1951) (and producer)*

Act of Love *(UA, 1953) (and producer, co-script)*

The Deep Blue Sea *(20th, 1955) (and producer)*

Anastasia *(20th, 1956)*

Mayerling *(NBC-TV, 1957)*

The Journey *(MGM, 1959) (and producer)*

Goodbye Again *(UA, 1961) (and producer)*

Five Miles to Midnight *(UA, 1963)*

A Shot in the Dark *(UA, 1964) (replaced by Blake Edwards)*

The Night of the Generals *(Col., 1967)*

The Lady in the Car with Glasses and a Gun *(Col., 1971) (and co-producer)*

Zachary Scott (second from left, and far right) in a curious double exposure. With (from left to right) David Hoffman, Steven Geray, Vince Barnett, and George Metaxa in a publicity pose for The Mask of Dimitrios *(WB, 1944)*

Finlay Currie, Andrew Ray, and Jean Negulesco on the set of The Mudlark *(20th, 1949)*

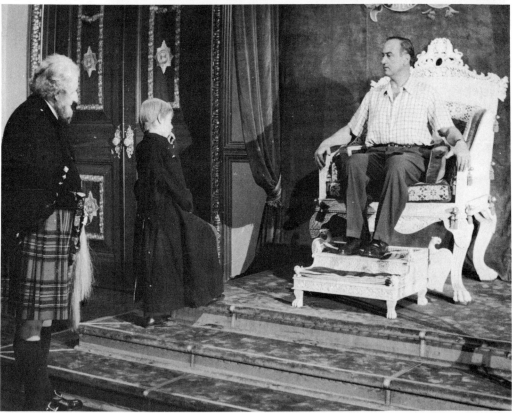

15

Jean Negulesco

ox was very different to work for from Warners," Jean Negulesco said a number of years ago. "It was not as tight or as strict; it was much more liberal. If they liked what you were doing, there was no limit to your budget, no restriction on your way of shooting, on your casting, or anything."

This leads to one of the great questions in Hollywood, and, indeed, the whole of filmmaking: Is quality always a by-product of freedom, or was the objective, cost-conscious analysis of studio executives a factor in eliminating artistic fat, and, in doing so, developing the strengths of directors?

If one looks at the evidence in the films of Jean Negulesco, it appears that Warner Brothers proved a much better environment for his talents than the more flexible Fox. The director made *The Mask of Dimitrios, Nobody Lives Forever, Three Strangers, Humoresque,* and *Johnny Belinda* under Jack Warner's aegis, while *Deep Valley, Road House, Under My Skin,* and *Three Came Home* are his best Fox works. Negulesco directed only seven films at Warner Brothers, as opposed to twenty-two at Fox. Perhaps, as Andrew Sarris has commented, Jean Negulesco was a victim of Cinemascope and its wide, rectangular screen which admittedly damaged the director's ability to create the intimacy that distinguishes his films from other Warner Brothers productions.

Jean Negulesco was born on February 29, 1900 in Craiova, Rumania. In 1914 he traveled to Paris to study art, learning much from his teacher Constantin Brancusi, and later from the great Amedeo Modigliani. Probably hearing that America was the place to be if he wanted to develop his interest in filmmaking, Jean sailed for New York City just as the country was struck by the Depression of 1929.

Around 1932 Negulesco entered the movie profession as a technical adviser for a rape to be committed in Paramount's *The Story of Temple Drake*. Jean made sketches illustrating how the scene could win approval from the censors. Producer Benjamin Glazer was impressed with Negulesco's ingenuity, and he made the 32-year-old man an assistant producer.

For the next decade Jean served as a liaison between the studio and its directors, and he received an invaluable education in the process by attending story conferences and screenings and working with editors in cutting rooms. In the late 1930s he began directing short films.

By 1941 Jean was offered a chance to guide a feature-length production. Jack Warner wanted to make a series of films budgeted at $300,000-$400,000, all to be handled by fresh young directors. Negulesco started *Singapore Woman* (1941), and his name appears on the finished version starring Brenda Marshall and David Bruce, but he was fired in mid-production. He then expressed his desire to film Dashiell Hammett's *The Maltese Falcon*, and he was given permission to do so. However, he didn't know that John Huston had been promised the opportunity to direct the project if his script of W. R. Burnett's *High Sierra* proved satisfactory. Negulesco worked two months on *The Maltese Falcon* before he was replaced when Huston reminded Jack Warner of their agreement. Then Jean's friend Anatole Litvak told him of a book by Eric Ambler called *A Coffin for Dimitrios*. Jean loved the story and arranged with Warner Brothers producer Henry Blanke (who was a staunch defender of many young studio directors, including John Huston) to adapt it for the screen.

With its title changed to *The Mask of Dimitrios*, Ambler's novel almost didn't get filmed at all. Negulesco's test of stars Peter Lorre and Sydney Greenstreet was so bad that Blanke became worried about the director's future at Warner Brothers. Then it was discovered that Lorre and Greenstreet had been acting with tongue strictly in cheek. Their next test proved acceptable.

"In *The Mask of Dimitrios*, I established a somber, low-key mood that I followed in a number of subsequent films," Jean said. "I learned that the public loves to share the actor's situation, to be a vicarious part of the action. It's curious that when you see actors moving and talking in semi-darkness it's always more exciting than seeing them plainly, because you identify with them more."

The Mask of Dimitrios (1944) is one of the best first features ever turned out by a Hollywood director. The story line is episodic, being a pieced-together puzzle of the rise and fall of arch-criminal Dimitrios, played with properly sinister dynamics by southerner Zachary Scott in his first big film role. Peter Lorre, Sydney Greenstreet, Victor Francen, and Steven Geray as the "poor, confused little man" provide a marvelous ensemble. They breathe life into Negulesco's shadowy, sweaty mystery which shows the grime in the streets of many backlot versions of the world's capitals, as well as the crime hatched in cold government offices and posh nightclubs. At the film's end, Lorre explodes with the words which lurk in the viewer's mind about the cold, traitorous Dimitrios. "You rotten insane brute," Lorre screams as he is about to pounce on the fiend. "Do you think you can go on murdering?"

According to the *New York Herald-Tribune*, *The Mask of Dimitrios* has "most of the ingredients of good film melodrama.... Where the film falters is in its arrangement of material.... Jean Negulesco has had more interest in the literary original than the imagery which might have been distilled from it." The *New York Times'* Bosley Crowther was more succinct in his negativism. "Clumsy, conventional," the critic clucked.

Warner Brothers attempted to follow up the success of *Casablanca* with *The Conspirators* in 1944. Starring Hedy Lamarr and a number of holdovers from Curtiz's classic, including Paul Henreid, Peter Lorre, and Sydney Greenstreet, the film does stylishly evoke the streets, train terminals, restaurants, and back rooms of Portugal, but Negulesco failed to transform the bland script into something striking, if not original.

Three Strangers (1946) was something else altogether. John Huston and Howard Koch scripted the film before the war, and the director originally intended to shoot it starring Humphrey Bogart, Mary Astor, and Sydney Greenstreet. After being mustered out of the service, Huston went on to other projects, and Negulesco assumed directorship, casting Peter Lorre and Geraldine Fitzgerald in place of Bogart and Astor. Jack Warner thought that Jean was crazy for handling Lorre a romantic lead, but the modest budget convinced the mogul that little could be lost.

Peter Lorre's fine performance and perfect aura (though atypical of Hollywood) as an alcoholic small-time hoodlum play an important part in the triumph of the bizarre *Three Strangers*. Lorre, Fitzgerald, and Sydney Greenstreet play the roles of three people whose lives are intertwined through the mutual ownership of a sweepstakes ticket. Each character is a criminal in his or her own way—Lorre as a bank robber, Fitzgerald as a scheming neurotic out to ruin her husband's career, and Greenstreet as an embezzler. Greenstreet ultimately murders Fitzgerald with a statue of Kwan-Yin, the Chinese goddess of mercy, and goes berserk in the street, while Lorre is redeemed.

Once more Negulesco does a fine job of interweaving separate units of narrative into a cohesive whole. The connecting element, over and beyond the sweepstakes ticket, is a glaze of mental illness which rules the strangers. Lorre has a weakness for liquor, Fitzgerald's flaw is consuming hatred, and Greenstreet is possessed by greed. Of the three, Greenstreet seems the most likely to survive with a degree of sanity, but by the end of the film he is completely buried inside his massive body, an idiot babbling something about murder to other strangers.

"Full-bodied melodrama of a shrewd and sophisticated sort," wrote Bosley Crowther in the *New York Times*. James Agee of the *Nation* made sense of *Three Strangers:* "A director I had never expected to praise is Jean Negulesco, who has always made me think of Michael Curtiz on toast. . . . I may be wrong in praising him now, since *Three Strangers* was smartly written . . . and is still more smartly played. But this rather silly story of three blemished people buzzing around a sweepstakes ticket is told with such exactly fancy terseness, even in casual street scenes, that I think nobody should be left out. It is one of few recent movies you don't feel rather ashamed about, next morning." "Jean Negulesco has staged more than one sequence in terms of cinematic excitement," wrote Howard Barnes in the *New York Herald-Tribune*, but he felt that *Three Strangers* "should be seen for its acting rather than its script."

"*Humoresque* (1947) was a very successful picture," Negulesco recalled in *The Celluloid Muse: Hollywood Directors Speak* (Signet). "It played one Mexican theatre continuously for three years—but I have occasionally been criticized for some of the fancy dissolves I used in it: the blind-roll dissolving into a piano keyboard, the soda-water dripping from the siphon and dissolving into a wave, etc. This was a period in which I was trying to be 'clever' and when such arty effects were all the rage."

Joan Crawford portrays a rich woman who becomes the patron of a poor violinist, played by John Garfield. The story isn't much, but Jean's camera style, along with the clipped exchanges between Crawford and Garfield, plus the sincerity of the rest of the cast, makes *Humoresque* a memorable film. The director's special talent for making a movie-goer feel as if he is peeking in on a very private scene recurs often in the production. The onset of the Crawford-Garfield relationship at a party, her visit to his disapproving parents' store, and the tension built during the restaurant scene are three examples of alternately delicate and explosive situations which seem to exist for the players' ears and their ears alone. In fact, Oscar Levant's position as Garfield's friend in *Humoresque* symbolizes that of the audience: Levant's wisecracking twists attention from the progression of the romance of Garfield and Crawford. It is as if his personality is in the way of the story, yet it provides needed relief from the guilt and violence propagated by the leads.

Alan Napier and Geraldine Fitzgerald in Three Strangers *(WB, 1946)*

Celeste Holm, Cornel Wilde, and Ida Lupino in Road House *(20th, 1948)*

The success of *Humoresque* was preceded by a fair reception for the tough, romantic melodrama *Nobody Lives Forever* (1946), starring John Garfield and Geraldine Fitzgerald. As a con-man who attempts to swindle Fitzgerald out of her fortune, but ruins his own well-laid plans by falling in love with the lady, Garfield simply transfers the characteristics of the violinist in *Humoresque* to the other side of the law. Ambition rules both men, and both are hurt by women, yet both emerge stronger and better because of it. As in *The Mask of Dimitrios* and *The Conspirators*, *Nobody Lives Forever* features Warner Brothers' dark, moody, smoke-filled backrooms where criminals plot and sometimes execute crimes. The seediness of such scenes practically jumps from the screen and crawls up the viewer's leg.

Johnny Belinda (1948) was Negulesco's last film at Warner Brothers. Jean thinks that it is his best film, and it may very well be so. Nevertheless, he was fired by Jack Warner after its release. The man who directed the film which went on to win twelve Academy Award nominations and praise from countless critics was probably let go as a result of the economy purge at Warner Brothers.

Essentially a gentle tale of a doctor's (Lew Ayres) concern for a deaf-mute (Jane Wyman), *Johnny Belinda* nevertheless has some of the

Jane Wyman and Lew Ayres in Johnny Belinda *(WB, 1948)*

most violent scenes in Jean Negulesco's oeuvre. The rape of the mute (by Stephen McNally) is fraught with tension, the tenderness of the doctor's concern for the girl is extremely touching, and images of sunrises, deep sun-framed skies, and the terrain around the farm beautifully punctuate the slowly unwinding tale.

Negulesco was originally assigned to direct *The Adventures of Don Juan*, with Errol Flynn in the title role. Jean wanted Flynn to act the part of one of the world's great romantic figures as a man who was constantly exploited by women. When Flynn panicked and complained to Jack Warner, the mogul decided that he needed Flynn for *Don Juan*, but not Negulesco, so the director came upon *Johnny Belinda* in a pile of scripts sent to him by Jerry Wald.

"Making it [*Johnny Belinda*] ... was the happiest experience of my life," he said in 1968. "We all loved what we did in it. This was the only time in my career when all the people connected with the film—including actors, cameramen, still-photographers, etc.—felt themselves an integral part of the project."

Jane Wyman's Oscar-winning performance was helped considerably by the concoction of wax placed in her ears. During rehearsals it was obvious from her eyes that she could hear Ayres speak, but the inserted wax rendered her deaf.

Nobody at Warner Brothers liked *Johnny Belinda*, and the studio executives were stunned when the production received a host of critical acclaim. "Quite moving," wrote the *Times'* Bosley Crowther. "Perhaps the foremost reason for this happy accomplishment is the sensitive and poignant performance of Jane Wyman." *Johnny Belinda* was nominated for a best picture Oscar, and made the *Times'* and *Film Daily's* Ten Best lists. Lew Ayres was also considered for best actor, but the fine performer's pacifism during the recent war may have sealed his fate with Academy members. Negulesco wasn't nominated for best director.

Later the director had the pleasure of receiving a personal apology from Jack Warner. This particular mogul usually admitted his mistakes and tried to rectify them. He made Jean a vague offer to continue directing for the studio, but Negulesco was gone from Warner Brothers for good.

Darryl Zanuck could get swept up in a director's enthusiasm for a project, and Jean liked that quality in him. In 1947 he directed *Deep Valley* for Fox, starring Ida Lupino and Dane Clark. This was another of the director's tough romances, dealing with an escaped convict who brings meaning to the life of a farm girl. There was a general strike at Fox, so Negulesco shot the production on location at Big Sur and Big Bear. At a time when the studio set and backlot competed with the natural locales of the "semi-documentaries," *Deep Valley* was in both camps, being an archetypal Hollywood concoction made away from the process screen.

Zanuck liked *Deep Valley* so much that he urged Jean to direct *Road House* (1948), even though Fox's number one man confessed that the poor script had been turned down by several directors. Zanuck told Negulesco that he wanted *Road House* to mimic the best fast-paced, sexy, violent yarns turned out by Warner Brothers.

Road House does that, and even more. It is a *film noir* transplanted from the city to a rural atmosphere. The road house itself is a nightclub abstracted from its usual home in dark, foreboding cities of concrete and steel. In the country death is no longer an anonymous function of crime, but it is just as real. As a husky-voiced singer who upsets the routine of the roadside bistro, Ida Lupino is the strongest and steadiest character around. Completing the second and third sides of the bizarre triangle are Cornel Wilde as a silent machismo type, along with a post-war mutant, the psychotic killer, chillingly etched by Richard Widmark.

In the tradition of Dietrich and Bacall, Lupino has little trouble defending her dignity against the sanctimonious pontifications of Wilde or the advances of Widmark. In fact, she is at odds with Wilde from the very moment of her arrival at the road house. It's Dietrich and Raft in *Manpower* all over again. Wilde is the club's manager, dedicated to keeping the place a "decent" spot for entertainment, and making sure that the furniture doesn't get broken or worn down (no cigarette burns on the piano). When Wilde tries to intimidate Lupino into leaving town, she clearly establishes her roots in the strong-willed independent female of the 1930s, as opposed to the love slave of the 1950s.

Richard Widmark's unbalanced child-like killer is drawn from the character of the gunsel Wilbur (Elisha Cook, Jr.) in *The Maltese Falcon*, often considered the first *film noir*. Yet it is Widmark, not Cook, who serves as the prototype for this brand of gunfighter. In *Road House* (as in *Kiss of Death*), Widmark replaces the strictly power-hungry killers—the Cagneys, Robinsons, and Munis—with a psychotic who is the victim of Hollywood's transition from Marx to Freud, from social analyses to psychological interpretation. If Cornel Wilde had stolen Paul Muni's girl in *Scarface* (or worse, his sister), he (Wilde) wouldn't have been framed for theft and tormented by his oppressor. The machine guns would have blazed and wiped out Wilde. This is the break with the Hollywood bad man of the 1930s.

The tension between the trio in *Road House* is as private as the love conflict in *Humoresque*. Although there are a number of supporting characters in the Fox film, the feeling persists that Lupino, Wilde, and Widmark are strictly alone. The emotions displayed are so direct, so deep-seated, that even co-star Celeste Holm cannot truly break into the charmed circle.

For the most part, the rest of Jean Negulesco's career is filled with comedy, a dash of romance, and a series of rather heavy melodramas. *The Mudlark* (20th, 1950) is one of the director's better films at the studio. Alec Guinness steals the show as British Prime Minister Benjamin Disraeli in a tale of Queen Victoria's (Irene Dunne) friendship with a bedraggled boy who steals into her castle. Jean later commented that Guinness was "so good, so different, that the rest of it [the film] was thrown a little out of balance."

Under My Skin (20th, 1950) is one of Jean's most touching dramas. Based on Ernest Hemingway's story *My Old Man*, about a corrupt jockey who reforms, the film stars John Garfield, Micheline Presle, and Luther Adler. Similar in theme to Hemingway's *To Have and Have Not* (as represented by Curtiz's *The Breaking Point* and Hawks' version of the same), *Under My Skin* is a much quieter story than the author's other tale. It doesn't have the same screen tension, undoubtedly due to Negulesco's more leisurely pacing and his emphasis on the relationship of the jockey and his son. Yet the underbelly of violence is always in the background, spoken or not.

Under My Skin received mixed criticism. In the *New York Herald-Tribune*, Howard Barnes called it a "singularly exciting romantic melodrama." However, Bosley Crowther of the *Times* destroyed the production with specifics: "The germ of a devastating drama which Ernest Hemingway conveyed in his story of a crooked jockey and his little boy under the title *My Old Man* has been pretty well doused with antiseptic by Casey Robinson (scenarist) and 20th Century-Fox."

Negulesco's favorite film at Fox is *Three Came Home*, also released in 1950. It is the first of four films he was to do with writer Nunnally Johnson. The story of British families in wartime Borneo who are held in Japanese detention camps stars Claudette Colbert, Patric Knowles, and Sessue Hayakawa.

In *The American Cinema* (E. P. Dutton), Andrew Sarris perceptively analyzes Negulesco's work: "Jean Negulesco's career can be divided into two periods labeled B.C. and A.C., or Before Cinemascope and After Cinemascope. *The Mask of Dimitrios, Three Strangers, Humoresque, Deep Valley, Road House, Johnny Belinda*, and *Take Care of My Little Girl* are all Before Cinemascope, and all rather competently and even memorably made. Everything After Cinemascope is completely worthless. Negulesco's is the most dramatic case of directorial maladjustment in the fifties."

Although Sarris is too severe with Negulesco's "A.C." productions, his point is well taken. Cinemascope caused a number of problems when the director first attempted to use the device in *How to Marry a Millionaire* (1953). "How, for example, were you going to do intimate scenes on that great wide oblong?" Jean asked. "And this was supposed to be a comedy." He did adapt the technique for later productions such as *Three Coins in the Fountain* and *Woman's World* (both 1954). However, those films which were designed as quiet, romantic, occasionally tense dramas became colder, more distant, more alienated from their warm conceptions, and consequently sapped the director's greatest strength.

Perhaps to make up for unwanted expansiveness, Jean tried to film in architecturally or naturally beautiful locations. He has an artist's eye for landscape and design, so the task was a mere utilization of his talent. The director told Charles Higham about his method of location shooting: "When I make a picture abroad, I always go to the best bookstore in town and look through every photographic book about that particular country. Usually foreign photographers do better work about a town or country than native photographers."

Yet the photography cannot make up for the occasional sterility of *How to Marry a Millionaire, Three Coins in the Fountain,* or *Woman's World*. As the 1950s progressed, Negulesco filmed scripts which were increasingly sentimental, without the bite of his material in the 1940s and early 1950s. The only redeeming features in *The Rains of Ranchipur* (1955) and *Boy on a Dolphin* (1957) are the locales of both and Sophia Loren in the latter. Jean went deeper into melodrama between 1958-64, with less and less success. The fine balance in *Humoresque* never surfaces in *The Gift of Life* (1958), and *The Best of Everything* (1959) and *The Pleasure Seekers* (1964) are sheer pap.

In the early 1970s the director attempted to make a series of films in Iran, but only *The Heroes* (also called *The Invincible Six*), starring Stuart Whitman and Elke Sommer, has surfaced to date. However, this 1970 variation on *The Magnificent Seven* is full of updated Negulesco virtues. For the most part the actors are properly cynical, the parched Iranian locations are chokingly arid yet picturesque, and well-cut violence is plentiful. On the whole, *The Heroes* is a tough little B film which doesn't quit, despite a contrivance or two and an ineffectual performance from Jim Mitchum as a native bandit. The dialogue almost always bites. Says Curt Jurgens to his cohorts, "The only man I ever murdered is standing before you, with a gun in his hand, defending his corpse to the bitter end." Whitman later says to Sommer about a buried leader, "If you've got a date with him, you're gonna need a shovel."

When last heard from, Jean Negulesco was living in England, doubtlessly trying to arrange new projects. In an age where violence and psychopathology are common cinema elements, producers should remember such works as *Three Strangers* and *Road House*, vital films today because they embody the very malaise of the 1970s in a rich, complex, and action-filled framework.

The Films of Jean Negulesco

Singapore Woman *(WB, 1941)*
The Mask of Dimitrios *(WB, 1944)*
The Conspirators *(WB, 1944)*
Nobody Lives Forever *(WB, 1946)*
Three Strangers *(WB, 1946)*
Humoresque *(WB, 1947)*
Deep Valley *(20th, 1947)*
Road House *(20th, 1948)*
Johnny Belinda *(WB, 1948)*
The Forbidden Street *(20th, 1949)*
The Mudlark *(20th, 1950)*
Under My Skin *(20th, 1950)*
Three Came Home *(20th, 1950)*
Take Care of My Little Girl *(20th, 1951)*
Phone Call from a Stranger *(20th, 1952)*
Lydia Bailey *(20th, 1952)*
Lure of the Wilderness *(20th, 1952)*
O. Henry's Full House *(episode: "The Last Leaf") (20th, 1952)*

Scandal at Scourie *(MGM, 1953)*
Titanic *(20th, 1953)*
How to Marry a Millionaire *(20th, 1953)*
Three Coins in the Fountain *(20th, 1954)*
Woman's World *(20th, 1954)*
Daddy Long Legs *(20th, 1955)*
The Rains of Ranchipur *(20th, 1955)*
Boy on a Dolphin *(20th, 1957)*
The Gift of Life *(20th, 1958)*
A Certain Smile *(20th, 1958)*
Count Your Blessings *(MGM, 1959)*
The Best of Everything *(20th, 1959)*
Jessica *(UA, 1962)*
The Pleasure Seekers *(20th, 1964)*
Hello—Goodbye *(20th, 1970)*
The Invincible Six (The Heroes) *(Continental, 1970)*

Irving Rapper (left), Fredric March, and producer Jesse Lasky discuss The Adventures of Mark Twain *(WB, 1944)*

James Stephenson (center) and Geraldine Fitzgerald (right) in Shining Victory *(WB, 1941)*

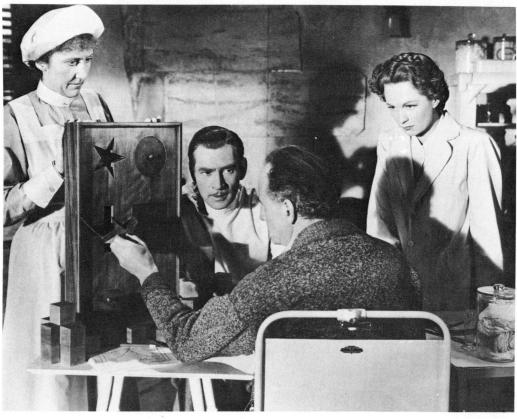

16

Irving Rapper

"I was so fascinated by it that I kept forgetting to give cues," Irving Rapper admitted in 1941. "We had two houses burning down and a whole block of traffic snarled up, with children running everywhere, fireman and crowds and terrific excitement. It was fascinating, and I kept looking at it. We had rehearsed it several times without setting the building on fire. Then we started the fire and it was even more exciting. Suddenly I realized people were calling to me, and they were asking about cues. I had forgotten all about directing."

The scene was for *One Foot in Heaven*. That enthusiasm had carried the director for over a dozen years in the theatre and a term as a Warner Brothers dialogue coach before he was able to turn down his first full-fledged directorial offer. When Irving Rapper finally accepted *Shining Victory*, most of Hollywood knew that the delay was worth it. Discriminating Rapper has a flair for directing actors, and, in his best films, for simultaneously framing them in their own worlds, whether it be the lab equipment in *Shining Victory*, the creaky, musty houses of *One Foot in Heaven*, or the museum-like penthouses in *Deception*. One can hardly wait for his return to the cinema as the director of *Sextette*, starring the indomitable Mae West.

Irving Rapper was born in 1898 in London, England. He came to America to study law at New York University after World War I, but he got caught up in the flourish of theatrical activity in the Manhattan of the 1920s. By 1928 he had clearly developed the intense approach to his work which swept him into the action of the aforementioned calamity in *One Foot in Heaven*. "How on God's earth one can even breathe during a stock season, I don't know," Rapper wrote to a friend. "Twice, I forgot to eat."

In the 1930s he directed such plays as *East River Romance* with Mildred McCoy and Gene Lockhart, and *Crime*. During this time the Walter Hershburn Agency tried unsuccessfully to sell Irving's talents to Paramount.* It was generally felt that his stage experience, particularly in directing Molnar plays, would be useless in Hollywood. This attitude was a far cry from the studio's hunger for theatrical talent after Al Jolson sang "Mammy" on the screen in 1927.

Rapper approached Warner Brothers himself in 1936, only to receive a carbon copy of his reception at Paramount. He then returned to the home of the crime and gangster film with a rave review from the play *Crime*, and the studio immediately hired him as a dialogue director. "I began working on a horror film called *The Walking Dead*, with Boris Karloff and just about the entire stock company of Warner Brothers," the director commented years later. "It was a bad story, but it was directed by the great Michael Curtiz, who was my mentor and guide for many years, and to whom I owe my knowledge of the cinema."

The dialogue coach also participated in the making of *The Story of Louis Pasteur, The Life of Emile Zola, The Sisters, Juarez*, and *All This and Heaven Too*. On the set of *Juarez* he stated: "Let me say that, having tasted of pictures, nothing in the world would induce me to forsake them entirely for my first love—the legitimate stage."

In 1938 Irving declined a directing offer from Warner Brothers, thereby shocking the entire studio, but he was waiting for the right project. *Shining Victory* (1941), a modest production about a research scientist, starring James Stephenson and Geraldine Fitzgerald, was the one. Rapper began his film career by sketching out the opening and closing moments of a scene, but he later changed his habit. "I would improvise a good deal, but I always followed the scripts I was given to the letter," he told Charles Higham and Joel Greenberg for *The Celluloid Muse: Hollywood Directors Speak*. "At Warners they would give you a finished script, and if you refused to do it, you were on suspension. Your contract specified that you must do anything you were assigned to. If a camera movement took an unusually long time, I would improvise a phrase or a line, but broadly speaking there would be no major reconstruction."

Rapper wasn't quite as docile as his statement to Higham implies. "I was known as the rebellious director at Warners.... I had ten suspensions in seven years! I would refuse, say, a crime picture I wouldn't even know how to begin, or some Nazi picture when I thought people were tired of them, or non-literate scripts." With Bette Davis, among others, backing him up, Irving enjoyed a little more freedom than the average new Warner Brothers director of the 1940s, such as Curtis Bernhardt.

*Although he assisted Robert Florey in directing *Hole in the Wall* at the studio in 1929.

Shining Victory was adapted from a Lloyd C. Douglas novel. Rapper's direction of the triangle formed by Stephenson, Fitzgerald, and Barbara O'Neil subtly evokes the real tensions of a woman entering what was then considered a man's world, along with the underplayed psychosis of the O'Neil character. The trio is something of a prophecy of the relationship shared by Bette Davis, Paul Henreid, and Claude Rains in *Deception*.

"Slow and generally unimpassioned," criticized the *New York Times'* Bosley Crowther, echoing the general critical reaction to *Shining Victory*.

When Anatole Litvak was taken off *One Foot in Heaven* (1941), the project was assigned to Irving. In 1935 Rapper had written of the film's star, Fredric March, that he couldn't "bear that strutting ham on screen." A half-decade later the two were close friends. "It's so rare that one finds an established actor so helpful to a 'young' director," he wrote.

"One of the finest pictures of the year," proclaimed the *Times'* Bosley Crowther, now an Irving Rapper cheerleader (for the time being), adding that it was "a cheerful and warmly compassionate film." Kate Carroll of the New York *Daily News* awarded *One Foot in Heaven* three and a half stars, and Howard Barnes of the *New York Herald-Tribune* felt that the "challenging subject matter has been handled with great skill and authority."

The "challenging subject matter" concerns the lives of a hard-working minister (March) and his perky wife (Martha Scott). The director distinguishes himself here through a penchant for absorbing Americana into artifacts of human experience, rather than envisioning old pictures, chairs, bric-a-brac, and even dust, as things to be seen and not understood. Some of the finest scenes in the film deal with the transformation of a house given to the minister and his wife by a small community. The dwelling belonged to a townswoman who slowly realizes the couple's need to rearrange the rooms to fit their basic living patterns.

Michael Curtiz was asked to direct Bette Davis in *Now, Voyager*, but he didn't like the script. The Hungarian may also have balked at the idea of working with an actress whom he reportedly loathed. Once again, Irving was second choice—and once again, what a glorious second choice! Yet the circumstances of his acceptance were unfortunate. The director's mother had just died, and he was planning to take a trip for a much needed rest, but producer Hal Wallis offered him the choice of taking the assignment or going on suspension.

Rapper had only two weeks between the finish of a bad film, *The Gay Sisters*, and the start of *Now, Voyager* to prepare. He insisted on casting the parts still open. Irving chose Claude Rains for the psychiatrist and Gladys Cooper as the mother, along with Ilka Chase and Bonita

Granville. Adapting Austrian star Paul Henreid to the English language and getting Bette Davis used to the foreigner took a full week of that short time.

Now, Voyager (1942) is a classic film of unrequited love, equal to other high-powered Bette Davis melodramas like *Dark Victory* (WB, 1939) and *The Letter* (WB, 1940). She stars as Charlotte, a middle-aged spinster who lives in a staid Boston mansion with her domineering mother. Charlotte's one passion is wood-carving until she has a nervous breakdown and meets Jerry (Henreid), a man burdened with an unhappy marriage, on a luxury cruise. On board ship Jerry ascends into movie history by placing two cigarettes in his mouth, lighting both, and giving one to Charlotte. By the end of the film, Charlotte has become a mistress in the shadows, functioning as a surrogate mother to Jerry's daughter. The final scene offers little hope of a change in the situation, but as the camera leaves a shot of the lovers to sweep into the sky, Charlotte muses, "Don't let's ask for the moon? We have the stars."

"A tale of unblushing sentimentality," announced the *New York Herald-Tribune* review. *Variety* analyzed *Now, Voyager* rather adroitly: "Has almost everything for excellent entertainment and boxoffice—plenty of romance, stark drama, expert direction and photography, a fine production, and a strong supporting cast."

Rapper didn't want to direct *The Adventures of Mark Twain* (1944), but once again he gave in to pressure from Hal Wallis, and later he was glad that he had. For one thing, the production provided Irving with another chance to work with Fredric March, and in addition the admittedly rambling biographical movie about one of America's greatest authors is now a favorite on television.

The 130-minute film is packed with pieces of Americana, from the jargon of Mississippi riverboat captains to the frog races in Bret Harte's California. The most memorable moment in the film is reserved for the finish, when the 75-year-old Twain dies peacefully and his soul slips into heaven. As in *Now, Voyager,* Rapper ends with a poetic reference to the mysteries of the universe.

In 1944 Rapper planned to direct *Winged Victory*, but the property only saw the light of celluloid at 20th Century-Fox in the hands of George Cukor. Irving was also supposed to film the life of stage star Marilyn Miller, but he wrote at the time, "Until I approve of the script... I will not direct it." Nor did he appreciate the studio's choice for the title role, a girl named Shirley Eldar. The assignment apparently was given to a number of filmmakers, including Busby Berkeley, before legal complications closed the production entirely.

The director liked *Rhapsody in Blue* (1945), the biography of George Gershwin, but the critics generally didn't agree. When Rapper suggested Tyrone Power for the title role, Jack Warner countered with Cary Grant or John Garfield. Everyone finally settled for Robert Alda, an unknown picked for his ethnic looks and sophisticated manner, but Alda failed to charm anybody as Gershwin. Today Rapper appreciates bits of *Rhapsody in Blue*, but rightly considers it choked with music.

Asked how he obtained so many fine performances from the female stars at Warner Brothers, Irving replied, "I handled them like a mother handles a child." Bette Davis must have liked the treatment, since she came back for more in *The Corn Is Green* (1945). Adapted from the successful play starring Ethel Barrymore, the director slightly changed the focus of the story through an alteration of the leading character, a dedicated school teacher, "We did make her a woman more interested in all the youth of the village rather than in one boy. That seemed important in the picture. The play showed her devoting herself to one gifted boy." The studio's realistic bent (as well as Rapper's good sense) is embodied in this decision. It's not difficult to accept the assumption that most teachers are dedicated to educating their students. Therefore, it is more likely that an educator working virtually alone in a mining town will have the interests of the entire class in mind, rather than those of an individual.

Originally Rapper wanted Richard Waring for the part of the mature schoolboy in the Welsh village inspired to study for college, but Waring was in the armed forces, and the studio selected John Dall instead. Irving at first guided the young actor with some disdain, but he soon came to like Dall's effervescent, somewhat vulgar, yet sweet interpretation of the role. The director did succeed in using a $150 a week contractee, Joan Loring, for the role of the slut, a character tagged for a $3,000 per seven days performer. Jack Warner loved him for that.

The Corn Is Green ends with a group of villagers carrying Dall off for a celebration in the night after he has been accepted for college. In this way Rapper begins a descent to earth for his finales, with Dall reaching for the sky from six feet off the ground. Although the village, classroom, and houses are finely detailed in the best Warner Brothers tradition, the director keeps all sets in the background, in favor of exploring the relationship between Davis and Dall. At one point, about two-thirds of the way through the film, Irving frames his stars in an extremely close shot, focusing on the teacher's face and words, with part of the student's profile in the foreground. Once, and once only, she speaks of their united commitment, and her motivations as a human being. The moment could have been extremely rhetorical, but it emerges as a sensitive plea for the triumph of the will to succeed, due to a very intimate image which features Davis' sincerity.

Deception in 1946 was quite a different matter. It appears that Rapper

Paul Henreid and Bette Davis in Now, Voyager *(WB, 1942)*

Bette Davis and Claude Rains in Deception *(WB, 1946)*

didn't care much for the property, yet he managed to film one of the most bizarre, compelling, and cynical melodramas ever to play under the Warner Brothers banner. The story deals with a triangle—a pianist (Bette Davis), a cellist (Paul Henreid), and the pianist's teacher, an ego-maniacal composer (Claude Rains).

"*Deception* ends with Bette shooting Claude dead and going to prison," the director recalled, "but it should have been concluded as a comedy, and the writer, John Collier, intended it that way. It was supposed to have a gay, light, natural, 'So what?' ending. The three people walk off as friends. But Bette wanted a dramatic conclusion; she insisted on it; and I didn't care much either way, so I gave in." The actress recently refuted the notion that she got her way in *Deception*, but whatever the case, it is difficult to imagine a steamy, bitchy, ornate film such as this treated like a comedy, especially by Irving Rapper. His best vehicles are melodramas tinged with humanism, a trait which probably endeared him to Bette Davis in the first place, inasmuch as the star herself brilliantly projects that quality on screen.

The *New York Herald-Tribune*'s Otis L. Guernsey, Jr. wrote that *Deception* "is a vast improvement over its Broadway counterpart. Its emotional agonies, however, almost never give one time to pause for breath." "Dreary ... has a thoroughly artifical look," carped Bosley Crowther of the *New York Times*. More recently, the film was damned by Ted Sennett in *Warner Brothers Presents* as "even more ludicrous [than *A Stolen Life*], as she [Davis] carried on operatically with Claude Rains and Paul Henreid to the loudest musical score Erich Wolfgang Korngold could devise."

Anna Lucasta (Col., 1949) is a disaster starring Paulette Goddard. Originally Susan Hayward signed for the title role, but Goddard proved that she had been promised the part earlier, so Rapper had no choice in the matter.

The Glass Menagerie (WB, 1950) is a fine screen version of Tennessee Williams' play about a plain young girl (Jane Wyman) who lives in the faded world of her mother (Gertrude Lawrence), and is subjected to her brother's (Kirk Douglas) ideals, until a gentleman caller (Arthur Kennedy) arrives to temporarily whisk her away from four southern walls and a collection of fragile glass miniatures.

Critics of the time didn't appreciate Irving's admittedly leisurely paced adaptation. "It is regrettable that director Irving Rapper was compelled, it appears, to kick around the substance of a frail, illusionary drama as though it were plastic and not Venetian glass," wrote Crowther of the *Times*.

The Glass Menagerie is Irving Rapper's last good Warner Brothers film as well as his swan song to the quality brand of melodrama dominated by women. When sagging box-office returns dictated a pairing of studio talent, he left to free-lance, and only one more top-grade production has followed since.

Fair to poor productions entitled *Another Man's Poison* (UA, 1952), *Forever Female* (Par., 1953), *Bad for Each Other* (Col., 1953), and *Strange Intruder* (AA, 1956) preceded *The Brave One* (RKO, 1956), which was shot on location in Mexico.

The director was advised against filming the script about a boy who runs away to Mexico City to find a pet bull. Scenarist Dalton Trumbo (under the assumed name of Robert Rich, since Trumbo was blacklisted during the McCarthy era) won an Oscar for his original story, and the film, which cost $430,000 raked in over $8,500,000 at the box office. "Compromises all the time," the director recently confessed. "But one picture of mine in recent years that wasn't compromised: *The Brave One.*"

The Brave One has an authentic look not unlike that realism of, say, the backgrounds of *One Foot in Heaven,* but this time the truth is recorded outdoors: not just on detailed studio sets, but in the bull ring, on ranches, in Mexican streets, and in the dry south-of-the-border dust. In this film Rapper moves from the upper and middle classes to deal with the classic proletarian existence so prevalent in Warner Brothers films.

Michael Ray and Rodolfo Hoyos in The Brave One *(RKO, 1956)*

Most critics loved the quiet film. *The Brave One* "is a delight in sight and sound," asserted Frank Quinn in the *New York Daily Mirror*, adding: "Irving Rapper has directed the beautiful story with understanding." The New York *Daily News'* Wanda Hale awarded the film four stars and praised its director "for getting so much suspense, excitement, and humor into the heart-warming story which works up to a terrific climax." *Variety* liked Rapper's "movingly sentimental tale."

Marjorie Morningstar (WB, 1958) is a turgid melodrama about a young girl (Natalie Wood) with show business aspirations. Adapted from Herman Wouk's best-seller, the overlong film lacks dramatic power and is too often bogged down in melodramatics, things that Rapper would have treated with more subtlety in the 1940s. In its day, however, *Marjorie Morningstar* was termed "a thoughtful, sympathetic work," by Paul V. Beckley in the *New York Herald-Tribune*, who described it as "a tender study of the growing up of a maiden of upper middle class background." Kate Carroll of the *Daily News* gave the film her highest rating, four stars, and commended Irving's "incisive direction." Even the title song was nominated for an Oscar, a fact that the director is particularly proud of, since he insisted that the original music be thrown out.

However, in *The Miracle* (WB, 1959) Rapper wasn't so lucky, since he had trouble with star Carroll Baker from the start. She, in turn, spoke of their on-set relationship: "I'm quite a strong woman and he's more or less a woman-hater. The result is we're like two cats." On the other side of the coin, Rapper remembered: "The whole thing was unspeakably bad because of her. I didn't even talk to her." It appears that Baker received the role of a nun courtesy of the new management at Warner Brothers without benefit of a test. Rapper hadn't even met her beforehand.

Two forgettable Italian productions followed before *The Christine Jorgensen Story* (UA, 1970). In the *Village Voice*, David Watts summarized the treatment of the man who became a woman: "Marginally employable veteran Irving Rapper has sealed it with the depressing glaze of old Hollywood," although he admitted that the director "does give the pulpy script certain disturbingly sinister accents by means of cheesy old-style lighting and a pseudo-Tchaikovsky score."

A short while later the director retired to Europe. He endeavored to promote several productions, such as *Ceferino Namuncura*, starring Anthony Quinn, Claude Rains, and Ricardo Montalban, but they all fell through. In 1976 Mae West requested Rapper to direct her in *Sextette*, a film version of the star's own 1927 play. Shooting was scheduled to start in August 1976. If anyone can project Mae West's saucy persona on a movie screen in the 1970s, it's Irving Rapper, a premier director of bombastic Bette Davis and a weaver of the best an actor can give.

The Films of Irving Rapper

Shining Victory *(WB, 1941)*

One Foot in Heaven (WB, 1941) (replaced Anatole Litvak) (and co-producer)

The Gay Sisters *(WB, 1942)*

Now, Voyager *(WB, 1942)*

The Adventures of Mark Twain *(WB, 1944)*

Rhapsody in Blue *(WB, 1945)*

The Corn Is Green *(WB, 1945)*

Deception *(WB, 1946)*

The Voice of the Turtle *(WB, 1947)*

Anna Lucasta *(Col., 1949)*

The Glass Menagerie *(WB, 1950)*

Another Man's Poison *(UA, 1952)*

Forever Female *(Par., 1953)*

Bad for Each Other *(Col., 1953)*

Strange Intruder *(AA, 1956)*

The Brave One *(RKO, 1956)*

Marjorie Morningstar *(WB, 1958)*

The Miracle *(WB, 1959)*

Giuseppe Venduto Dai Fratelli *(Italian, 1960) (co-directed by Luciano Ricci)*

Pontius Pilate *(Italian, 1961)*

The Christine Jorgensen Story *(UA, 1970)*

Sextette *(project, 1977)*

Jeffrey Lynn and Kaaren Verne in Underground (WB, 1941)

Ann Sheridan, Kent Smith, and Vincent Sherman on the set of Nora Prentiss (WB, 1947)

Vincent Sherman

"In my thirty films I have worked closely with the writers. Of those thirty only six required very little work, were ready to go to the post when I first read them," Vincent Sherman recalled for me recently. "After the films were completed I liked to have a first look with the cutter, then make a few changes before it was shown to the producer and Warner. We all then discussed various cuts, trims, changes which were usually agreed upon. Sometimes, of course, I would differ seriously with certain cuts but you can't have everything your way. You must still defer to the man who puts up the money, unless you are strong enough to have it otherwise in your contract."

A reasonable man, Vincent Sherman spent a profitable decade as a Warner Brothers director, moving from war to women, to gangsters, to show business, to comedy, then back to women and war. As such, he cannot be classified with Edmund Goulding and Irving Rapper as a director of "women's" vehicles, nor does he fit into the Hawks-Wellman-Curtiz-Walsh pattern of the action filmmaker. Sherman is something of a hybrid. When the project is right, as in *Underground, The Hard Way, Old Acquaintance,* or *The Hasty Heart,* the director gives the best to both worlds. In the 1950s he didn't get lost in the changing Hollywood, as did so many of his friends behind the camera. *The Garment Jungle* and *The Young Philadelphians* rank with the best Sherman efforts of the 1940s.

The man's métier has been stories in which hero and villain are clearly defined, yet influenced by a pathological overcast, a fear, or an obsession which may either build or break. If there is a quintessential Sherman protagonist, it is the man or woman who overcomes the weight of a severely oppressive world.

Vincent Sherman was born on July 16, 1906 in Vienna, Georgia. He took his A.B. at Oglethorpe University in Atlanta, where he was president of the debating team, a broad jumper, and an amateur boxer. Young Vincent attended law school and labored at many jobs, including journalism in Atlanta and selling films.

In the early days of the Depression, Sherman moved to New York City in hopes of becoming a playwright. He married Hedda Comoro in 1930 and was swept up into the theatrical world, making his acting debut in a Theatre Guild production of *Marco Millions* ("I actually carried a spear. No kidding!"), followed by roles in *Elizabeth the Queen*, *The Good Earth* (as a young revolutionary, a role he repeated in MGM's 1937 film), *Counsellor at Law, Sailor of Cattaro, Black Pit, Waiting for Lefty, Paradise Lost, Bitter Stream*, and others. He also toured in a road company of *Dead End* for six months as Baby Face Martin.

In 1937 Vincent staged Sinclair Lewis' *It Can't Happen Here* at the WPA theatre in New York. Of the production, *New York Times* critic Brooks Atkinson wrote, "It hardly fulfills the opportunity Mr. Lewis has given to the stage, for the characters are meagerly defined, the dialogue is undistinguished, and many of the scenes dawdle on one foot." A notable occurrence took place when the curtain rang down at 11:30 on opening night. The show received a standing ovation, and the audience called for the author to make a speech. Lewis came into view, simply said, "I've been making a speech since seven minutes to nine," and then disappeared. That was the quality of social activist theatre in New York of the 1930s.

Although the New York critics weren't enthusiastic about Sherman's direction, Sinclair Lewis thought enough of the young man to consider co-authoring a play with him. Despite the impression that the author must have made on the budding writer, however, Vincent's career was permanently welded to Hollywood in June 1937 when he signed with Warner Brothers as a writer-director-actor.

Producer Bryan Foy told Sherman, "Well, I talked to Mr. Warner and he says that if you are willing to sign a seven-year contract (a standard at the studio) to act, write, or direct, then we'll start you with two hundred dollars a week." Wanting to cover all of the young man's talents at the same salary, Foy added, "If you don't turn out all right as a writer, we'll use you as an actor."

Vincent had appeared in a number of films prior to being engaged by Warner Brothers, such as *The Old Doll House* and *Girl in Danger*, but it was as a writer that he received his first Warner Brothers screen credit. Script contributions to *Crime School, My Bill, Heart of the North*, and *Gantry the Great* preceded his first directorial assignment in 1939, *The Return of Dr. X*.

The most memorable element in that lackluster entry into the horror genre is Humphrey Bogart's bizarre performance as a zombie. The remaining cast and the plot are eminently forgettable. "A cheerful little picture," quipped *New York Times* critic B. R. Crisler.

Although Vincent is an even-tempered man, his patience was severely tested on the set of *The Return of Dr. X*. The first time he looked through the camera he found the arc lights placed in view of the lens. Precocious assistants asked the rookie filmmaker if he wished the lights to be in the shot, and more put-ons followed throughout the day. That was Vincent Sherman's baptism into the frolics of the colorful, super-fast section of Hollywood called Warner Brothers.

John Garfield and the director were set to work together in 1939's *Bad Boy*, after Vincent replaced Michael Curtiz. The production was canceled, but the two finally teamed during the following year in *Saturday's Children*, produced in 1929 and 1935 as *Maybe It's Love*. Based on Maxwell Anderson's play of a young married couple struggling against poverty in New York City, the film stars Garfield and Anne Shirley, but Claude Rains as Shirley's father dominates the proceedings with his stiff-upper-lip sense of duty to his daughter.

Once again the director had to smile through difficulties during the production of *Saturday's Children*. While shooting a difficult scene on a Warner Brothers process stage, somebody walked onto the set and ruined the take. Rather than exploding in anger, the director quietly inquired why the person had entered a studio when the red light at the front door was flashing, thus indicating that the cameras were rolling. The answer was that the light was out. After remedying the situation, Sherman then reshot the scene. "I still have a lot to learn about directing moving pictures," Vincent said in 1940, "and feel that only by doing a lot of them will I be able to attain near perfection." He knew that the education process also consisted of learning to deal with on-set errors, innocent mistakes which destroyed beautiful scenes.

In addition Sherman got used to being associated with projects that were never produced. Among them was a 1940 Charles Kaufman story called *Fiesta in Manhattan*, to star John Garfield, and 1941's *Klondike* with Ann Sheridan. Nevertheless, the filmmaker informed me recently, "Warner Brothers, being my home lot, was, I thought, the best. A big family, in its heyday, with two thousand people walking through the gate every morning, all of us knowing each other by sight or name. All departments were of the best."

After directing an unsuccessful remake of *The Mouthpiece* (1932), retitled *The Man Who Talked Too Much*, Vincent filmed the touching little drama *Flight from Destiny*, released early in 1941. Starring Geraldine Fitzgerald, Thomas Mitchell, James Stephenson, and Jeffrey Lynn, the film originally titled *Trial and Error* concerns the sacrifices made by an older man (Mitchell) to clear a young husband (Lynn) of criminal charges.

Underground (1941) is one of Sherman's best films. The taut tale of anti-Nazi operations in wartime Germany features Philip Dorn (as a conspirator) and Jeffrey Lynn (as his one-armed brother, a Nazi hero), along with Kaaren Verne, Mona Maris, and menacing Martin Kosleck as a brutal Nazi officer.

"Much credit for the gripping story must be given to Vincent Sherman's excellent staging and direction," read the *New York Herald-Tribune* review, but others weren't as kind. "I'm afraid, in the end, that *Underground* is just as fictional, just as fantastic, as anything that Hollywood has cooked up," carped Leo Mishkin in the *New York Morning Telegraph*.

Of course it is now known that there were many fervent anti-Nazis in Germany from Hitler's rise to power onward. The sinister end which meets a group of the conspirators was a dim prophecy of the real fate of others who attempted to overthrow the Third Reich toward the end of the war. The only scene in *Underground* which rings false is between Lynn and Mona Maris outside a cell where Lynn's brother and father are being tortured. Maris is a member of the underground who works as a secretary to Kosleck. It is simply not believable that she would convince Lynn to join the anti-Nazi forces less than fifty feet away from the inferno where others are being bloodied. For a group of conspirators who up to that point operated so intelligently, such a blunder is unthinkable.

Aside from that flaw, *Underground* is a topical, terror-inspiring odyssey into human relations in Nazi Germany, where no one is safe from the lies of another, and loyal friendships and working relationships disintegrate in the face of the Nazi whip, or even that cold Aryan face, that penetrating Kosleck stare. In a world where even looking away from a Nazi figure is deemed suspicious, anything can happen, and a hero of the resistance one year may be a cowering lackey of the Third Reich the next. The scenes in which an imprisoned underground leader is brought from his cell into the light of the Nazi shadow, becomes an informer, and ultimately commits suicide symbolize the struggle for dignity in a fascist dictatorship. All the intrigues of *Underground* were found to be accurate inside Germany after the war. As Sherman declared, "There was a special vitality at the studio that expressed itself in trying to make films about the times."

All Through the Night (1942) concerns underground operations in America, featuring a light mix of underworld activity to keep the pace fast-moving and bright. Humphrey Bogart stars as a likable gangster with a mother, funny cohorts (William Demarest, Jackie Gleason, Frank McHugh, and Phil Silvers), and a budding love relationship (with

Kaaren Verne). Throw in some cloak-and-spy stuff courtesy of Conrad Veidt, Peter Lorre, and Judith Anderson, and what emerges is a double-edged film that balances laughs with the direst implications of Nazi sabotage strategy in America. An airy follow-up to Warner Brothers' hard-hitting *Confessions of a Nazi Spy* in 1939, *All Through the Night* was released shortly before the FBI arrested a nest of German saboteurs operating along the Eastern seaboard.

Variety's review was clipped and to the point: "Gripping espionage thriller." The *New York Sun* called *All Through the Night* "bright and brittle entertainment, jam-packed with spurting automatics, steaming left hooks, wisecracking mobsters and as leering a lot of Gestapo agents as ever cheated the hot seat."

The high point of *All Through the Night* encompasses spy, gangster, and, above all, comedy territory. Bogart and William Demarest have infiltrated the secret organization and are mistaken for two explosives specialists. The pair's doubletalk as they try to explain their way out of certain death has to stand as one of the memorable moments of war-oriented films in Hollywood.

In 1943 Sherman started shifting his emphasis to stories with strong roles for women. *The Hard Way* is a tingling tale of a snakish female (Ida Lupino) who positions herself with teeth clenched and fingernails sharpened to destroy anyone who gets in the way of her sister's (Joan Leslie) ascent to Broadway stardom. Dennis Morgan and Jack Carson play small-time vaudevillians who give Leslie a start and are then discarded when better things come.

In this film, called "a disagreeable and purposeless charade" by Theodore Strauss of the *New York Times*, Sherman excels in directing scenes of high intensity which are colored by a foreboding obsession. The two-sided neurosis is filled by Leslie's thoughtless ambition and Lupino's vicarious thrills at seeing her sister become the toast of Broadway. Suicide is both a crime and a penalty in *The Hard Way*. Jack Carson marries Leslie and the couple tour American theatres. Soon they split professionally, and it is only a matter of time before she abandons him altogether. When he is practically ejected from a posh party given in his wife's honor, the dejected vaudevillian attempts to fill a final engagement, but he ends up committing suicide to the strains of her melodious recorded voice. Lupino's death is a lingering one as she attempts to end her life on a lonely, mist-filled pier. From the smoke-filled mines of Pittsburgh, to the shrouded docks of New York, Lupino has come to a belated recognition of the damage she has done. She dies an anonymous patient in a hospital, forgotten by all, rejected even by white-clad attendants as a "crazy rich dame."

During the war years Warner Brothers attempted to provide a catharsis of sorts for women whose sons, husbands, and sweethearts were

287

fighting in bloody theatres throughout the world. The result for Vincent Sherman was *Old Acquaintance* (1943), *In Our Time* (1944), and *Mr. Skeffington* (1945)—all tear-jerkers of the highest order, generally films with solid production values, top casts and performances, and female all the way. In quality, they rank as follows—*Old Acquaintance, Mr. Skeffington*, and *In Our Time*.

Old Acquaintance stars those two battling professionals, Bette Davis and Miriam Hopkins, with poor John Loder caught between their lifetime squabbles. Davis loses two loves due to the selfish Hopkins and Dolores Moran (Davis' screen daughter), but at the end of the film the stalwarts sit in a cozy room and reminisce. Old acquaintances can do that.

According to the *Nation*'s James Agee, "*Old Acquaintance* is a topical women's duet on the standard musical saws favored by any housewives' magazine.... What perplexes me is that I could sit through it with some interest." *Variety* wasn't puzzled by great contradictions. "A strong attraction for the women," the show business journal contended.

Like its predecessor, *Mr. Skeffington* unwinds over a long period of time. Bette Davis plays a vain woman who marries an older man (Claude Rains) for reasons of convenience. Ultimately, after she has lost her hair from a bout with diphtheria, Rains returns as a blinded victim of World War II, yet still "sees" his wife as a great beauty. She reforms, and hungry audiences got a good cry, despite the rambling nature of the film which loses much punch due to excessive length.

In Our Time has all the soap and little of the dramatic surge of the previous films, while *Pillow to Post* (1945) is an innocuous comedy about a salesgirl and a soldier. *Nora Prentiss* and *The Unfaithful* (both 1947) were the final attempts by Warner Brothers to embroil Ann Sheridan in melodrama before she left the studio. *Nora Prentiss* could have been a scorching film but for a huge catch: one has to believe that Nora wouldn't recognize a doctor (Lew Ayres) whose lover she was and whose life she ruined, even with a changed face. *The Unfaithful* is a fair remake of *The Letter,* but it can't match the original on the levels of performance (Sheridan is not Bette Davis) or properly florid direction. Sherman's camera just doesn't move enough.

The Adventures of Don Juan (1949) is Sherman's only released foray into the swashbuckler. The 110-minute color spectacle contains a fine tongue-in-cheek performance by Errol Flynn as the title character, laughing and loving as before, but with a sense of the absurdity of it all. The film's main problem is pace. Slowness dulls an absorbing adventure, as Douglas Fairbanks found out after making *The Thief of Bagdad.* Amid flashy swordplay and cocky love-talk, Flynn and Alan Hale counterbalance newer, less suitable villains (Robert Douglas and

Raymond Burr) and less publicized lovelies (Viveca Lindfors and Ann Rutherford).

"Vincent Sherman has directed for eye-filling pictures and speed," insisted Bosley Crowther in the *New York Times*. "A number of swashbuckling costume films have reached the screen recently," observed *Variety*, adding: "*The Adventures of Don Juan* measures among the best of them."

The Hasty Heart (1949) is in many ways Vincent Sherman's most sensitive drama. Adapted from John Patrick's play, the film centers around an anti-social Scottish soldier (Richard Todd) who discovers he only has a few months to live. Others in the remote hospital setting attempt to make friends with the stubborn serviceman, but his pride won't allow it. Patricia Neal as a nurse and Ronald Reagan as a GI both etch characters who don't relent in the strain of a harsh environment, yet manage to display genuine human concern. Todd's Scottish kilts provide a telling refrain, symbolizing his alienation, then acceptance of his fate, along with the friendship of other ailing soldiers. Despite the fact that the proceedings occur almost entirely in one area, *The Hasty Heart* isn't one bit stagebound. That's quite a feat during a period of emphasis on location work and realistic settings.

"Vincent Sherman has done a wonderful job of maintaining fluidity in the progress of his drama," asserted Otis L. Guernsey, Jr. of the *New York Herald-Tribune*, while the *Times*' Bosley Crowther termed *The Hasty Heart* a "winning and poignant film."

Backfire (1950) is a lackluster mystery starring Gordon MacRae, but Sherman's other films of that year, *The Damned Don't Cry* and *Harriet Craig* (Columbia), mark a return to the garish melodramas of the 1940s.

The Damned Don't Cry, starring Joan Crawford, was originally titled *The Victim* and described by Warner Brothers producer Jerry Wald as "the story of a modern bad girl." Crawford is in fine form as a gangster's moll who discovers the virtuous life a little too late to live it. *Harriet Craig* is a remake of *Craig's Wife* (1936), and again features Crawford as a bad girl, this time on the right side of the tracks. In the *Herald-Tribune* Otis L. Guernsey, Jr. called *Harriet Craig* "as smooth as the silk in its namesake's well-guarded salon," which is rescued from a "lack of warmth and personality by the presence of a star who does not know how to do anything except shine."

Harriet Craig caused Sherman much consternation. Joan Crawford asked him to read the script, but the director didn't like it. When Warner Brothers executive Steve Trilling asked Vincent to direct the film, Sherman only consented when he discovered that Trilling had loaned out his services anyway. At Warner Brothers, to balk at a film meant suspension. "Well, it was much later that I discovered that Jack Warner had set

Ida Lupino,
Dennis Morgan,
and Joan Leslie
in The Hard Way
(WB, 1943)

Frank McHugh,
Judith Anderson,
Humphrey Bogart,
and Kaaren
Verne in All
Through the
Night *(WB, 1942)*

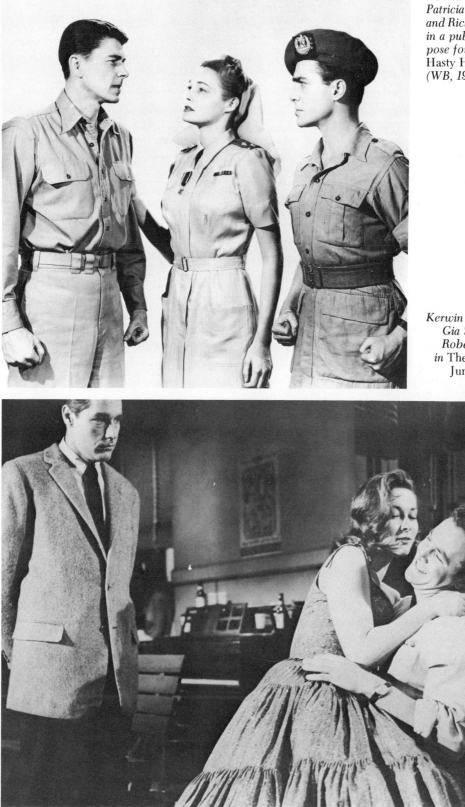

Ronald Reagan, Patricia Neal, and Richard Todd in a publicity pose for The Hasty Heart (WB, 1950)

Kerwin Mathews, Gia Scala, and Robert Loggia in The Garment Jungle (Col., 1957)

up a new policy," Sherman told author James Silke for *Here's Looking at You, Kid* (Little, Brown). "The picture business was in the process of changing and Warner was trying to reduce his overhead and costs as much as possible. People were making $3,500 a week and he didn't have pictures for them; he was just trying to get rid of those heavy contracts."

Goodbye, My Fancy (WB, 1951) is in a way a reflective look at a genre grown up. Joan Crawford has the role of a Congresswoman who returns to her alma mater to receive an award, and also to engage in a fling with a former sweetheart (Robert Young). It's as if the film is saying, "In a post-war world, everybody's an adult, and there's no room for high society or proletarian soap operas, but we can look back just once."

In the 1950s Sherman free-lanced, although he made all but two of his remaining films at Warner Brothers or Columbia. Unlike many directors, Sherman liked working for strong-willed Harry Cohn at Columbia. The director recently wrote to me: "I especially enjoyed working at Columbia because I got along well with Harry Cohn and we became quite friendly. He was a strange and difficult man to know, contradictory but talented, crude and coarse at times but with impeccable taste when it came to films."

After filming his first and only Western to date, *Lone Star* (MGM, 1951), starring Clark Gable, Ava Gardner, and Lionel Barrymore, Vincent directed *Affair in Trinidad* for Cohn. Most of the sparks in the film come from alluring Rita Hayworth.

It wasn't until 1957 that Sherman's name was again listed on a movie as a director. *The Garment Jungle* is the oddest film of the director's career, and it was started by Robert Aldrich. Released during a period of exposé films such as *On the Waterfront, The Phoenix City Story*, and *Slaughter on Tenth Avenue, The Garment Jungle* explores gangster infiltration into the dressmaking industry. Featuring Lee J. Cobb, Kerwin Matthews, Gia Scala, and Richard Boone, the film has the very real look of its predecessors, as well as the extreme violence, which is occasionally tempered by romantic interludes between Matthews and Scala. One of the most frightening scenes occurs when a man falls to his death down an elevator shaft, fulfilling a grim prophecy and marking the consolidation of the rule of criminal lords.

Paul V. Beckley of the *New York Herald-Tribune* called *The Garment Jungle* "a well-made minor film," while the *New York Times'* Howard Thompson wrote: "This challenging bold picture does have color, it moves, and the acting is generally first rate."

The making of *The Garment Jungle* was as exciting as the film itself. The director recently informed me about the problems: "This is a painful subject to me since Bob Aldrich, whom I like and respect, was hurt. The facts in brief are: Cohn summoned me to his office one day to say he wanted a few scenes reshot as soon as the film was completed. I suggested that Aldrich redo them, but Cohn said he was not happy the way things were going on the set. Aldrich and the writer-producer, Harry Kleiner, he said, were not getting along and Lee Cobb, the star, was unhappy. I tried to beg off but he said if I didn't do them he would get someone else. I finally agreed but told him he would have to let Aldrich know and I would also discuss it with him.

"The next morning about 6:00 I received a call from the production head, Jack Fier, saying that Aldrich was ill, and would I come in for the day to take over? I went in and called Aldrich from the studio. I was to pick up on a scene that was not completed. By talking to Aldrich, getting his ideas on how he intended to complete the scene, I proceeded to do so. I also asked him what his thoughts were on the other scenes to be done that day and he told me. I tried to follow through with his ideas as best as possible.

"This I believe was on a Friday and Bob was supposed to return to the set on Monday. On Friday night I had a chance to read the script thoroughly which I had not been able to do before and found some glaring errors, so far as I was concerned.

"Saturday morning I received a call from Cohn asking me to come to his house to see Friday's work. I went. He seemed pleased with the rushes, then asked me what I thought of the script. I told him what I thought was wrong but I added perhaps these discrepancies had been taken care of by Aldrich in the way he had rewritten the scenes or conceived them.

"Cohn stood up and in a burst of anger turned on Lillian Sydney who was his assistant at the time and said, 'He's right, that's what's wrong with the picture. This area doesn't make sense.' After a lengthy discussion between them, he turned to me and said the situation between Aldrich and the writer and Lee Cobb was not very good, they were not getting along, and he thought it hopeless to expect any improvement.

"Again I did not want to become involved since Aldrich had already been shooting for thirty days and the film was almost completed. I forget the details here but as I recall I was told to report to the set again on Monday. I was under the impression that Aldrich was still sick. Then I heard that Aldrich had come through the front gate and I left the set and went to my office. I was angry with Jack Fier for putting both Aldrich and myself in this awkward position. What I did not know was that Cohn had decided on Sunday to take Aldrich off the film.

"Later I was called into Cohn's office. He explained that he could not go on under the present situation. He asked me to look at the cut film so far, tell him what I thought could be saved and what would have to be rewritten. I could not turn him down because of past favors, and he also informed me that he had explained the situation to Aldrich. Aldrich came to the studio, he said, merely to say goodbye to the actors.

"I sat with Harry Kleiner, the writer-producer, and told him what I thought we could save and what I thought had to be rewritten. He accepted the ideas and we took off a day or two to rewrite. I do not know to this day who was responsible for what. When I talked to Lee Cobb about the changes he indicated that there was a disagreement about the script between Aldrich and Kleiner and Cohn. Who knows? I was in the middle but had to proceed. It was costing the studio money.

"I reshot for eleven days—sixty or seventy percent of the total. Cohn then said he was putting my name on the film. I told him I thought that was unfair, that Aldrich, if he wished, should certainly share the credit. Before anything was settled I had to leave for London where I had a commitment to direct *The Naked Earth*.

"It is always a thankless and awkward task to take over another director's picture. Aldrich wrote a letter of protest to the Guild. I think he felt I had not done right. I sent a long letter explaining my position."

The Naked Earth (20th, 1958) features Richard Todd and budding studio starlet Juliette Greco, but it remains one of Sherman's lesser efforts. However, his next film, *The Young Philadelphians* (WB, 1959), stands as one of his finest. A harrowing drama of the rise of an unscrupulous lawyer (Paul Newman) who turns honest in the face of love (for Barbara Rush) and an innocent friend charged with murder (Robert Vaughn), *The Young Philadelphians* is the director's last quality film to date. Fine performances by the aforementioned performers and excellent support by Alexis Smith as the dissatisfied wife of an attorney help to unify the threads of conflict. The film's highlights don't take place in offices and boudoirs or at the stuffed dinner tables of rich Philadelphians, but rather in Vaughn's lonely prison cell and in the courtroom during his explosive trial.

Ice Palace (WB, 1960) is Sherman's weakest film, dealing with a lifelong (and filmlong) battle between two titans of industry (Richard Burton and Robert Ryan) in the wilds of an Alaska which becomes part of the twentieth century as the long, long narrative collapses to a close. *A Fever in the Blood* (WB, 1961) is another courtroom drama which has its moments, but the Warner Brothers-Seven Arts stock company of the time (Efrem Zimbalist, Jr., Jack Kelly, Ray Danton, *et al.*) were no match for their illustrious predecessors. *The Second Time Around* (20th, 1961) is a comedy with little charm. The director's last film to this writing, *Cervantes—The Young Rebel* (1967), is still unreleased.

During his absence from the cinema Vincent Sherman has been busy in television. Among his recent entries on the small screen were numer-

Paul Newman and Paul Picerni in The Young Philadelphians *(WB, 1959)*

ous episodes of CBS' *Medical Center*, along with work on the continuing drama *Executive Suite*, based on the novel and film of the same name. Not one to neglect his past during the wave of nostalgia and appreciation of Hollywood, in 1972 the director did an oral history for the American Film Institute, under a $150,000 grant from the Louis B. Mayer Foundation.

Sherman summed up his present status for me: "I consider my TV experience most invaluable. Naturally I would prefer to do a good film but they seem to be few and far between."

The Films of Vincent Sherman

The Return of Dr. X *(WB, 1939)*
Saturday's Children *(WB, 1940)*
The Man Who Talked Too Much *(WB, 1940)*
Flight from Destiny *(WB, 1941)*
Underground *(WB, 1941)*
All Through the Night *(WB, 1942)*
Across the Pacific *(WB, 1942) (replaced John Huston)*
The Hard Way *(WB, 1943)*
Old Acquaintance *(WB, 1943)*
In Our Time *(WB, 1944)*
Mr. Skeffington *(WB, 1945)*
Pillow to Post *(WB, 1945)*
Nora Prentiss *(WB, 1947)*
The Unfaithful *(WB, 1947)*
The Adventures of Don Juan *(WB, 1949)*

The Hasty Heart *(WB, 1949)*
Backfire *(WB, 1950)*
The Damned Don't Cry *(WB, 1950)*
Harriet Craig *(Col., 1950)*
Lone Star *(MGM, 1951)*
Goodbye, My Fancy *(WB, 1951)*
Affair in Trinidad *(Col., 1952)*
The Garment Jungle *(Col., 1957) (replaced Robert Aldrich)*
The Naked Earth *(20th, 1958)*
The Young Philadelphians *(WB, 1959)*
Ice Palace *(WB, 1960)*
A Fever in the Blood *(WB, 1961)*
The Second Time Around *(20th, 1961)*
Cervantes—The Young Rebel *(1967, unreleased)*

Raoul Walsh in the late thirties

Raoul Walsh

$\mathcal{S}$hortly before the first shots were fired in World War I, Raoul Walsh was playing the title role in a one-reel Pathé production called *Paul Revere's Ride*. Astride the horse, Raoul received instructions from French director Emile Couteau.

"Come around ze corner, and come down ze street as fast as you can," the man said. "Stay in the middle so we can see you."

Walsh was astonished. He had to ride near trolley tracks which would surely intrude into the frame. "Say, they didn't have any trolley tracks in tho...."

"Who ze hell is directing theez picture," the filmmaker with the dramatic license retorted, "you or me?"

"That's when I decided I'd have to become a director," Raoul Walsh recalled a half-century later. "Paul Revere and the trolley tracks."

He certainly accomplished what he set out to do that day. Raoul Walsh is the action director's action director. Social themes and psychoanalysis have little place in the oeuvre of a man whose best works are exciting, unpretentious crime films such as *White Heat, The Roaring Twenties*, and *They Drive by Night*, the Western *They Died with Their Boots On*, the melodramatic *Manpower*, the comic *The Strawberry Blonde*, and the charmingly biographical *Gentleman Jim*. Even when his characters beg for psychological interpretation, as in *White Heat* and *Pursued*, Walsh prefers to concentrate on the pure level of narrative.

On March 11, 1892 Raoul became the second child born to Elizabeth and Thomas Walsh of New York City. Another son and daughter followed, and the six Walshes lived in a three-story brownstone at 128 East 48th Street bustling with servants, and guests who were the talk of the day. Young Raoul hobnobbed with the likes of Edwin Booth, Maurice Barrymore, and John L. Sullivan around the dinner table, and when he and his brother George weren't raising hell on the streets of Manhattan, they traveled the byways of America and raised hell there.

"Life was good when I was a boy," the director remembered. "I was born in New York but raised in different cities. My father was a clothing designer, but when I was a young fellow I hated the life of the city. I ran away to sea." That was big adventure number one for Raoul Walsh. "My uncle Matt owned a sailing vessel. We were broken up in a hurricane, so I went ashore in Mexico and joined a cattle drive across the Texas panhandle. I learned breakin' horses, mendin' fences, and went on to Montana, where I broke more horses for the wagons. They had tough boss fellas in those days. Toughest guys in the whole wide world, in Butte."

Living the existence of a knock-about cowboy was an exhilarating one for Walsh. Yet it was the temporary halt in that trade which brought the director into show business. When he fell off a horse and injured his right knee, he required hospitalization in San Antonio, Texas. While recuperating on the porch of a hotel, a man dressed in a natty suit approached him. The enigma in question was theatrical producer Sid Green. Green offered the lame cowboy the part of a Ku Klux Klan rider in his show *The Clansman*.

"That's how I came to be loping around a horse on a treadmill at eight o'clock that night," wrote Raoul Walsh in his autobiography *Each Man in His Time* (Farrar, Straus & Giroux). "The treadmill was being towed across a stage by a rope attached to a windlass in the wings. I, the bronco wrangler, Uncle Sam's remount trooper who never walked away from the worst outlaw, riding an old, flea-bitten circus jughead that was dressed up in a sheet with eye-slits. I was too but I also had a peaked top and carried a burning cross. I think I made up my mind to take the job when Green, who owned the horse and gear, informed me that the last rider had been thrown into the orchestra pit. I had taken my quota of falls, but so far I had never landed on top of a brass drum."

From this experience, Raoul decided that he wanted to become an actor, maybe as famous as his father's friend Edwin Booth. Back in New York, the future director and a friend, George Center, made the rounds of casting agencies, but without any luck until somebody recommended Pathé Productions. Walsh went for an interview and was hired on the spot, possibly because the company's representative liked Raoul's suit. Told to report at eight o'clock the next morning, he cracked to Center, "I don't believe it was me they hired. I think it was the suit."

That's not so far-fetched either. Since the early days of filmmaking weren't exactly strewn with sophisticated, fully equipped production companies, directors often worked in the street, using people around them who were dressed in whatever clothes they owned.

In reality Raoul had no conception of Pathé Productions, since he had only seen one movie in his life, *The Great Train Robbery*. Induced to sign a contract for three films, Raoul was introduced to make-up by the other actors. "I got my baptism of greasepaint and felt half Indian, half idiot."

His first films at the Union Hill, New Jersey studio were the unmemorable *The Banker's Daughter* and *A Mother's Love*. Walsh was hired to ride horses, but had yet to see one. However, he did see a great deal of the sexual gymnastics of fellow performer and former burlesque queen Dolly Larkin. Apparently the filmmaking profession could be as colorful and stimulating as busting broncs or sailing the seas!

Walsh was directed by Emile Couteau in the Pathé one-reelers, but the cowboy-turned-actor soon met a filmmaker named Christy Cabanne who worked at Biograph. Cabanne obtained roles for Walsh in the studio's one- and two-reel productions shot nearer the family home, on 14th Street. There Raoul acted with Lionel Barrymore, one of the first stage stars to do screen roles under his own name, as well as with the Gish sisters and Blanche Sweet, and later with Henry B. Walthall and Donald Crisp.

Soon afterward Cabanne and Walsh joined Biograph's leading director, D. W. Griffith, in Griffith's California-bound Fine Arts Production company. Walsh's first assignment for Griffith was to photograph revolutionary Pancho Villa and his men in Mexico.

"My first taste of battle was in 1911, when I was 22. I'd gotten a job with D. W. Griffith in New York and he sent me down with a camera to ride with Pancho Villa in Mexico. I rode alongside Pancho all the way from Juarez to Mexico City. We paid him $500 a month and gold to let us film him. I was in direct line of fire. I damn near got the bullets through my hat. When Pancho would line up the Federales along a wall to shoot them, I'd say, 'I haven't got enough light to photograph them. Bring 'em back a couple of hours from now!' So they'd take those poor sons of bitches out and bring 'em back and I photographed 'em as they died. And then Pancho Villa's men would run over to see if they had any gold in their teeth.

"Griffith liked the stuff I shot—unfortunately, it's all been lost—and he put me on directin' shorts and actin'."

The Life of Villa (1912) was Raoul Walsh's first film as director. Real footage shot in Mexico was blended with film taken at the Fine Arts studio and on location in San Francisco. Like other film pioneers, Walsh became an expert at the semi-documentary long before the style was proclaimed a style. Walsh's biggest acting success for Griffith was in the role of John Wilkes Booth in *The Birth of a Nation*.

Raoul's starting salary at Fine Arts was $30 a week, and he had been raised to $40 by the time he accepted an offer by William Fox in 1915. Fox lured the young director from Griffith with the promise of $400 a week. The founder of the Fox film studio liked Walsh's *Home from the Sea*. Walsh considers that film and *The Life of Villa* to be "the only pictures I made that amount to anything" in his early period.

Walsh's debut at Fox was *The Regeneration*, released in 1915, and considered by the director to be "the first feature-length gangster picture ever made." Walsh also served as scenarist and producer for what he termed a typical story of the day. Swedish Anna Q. Nilsson acts the role of a dedicated woman who runs a Bowery soup kitchen, with Rockliffe Fellow as a gangster who develops a heart of gold. From that point, Walsh wanted a little more zip in his production than the script indicated.

Griffith taught him not to follow the early cinema practice of shooting a film in sequence, so Walsh devised his own production schedule, trekking to the Bowery to film winos, prostitutes, and varied criminals before shooting additional footage in Fort Lee, New Jersey. Interiors were left for last. A big scene took place on a boat sailing up the Hudson River, and the director recruited unseemly extras from Hell's Kitchen, on the condition that each could swim. A rented boat was to be set afire, and the hundred-odd passengers would then leap into the river. A couple of toughs manned the smoke pots, and at Walsh's command the vessel was put to the torch. The passengers frantically dove over the side, with those reluctant to hit the water receiving a lift from several burly criminal types.

The city of New York had not been informed of Walsh's plans, and launches were sent to rescue the victims of what was thought to be a real disaster. When the police discovered that the scene was movie reel life instead of reality, they arrested Walsh, and only some fast talking by Fox cohort Winfield Sheehan freed the director from his prison cell.

William Fox was ecstatic about Raoul's arrest: "What you pulled today has never been done in the history of motion pictures. The papers alone will give us more publicity than if we were paying them. And all those people—boy, what more could we ask?" Apparently young Walsh had executed one of the first movie publicity stunts without even knowing it!

By the end of the film, the reformed gangster is killed by former associates. His tombstone reads, "To Lefty, a sinner who found peace," and the inscription was written by Walsh. The last shot of the film is a close-up of Nilsson's tear-wet face. "It was so harrowing that I almost bawled with her," the director wrote. *The Regeneration* ran at

Manhattan's Academy of Music theatre (owned by William Fox) for three weeks at a time when the average film stayed only two or three days.

When America declared war on Germany, Walsh was commissioned as a second lieutenant in the Army Signal Corps and assigned to put together reels of war film shot in France. While in the service, he suggested that the Army contact stars such as Mary Pickford to make public statements in support of the war and to sell war bonds. Although Raoul wanted to serve in Europe, he never got past Fort Dix, New Jersey. Within the month he was discharged—the result of some string-pulling on the part of Fox and Sheehan, he suspected.

Walsh's star soon was on the rise at Fox. One day William Fox summoned the director into his office, announced plans to move the studio to the corner of Sunset and Western Avenue in Hollywood, and offered him a whopping $1,000 a week to relocate and direct *The Honor System*.

Raoul's younger brother George, a budding actor, is featured in the production of *The Honor System* (1916). Milton Sills stars with Miriam Cooper, whom Raoul married in 1915. Their first child was born that year.

A good deal of *The Honor System* was shot in the Arizona State Prison (Walsh would go back to prison in 1949 for scenes for *White Heat*) and on nearby outdoor locations. Raoul wrote the script, and George played Jack, "who died that others might live."

The Serpent (1916) stars the screen's first vamp, Theda Bara, whom Walsh considered to be a real trouper. One scene called for about four extras to row the star across the lake. The director told several men in the area to get into the boat when the cameras started rolling, but the pay offered by Walsh persuaded almost two dozen extras to jump into the boat once the command was issued. The boat rapidly sank, and Bara, who couldn't swim, had to be rescued. Contrary to the endless delay that such an accident might cause today, the star got up dripping wet, changed her clothes, and continued shooting.

Walsh continued to direct, write, and produce films for Fox until 1920, when he switched to Realart for *The Deep Purple*, and the following year he shot *The Oath* for Mayflower Productions and *Serenade* for Associated First National. Few of the director's works from the late teens and early 1920s appear to have survived. Perhaps one of his most significant films of the time is *Evangeline* (Fox, 1919), which he wrote, produced, and directed, and which reportedly stands as Walsh's one financially unsuccessful foray into the "art" film, a field he vowed never to touch again.

By the early 1920s Hollywood studios such as Paramount and Fox had grown into major corporations with sophisticated production machines. Metro-Goldwyn-Mayer and Warner Brothers soon followed the example. United Artists was founded in 1919 by Charlie Chaplin, D. W. Griffith, Mary Pickford, and Douglas Fairbanks.

In 1924 Walsh became associated with his first agent, Harry Wurtzel. Within a week, Wurtzel arranged to have the director film a Douglas Fairbanks spectacle at United Artists called *The Thief of Bagdad*. Fairbanks escorted Walsh around the sets of the director's first million dollar production, lavishly designed by William Cameron Menzies.

Of course Fairbanks essayed the title role, and he even wrote the script under a pseudonym. A fresh face, Julanne Johnston, was chosen to play the princess. The combination of a huge budget and totally new material made Raoul quite nervous, yet he wasn't too timid to suggest disguising Mexicans as Arabs when Fairbanks failed to solve the rather large problem of hiring suitable extras.

The Thief of Bagdad was shot in thirty-five days. Among the many distinguished visitors to the set were Charlie Chaplin, John Barrymore, John Gilbert, and Bill Tilden, and the director with the heavy production costs often had trouble keeping the playful celebrities out of camera range.

Raoul also had to plan Fairbanks' trip on the magic carpet, and the troublesome scene was saved for last. "I found the answer while watching a construction job," Raoul recalled. "The steelworkers were topping out, and one of them was riding a load of girders up from the ground level, hoisted by a large crane. That gave me a clue. If he could ride the steel, then the thief and the princess could ride the flying carpet. I would stretch it over a framework of supporting cables and find some way to avoid showing the support." The way was to hang the carpet by airplane wire. Attached to an eighty-foot boom, plucky Fairbanks and a double for Julanne Johnston "rode" the carpet long enough for Walsh to take long-angled shots which he edited in with close-ups and several slow, lateral takes. The wire, painted white, was not even visible in the closer shots. The danger to Douglas Fairbanks was very real, however, since he and the stuntman performed the feat without benefit of a net!

Debuting at the Liberty Theatre in New York City, *The Thief of Bagdad* cost three dollars per ticket. The opening night moviegoer was treated to a speech by Fairbanks, and the star and director then took center stage to bow to the fans' standing ovation.

Critics cheered the loudest. "The danger in writing about *The Thief of Bagdad* is in too great use of superlatives," cautioned *Cinema Art* magazine. "Yet this new production of Douglas Fairbanks is such a marvelous creation and is so unlike any other offering of the screen that the reviewer is justified in ecstasies. Raoul Walsh directed and to him must go a big portion of the honors." According to the *Boston American*,

The Thief of Bagdad "cannot be described in words—it must be seen."
"Imagine a clever satire on *Arabian Nights*," wrote the *New York Times*
critic, "with marvelous photography, and you have an inkling of ... *The
Thief of Bagdad*."

Although the film is certainly visually exciting, the plot drags for
much of the production's 135 minutes. There is a long section which
features an uncharacteristically solemn Fairbanks, and fans found it
difficult to reconcile their bouncy hero with his more human reactions
and less gymnastic gyrations. *The Thief of Bagdad* didn't come close to
matching the financial success of Allan Dwan's 1922 Fairbanks spectacle,
Robin Hood, even though the latter cost but one-third the amount of the
Walsh film.

After a group of 1925 Paramount adventure films, *East of Suez*, *The
Spaniard*, and *The Wanderer*, and a couple of others, Walsh signed a
lucrative seven-year contract at Fox. His first assignment was to adapt
Lawrence Stallings' and Maxwell Anderson's hit play *What Price Glory?*

"Write a shooting script around the story and don't pull any
punches," said Winfield Sheehan. Fox had a $100,000 fee for the screen
rights to the play riding on Walsh's talents—the highest price a studio
had ever paid for a property up to that time.

The first thing Raoul did was to alter the pacifist tone of the drama.
"The Army loved it," he recalled. "I always stood in good with the Army
after that. They had more recruits after that picture than they'd had
since World War I."

Yet the director's reason for the radical shift was cinematic, not
hawkish. He felt that the film had to be directed in terms of action,
therefore necessitating the elimination of much of Stallings' and Anderson's anti-war dialogue.

The role of Captain Flagg, who was described as being "straight as a
mast, muscled like a gorilla, and Christian as hell," was given to Victor
McLaglen, while Flagg's friendly nemesis, Sergeant Quirt, "the lousiest, filthiest bum who ever wore a uniform ... who has forgotten more
about being a soldier than any ... college boys will ever know," was
portrayed by Edmund Lowe.

The director asked McLaglen, Lowe, and co-star Dolores Del Rio to
read the play in order to absorb the mood of the characters. The realistic
sets and a fine, fast-paced script do the rest. Walsh used a dolly for the
first time in *What Price Glory?* in order to shoot flowing camera movements through the muddy trenches that had been dug by Fox workers.
One of the shots is of the bombing and collapsing of a long trench, with
scenes of the wounded being patched up and the critically injured dying
providing an almost unbearable realism to the film. The grim atmosphere is heightened by Walsh's refusal to show the enemy until the

very end, concentrating instead on the suffering of Quirt, Flagg, and the rest. The director alludes to the Germans via the smoke of battle, but nothing more.

An additional touch is the salty dialogue often ad-libbed by the actors in place of the lines on title cards. "The only trouble came from lip-readers," Walsh remembered. "Victor McLaglen would say to Edmund Lowe, 'You great big fat son of a bitch,' but the title would say 'How are you today?' Well, the lip-readers picked it up, and there was a hell of an explosion over it. But the result was that everyone went back a second time to see if they could read the lips—and that helped make the picture one of the biggest hits Fox ever had."

What Price Glory? opened at the Roxy Theatre in New York and grossed $780,000 in the first four weeks. During the last two weeks of the film's run it was shown twenty-four hours a day by popular demand. Critics raved. "It is because Raoul Walsh has with uncanny skill caught the spirit of the humans of the play that *What Price Glory?* has emerged an epic on screen," wrote the *New York Telegram*. Mordaunt Hall of the *New York Times* called Walsh's film "a powerful screen effort," and picked it as one of the Ten Best of 1926. More recently, Manny Farber deemed the film "an air-filled lyrical masterpiece: the haphazard unprecious careers of two blustery rivals who swagger around trench and village exquisitely scaled in human terms to the frame of the screen, suggesting, in their unhesitating grace, the sweet-tough-earthy feeling that is a Walsh trademark."

Sadie Thompson (UA, 1928) stars Gloria Swanson and Walsh himself in the role of O'Hara, the tough Marine. The director changed the tone of the story by Somerset Maugham from a strictly passionate affair to one containing a heavy dose of robust comedy. Raoul couldn't do any other kind of humor, it seemed. As his friend Jack Pickford once said to him, "I always thought your idea of light comedy was to burn down a whorehouse."

Walsh was drawn to Gloria Swanson, and the star reportedly returned the interest. She also helped him to make his "comeback" before the cameras. According to Raoul, Swanson turned down "some of the best actors in Hollywood" in order to have the director "play her champion," Tim O'Hara.

Mordaunt Hall of the *Times* was pleased by Walsh's performance in front of and behind the camera. "A stirring pictorial drama," claimed Hall, "with a shrewd development of the plot and admirable characterizations," adding that Raoul Walsh "does exceedingly well with his portrayal of the Marine."

The Cockeyed World (Fox, 1929) was essentially the new talking adventures of Flagg and Quirt. It retained McLaglen and Lowe, the stars of *What Price Glory?* Studio executive Winfield Sheehan warned Walsh not to film anything that the censors would scissor. Nevertheless a scene between comic actor El Brendel, a starlet, and Victor McLaglen came close to dying in the editing room. When Brendel and the girl approach McLaglen, the comic quips, "I brought you the lay of the land," and pulls out a map!

Walsh's first big sound opportunity came with the assignment of *The Big Trail* in 1930. The previous year could have featured one of Walsh's finest efforts, *In Old Arizona,* in which he starred as well as directed, but a leaping jackrabbit ruined his chances.

The arrival of the talkie signaled the ascension of the microphone as the new god of Hollywood. Actors were forced to scramble under the long silver monster or hover over a floral arrangement hiding the mike in order to speak their lines. Consequently film production was strictly inhibited, limited more than ever to a sound stage photographed by a static camera.

Raoul Walsh was a man of action who wanted his productions to move. An idea presented itself one day as he sat in a movie theatre watching a talking newsreel. Walsh then approached Winfield Sheehan with a request for a Western script and a newsreel truck. He would film a rip-snorting action drama on location, thus giving the public movement as well as sound. Sheehan chose an O. Henry short story called *The Caballero's Way* and changed the title to *In Old Arizona.* The executive also suggested that Walsh play the leading role of the Cisco Kid, and he concurred.

In Old Arizona was to be filmed entirely in Zion County, Arizona. One night while driving through the Mojave Desert in a jeep in order to familiarize himself with the country, the director's right eye was seriously injured when a jackrabbit, scared by the vehicle's headlights, leapt through the windshield. Actor/director Irving Cummings assumed directorial chores on the Western, and Warner Baxter replaced Walsh as the Cisco Kid. Baxter won an Oscar for his portrayal, and Raoul recovered in time to finish the film. (He had the eye removed in later years and donned a black patch.) Much of the footage that Cummings shot was incorporated into the release print. The sound of *In Old Arizona* emerged erratic in quality, prompting some film historians to assume that the effect was originally mistaken for stylization.

The Big Trail was in production for four months. Twenty thousand people worked hard to make the epic jell, traveling a total of 4,000 miles, from Yuma to Utah, to Lake Moiese, Montana, and then back to Hollywood. Fifteen cameras shot the initial exodus, with Raoul Walsh up twenty feet in the air directing the movement.

When Walsh said that he didn't like the original script, Winfield

Julanne Johnston (left) and Douglas Fairbanks in The Thief of Bagdad *(UA, 1924)*

Dolores Del Rio, Edmund Lowe, and Victor McLaglen in What Price Glory? *(Fox, 1926)*

Dorothy Burgess and Edmund Lowe in In Old Arizona *(Fox, 1929)*

Gloria Swanson in Sadie Thompson *(UA, 1928)*

Sheehan retorted: "Make your own action. And remember, this is going to be the first outdoor Western." "What about *In Old Arizona?*" asked the confused filmmaker. "O. Henry never intended his story to be a Western," Sheehan explained. "That was your idea."

One of the film's ninety-three speaking roles was taken by an inexperienced actor named Marion Michael Morrison, whose name became John Wayne during *The Big Trail.* Wayne tested for the part of the trail driver three times, reading more melodramatically on each take. Walsh had a feeling about the capabilities of the tall, sincere-looking collegiate football star turned actor, and Wayne got the role.

The Big Trail received good reviews in its day. Mordaunt Hall of the *New York Times* praised the "magnificent panoramic views on an enlarged screen, with a host of performers and paraphernalia, cattle, horses, buffalo, and redskins ... beheld in the ambitious Fox grandeur production."

Although the film looks as tough as rawhide, with little in the way of a musical underscore, its plot machinations creak like old bones and don't hold up well today. The strength of *The Big Trail* on modern audiences is the realistic effect that literally filming the production on the trail had on Walsh's direction. It is not surprising that when a Kansas historical society found stills from the film a decade or so ago, it enthusiastically believed that some lost photographic records had been unearthed.

The Big Trail proved to be a short-lived booster to the careers of both Walsh and Wayne. Wayne followed the epic with a decade of starring roles in B films, largely Westerns, until John Ford plunked him into the saddle of *Stagecoach,* one of the screen's great Westerns. Walsh continued to direct almost exclusively at Fox for the next five years, occasionally making a notable yarn such as *The Bowery* (UA, 1933— here Walsh employed his experience from shooting on the Lower East Side for *The Regeneration* twenty years earlier) or *Going Hollywood* (MGM, 1933—where he met Marion Davies). Sadly most of his films during this period are melodramas and comedies with which he seemed to have little sympathy. There was some talk of his directing a film called *Soldiers Three* for Gaumont-British in 1936 (he did lense *O.H.M.S.* for that studio), but that project fell through. Other prospective projects included *Marco Polo* with Douglas Fairbanks, Sr., but the production was shelved. Archie May eventually directed Gary Cooper in the bulky *The Adventures of Marco Polo* for Goldwyn in 1938.

Raoul's former wife Miriam did little to retain the quality of his press image. During the 1930s she was found guilty of disorderly conduct by a Manhattan court. But Raoul's friendship with William Randolph Hearst and the newspaper magnate's mistress, Marion Davies, kept the director's name in cheerful lights. In his autobiography, Walsh delights in telling stories of socializing with Hearst, sleeping in Napoleon's bed in one of the millionaire's guest houses, meeting the likes of Winston Churchill (who called him "Walshie"), Douglas MacArthur, Howard Hughes, J. Edgar Hoover, and others. For the director it was something of a throwback to the dinner table on West 48th Street in Manhattan where Thomas Walsh used to eat and drink with many turn-of-the-century celebrities.

The year 1939 was a watershed in Raoul Walsh's career. He signed a seven-year contract with Warner Brothers and finally found the properly sizzling, hair-trigger scripts that his directorial touch could turn into action gold. Ironically, Jack Warner had been trying to secure Walsh's services for years.

The Roaring Twenties was Walsh's first Warner Brothers film. Written by journalist-producer Mark Hellinger, the gangster film stars James Cagney, Humphrey Bogart, Priscilla Lane, and Gladys George. Hellinger's topical script deals with the period of World War I, the high unemployment rate of returning soldiers, Prohibition, and the rise and simultaneous fall of hoodlums Cagney and Bogart.

Otis Ferguson insisted that *The Roaring Twenties* "is a great deal more than the melodrama it has been carelessly advertised as." The New York *Daily Mirror* agreed, stating: "It has a glittering quality which distinguishes it from previous bootleg melodramas." Writing in the *New York Times*, Frank S. Nugent hailed the return of Warner Brothers "to the profitable and visually exciting field" that had once produced "such horrendous nosegays as *Public Enemy* and *Little Caesar*." *Variety* praised Walsh's "fine directing job" and the "uniformly excellent performances," but the *New York Herald-Tribune* brought up the valid point that Cagney's acting "keeps the new ... presentation from unraveling."

If *The Roaring Twenties* has a visible flaw, it is that very sprawling nature which Walsh generally compacts professionally, but which does surface on the occasion of long chronological transitions. Furthermore, Hellinger's narration is completely unnecessary.

In 1940 Miriam Cooper Walsh filed suit for $56,000 in alimony, citing the director's failure to maintain the payments of a $500 per week settlement agreed on during the divorce proceedings in 1927. Arbitration finally reduced the amount to $325 a week, providing that Raoul didn't miss three straight payments.

Such personal problems may have temporarily halted the director's progress at Warner Brothers. He was to direct *City for Conquest* starring Cagney, but the project ultimately came to life in the hands of Anatole Litvak, while a proposed remake of 1927's *The Patent Leather Kid* with George Raft in Richard Barthelmess' role was shelved.

*Ian Keith,
Margueritte
Churchill, and
John Wayne in*
The Big Trail
(Fox, 1930)

*George Raft,
Jackie Cooper,
and Wallace
Beery in a
publicity pose
for* The Bowery
(UA, 1933)

*Humphrey
Bogart and Ida
Lupino in* High
Sierra *(WB,
1941)*

*Priscilla Lane,
Frank McHugh,
and James
Cagney in* The
Roaring Twenties
(WB, 1939)

They Drive by Night (1940) was Raoul's second Warner Brothers film. Ironically it is the story of love and jealousy acted out against a gritty truck-driving background, with Raft and Bogart as brothers trying to establish a trucking business. After a series of numbing incidents, Raft accepts a position with an old friend's trucking firm, but the friend is married to one of Raft's old flames (Ida Lupino). She is obsessed with Raft, and her obsession leads to tragedy.

Bosley Crowther of the *New York Times* quoted a George Raft line regarding *They Drive by Night*: "'We're tougher than any truck ever come off an assembly line!' That goes for the picture, too." *Variety* deemed the seamy production "fast-moving and action-full ... clicks with plenty of entertainment content." On the negative side, the *New York Herald-Tribune*'s Howard Barnes correctly claimed: "There is so much power and honesty in the early sequences of *They Drive by Night* that its synthetic ending becomes doubly disappointing."

Paul Muni was scheduled to star in *High Sierra*, a very old-fashioned screenplay by John Huston (from W. R. Burnett's novel) about an aging gangster who decides to pull one more job to finance an operation for a girl he loves. Muni simply refused to play the role, and his contract was terminated because of it. Walsh tried to talk George Raft into accepting the part of gunman Roy Earle, but the star of *They Drive by Night* didn't want to die in the film. Raft went on to a mediocre project, and Humphrey Bogart finally achieved a long-desired and deserved stardom in Walsh's classic gangster film.

Released in January 1941, Bosley Crowther of the *Times* said of *High Sierra*: "As gangster pictures go, this one has everything, speed, excitement, suspense, and that ennobling suggestion of futility which makes for irony and pity." Otis Ferguson was reserved in his praise. "It has faults," he wrote, "but it is fine and exciting."

High Sierra is important for two reasons. First, it may contain the purest example of Robert Warshow's view of the modern bad man in his essay "The Gangster as Tragic Hero." Is Bogart's Roy Earle a tragic hero in the Greek sense? In a way, yes. Earle certainly had a choice, in the beginning at least, to escape his fate. Paroled quite suddenly, Earle could have gone straight, yet he became entangled in that one last chance to "make it" and perform a noble gesture at the same time. Does he make a fatal mistake? His love for crippled Joan Leslie qualifies. Is his fate pre-ordained? Yes, by both Huston's doom-ridden narrative and Hollywood convention. Does he gain knowledge from his experience? Earle's "come and get me" attitude while high atop the mountain suggests a realization that ruthless behavior has only one termination—death.

High Sierra is the mid-point in Walsh's trio of gangster films. Centered between *The Roaring Twenties* and *White Heat* (1949), *High Sierra*'s protagonist is psychologically one step removed from the cockiness of Rocky in the earlier film and one step behind the insanity of Cody Jarrett in the later production, although Earle is certainly tottering on the verge of lunacy as he is gunned down.

Released in 1941, *Manpower* "has a really bad script," according to Howard Barnes of the *Tribune*. The *New York Sun* called it "sentimental but tough," while the *New York Times* regarded it as "a tough, fast, exciting adventure film." *Manpower* confirmed Walsh's reputation as a man's director, yet he proved that he could handle the ladies as well.

"I was glad when *Manpower* . . . gave me a chance to direct a female star," Raoul Walsh said at the time. That star, Marlene Dietrich, fit neatly into Walsh's world of gangsters, truck drivers, and cowboys. She sits pretty and laconic between Raft and Edward G. Robinson as two linemen attracted to her character Fay, the embittered clip-joint chanteuse. Dietrich puts her uniquely feminine touch to two new Frederick Hollander songs, "I'm in No Mood for Music Tonight" and "He Lied and I Listened," while Robinson and Raft break up Barton MacLane's nightclub, a hospital and Robinson's wedding.

Charles Higham credits Warner Brothers executive/writer Jerry Wald with conceiving the hard-bitten melodramas such as *They Drive by Night* and *Manpower*, which contained characters right off the street who led relatively honest lives. Wald wanted the average male moviegoer to be able to step into the shoes of a Raft or a Robinson in these films while sitting in a darkened theatre.

Walsh soon felt a need for variety in his work, and he got some in the quasi-biographical *They Died with Their Boots On*, which purports to tell the life story of George Armstrong Custer. A typical Hollywood biography in terms of truth-stretching and plain distortion, the fast-paced 140-minute epic covers as much ground as *The Roaring Twenties*, but the script is much more graceful—perhaps befitting its heroic view of the controversial Custer.

Raoul replaced Michael Curtiz on the project when the Hungarian's running battle with star Errol Flynn became too hot for the studio to handle by 1941—and the property was costly enough to preclude such cavalier preparation. Most of Walsh's Warner Brothers films were budgeted around $1,000,000 until this biographical film doubled that figure. In addition to Flynn, the stars are Olivia de Havilland as Mrs. Custer and Arthur Kennedy as the traitorous Sharp, with support by Anthony Quinn as Chief Crazy Horse.

In describing part of the story, the director revealed his approach to the script: "Most Westerns had depicted the Indian as a painted, vicious savage. In *They Died with Their Boots On*, I tried to show him as an individual who only turned vindictive when his rights as defined by treaty were violated by white men. The best action came after the Civil War, when Custer was given command of Fort Lincoln in the Dakota Territory. In disgrace, because Sharp has engineered the failure of his agreement with the tribes, Custer's command is restored by President Grant. He is sent to fight Crazy Horse and his embattled confederates."

Aside from the solid script and fine ensemble acting, little touches help make *They Died with Their Boots On* a subtle yet spectacular film. For instance, the scene where Crazy Horse is brought into the fort as a prisoner may be very revealing, for he fears that the soldiers will hang him. While working out West in the early twentieth century, Walsh had learned that hanging was anathema to the Indian, and he may have created the bit in this film. The final moments between Flynn and de Havilland are much more than a "little touch," but they are so uncharacteristic of Walsh's work that they are worth noting for oddity's sake alone. Custer is about to go off with the Seventh Cavalry to fight the Sioux. Somehow both the general and his wife know that they will never meet again and that Custer will die in battle. He breaks his pocket watch on purpose and gives it to his wife to have it repaired. She knows what he has done but says nothing. The memento will have to last. There are no tears. Custer exits quietly, and Mrs. Custer collapses to the floor. This scene is one of the most powerful in Walsh's oeuvre, and there isn't a hint of slapstick, wisecracking, or bitterness to be found. Let this dispel forever the illusion that the director's *only* vision of a passionate love affair is "a whorehouse burning down," as related by more than one source.

They Died with Their Boots On received mixed reviews. "An adventure tale of frontier days which, for screen scope if not dramatic impact, it would be hard to equal," wrote Thomas M. Pryor in the *New York Times*. "The occasional lapses in the story can be attributed to the neglect of the film editors to cut excessive portions of the film rather than to Mr. Walsh," stated the qualifying *Herald-Tribune* critic.

Jack Warner wanted to cast Ann Sheridan as dazzling Virginia Brush in *The Strawberry Blonde* with James Cagney, Olivia de Havilland, and Jack Carson. However, Sheridan wasn't on speaking terms with the mogul, and Raoul couldn't persuade her to take the role. Then the director remembered a young dancer he had seen at the Caliente and whom he had recommended to Winfield Sheehan at Fox. The young lady subsequently floundered in B films until Walsh cast her in the title role of *The Strawberry Blonde* (1941), a charming turn-of-the-century comedy. With that picture, Rita Hayworth was on her way.

"Lusty, affectionate, and altogether winning," said *Times* critic Bosley Crowther. *Time* magazine felt that "*The Strawberry Blonde* is a blithe, turn-of-the-century buggy ride. Cagney makes the hero a tough but obviously peachy fellow.... Rita Hayworth takes the picture away from him, and dark-eyed Olivia de Havilland takes it away from both of them." In the *New Republic*, Otis Ferguson called Walsh's direction "heavy slugging," and believed the pixieish tale "could have been a far better thing than it is."

Another biographical film followed. *Gentleman Jim* (1942) recounts the training and triumph of Jim Corbett as the heavyweight defeats the world's last bare-knuckled champion, John L. Sullivan, and wins Alexis Smith in the process. Walsh's final cinema biography marks the end of Warner Brothers' really fine film versions of the lives of notable people. Biographical presentations of Mark Twain, George Gershwin, and the Brontes followed, but in one way or another they failed to measure up to earlier biographies by Walsh and William Dieterle.

Gentleman Jim contains a poignant scene between Errol Flynn and Ward Bond involving Sullivan's handing over of the heavyweight champion's belt to Corbett. The two men exchange a few quiet, polite words, in marked contrast to their previous braggadocio style. The bit serves as a brief break in the action, and Sullivan solemnly exits. However, unlike the aforementioned emotional segment in *They Died with Their Boots On*, the tone is quickly dashed in the final scene. Corbett and his girl-to-be have a lovers' quarrel, and then the boxer's father and brother start brawling. "The Corbetts are at it again!" screams one interested party. The shock of the bawdy conclusion following such sentimentality is akin to that of a naked man being thrown into an ice-cold lake—but it works.

Objective Burma (1945) didn't work out as well, especially in the minds of the British. Our allies across the sea felt that the Warner Brothers war film showed Americans capturing Burma single-handedly, and the film was banned in England after an initial screening at the Warner Theatre in London. Walsh has since explained his feeling about *Objective Burma*: "The film's real purpose was to convey a graphic, firsthand portrait of men at war. Errol Flynn was impressively stalwart as the paratrooper leader, George Tobias had his Bronx-dialect jokes, and George Tyne (his name is now Buddy Yarus) was fine as Soapy Higgins from Flatbush." As such, the production's single-mindedness could be explained by a heavy concentration on the American soldiers, at the expense of a necessarily brisk narrative.

Objective Burma drew as much controversy from critics in America as in England. Thomas M. Pryor of the *Times* hailed the production as "one of the best war films yet made in Hollywood." However, James Agee thought that it should have been so, but decidedly wasn't: "The main reason is that the players, by always saying the apt line at the apt

Robert Mitchum and Teresa Wright in Pursued *(WB, 1947)*

Charles Winninger, Olivia de Havilland, and Errol Flynn in They Died with Their Boots On *(WB, 1941)*

Sara Shane,
Clark Gable,
and Eleanor
Parker in The
King and Four
Queens *(WB,*
1956)

Virginia Mayo
and James
Cagney in
White Heat
(WB, 1949)

moment and by almost every other means possible, continually remind you that they are, after all, just actors, and that none of this is really happening." The *Nation* reviewer thought that the script was too glib and too long. *Objective Burma* was often compared unfavorably to *The Story of G.I. Joe*, directed by William Wellman and released in 1945.

Raoul Walsh himself terms *Pursued* (1946), starring Robert Mitchum, a "psychological Western," although he doesn't explore the ramifications of that determination in the film. He is a director of action and has summarized the film well: "The picture was helped along by the strong performances of Judith Anderson, whose infidelity was the cause of the father's sin, and Teresa Wright, her sensitive daughter. We made a great wide-angel shot of Mitchum being followed by Judith's son (John Rodney), showing him small but relentless, crouching on top of a mountain, waiting to line his rifle sights and fire. The climax was appropriately violent."

The *New York Times* called *Pursued* "a novel and vastly effective Western." Writing in *Warner Brothers Presents* (Castle), Ted Sennett put the film in the perspective of studio Westerns of the 1940s: "Only one Warners Western of those years had genuine merit.... Clouded in motivation and heavy-handed in the dialogue of Niven Busch's original screenplay, *Pursued* is still interesting in parts." *Variety* asserted that the "entertainment elements are put solidly together."

Walsh's next important production was *White Heat* in 1949, the third of his trio of tough Warner Brothers crime films. The director was going through a pile of scripts when he found this action-filled account of an FBI agent who infiltrates the gang of psychopathic criminal Cody Jarrett. Walsh immediately thought of James Cagney for the lead, and the actor welcomed the chance to step back into the type of no-nonsense bad-guy he had played at Warner Brothers in the 1930s. *White Heat* is a perfect illustration of the plans of Jack Warner and studio executive Steve Trilling to return Warner Brothers to the kind of hard, clipped production it shot off the assembly line at a record rate in the previous decade.

White Heat is harshly told, harshly photographed (in barren natural vistas, a real prison, offices, and shoddy hideouts), harshly lit, and harshly played. No one lets up for a minute until Cody Jarrett gets blown sky-high atop an oil derrick. "Made it, Ma, top of the world," he screams to his murdered mother, right before FBI bullets blow the derrick into oblivion.

Cagney is brilliant as the gang leader with the severe mother complex. Jarrett's wife, played by Virginia Mayo, is the little tart she is expected to be, a woman difficult to have sympathy for, even though her man is so obviously ill and abusive. Steve Cochran portrays her slimy paramour, a man not any less likable than Jarrett, but the one who holds the audience's contempt because he causes the death of Cody's mother and breaks up the murderer's "marriage." The only sanity in the film at all exists in the incognito FBI man portrayed by Edmond O'Brien.

The *Time* magazine critic said that Raoul Walsh was the only director in Hollywood who could have successfully filmed a scene which features James Cagney sitting on his screen mother's lap. The bit takes place after one of the gangster's frequent headaches, "a buzz saw in my head," as Cody delineates it, which lasts but a moment, yet is indelibly imprinted in the viewer's consciousness.

"Red-hot box-office," proclaimed *Variety* regarding *White Heat,* adding: "Raoul Walsh's direction has kept the pace sharp and exciting for the nearly two-hour length." According to Crowther of the *New York Times,* "Mr. Cagney has made his return to a gangster role in one of the most explosive pictures that he or anyone else has ever played."

The 1950s contain a disproportionate amount of disappointing Raoul Walsh productions. Out of the nineteen films he directed during that decade, only a handful, including *Captain Horatio Hornblower* (WB, 1951), *A Lion Is in the Streets* (WB, 1953), and *The King and Four Queens* (UA, 1956), are among his better productions.

Based on the novel by C. S. Forester, *Captain Horatio Hornblower* was shot in Warner Brothers' London studio. A forty-gun frigate of the early nineteenth century was constructed, and the director had been filming with his cast of Gregory Peck, Virginia Mayo, and Robert Beatty for about three weeks when Princess Elizabeth and Princess Margaret came to watch him shoot battle sequences. The most memorable shot in the film frames Gregory Peck standing in his Hornblower costume on the deck of the frigate. As Andrew Sarris has written, all the gallantry and loyalty implicit in the film are evoked in that one image.

The King and Four Queens starring Clark Gable, Eleanor Parker, and Jo Van Fleet stands out as one of Walsh's two most unusual Westerns (the other was *Pursued*). Gable was on the way out at MGM, so the studio loaned him to United Artists for what was one of the most engaging roles of his later career. As a gambler who stumbles upon four women, three wives and the mother of their outlaw husbands who wait for the men's return, Gable is charming to the hilt. A tantalizing sequence in the film is built around a square dance where Gable does some do-si-dos with the wives, much to the consternation of the mother.
mother.

In 1945 James Cagney paid $250,000 for the right to a novel by Adrian Locke-Langley called *A Lion Is in the Streets.* Walsh directed Cagney as the Huey Long-type politician in a tale of power and retribution which runs an honorable second to Robert Rossen's *All the King's Men*

(Col., 1949). Otis L. Guernsey of the *New York Herald-Tribune* called the production "a live wire of a movie" which was "directed by Raoul Walsh in as earthy a fashion as technicolor permits."

From this point on, Walsh's career is laden with failed epics, hackneyed comedies, an extremely outdated war film, and a serviceable Western (*A Distant Trumpet*, WB, 1964). The director was peripherally involved in *PT 109*, the story of then President John F. Kennedy's wartime Pacific adventures, but the film eventually came under the direction of Leslie Martinson. In the 1950s he was scheduled to make *Patton* as part of a long-term deal with Warner Brothers, but that too came to nothing until Franklin Schaffner guided George C. Scott to his Oscar-winning performance in the 1970 film.

Marines, Let's Go (20th, 1961) resembles *What Price Glory?* gone out of style, although Walsh didn't think so at the time: "The audiences will really go for what these characters do, no matter how outlandish. These are sympathetic characters because they're on borrowed time. They're going right back into war." Be that as it may, stars Tom Tryon, David Hedison, and Tom Reese cannot duplicate the heroics and humor of Victor McLaglen and Edmund Lowe, simply because those heroics and that humor were archaic by the 1960s, and because the younger

Tom Reese in Marines, Let's Go *(20th, 1961)*

actors weren't anywhere near as talented as the earlier duo. According to Howard Thompson of the *New York Times, Marines, Let's Go* "lets go with most of the furlough and battlefield clichés that have been developed since the invention of talking pictures, adding some ripe foolishness of its own."

Raoul Walsh is currently living in retirement in a white clapboard farmhouse in the middle of 1,500 acres of land in the mountain area northwest of Los Angeles, California. He and his wife take care of orange trees, horses, ten cats, and four dogs. Yet the director's creative instincts remain intact. The latest outlets are his 1972 novel *Wrath of the Just,* as well as the autobiographical *Each Man in His Time,* published in 1974.

From April 17 through July 11, 1974, the Museum of Modern Art in New York offered a retrospective of sixty-seven of Raoul Walsh's more than one hundred films, a fine tribute to a genuine American classic both privately and professionally.

The Films of Raoul Walsh

The Life of Villa *(Biograph, 1912)*

The Regeneration *(Fox, 1915) (and producer, co-script)*

Carmen *(Fox, 1915) (and producer, script)*

The Honor System *(Fox, 1916)*

Blue Blood and Rex *(Fox, 1916) (and producer, story, script)*

The Serpent *(Fox, 1916) (and producer, co-script)*

The Conqueror *(Fox, 1917)*

Betrayed *(Fox, 1917) (and producer, co-story, script)*

This Is the Life *(Fox, 1917) (and co-story, co-script)*

The Pride of New York *(Fox, 1917) (and story, script)*

The Silent Lie *(Fox, 1917)*

The Innocent Sinner *(Fox, 1917) (and script)*

The Woman and the Law *(Fox, 1918) (and script)*

The Prussian Cure *(Fox, 1918) (and story, script)*

On the Jump *(Fox, 1918) (and story, script)*

Every Mother's Son *(Fox, 1918) (and story, script)*

I'll Say So *(Fox, 1918)*

Evangeline *(Fox, 1919) (and producer, script)*

The Strongest *(Fox, 1919) (and script)*

Should a Husband Forgive? *(Fox, 1919) (and story, script)*

From Now On *(Fox, 1920) (and script)*

The Deep Purple *(Realart, 1920)*

The Oath *(Mayflower, 1921) (and producer, script)*

Serenade *(Associated FN, 1921)*

Kindred of the Dust *(Associated FN, 1922)*

Lost and Found on a South Sea Island *(Goldwyn, 1923)*

The Thief of Bagdad *(UA, 1924)*

East of Suez *(Par., 1925) (and producer)*

The Spaniard *(Par., 1925)*

The Wanderer *(Par., 1925) (and producer)*

The Lucky Lady *(Par., 1926) (and producer)*

The Lady of the Harem *(Par., 1926)*

What Price Glory? *(Fox, 1926)*

The Monkey Talks *(Fox, 1927) (and producer)*

The Loves of Carmen *(Fox, 1927)*

Sadie Thompson *(UA, 1928) (and script, actor)*

The Red Dance *(Fox, 1928) (and producer)*

Me, Gangster *(Fox, 1928) (and co-script)*

Hot for Paris *(Fox, 1929) (and story)*

In Old Arizona *(Fox, 1929) (co-directed by Irving Cummings)*

The Cockeyed World *(Fox, 1929) (and script)*

The Big Trail *(Fox, 1930)*

The Man Who Came Back *(Fox, 1931)*

Women of All Nations *(Fox, 1931)*

The Yellow Ticket *(Fox, 1931) (and producer)*

Wild Girl *(Fox, 1932)*

Me and My Gal *(Fox, 1932)*

Hello, Sister! (Walking Down Broadway) *(Fox, 1933) (not credited)*

Going Hollywood *(MGM, 1933)*
Under Pressure *(Fox, 1935)*
Baby-Face Harrington *(MGM, 1935)*
Every Night at Eight *(Par., 1935)*
Klondike Annie *(Par., 1936)*
Big Brown Eyes *(Par., 1936) (and co-script)*
Spendthrift *(Par., 1936) (and co-script)*
O.H.M.S. *(Gaumont-British, 1937)*
Jump for Glory *(Criterion, 1937)*
Artists and Models *(Par., 1937)*
Hitting a New High *(RKO, 1937)*
College Swing *(Par., 1938)*
St. Louis Blues *(Par., 1939)*
The Roaring Twenties *(WB, 1939) (replaced Anatole Litvak)*
Dark Command *(Republic, 1940)*
They Drive by Night *(WB, 1940)*
High Sierra *(WB, 1941)*
The Strawberry Blonde *(WB, 1941)*
Manpower *(WB, 1941)*
They Died with Their Boots On *(WB, 1941)*
Desperate Journey *(WB, 1942)*
Gentleman Jim *(WB, 1942)*
Background to Danger *(WB, 1943)*
Northern Pursuit *(WB, 1943)*
Uncertain Glory *(WB, 1944)*
Objective Burma *(WB, 1945)*
Salty O'Rourke *(Par., 1945)*
The Horn Blows at Midnight *(WB, 1945)*
The Man I Love *(WB, 1946)*
San Antonio *(WB, 1946) (not credited: directed by David Butler)*
Pursued *(WB, 1946)*
Stallion Road *(WB, 1947) (not credited: directed by James V. Kern)*

Cheyenne *(WB, 1947)*
Silver River *(WB, 1948)*
Fighter Squadron *(WB, 1948)*
One Sunday Afternoon *(WB, 1948)*
Colorado Territory *(WB, 1949)*
White Heat *(WB, 1949)*
Montana *(WB, 1950) (not credited: directed by Ray Enright)*
Along the Great Divide *(WB, 1951)*
Captain Horatio Hornblower *(WB, 1951)*
Distant Drums *(WB, 1951)*
The Enforcer *(WB, 1951) (not credited: directed by Bretaigne Windust)*
Glory Alley *(MGM, 1952)*
The World in His Arms *(Univ., 1952)*
The Lawless Breed *(Univ., 1952)*
Blackbeard the Pirate *(RKO, 1952)*
Sea Devils *(RKO, 1953)*
A Lion Is in the Streets *(WB, 1953)*
Gun Fury *(Col., 1953)*
Saskatchewan *(Univ., 1954)*
Battle Cry *(WB, 1955)*
The Tall Men *(20th, 1955)*
The Revolt of Mamie Stover *(20th, 1956)*
The King and Four Queens *(UA, 1956)*
Band of Angels *(WB, 1957)*
The Naked and the Dead *(RKO, 1958)*
The Sheriff of Fractured Jaw *(20th, 1958)*
A Private's Affair *(20th, 1959)*
Esther and the King *(20th, 1960) (and producer, co-script)*
Marines, Let's Go *(20th, 1961)*
A Distant Trumpet *(WB, 1964)*

William Wellman and friend on the set of Wings *(Par., 1927)*

19

William Wellman

Here's a unique method of becoming a Hollywood director without really trying: "Go to France, learn to fly, and have your ass shot off." The speaker is William Augustus "Wild Bill" Wellman, and the remark is obviously facetious, yet strangely indicative of what it took to launch a directorial career in pre-World War II Hollywood. Guts, imagination, and a flair for the cinema were three qualities that all American directors possessed to a certain degree. The guts weld the content of Wellman's declaration, the imagination is in saying it, and the cinema provides the image in film many times over a forty-year career.

That image can be seen in classics such as *Wings, Public Enemy, Wild Boys of the Road, A Star Is Born, Nothing Sacred, The Ox-Bow Incident,* and *The Story of G.I. Joe,* models of almost every genre made in Hollywood. Wellman was a fast worker, turning out five films for Warner Brothers in 1931, the year in which Cagney forever washed Mae Clarke's face with grapefruit in *Public Enemy.* "Wild Bill" hated anything that slowed down his beloved filmmaking—retakes, producers, stars, make-up men—but he respected the courage of men and women and their loyalty, qualities which made Wellman a war hero and which emerge again and again in the director's nearly eighty films.

Born on February 29, 1896 in Brookline, Massachusetts, Wellman received the moniker "Wild Bill" at an early age. A high school discipline problem, he let more than one teacher know of his disdain for authority. Once his aggression resulted in a stink bomb being thrown in the face of one of his educators. Consequently Bill spent many hours with the local police. Long talks with corrections officers must have seemed like discussions with mom at home; as a matter of fact, Mrs. Wellman was one of the authorities in question! The youthful wild one managed to sublimate some of his energies by playing professional hockey for the Boston Athletic Association, but a point was reached where fights off the ice outnumbered the more legal pugilistics with fists and hockey sticks. It was through the sport (hockey, that is) that Wellman met Douglas Fairbanks, Sr., a great athlete and something of a celebrity in the first decades of the twentieth century. Backstage at the Fairbanks production of *Hawthorne of the U.S.A.*, America's idol and the rough-and-tumble Wellman became friends, a bond which benefited Bill greatly a few years later.

At the time Wellman yearned for adventure, something more than slapping a teacher, policeman, or hockey puck, and he ducked out of the house to join the Norton-Harjes Ambulance Corps which sailed for France in April 1917. He enlisted as a corporal, but within a month he shifted service and won his wings as a sergeant. Serving with the Spad 87, Bill was credited with shooting down three German planes, and he was sent crashing to the ground an equal number of times. He was awarded the Croix de Guerre for bravery in action, and that medal was later adorned with four palms for additional courage. However, the gallantry did have a price. Once a control stick smashed the roof of Bill's mouth, ending all thoughts of further vocal training at the Boston Conservatory which he had attended before the war. After his third plane was shot out from under him, Bill was sent to a Boston hospital with a broken back and told that he had but six months to live. He returned to America a real-life hero, just like Fairbanks in the movies, yet a tragic figure to his fellow Bostonians. A series of newspaper articles told of Wellman's exploits, and it was through the printed media that his parents discovered their son's deceit. They had assumed that he was still an ambulance driver.

Since Kaiser Wilhelm's forces couldn't kill Bill, it was reasonable to assume that a broken back wouldn't keep him in traction for long. During his hospital stay he wrote a novel of the air war called *Go Get 'Em*. As an experienced flyer he was welcomed into the American Air Corps and sent to Rockwell Field in San Diego, California to instruct budding flyers. Being in close proximity to Hollywood allowed him to mingle with celebrities, and one day Bill landed his Spad in the back yard of his old friend Doug Fairbanks. Wellman didn't know how he wanted to spend the rest of his life, but right then he wanted to be in the movies. Fairbanks tried in vain to secure the young man a position at a studio, but nothing developed, and Bill Wellman returned to Boston to enter the wool business.

At the tender age of 22, Wild Bill was locked out of several fields of endeavor. With the war finished his flying days were limited to teaching, the control stick of the shattering Spad had ended a possible singing career, and wool was definitely not the answer.

Fortunately it didn't have to be, for in 1919 Fairbanks landed Wellman the juvenile lead in *Knickerbocker Buckaroo*, after which Raoul Walsh used Bill's thespian talents in the artistic but unsuccessful *Evangeline*. Through these jobs Bill Wellman discovered that he didn't like acting. Perhaps this is the root of a statement he made many years later: "I'm not very fond of actors. They spend years looking in the mirror, studying their angles, and so forth. You do that for any length of time and there are only two things that can happen. Either you love what you see or you hate it. So far I've never met anyone who hated it."

Nevertheless Bill hated it. He hated putting make-up on. When he saw himself in *Knickerbocker Buckaroo* his suspicions were confirmed. "I went through two-thirds of the picture, then I went outside and was violently sick," he admitted to Julian Fox of *Films and Filming* (March 1973)—the first time in my life this had happened without good reason." (Booze and high adventure made for many good reasons.)

Bill pleaded with Fairbanks on the set of *Knickerbocker Buckaroo*: "Look, Doug, I don't want to be an actor—let me be something else." In the back of his mind was an image of a man with a megaphone—perhaps Al Parker, the director of Bill's first film. "I'd like to do what that guy does," he said, indicating Parker.

The path to the director's chair wasn't too long, but it had several detours. Fairbanks arranged to get Bill work as a Goldwyn messenger. From there he was promoted to the job of prop boy, and then he became an assistant director. Short associations with T. Hayes Hunter, Clarence Badger, and E. Mason Hopper led to a formative relationship with director Bernard Durning, whom Bill assisted for two years. In 1923 Durning talked Fox into giving Bill the directorial reins of *The Man Who Won*, a Western starring the fading box-office star Dustin Farnum. Fox liked the film and rewarded Wellman with six more Westerns, this time starring Buck Jones, and often featuring Marian Nixon.

After winning his director's spurs at Fox, Wellman filmed Columbia's *When Husbands Flirt* in 1925. The next year MGM assigned Bill to direct *The Boob*, featuring young Joan Crawford. It was his first important production.

Bill then moved on to Paramount. Several insignificant films followed until he grabbed the opportunity to direct *Wings* in 1927. "They gave me *Wings* because I was the only director who had been a flyer in action," Wellman said decades later. "I was the only one who knew what the hell it was all about." Wellman was almost right. Scenarist John Monk Saunders, another ex-flyer and a bosom buddy of the director, also knew a good deal about the daredevil pilots of World War I.

Wellman and Saunders created a masterpiece whose example was followed by Hollywood action directors for decades. Originally released in a red and blue tint, *Wings* artfully combines the camaraderie of men in action with beautifully photographed aerial battle scenes *and* an admittedly sentimental but nonetheless moving tribute to the courage of men and women in war.

Dedicated "To those young warriors of the sky whose wings are folded about them forever," *Wings* is quite simply *the* classic aerial war film—*The Big Parade* of the sky.

Being a spectacular production, *Wings* suffered some minor catastrophes due to studio interference. One such incident occurred on the set of the most intricate scene in the film. At the time, Bill stated: "The greatest problem one has in directing a picture which deals with the air is that of photography. Airplanes might be called 'camera shy' because of the difficulty of getting them in range of the lens." Wellman was filming the battle of St. Mihiel (France) in San Antonio, Texas, a barren area capped by luminous cloud formations and stark skylines. The scenes were to be shot by fifteen cameramen from a series of platforms seventy-five feet high. The director stood on top of one of the structures, completely oblivious to the ground below. Several New York bankers were visiting the set that day, and one of them innocently yelled to Wellman. The production crew took the call to mean that the battle should begin, and immediately bombs began to explode, smoke filled the area, and men ran, screamed, and "died." Above all the noise, however, could be heard the shouts of director Wellman as he frantically tried to stop the battle before all the damage was done without the benefit of a turn of a single camera. Bill finally got things under control in time to salvage the film's budget. The shooting proceeded as planned and the photographers filmed one of the great war scenes in cinema history.

When the battle was shown to thrilled moviegoers, it was on a screen twice the size of the one holding the rest of this great film. Bill and Roy Pomeroy, head of the special effects department, begged Paramount executives to employ such a device, and their triumph was shared by audiences and critics.

Wings went on to win the first Academy Award as best picture. Quinn Martin of the *New York World* summed up America's reaction to *Wings:* "There has been no movie so far as I know which has surpassed it in impressing upon an audience a feeling of personal participation ... and its climax, when the magnascope device enlarges the curtain to twice its normal size and carries the spectator head-on into the action of an airplane battle in the clouds, there is no escaping the thrill."

Wellman shows stars Buddy Rogers, Richard Arlen, and Clara Bow at their very best. *Wings* also showcases young Gary Cooper, whom Wellman tagged for early stardom. Cooper wasn't so sure of his fate, and he requested a retake of a scene in which he had been picking his nose. Wild Bill ended the conversation by saying, "Listen, you son of a bitch, you keep right on picking your nose and you'll pick your nose right into a fortune." He was right. Cooper's natural look in front of the camera kept him on top until his death.

Cooper received a starring role in Wellman's next Paramount aerial thriller, *Legion of the Condemned* (1928). The studio attempted to team Cooper with starlet Fay Wray, a combination that moviegoers found less than electrifying. However, according to Mordaunt Hall of the *New York Times*, people seemed to like the film: "The suspense is piled on in the last chapter; but judging by the demonstrative approval of the audience at one juncture, this was more than moderately successful."

Although *Beggars of Life* (1928) wasn't generally popular, it did continue Wellman's slowly building reputation for "documentary realism," first spotted in *Wings*. The film also has the same dreary, downbeat look of his later *Wild Boys of the Road*. Both that picture and *Beggars of Life* are about hobo life and contain a female drifter who masquerades as a man. A particularly haunting shot in the earlier film is the slow camera movement from blood on the floor to a dead man's upright body.

Starring Wallace Beery, Richard Arlen, and beautiful Louise Brooks, *Beggars of Life* was called "a dull and unimaginative piece of work, which is largely confined to scenes of tramps hopping freight trains" by Mordaunt Hall of the *Times*. The reviewer also felt that the director "reveals little intimate knowledge of his subject."

In 1929 *Film Daily* listed Bill Wellman as one of the world's ten best directors. As one of the top in his sphere, he was expected to contend with an item which hurt or ended the careers of other well-known directors like Herbert Brenon, Rex Ingram, and Fred Niblo—namely, the sound film. However, the challenge didn't faze Wellman. He once responded in this way to a question about whether the cinema lost some of its art when it learned to talk: "I didn't have an opinion one way or another. My reputation was based on shooting pictures very quickly."

The only thing which bothered the director was the plodding method of filming early sound movies. He declared: "Whether a film talks or not is immaterial, and, anyhow, I don't like this word 'film.' Film is just an ugly little strip you hold up in the light. I prefer 'motion picture'—a picture which moves—and movement is the most important thing." And that important thing was strangled by cumbersome sound equipment, so Wellman did what many other directors of the era claimed to have done—he invented the boom mike! One day Bill told his crew, "I've got news for you guys this morning. I'm moving that goddamned mike." Wellman was tired of hiding the instrument in a fruit bowl or having his actors scoot within range to speak their lines. "The guys gave me a big

Charles "Buddy" Rogers, Clara Bow, and Richard Arlen in Wings (Par., 1927)

Louise Brooks, Richard Arlen, and Wallace Beery in a publicity pose for Beggars of Life (Par., 1928)

ladder and I went up and got the thing and put it on the end of a broom-stick. It worked! That was the first boom, and it changed the studio overnight."

Paramount was appreciative of Wellman's efforts to speed up production, but it wanted one of several stage directors flown out from the East to help him handle dialogue. The film director exploded: "Look here, I've got a seven-year contract. There's nothing here that says I have to divide responsibility with anyone. I shoot in my own way and on my own." He finally agreed to let some of the Broadway talent—including, at one time or another, George Abbott, John Cromwell, and George Cukor—witness his productions, "if they sit quietly at the back where I can't see them." Wellman's future at Paramount may have been jeopardized by his stubborn stance, but the early talkies he directed for the studio would have been immeasurably slowed down by the inch at the time pace of a Cukor, and the two would have almost certainly come to blows.

Chinatown Nights (1929) was Wellman's first sound film, but it also surfaced in a silent version. Critics and audiences responded well to Bill's talkie. Yet four films later Wellman's contract with Paramount was canceled and he stood on the unemployment line with millions of other Americans.

At the suggestion of Darryl F. Zanuck, then head of production at Warner Brothers, Wellman's services were retained for four years, commencing in 1930. Zanuck and Jack Warner felt the need for a new look to fit the fresh mode of cinematic expression. Wild Bill directed one distinctly tame Warner Brothers football comedy in 1930, *Maybe It's Love*, which the *New York Times* tagged "ingenious but scarcely stimulating," before his talents as a documentary realist were exploited in the tough but melodramatic *Other Men's Women*, also known as *Steel Highway*. One of five Wellman films released in 1931, the film contains the nucleus of Zanuck's plan to shoot stories straight out of newspaper headlines. The steamy tale is set against the backdrop of railway workers, the common men who run the train lines. The plot centers around a conflict between blue collar worker Grant Withers and Regis Toomey for the favors of the titled lady, played by Mary Astor. The love angle dominates, but one can feel the essence of life among working men who dirty their hands seeping through the slickly evoked passion and jealousy.

Zanuck could see that Bill Wellman was the kind of director he needed to rivet topical happenings into Warner Brothers productions, so the executive was always willing to listen to a man as strong-willed as himself. Since Warner Brothers had just triumphantly released Mervyn LeRoy's *Little Caesar* and Archie Mayo's *Doorway to Hell*, Wellman confidently approached Zanuck with an idea to film an unpub-

Mary Astor and Grant Withers in Other Men's Women *(WB, 1931)*

lished novel by Chicago soda jerks Kubec Glasmon and John Bright, called *Beer and Blood*. Although the gangster cycle had just started, Zanuck felt that it was to be short-lived.

"Hey, look, Bill, the gangster picture's dead," Zanuck said. "We've had *Little Caesar* and *Doorway to Hell*. What do you think you can bring to this one that will possibly make it different?" Wellman replied firmly: "What I'll bring you is the toughest, the most violent, most realistic picture you ever did see." That convinced Zanuck, and he said: "OK, Bill. Do it." This episode marked the beginning of a mutual respect that Wellman and Zanuck shared for decades, even though they often had bitter fights and at one point wouldn't speak to each other for years.

The episode which probably solidified their camaraderie took place in the Warner Brothers screening room. Wellman, Zanuck, Jack Warner, and another new studio director, Michael Curtiz, had just viewed the final version of *Public Enemy*, adapted from Glasmon's and Bright's book by the authors themselves. Everyone was generally happy with the picture, but there was a disagreement over the quality of the ending. One of the most brutal moments in American cinema history begins with gangster Tom Powers (James Cagney) being shot down in the gutter, wrapped in blankets, and then dumped through his mother's door. Warner didn't like it, and when he asked Curtiz about the scene, the director concurred. At that point, according to Wellman, Zanuck jumped up and punched Curtiz in the mouth, knocking the Hungarian's cigar halfway down his throat. Bill thought to himself, "I can love this guy Zanuck. I don't care what he does from now on."

It was that kind of beautiful friendship which allowed Wellman great flexibility in adapting Glasmon's and Bright's screenplay. After seeing a day's rushes, the director wasn't satisfied with the performance of Edward Woods in the role of Tom Powers, and he immediately decided to switch the actors portraying the gangsters who had learned their criminal ways together in the slums. Cagney, the original sidekick of the public enemy, became the top villian himself, and Hollywood watched closely to see if there would be any repercussions from the move, since Woods planned to marry the daughter of powerful columnist Louella Parsons.

Even the famous grapefruit scene wasn't in the original script. Wellman believed that the breakfast moment needed a lift, but he found Mae Clarke extremely unreceptive to the addition. She had a bad cold and didn't want anything crushed in her face. Finally they compromised. Bill assured her that Cagney would only mime the move, and the camera would cover the deception. In reality, Wild Bill had other ideas. "We needed something big right there in the picture," he recalled. "That grapefruit on the table looked inviting and I didn't like the dame much

335

anyhow. So I told Jimmy to try socking her with it—but hard. He did." The rest, as they say, is screen history. Clarke's shocked and hurt countenance wasn't an act—the blow was painful—but it made an indelible footnote in film lore.

Public Enemy became a popular success, despite mixed reviews when it was released in April 1931. Thomas Delehanty of the *New York Evening Post* wrote, "In its cold-blooded realism, *Public Enemy* is a better picture than *Little Caesar*. It moves swiftly and fiercely, and the only bogus thing about it is its pretense to sermonize." However, Andre Sennwald was unimpressed in the *New York Times*, labeling Wellman's action drama "just another gangster film ... weaker than most in story." Thirty years later, noted film critic Dwight MacDonald saw *Public Enemy* at a revival and decided, "I had remembered it as good, but not as good as it now appears to be. . . . Its realism is blunt, direct, unsparing, as against the romanticized kind. . . . There is none of the usual pornography of violence; the killings take place out of camera range, as in the shooting of Putty Nose, where we hear the shots while the camera is on the horrified face of the accomplice."

Bill Wellman's style was now set, and Warner Brothers was the studio where he could implement his personal stamp of stark, melo-dramatic realism. *Public Enemy* was followed by a series of hard-bitten films such as *The Star Witness, Night Nurse, Safe in Hell,* and *Love Is a Racket.* These productions were filmed quickly. Wellman as a rule didn't take cover shots, yet he was not averse to shooting a scene a dozen or more times to get it perfect. His stars in these pot-boiling tales are 24-year-old Barbara Stanwyck, Walter Huston, a clean-shaven Clark Gable on loan from MGM, and lesser luminaries Donald Cook, Ben Lyon, and Dorothy Mackaill. There wasn't a tantrum-throwing per-former in the group.

The biggest name at the time was Barbara Stanwyck, although she was a decade from her peak. Stanwyck and Carole Lombard were Well-man's favorite actresses. "A magnificent actress, Stanwyck," he said of the woman he directed in five films. However, he could be a devil with others. In an impish mood, the director once admitted: "I liked to fool actors. I always did camera rehearsals. But we'd shoot the camera re-hearsals without telling the actors. Then we'd do another take so the actor could adjust to things he didn't like. But I'd print the camera rehearsal."

In 1933 Warner Brothers put social comment in musical form with the film *Gold Diggers of 1933.* The "Forgotten Man" production number in that picture is at once one of the most bizarre yet eloquent evocations of the neglected "everyman" in cinema history.

In his own way Wellman matched that empathy in two films also shot

336

that year, *Heroes for Sale* and *Wild Boys of the Road*. Released in June, *Heroes for Sale* stars Richard Barthelmess as a war hero who finds it impossible to establish a life for himself in depression-ridden America. Like Jim in *I Am a Fugitive from a Chain Gang*, he is cheated and victimized at every turn by capitalists and communists alike. He becomes a drug addict, reforms, makes a fortune, and then gives it up for life on the open road—and that's only part of the plot! Wellman packs the 70-minute melodrama with twists and turns which would have crippled a lesser director. The pace is swift and the performances are believable. Barthelmess is extremely effective in his quiet way, and he is well supported by Loretta Young and Charley Grapewin and especially by Aline MacMahon.

The reviews of *Heroes for Sale* were less than ecstatic. Richard Watts, Jr. of the *New York Herald-Tribune* lamented, "What might have been a courageous picture ends by seeming just another futile essay in liberalism." The *Times'* Frank Nugent saw the film as two separate stories, adding: "Both plots are good, but not in the same picture." *Variety* dubbed Wellman's sincere effort "a bitter and rather logy yarn."

Wild Boys of the Road, which fared a bit better, is a classic example of film as social document and a fine illustration of Warner Brothers' concern with the ills of the day. *Heroes for Sale* details the repercussions of the Depression on adults, while *Wild Boys of the Road* is about the efforts of young people to make a living in a country where there are few jobs and fewer people who really care. Not one of the actors in major roles was over twenty years old. Stars Frankie Darro, Dorothy Coonan (soon to be Wellman's wife), and Edwin Phillips hold their own with more mature performers such as Grant Withers, Sterling Holloway, and Ward Bond.

Wild Boys of the Road is a wonderful testament to the director's dictum that "you can't make a picture unless you have beautiful writing." The courage of young men and women is explored, as well as the brutal conditions which force homeless youths to take to the road. They band together in trains and hobo camps throughout America, meting out their own justice to a railway worker who rapes one of their female members. The teenage troops are finally scattered by local authorities with billy clubs and high-power water hoses. The destruction of their little shanty town was perhaps the country's last chance to make amends with those on the edge of society. Even when Frankie Darro is adopted by a loving family, he makes a stirring and disturbing speech about the jobless and the homeless, those about whom the average American doesn't want to know. "You don't want to see us," he tells a smug judge whose attitude may be changed by the boy's words. At the film's end, Darro does a rather gymnastic flip at the reversal of his fortunes. He

James Cagney, Jean Harlow, Leslie Fenton, and Louise Brooks in a publicity pose for Public Enemy *(WB, 1931)*

Loretta Young, Richard Barthelmess, Robert Barrat, and Aline MacMahon in Heroes for Sale *(WB, 1933)*

Dorothy Coonan and Frankie Darro in a publicity pose for Wild Boys of the Road *(WB, 1933)*

immediately places his hand on Phillips' shoulder. The friend's leg had been severed by a speeding train, and the feeling persists that Darro is comforting the rest of America as well.

Richard Watts, Jr. compared *Wild Boys of the Road* to the Soviet *Road to Life*. Of Wellman's film he wrote in the *Tribune*: "This account of American youth in a similar plight has received a definite softening in outline and manner and the vagabond young of the narrative are less fiercely real than was the case with the Muscovite edition, but, for all that, the new picture ... has a rough vitality and, beneath its incidental sugar-coating, a suggestion of bitterness about it." He praised Bill for never allowing the film "to drift into flabbiness." However, Nugent of the *Times* criticized Wellman's direction: "He has taken a theme with broad social implications and has converted it into a rather pointless yarn about three wandering youngsters." The *Times'* reviewer called *Wild Boys of the Road* "disappointing, primarily because it might have been so much more than it is." *Variety* found it "thoroughly depressing and lacking in entertainment."

Wellman left Warner Brothers in 1934, not to return until *Island in the Sky* in 1953. Back at Paramount, Bill directed one of his oddest, most effective, and timeliest films, *The President Vanishes*, also called *The Strange Conspiracy*. This prophetic little production concerns a pacifist President who attempts to keep profiteers from involving the United States in a European war. Played by Arthur Byron, the President arranges to have himself kidnaped in order to arouse the sympathy of the populace. After he is miraculously "found," the Chief Executive pleads for world peace over the radio, and the Fascists and profiteers are defeated.

The President Vanishes caused much controversy. It was released at a time (1934) when Hitler had just consolidated power in Germany, and possibly it made audiences and critics quite uncomfortable about such a possibility in America. Andre Sennwald of the *New York Times* called Wellman's glum parable "an absorbing essay in topical melodrama" and asserted that the director "has paced the narrative briskly and he gives the film a helpful realistic atmosphere by inserting timely newsreel scenes of street fighting." Richard Watts, Jr. of the *Herald-Tribune* was more political: "In good, rousing melodramatic terms, *The President Vanishes* pillories the munitions' interests, the international bankers, the uniformed Fascist organizations, and other sinister groups and individuals concerned with getting the United States into a new world war." Film historian Richard Griffith wasn't stirred by the film's rhetoric, calling it "a heavy-handed anti-Fascist parable." However, Eileen Creelman of the *New York Sun* wasn't planning to offend anyone, asserting that the film "combines all the excitement of war, kid-

340

naping, and a hotbed of political intrigue, and makes of them a smashing good melodrama."

After half a decade of social relevance and realism, often edged in violence and mostly shot at Warner Brothers, Hollywood started to swing back to the simpler, more innocent (at least in terms of social comment) days of the 1920s. Adventure, romance, and lavish costume spectacles, along with a dash of apolitical idealism courtesy of Frank Capra and Warner Brothers biographies, set the standards for 1935-40 productions. Wellman could do another tough gangster yarn, but it had to be set in the guise of a Western, dubbed *Robin Hood of El Dorado* (MGM, 1936) and claim to be the biography of legendary Mexican bandit Joaquin Murietta. Portrayed by Warner Baxter (the screen's first Cisco Kid), Murietta only becomes a criminal after his wife is raped and murdered by bigoted miners in the California gold country of the 1850s. Yet Bill's realistic touches, the empathy for the underprivileged and several very violent shoot-outs are reminiscent in general of the most uncompromising gangster and social films that Warner Brothers had made a few years earlier, and in particular of two 1932 MGM films, *Law and Order* and *Beast of the City*, which have extremely gory endings. It seemed that Hollywood could get around Will Hays morality and the anti-violence Code of 1934 with a little window-dressing.

Bill didn't avoid sheer entertainment films, but he added a little grit to the characters, stories, and locales of such productions. Being an adventurous fellow himself, he was the perfect choice to film Jack London's *Call of the Wild* (1935). The production reunited Wellman and Darryl F. Zanuck, by then chief of 20th Century-Fox. The film, released through United Artists, was the scene of many loud arguments between the executive and the director. Consequently Wild Bill refused to enter the Fox lot again until he had to shoot some footage there for *A Star Is Born* in 1937.

Robin Hood of El Dorado and *Small Town Girl* (both 1936) were the only films Wellman directed under his MGM contract. He hated autocratic studio head Louis B. Mayer, and he relished telling a story of how he and W. S. Van Dyke reacted to one of the mogul's propositions. Mayer was impressed with the prolific outputs of the two men, and he asked them to keep an eye on other Metro directors. In effect, Louis B. was the "lieutenant," and Wellman and Van Dyke were to be his "sergeants." "Now I'd been in the Flying Corps and the Foreign Legion when this punk was still selling scrap medal," he recalled, "so I told him I wasn't going to be anybody's sergeant ... and I wasn't going to work with him to cut the throats of other directors."

Mayer was a vindictive man, and he "punished" Wellman by keeping him inactive. Therefore Bill schemed with studio executive Eddie Mannix to have Metro film any story the director might write. Since Wild Bill was in disfavor with Mayer, none of MGM's established writers were permitted to work with him. As a result he established an association with fledgling Robert Carson, which soon benefited both men.

Edward Ludwig directed one Wellman/Carson script, *The Last Gangster,* but their collaboration really sparked with an original story called *It Happened in Hollywood.* Carson completed the script with the help of fifteen other writers, including Ring Lardner, Jr., Budd Schulberg, and Dorothy Parker. Wellman became tired of wasting away at MGM, and he signed with Selznick/UA to direct *It Happened in Hollywood,* retitled *A Star Is Born,* and *Nothing Sacred.*

Although Bill never soft-pedaled his hatred for producers, he had great respect for David Selznick. "He and Thalberg were great. They gave you your head." In contrast, he compared Mayer to a praying mantis: "[It] feeds upon other insects and clasps its prey in its forelimbs as if in prayer." One can only wonder how long Wellman's career at MGM would have lasted if Thalberg had not died just as Bill began to work at the studio.

A Star Is Born (1937) is one of the finest films Hollywood ever made about itself. Wellman packed the drama of a woman (Janet Gaynor) who rises to dizzying heights in Hollywood, while attached to a rapidly falling star (Fredric March), with almost twenty years of memories of tinsel town. The descending matinee idol mired in a maze of alcoholism was a composite of many real-life actors, including John Gilbert and John Barrymore. The final scene of Norman Maine (March) walking into the ocean was a suicide actually committed by a lesser known leading man named John Bowers. To bring the nightmare of shattered lives in Hollywood further into bleak reality, Wellman hired a top silent screen director, Marshall Neilan, himself an alcoholic, for the role of a film director.

Aside from the emotional power of *A Star Is Born* and the speculation as to the real-life identities of the fictional characters, the film is distinguished as Bill's first technicolor production, and the first to play three weeks at the Radio City Music Hall in New York City.

United Artists made much of Wellman's interest in color, and studio publicists placed several newspaper stories hyping the new technicolor. Bill told one reporter, "I honestly believe that the black-and-white film is as obsolete—or will be in a few seasons—as the silent screen. But more important to me is the fact that color can give a director what might be called new tools." Several journals published the "Wellman Chart of Colors and Their Associated Emotions." Color values were identified with emotion rooted in primitive environmental association.

Under headings such as "Chief Auxiliary Influence" were "snow, sea, sunlight," while "Prime Factor of Color" was supported by "affirmation, death, life."

The critical and popular reception to *A Star Is Born* was excellent. Otis Ferguson of the *New Republic* immediately tagged Wellman's tale of Hollywood "a good picture and the first color job that gets close to what screen color must eventually come to." In the *New York Herald-Tribune*, Howard Barnes exclaimed: "Hollywood has turned brilliantly introspective," and he added that Bill "directed the script superbly, employing technicolor without affectation and bridging a variety of moods triumphantly." *New York Times* critic Frank S. Nugent called the direction "expert" and labeled the film "a good entertainment by any standards, including the artistic and convincing proof that Hollywood need not travel to Ruritania for its plots."

In a final flourish, Wellman impressed all of egotistical Hollywood at the Academy Award ceremonies by taking the Oscar that he and Robert Carson had just won for the story of *A Star Is Born* and placing it at David Selznick's table, saying, "You deserve this more than I do."

Nothing Sacred (1937) is a dazzling exposé of yellow journalism scripted by Ben Hecht. The film satirizes everything it touches, including reporters, country hicks, medicine, and get-rich-quick schemes. Carole Lombard stars as Hazel Flagg, a woman believed doomed by radium poisoning, and Fredric March is a reporter sent to cover Hazel's dying days. Subsequently she discovers that her medical diagnosis is incorrect, but she proceeds to take March's newspaper and America for all they are worth.

The set of *Nothing Sacred* was as dizzy and laugh-filled as the movie itself. Wellman and Lombard established a tremendous rapport. Once she even had studio technicians wrap the director in a straitjacket during one of their arguments so that he couldn't walk away. At other times Lombard and co-star March could be seen zipping around Selznick's lot on a fire engine, with sirens blaring. Such antics complied perfectly with Wellman's declaration that "a little fun is the best tonic between scenes." Even during the shooting, Bill used humor to break Lombard or March from a dry spell in motivation, or to comfort a concerned actor who had dropped his lines. At least once he told his leading lady, "Miss Lombard, I know it must be tough for a woman to look into Freddie March's frozen puss and pretend to be in love with him. But close your eyes or something and let's do it just once more."

Nothing Sacred was a hit. Barnes of the *Tribune* called it "an extravagant lampoon, made exceedingly amusing by expert craftsmanship.... Wellman ... has molded it to a true film continuity in his direction and the performances are in perfect keeping with a wildly farcical mood."

343

*Arthur Byron and
Janet Beecher in*
The President
Vanishes *(Par.,
1934)*

*Ann Loring and
Warner Baxter in*
Robin Hood of
El Dorado *(MGM,
1936)*

Carole Lombard and Fredric March in Nothing Sacred *(UA, 1937)*

Fredric March and Janet Gaynor in A Star Is Born *(UA, 1937)*

The *Times*' Frank Nugent deemed *Nothing Sacred* "an impishly impious comedy" and commended Bill's "alert" direction.

From Selznick, Wellman moved once again to Paramount to produce and direct four films, *Men with Wings, Beau Geste, The Light That Failed,* and *Reaching for the Sun.* His remake of *Beau Geste* is solid if not classic like the original 1926 version directed by Herbert Brenon. Gary Cooper, Ray Milland, and Robert Preston play the Geste brothers, and Brian Donlevy essays the role of Sergeant Lejaune, a scarfaced, dictatorial Prussian with more than a taint of the Nazi mentality.

Adapted from Rudyard Kipling's first novel, *The Light That Failed* (1939) at first didn't intrigue Wellman. "Now I didn't think I could bring anything to Kipling, or that *The Light That Failed* was my kind of thing. But I said OK." Originally the film was announced as a technicolor production starring Ray Milland and newcomer Ida Lupino, but Ronald Colman was signed for the role of Dick Heldar, an artist who goes blind, and Colman planned on co-starring with another new face named Vivien Leigh. Sparks between the director and his star flew around the studio, but Wellman's insistence that Lupino play the street urchin who ruins Heldar's one great painting was honored. The two men, both gentlemen, but of very different orders, patched up their differences.

Mixed reviews followed the release of *The Light That Failed.* Nugent of the *Times* said it was "a letter-perfect edition of Kipling's novel," but Barnes of the *Tribune* lamented that "Mr. Wellman took the Kipling yarn too literally and fell into the same errors that the author did in composing his first novel." Today the film is regarded as a flawed, slightly out of place, but decidedly worthy entry in Wellman's filmography.

For the next few years Bill directed competent, occasionally memorable films such as *Reaching for the Sun* (1941) and *Roxie Hart* (1942). Announced projects *The City That Never Sleeps* (1940) at Paramount and *The Full Glory* (1942) for MGM never materialized. The most notable thing about Wellman's life during this period was his 1941 effort to defend Tahiti from raider vessels.

It wasn't until 1943, when Wellman met Walter Van Tilburg Clark, author of the novel *The Ox-Bow Incident,* that the director was to put another classic on the screen. Bill's enthusiasm for the book reunited him with old sparring partner Darryl Zanuck at Fox. After being rejected by every other major studio, Wellman got Zanuck to agree to film Clark's examination of mob violence. Wellman and Lamar Trotti started planning the production. A number of Fox executives tried to talk Zanuck out of his promise to Wellman, but the handshake of a man was his bond, so a shooting schedule was arranged. Wellman reportedly agreed to direct any two projects Fox gave him in return for the opportunity to film the non-commercial *The Ox-Bow Incident.*

The story revolves around the murder of a rancher named Kincaid and the theft of his cattle. The sheriff is out of town, so a retired Confederate officer organizes a mob to hunt Kincaid's murderer. They happen on three men on the trail, a cowboy (Dana Andrews), a Mexican (Anthony Quinn), and an old man (Francis Ford). The men are driving fifty of Kincaid's steers over the prairie, and when they cannot produce a bill of sale, the mob decides that they are guilty and must die. Caught in the swirl of madness and the craze for revenge are two aimless cowboys, Gil Carter (Henry Fonda) and Art Croft (Harry Morgan). They witness the proceedings from beginning to end, confused, enraged, but utterly helpless to prevent the deaths of the three men. It is later discovered that Kincaid is alive and that the men had indeed purchased the cattle from him. The film ends with Carter reading a letter written by the lynched cowboy to his wife. Carter and Croft then ride out of a very quiet town. The only sounds are a hint of drifting dust and a dog scurrying across the street.

The Ox-Bow Incident was certainly one of Hollywood's most atypical productions during the war years. At a time when the studios attempted to uplift the spirits of war-torn Americans, Fox chose, reluctantly, to release a very depressing, unrelenting exploration of the insanity which grips men's souls when they seek to mete out "justice" outside the law.

Years later Wellman was still reacting to the reception that the film received in 1943. "Well, it didn't make money, but they finally got hold of it in Europe (under the title *Strange Incident*), and it was a great success. One of the great critics of the time in the States—he was the biggest voice of them all—he went against the mainstream at that time. He said it had less merit than the smallest 'B' Western. I've still got that review. I have it in my safe deposit box—it's reading something like that that can still turn an artist's insides into knots. But mostly the reaction was favorable. I'm proud of it."

Bosley Crowther of the *New York Times* called *The Ox-Bow Incident* "an ugly study in mob violence, unrelieved by any human grace save the futile reproach of a minority and some wild post-lynching remorse. . . . William Wellman has directed the picture with a realism that is as sharp and cold as a knife." Writing in the *Nation*, James Agee took an opposite, yet not completely unsympathetic view of the film: "*Ox-Bow* is one of the best and most interesting pictures I have seen for a long time, and it disappointed me. . . . It seems to me that in *Ox-Bow* artifice and nature got jammed in such a way as to give a sort of double focus, like off-printing in a comic strip. Here was a remarkably controlled and intelligent film; and in steady nimbus, on every detail, was the stiff over-consciousness of those who made of it the excellence of each effect, to such a degree that the whole thing seemed a mosaic of over-appreciated effects which continually robbed nature of its own warmth and energy."

In recent years Andrew Sarris has attacked the painted sets which dominated the night scenes in *The Ox-Bow Incident*. At first it may appear that they contradict the grey but natural vistas of the town and the trail and thus circumvent the enormous power of the film, but if the story is taken on an allegorical plane, the painted backdrops enhance the unreal nightmare suffered by the victims of mob madness and the executioners themselves.

Buffalo Bill (1944) followed *The Ox-Bow Incident*, and, like its predecessor, it started out as an uncompromising biography of a great Western hero, with an attack on the inequities perpetrated on Indians by the United States government. Wellman and his friend Gene Fowler wrote a realistic script about Bill Cody's life, and they were almost ready to present it to Zanuck, when Fowler said, "Look, Bill, you know you couldn't kill Dempsey, you couldn't stab Babe Ruth, and you can't kill these heroes our children and grandchildren worship. We can't do it. What do you say we burn the whole goddamn thing?"

Early the next morning Wellman and Fowler got drunk. Page by page, they dropped the original script for *Buffalo Bill* into Fowler's crackling fireplace. "Some of the best work I've done as a writer," Bill later lamented. "And he was right."

After the two cinematic sojourns through various sections of the West, Bill Wellman returned to the twentieth century and up-to-the-minute headlines to film *The Story of G.I. Joe* in 1945 for Fox. Based on journalist Ernie Pyle's book about the soldier in war, Wellman's film faithfully transfers the spirit of the author's writing to the screen. There are no heroics, mock or otherwise, no heroes, no villains, but simply soldiers out to do a job. The war is seen through their eyes. *The Story of G.I. Joe* is one of the great war films, comparable in quality to, and perhaps even better than, Wellman's own *Wings*, since *The Story of G.I. Joe* isn't affected by the streak of sentimentality running through the air film.

Sadly the film is rarely shown in theatres or on television. In 1973 Wellman explained, "The man who owns it is a crook, and he owes me a lot of money. But he's in the hospital—what can I do? Sue him? How can he pay me if he's sick and in jail?"

Nevertheless the memory of *The Story of G.I. Joe* has not dimmed for those who have seen it once, even three decades ago. Soldiers of the Fifth Army in Italy who viewed the film in 1945 uniformly declared, "This is it." Wellman's essay on the day-to-day life of American soldiers was "the finest tribute accorded any of our armed forces," accord-

*Dana Andrews,
Paul Hurst,
and Henry Fonda
in a publicity
pose for* The
Ox-Bow Incident
(20th, 1943)

*Burgess Meredith
in* The Story of
G.I. Joe *(UA,
1945)*

ing to *New York Herald-Tribune* critic Howard Barnes. Thomas M. Pryor praised Bill's approach to the subject as "starkly realistic." In the *New York Times,* Pryor wrote that the film "moves across the screen with tremendous emotional impact. It is humorous, poignant, and tragic, an earnestly honest reflection of a stern life and the dignity of man." *Nation* critic James Agee was overwhelmed by *The Story of G.I. Joe:* "Coming as it does out of a world in which even the best work is nearly always compromised, and into a world which is generally assumed to dread honesty and courage and to despise artistic integrity, it is an act of heroism, and I cannot suggest my regard for it without using such words as veneration and love."

In 1949 Bill returned to MGM to find Dore Schary installed as the studio's new artistic head. Schary and Louis B. Mayer had completely different philosophies of film, and it was through Schary's influence that Wellman directed another gritty war film, *Battleground* (1949). Similar to *The Story of G.I. Joe* in its focus on average foot soldiers, the Metro film does occasionally engage in heroics which would have been anathema to its predecessor.

Battleground was the biggest box-office hit of the year, and it impressed critics as well. In 1950 Bill Wellman received *Look* magazine's Achievement Award as the director of the year.

Perhaps William Wellman's last great film was *Track of the Cat,* released by Warner Brothers in 1954. Finished near the end of the reign of the Warner brothers over the company where Bill solidified his directorial reputation, this strange little Western was shot in color, yet is almost entirely black and white, with occasional brushes of red and yellow. True to the publicity for *A Star Is Born* seventeen years earlier, Wellman was still fascinated by the possibilities of color in the cinema. "It was breathtaking," he remembered of the color in *Track of the Cat,* "but no one recognized what we had tried to do. This is a dream, finally it came true, and nothing. But God, I'm proud of the fact that I thought of it and had guts enough to try it."

Starring Robert Mitchum, who had copped an Oscar for his performance in *The Story of G.I. Joe,* along with Warner contractee Tab Hunter, Wellman's film of Walter Van Tilburg Clark's novel was considered an "oddly potent tale" by Bosley Crowther of the *New York Times.* He further stated that the film was "a heavy and clumsy travesty of a deep matriarchal melodrama or Western with Greek overtones." Indeed, *Track of the Cat* has often been termed a "Eugene O'Neill Western." Otis L. Guernsey of the *New York Herald-Tribune* was taken by the production, asserting that it was "touched with the icicle finger of nightmare.... It isn't what Wellman has done but how he has done it that makes *Track of the Cat* so fascinating."

Even though Wellman was nominated for best director of the year by the Directors Guild (which he helped start) for *The High and the Mighty* (WB, 1954), Bill's final four films, *Blood Alley*, *Goodbye, My Lady*, *Darby's Rangers*, and *Lafayette Escadrille*, were either ignored, butchered, or mediocre. He called *Goodbye, My Lady* "one of the best I ever made." It is also one of his most sentimental. However, the director recognized a failure when he saw it, and he considered *Darby's Rangers* his worst film. Failure bothered him: "A bad picture is like a frightful birthmark on your face—it never leaves you, first run, second run, reruns, TV prime time, late time, lousy time. . . ."

Lafayette Escadrille (1958), another autobiographical effort about American fliers in World War I, was Wellman's last film. It's a gentle, nostalgic, occasionally exciting, and even bitter piece of memorabilia. Starring Tab Hunter as the boy who leaves home to join the war in France, much as the director himself did, *Lafayette Escadrille* underwent heavy changes at the insistence of the new heads of production at Warner Brothers. Bill later disassociated himself from the film. "The story was too close to me, and it nearly broke my tough old heart when they wouldn't let me make it the way it really had happened," he lamented. "The screenplay was adapted from a true story I wrote called *C'est la Guerre.*"

Efforts to get new projects underway were unsuccessful. In 1960 he wrote a screenplay called *Footprints*, but it never sold. Two possible productions, *The Rounders* and *Flight of the Phoenix*, were taken over by Burt Kennedy and Robert Aldrich, respectively. A typically titled proposal, *The SOB's*, never materialized.

Wellman retired from filmmaking due to illness and a general dislike for the "new" Hollywood. In 1973 he received the D. W. Griffith Award "for distinguished achievement in motion picture directing." A month-long retrospective of thirty-eight of the 77-year-old director's films was held at the Royal Theatre in Los Angeles. For many years Bill suffered from a rare bone disease called ridiculitis, a name which constantly amused him. Bill ignored the problem for a long time, probably reasoning that a man of his wide experience wouldn't be felled by something as ridiculously named as ridiculitis—and he was right. While bending over to pick a flower on his six-acre Brentwood, California estate, Wild Bill Wellman received a back injury severe enough to hospitalize him. "After sixty-five years of fighting and flying and directing and living and marrrying, I get it reaching for a flower," he quipped.

While recovering, Bill wrote the first installment of his autobiography, *A Short Time for Insanity*, almost completely under the influence of pain-killing codeine. Thomas M. Pryor of *Variety* appropriately called Bill's book a "crazy quilt of recollections." A second volume,

Guy Anderson,
Denise Darcel,
and Van Johnson
in Battleground
(MGM, 1949)

Diana Lynn,
Robert Mitchum,
and Teresa
Wright in Track
of the Cat *(WB,*
1954)

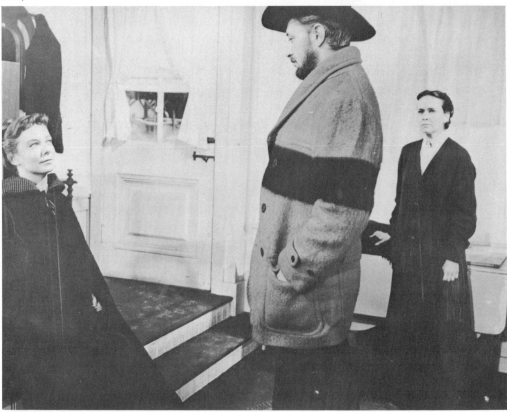

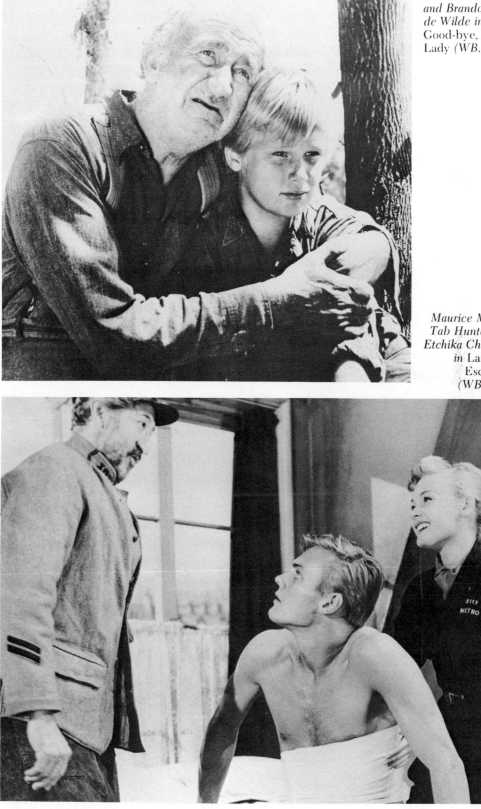

Walter Brennan and Brandon de Wilde in Good-bye, My Lady *(WB, 1956)*

Maurice Marsac, Tab Hunter, and Etchika Choureau in Lafayette Escadrille *(WB, 1958)*

entitled *Growing Old Disgracefully,* was completed during a final illness which took his life.

William Wellman died on Tuesday, December 11, 1975, after a bout with leukemia. A rugged individualist to the last, the 79-year-old filmmaker asked friends Ernest Gann and Ed Mack Miller to scatter his ashes in the clouds.

The Films of William Wellman

The Man Who Won *(Fox, 1923)*
Second Hand Love *(Fox, 1923)*
Big Dan *(Fox, 1923)*
Cupid's Fireman *(Fox, 1923)*
The Vagabond Trail *(Fox, 1924)*
Not a Drum Was Heard *(Fox, 1924)*
The Circus Cowboy *(Fox, 1924)*
When Husbands Flirt *(Col., 1925)*
The Boob *(MGM, 1926)*
The Cat's Pajamas *(Par., 1926)*
You Never Know Women *(Par., 1926)*
Wings *(Par., 1927)*
Legion of the Condemned *(Par., 1928)*
Ladies of the Mob *(Par., 1928)*
Beggars of Life *(Par., 1928)*
Chinatown Nights *(Par., 1929)*
The Man I Love *(Par., 1929)*
Woman Trap *(Par., 1929)*
Dangerous Paradise *(Par., 1930)*
Young Eagles *(Par., 1930)*
Maybe It's Love *(WB, 1930)*
Other Men's Women *(WB, 1931)*
Public Enemy *(WB, 1931)*
The Star Witness *(WB, 1931)*
Night Nurse *(WB, 1931)*
Safe in Hell *(FN, 1931)*
The Hatchet Man *(FN, 1932)*
Love Is a Racket *(FN, 1932)*
So Big *(WB, 1932)*

The Purchase Price *(WB, 1932)*
The Conquerors *(RKO, 1932)*
Frisco Jenny *(FN, 1933)*
Central Airport *(FN, 1933)*
Lily Turner *(FN, 1933)*
Heroes for Sale *(FN, 1933)*
Wild Boys of the Road *(FN, 1933)*
Midnight Mary *(MGM, 1933)*
College Coach *(WB, 1933)*
Looking for Trouble *(UA, 1934)*
Stingaree *(RKO, 1934)*
The President Vanishes *(Par., 1934)*
Call of the Wild *(UA, 1935)*
Robin Hood of El Dorado *(MGM, 1936) (and co-script)*
Small Town Girl *(MGM, 1936)*
A Star Is Born *(UA, 1937) (and co-story)*
Nothing Sacred *(UA, 1937)*
Men with Wings *(Par., 1938) (and producer)*
Beau Geste *(Par., 1939) (and producer)*
The Light That Failed *(Par., 1939) (and producer)*
Reaching for the Sun *(Par., 1941) (and producer)*
Roxie Hart *(20th, 1942)*
The Great Man's Lady *(Par., 1942) (and producer)*

Thunder Birds *(20th, 1942)*
Lady of Burlesque *(UA, 1943)*
The Ox-Bow Incident *(20th, 1943)*
Buffalo Bill *(20th, 1944)*
This Man's Navy *(MGM, 1945)*
The Story of G.I. Joe *(20th, 1945) (and producer)*
Gallant Journey *(Col., 1946) (and producer, co-script)*
Magic Town *(RKO, 1947)*
The Iron Curtain *(20th, 1948)*
Yellow Sky *(20th, 1948)*
Battleground *(MGM, 1949)*
The Next Voice You Hear *(MGM, 1950)*
The Happy Years *(MGM, 1950)*

It's a Big Country *(MGM, 1951) (co-directed by Clarence Brown, Don Hartman, John Sturges, Richard Thorpe, Charles Vidor, Don Weis)*
Across the Wide Missouri *(MGM, 1951)*
Westward the Women *(MGM, 1951)*
My Man and I *(MGM, 1952)*
Island in the Sky *(WB, 1953)*
The High and the Mighty *(WB, 1954)*
Track of the Cat *(WB, 1954)*
Blood Alley *(WB, 1955)*
Goodbye, My Lady *(WB, 1956)*
Darby's Rangers *(WB, 1958)*
Lafayette Escadrille *(WB, 1958) (and story)*

Index

262, 289, 292, 329

365

Hawks, Howard, 12, 18, 21, 99, 121, 156-77, 267
Hawks, Kenneth, 157
Hawks, William, 157
Hawthorne of the U.S.A., 328
Hay, Will, 144
Hayakaua, Sessue, 267
Hayden, Sterling, 188-89
Hayes, Alfred, 255
Hays Office, 89
Hays, Will, 66
Hayward, Susan, 277
Hayworth, Rita, 136, 292, 316-17
He Walked By Night, 218
Hearst, William Randolph, 310
Heart of the North, 284
Hearts and Dollars, 246
Heaven Knows Mr. Allison, 196
Hecht, Ben, 160, 164-65, 210, 343
Hedison, David, 322
Heflin, Van, 53-5, 114
Hellinger, Mark, 184, 216, 311
Helvick, James, 191
Hemingway, Ernest, 99, 100, 167, 184, 205, 267
Henreid, Paul, 13, 52, 92-3, 96, 261, 273-74, 276
Henry, Mae, 141
Hepburn, Audrey, 196-97, 255
Hepburn, Katharine, 163-65, 190, 192
Herald, Heinz, 123, 128
Herczeg, Geza, 123
Here's Looking At You, Kid, 146, 213, 292
Hernandez, Juano, 99, 102
Heroes, The, 268
Heroes for Sale, 337-38
Heston, Charlton, 131
Heydt, Louis Jean, 215
Higham, Charles, 49, 57, 122, 250, 272, 315
High and the Mighty, The, 351
High Noon, 112, 115, 174
High Sierra, 313-14, 182
High Wall, 55, 57
Highway By Night, 136

Hill, Arthur, 241
Hill, Gladys, 205
Hills of California, 16
Hilton, James, 237
His Girl Friday, 159, 165-66
Hitchy-Koo of 1923, 31
Hitler, Adolf, 48, 254
Hobart, Rose, 50
Hochhuth, Rolf, 256
Hodiak, John, 25
Hoffman, David, 258
Hole in the Wall, 272
Holiday Inn, 100
Holka, Polka, 31
Holloway, Sterling, 337
Hollywood Canteen, 111
Hollywood Directors: 1914-1940, 146
Hollywood Hotel, 37
Hollywood in the Thirties, 82
Hollywood Professionals, Volume 1, The, 81, 99
Holm, Celeste, 263, 266
Holt, Charlene, 174-75
Holt, Tim, 185-86
Holumbar, Allen, 158
Home from the Sea, 302
Home Sweet Homicide, 25
Honeymoon, 217
Honeymoon for Three, 24
Honor System, The, 303
Hoover, J. Edgar, 311
Hopkins, Anthony, 150
Hopkins, Charles, 210
Hopkins, Miriam, 12, 49, 91, 127, 152, 164, 248, 288
Hopper, E. Mason, 329
Hopton, Russell, 214
Hot Nocturne, 50
Hot Stuff, 227
Hotel Berlin, 136-37
House Divided, A, 181-82
House I Live In, The, 238
House of Wax, 81
House on 92nd Street, The, 218
House Un-American Activities Committee, 97, 187

McGrath, Joseph, 200
McGuire, Dorothy, 143, 151, 153
McHugh, Frank, 90-1, 211, 252, 286, 290, 313
McKee, Raymond, 63
McLaglen, Victor, 156, 159, 305-06, 308, 322
McNally, Stephen, 265
Medical Center, 296
Melville, Herman, 18-9, 187, 194-96
Men with Wings, 346
Menjou, Adolphe, 34, 210
Menschen an Wege, Der, 120
Menzies, William Cameron, 304
Meredith, Burgess, 349
Merry Widow, The, 56
Mervyn LeRoy: Take One, 226
Metaxa, George, 258
Meyerhold, Vsevolod Emilievitch, 246-47
Midsummer Night's Dream, A, 12, 119-22, 124
Mildred Pierce, 75, 81, 98
Miles, Bernard, 193-94
Milestone, Lewis, 101, 166
Milland, Ray, 346
Miller, Arthur, 197
Miller, Ed Mack, 354
Miller, Marilyn, 274
Miller, Seton I., 211
Million Dollar Baby, 50
Miracle, The, 279
Misfits, The, 179, 197-98, 201-02
Miss Pinkerton, 19
Miss Sadie Thompson, 56
Mission to Moscow, 96-7
Mr. Bones, 79
Mr. Deeds Goes to Town, 165
Mister Dynamite, 70
Mister Roberts, 239
Mr. Skeffington, 288
Mr. Smith Goes to Washington, 90, 165
Mitchell, Thomas, 285-86
Mitchum, Chris, 175
Mitchum, Jim, 268

Mitchum, Robert, 173-74, 198, 318, 320, 350, 352
Moby Dick, 18, 19, 79, 179, 183, 187, 194-96, 200
Modiglianii, Amedeo, 259
Mohegan Lake Military Academy, 30
Mohr, Hal, 122
Molnar, Fredric, 77
Moment to Moment, 239, 241
Monkey Business, 170
Monroe, Marilyn, 197, 202
Montalban, Ricardo, 279
Montgomery, Elizabeth, 150
Montgomery, James, 31
Mooney, Martin, 211
Moore, Colleen, 226
Moorhead, Agnes, 112, 139
Moorhead, Natalie, 70
Morgan, Dennis, 93, 137, 287, 290
Morgan, Harry, 347
Morgan, Ralph, 136
Morin, Relma, 35
Morley, Karen, 86
Morris, Oswald, 195
Morris, Wayne, 85, 213
Mose, Marjorie Violet, 145
Moszhukin, Ivan, 246-47
Mother Is a Freshman, 25
Mother's Love, A, 301
Motion Picture Daily, 69
Moulin Rouge, 187, 191, 195, 198
Mouthpiece, The, 285
Mrs. Miniver, 237
Mudlark, The, 258, 267
Muir, Jean, 212
Muni, Paul, 12, 13, 84, 86, 121-25, 127, 161-62, 230, 232, 248, 266
Murders in the Rue Morgue, 181
Murnau, Friedrich Wilhelm, 120
Murphy, Audie, 188, 192-93, 197
Musmanno, Richard, 84
Museum of Modern Art, 176, 323
My Bill, 284
My First Hundred Years in Hollywood, 69
My Love Came Back, 46, 49

978